TERRIBLE
JUSTICE

TERRIBLE JUSTICE

Sioux Chiefs and U.S. Soldiers on the Upper Missouri, 1854–1868

DOREEN CHAKY

UNIVERSITY OF OKLAHOMA : NORMAN

Library of Congress Cataloging-in-Publication Data
Chaky, Doreen, 1944–
Terrible justice : Sioux chiefs and U.S. soldiers on the upper Missouri,
1854–1868 / Doreen Chaky.
p. cm.
Includes bibliographical references and index.
ISBN 978-0-8061-4652-2 (paper)
1. Blue Water Creek, Battle of, Neb., 1855. 2. Harney, William S. (William
Selby), 1800–1889. 3. Dakota Indians—Wars. 4. Dakota Indians—Treaties.
5. Dakota Indians—Government relations. I. Title.

E83.854.C43 2012
978.2′02—dc23

2011050178

The paper in this book meets the guidelines for permanence and durability
of the Committee on Production Guidelines for Book Longevity of the
Council on Library Resources, Inc. ∞

Contents

Part III. Resolutions with Reservations: 1865–1868

Illustrations

Preface

THE AUGUST 3, 1865, *FRONTIER SCOUT*, A NEWSPAPER PUBLISHED BY officers of a "galvanized Yankee" unit stationed at Fort Rice, Dakota Territory, reported a skirmish outside the stockade between U.S. soldiers and Sitting Bull's band of Sioux. One hundred and forty years later, during the summers of 1994 and 1996, U.S. Army Corps of Engineers archeologists directing volunteers unearthed features of a traders' complex that stood outside the fort's walls, evidence of an icehouse, and a horse buried near the riverbank still wearing cavalry trappings. I participated in these archeological digs as a volunteer in order to write about them for a state publication, and I became intensely curious about who had lived at Fort Rice and other posts like it.

Finding few books or other published material to enlighten me about the history of such Upper Missouri River posts, I began my own research. As I delved into military records and other primary documents, I realized this was not the soldiers' story I had set out to tell. The brief time these men spent on the Upper Missouri was merely an adventure they could tell their grandchildren about. The story belonged to the Sioux, who witnessed wave after wave of soldiers and other whites encroaching into their homeland—whites who made and often broke conflicting promises. The real story was a long one that would not fit into an article. Doing justice to the subject required studying the period between two seminal events—the Grattan Affair of 1854 and the Fort Laramie Treaty of 1868. However, I came to realize that merely knowing what happened was not enough. I wanted to answer the question, What did these Upper Missouri Sioux and the mostly volunteer soldiers they encountered intend both for themselves and for their respective people, nations, and progeny? In this book I examine contemporary ideas held during those years by the Sioux and the soldiers and attempt to discover a greater depth of understanding of their actions and reactions.

On October 7, 2009, the U.S. Senate passed a resolution amended to the 2010 Defense Appropriations bill offering American Indians an

9

apology for "the destructive policies our government has too often followed regarding them." Similar resolutions, introduced multiple times in prior years, never became law. This time it did when President Barack Obama signed that defense bill. However, as Senator Byron Dorgan (D-N.Dak.) and co-sponsor Senator Samuel Brownback (R-Kans.), explained, "The resolution of apology does not authorize or serve as a settlement of any claim against the United States and does not resolve many challenges still facing Native Americans."

Terrible Justice: Sioux Chiefs and U.S. Soldiers on the Upper Missouri, 1854–1868 illuminates why the Sioux tribe deserves such an official apology, but it is not a diatribe about white-on-Indian injustice. Rather, I unearth conflict that is more complicated than many historians have revealed, and I try to explicate that complexity.

Acknowledgements

I WISH TO THANK—BY NAME, BUT THAT'S IMPOSSIBLE IN THE SPACE allowed—the many librarians, archivists, and image specialists who have gone beyond their ordinary duties to help; the military experts and buffs, tribal historians, and American Indian authors who shared their knowledge with me personally or share it with the world on the Internet; as well as the many authors whose books, articles, and other publications laid the groundwork for *Terrible Justice*. Among the librarians and archivists, Jim Davis at the State Historical Society of North Dakota, Ken Stewart at the South Dakota State Historical Society, and the entire staff at my hometown Williston Community Library—especially Yvonne Topp, who performed magical feats of interlibrary loan—were particularly helpful. Considerable help came from Julian Shields, who, if he could not answer some of my Lakota, Nakota, and Dakota questions himself, found someone who could. Invaluable help came from brief or extensive e-mail communications with such distinguished authors as Eli Paul, John Ludwickson, Paul Hedren, Michèle Tucker Butts, George Rollie Adams, and others.

I am especially grateful to my friends who read either all or portions of my manuscript or, in the case of my fellow Toastmasters club members, listened to and critiqued many speeches based on my research. My author friend Lesley Wischmann read and edited an early (and wordy) draft, and my author friend Sandra Sagala has commented on multiple versions of *Terrible Justice* over the eight or more years it took me to write it. They and my membership in the Western Writers of America (WWA) organization have provided not only practical help, but also a community of people who do what I do and understand the difficulties and joys a writing life involves.

Publisher Bob Clark has stuck with me since I broached the idea of *Terrible Justice* to him at a WWA convention in 2003. More than anyone else, he has taught me how to write a book like this. Thanks also to

Kimberly Kinne, Jean Middleton, Amy Hernandez, Bill Nelson, Alice Stanton, and Ariane Smith for their painstaking work on *Terrible Justice* and for their extraordinary patience and kindness.

To all these people, and to many more who regrettably shall remain nameless, I am grateful, but to no one so much as my husband, Alex, who has supported me in the style to which I have become accustomed—and in many other non-material ways—during the research and writing of *Terrible Justice*. Our son Damon has been an encouraging cheerleader. Sometimes, that encouragement was what I needed most to complete this project.

Introduction

"You cannot begin to understand Indian people until you know something about their culture and heritage. Their language, philosophy, values, beliefs, and the way they process information are at the opposite end of a continuum with the American mainstream. No two cultures are more different."[1] If that statement was true in 2006, when Sisseton Wahpeton Sioux educator and author Elden Lawrence wrote it, it seems hopeless indeed to try to understand differences between the American military culture and Sioux culture during the mid-nineteenth century. However, as historian Elliot West argues, "Reconstructing the Indian perception of contact, exchange, and conflict is one of the most challenging, and essential, tasks before us."[2]

The pitfalls of interpretation are many, particularly when primary source material, as in this case, is from a time when most interactions between the Sioux and the military were recorded by, or filtered through, white observers.[3] Indian accounts and reminiscences are rare, and Sioux winter counts—depictions of a band's most important event during the year—are sometimes inscrutable even to Sioux. Conventions used by both sides during treaty conferences or other public performances might dilute or skew an American soldier's or a Sioux chief's true message. Even discerning what common English words meant in the nineteenth century versus today can be problematic. To be paternalistic in the 1850s and 1860s at least implied good intentions, although it meant treating Indians as children or dependant wards while "civilizing" and Christianizing them, supposedly for their own good. "Paternalism" today has a connotation of demeaning the recipient and condemning the "parent."

When parties to a conflict hold widely differing perceptions of justice, misunderstandings can turn slight difficulties into major problems. Furthermore, because the principals' personalities also influence any

[1]Lawrence, "Missing Voices," 33.
[2]West, "Shadow of Pikes Peak," 208.
[3]Ibid.

quarrel, historians should scrutinize the prejudices and characters of the interpreters, agents, fur traders, soldiers, and adventurers who wrote the reports, letters, diaries, treaty transcripts, and other documents they use. Such scrutiny, though, is not always possible or practical.

Those studying the Sioux of this period must, however, consider how varied was each subgroup's knowledge of, attitude toward, and experience with whites. Whereas European and Euro-American traders aimed to win over the Sioux as customers, military officers arrived intending to make the Upper Missouri country safe for white expansion. Before long, the Sioux realized that if they objected to or fought against a future preordained by white society, the United States would push them back by force. Some Sioux leaders reacted by using diplomacy to state their case; this book pays them overdue attention. Others led their bands away to where they hoped to have little or no contact with whites. Which faction was right is forever debatable; no one way led to a satisfactory outcome. Often, those attempting to take a middle road were marginalized, their power lost to a noisier solution involving "terrible justice."

With these and other limitations in mind, then, *Terrible Justice* ventures to interpret conflicts between Sioux leaders and American soldiers during the tumultuous era of 1854 to 1868. This period of conflict brought unprecedented change to the Sioux and was also remarkable for modifications it wrought in U.S. Indian policy.

In 1854, Sioux country was a land of woodlands, plains, prairies, alpine forests, and sagebrush deserts with climates to match. Such geographical diversity dictated a diversity of lifestyles among the four eastern, two middle, and seven western Sioux divisions. At the beginning of the period, Sioux who called themselves *Titonwan* (or *Lakota*) lived west of the Missouri River, or *Mnisose*, making their living primarily by hunting.[4] Those who called themselves *Nakota* lived between the Missouri River and Minnesota and planted crops to supplement their hunting. Those eastern Dakotas (or Santees) who farmed and occupied reservations were beginning to live much as did their Euro-American neighbors.

By 1868, the United States had added six new states—all but one west of the Mississippi—to the thirty-one present in 1854. Similarly, Lakota Sioux continued to fight the Crow tribe for dominion over the country west of the Black Hills and south of the Yellowstone River; thus, by 1868 the Lakota Sioux had considerably expanded their territory by conquest

---

[4]Howe and TallBear, "Introduction," ix, x.

beyond the Black Hills to the Bighorn Mountains. During this time, though, the three Nakota Sioux bands occupying the wedge between the Missouri and Minnesota in 1854 lost land. The four Dakota Sioux bands that had already lived on reservations in southwestern Minnesota in 1854 started a brutal war in 1862 that prompted white Minnesotans to banish them to Dakota Territory, where they encroached on Lakota and Nakota tribesmen.

In the 1860s, conflict with whites repeatedly brought the vast and divergent Sioux Nation together in common cause and then, through internal dissention, split it again into new configurations. After Sioux chiefs, soldiers, and their respective cultures wrestled one another for justice multiple times and in multiple ways, the U.S. government encouraged, cajoled, and finally persuaded those Sioux leaders who signed the 1868 Fort Laramie Treaty to settle their bands near the Upper Missouri River. In a similar manner, the American government had split into factions over the so-called Sioux problem, with the war faction dominating in 1854; by 1868, peace advocates wielded power, if only temporarily.

The story of Sioux chiefs and soldiers on the Upper Missouri is a riveting one of parties in conflict with different ideas of what constitutes justice. In this book, part one examines how the escalating conflict sparked by a cow and ignited by the Grattan and Ash Hollow affairs spread to the Upper Missouri and culminated in the assassination of a Lakota peace chief. Part two considers what occurred after Dakotas in Minnesota erupted in anger in 1862 over accumulated injustices and how the resulting three-year-long military conflict on the northern plains affected the entire Sioux Nation. Part three examines U.S. peace policy as it developed toward what seemed like a satisfactory solution to the so-called Sioux problem and was encapsulated in the Laramie Treaty of 1868. The treaty created the Great Sioux Reservation, the purpose of which was to concentrate the entire Sioux Nation near the Upper Missouri River, conveniently out of the way of settlers and travelers. A concluding chapter examines how events taking place during the 1854–68 era fit into Sioux and U.S. military history.

Abbreviations

AFC	American Fur Company
AGO	Adjutant General's Office
CIA	Commissioner of Indian Affairs
Cir	Circular
fr	frame
FS	Fort Sully
GO	General Order
LR	Letters Received
LS	Letters Sent
MNHS	Minnesota Historical Society
MOA	Cornell University's "Making of America" database: http:// cdl.library.cornell.edu/moa/
MOLLUS	Military Order of the Loyal Legion of the United States
NA	National Archives
NARA	National Archives and Records Administration
OCRFP	"Official Correspondence Relating to Fort Pierre"
OR	*The War of Rebellion: A Compilation of Official Records of the Union and Confederate Armies*
ORN	*Official Records of the Union and Confederate Navies in the War of the Rebellion*
PR	post returns
RG	Record Group
SC	small collection
SDSHS	South Dakota State Historical Society
SHSND	State Historical Society of North Dakota
SE	Sioux Expedition (Harney's)
SO	Special Order
USV	United States Volunteer

PART I

A Clash of Cultures

1854–1862

Sioux Country 1854–1862. *Map by Bill Nelson.*

Legend:
- Harney 1855
- Warren 1857
- Raynolds 1859
- Raynolds 1860
- ■ Military forts
- ▲ Trading forts
- ● Towns and settlements

0 25 50 mi

N

MINNESOTA

IOWA

NEBRASKA

INTERNATIONAL BORDER

DAKOTAS

NAKOTAS

LAKOTAS

DAKOTA

UPPER DAKOTA RES.
LOWER DAKOTA RES.
NON-RES. DAKOTAS
YANKTONS
Yankton Res.
CUTHEADS
UPPER YANKTONAIS
LOWER YANKTONAIS
HUNKPAPAS
SANS ARCS and SIHASAPAS
MINICONJOUS
TWO KETTLES
BRULÉS
OGLALAS
BLACK HILLS
BADLANDS

Ft. Snelling
Ft. Ridgely
Ft. Abercrombie
Pembina
Ft. Berthold
Ft. Atkinson
Ft. Clark
Ft. William
Ft. Union
Ft. Sarpy
Ft. La Framboise
Ft. Pierre II
Ft. Pierre
Ft. Lookout
Handy's Point (aka Ft. Randall)
Ft. Laramie
Sioux City
Sioux Falls
Vermillion
Omaha
Spirit Lake
Devil's Lake
Lake Traverse
Big Stone Lake
Kettle Lakes
Pipestone Quarry
Bear Butte
Wounded Knee Cr.

Rivers and trails:
Mississippi R.
Red R.
Sheyenne R.
Mouse R.
White Earth R.
Little Muddy R.
Poplar R.
Milk R.
Missouri R.
Yellowstone R.
Powder R.
Tongue R.
Rosebud R.
Big Horn R.
Musselshell R.
Little Missouri R.
Knife R.
Heart R.
Cannonball R.
Grand R.
Moreau R.
Beaver Cr.
Bad R.
Cheyenne R.
Belle Fourche R.
White R.
Niobrara R.
N. Platte R.
Loup R.
Whetstone R.
Minnesota R.
James R.
Big Sioux R.
Noble's Road
Ft. Laramie-Ft. Pierre Trail

Chapter 1

"Terrible Justice"

WHEN ONE CULTURE INFRINGES ON ANOTHER'S PERCEIVED RIGHTS and traditions, conflict is inevitable. When each party's sense of justice differs from the other's and they find no common ground, escalation ensues. Often, internal polarization burgeons until discord within can become as devastating as the external threat. What follows is the story of a tumultuous decade and a half—1854 through 1868—during which indigenous Sioux culture confronted, resisted, and adapted to the American army and to new ideas of justice.

First contact with white traders and explorers came for people calling themselves *Dakota* when they were living along the Mississippi River and its tributaries in the sixteenth century. Explorers and fur traders called them by a corruption of the name their enemies called them, which has come down through history as *Sioux*. Eastern Sioux met their first American military men—Lieutenant Zebulon Pike's expedition—in 1805 and 1806 and were among American Indians who fought against the United States during the War of 1812. They saw a military post, Fort Snelling, established in their country in 1819.

Sioux had acquired guns by the eighteenth century, and some ventured west toward the Missouri where the Arikara tribe held sway. In time, Iowa and Fox tribes forced other Sioux bands west onto the prairie east of the Missouri River. In the nineteenth century, smallpox and war decimated the Arikaras (the *Rees*), who then moved upriver closer to Mandan and Hidatsa nations claiming territory near the sharp southward bend of the river. Sioux replaced them, eventually expanding west beyond the Missouri.

Northern bands living along the Missouri met American military men when Meriwether Lewis and William Clark led the Corps of Discovery through their country in 1804 and 1806. In 1823, some 750 Upper Missouri Sioux joined U.S. forces under Colonel Henry Leavenworth in fighting their own traditional enemies, the Arikaras. In 1825, northern Sioux leaders signed treaties of friendship presented to them by U.S. military men of the Long Expedition exploring the Missouri River.

Beginning in the 1830s, the advent of steamboats introduced a period of Sioux adjustment to increased American travel through Upper Missouri country. However, at mid-century they lived a relatively quiet existence, a roaming lifestyle not unlike that of their grandfathers' generation, punctuated often by intertribal warfare.

Conflict with civilians developed for the southern Sioux bands at mid-nineteenth century when non-Indian travelers first made their way to Oregon, Utah, and the California gold fields. Americans entering Sioux country north of the North Platte River knew this vast country as "unorganized territory" and considered it theirs, not only by the Louisiana Purchase but also by a natural providence white Americans called "manifest destiny." The Sioux populating the area did not believe they owned this land; instead, they belonged to it. To them, it was *Unki Maki*, Grandmother Earth. It was theirs because it was where the bones of their ancestors lay, and they were ready to defend it with their lives. They sought justice from travelers who used up or defiled it.[1]

Aside from encountering small military details escorting emigrants, the southern Sioux bands first experienced a notable American military presence in 1845, when Colonel Stephen Watts Kearny led a large wagon train escort force of dragoons (military units trained and equipped to fight both on horseback or afoot) from Fort Leavenworth as far west as South Pass. Minnesota was already a U.S. territory in 1849 when the increase in traffic on the overland trails through southern Sioux country began to alarm the Sioux bands who lived there.

In all of Sioux country, travelers whose journeys were interrupted by Indians demanding tolls, or, in rare cases, by Indians attacking them, wanted justice. A young American nation caught up in what its citizens considered the inevitability of sea-to-sea expansion craved it and sent soldiers to protect and defend its people as they fulfilled that destiny.

By mid-century, the many Sioux bands were so widespread that three dialects had developed. The four groups of Minnesota, or Santee, Sioux (comprising Sisseton, Wahpeton, Wapekute, and Mdewakanton bands) living in the southwestern part of Minnesota Territory called themselves *Dakota*. Two of the seven bands calling themselves *Lakota*, or *Titonwan* (Teton)—the Oglalas and, east of them, the Brulé, or Sicangu,

---

[1]Oak Lake Writers, *This Stretch of the River*, 113.

bands—lived near the North Platte River and were considered southern Sioux. The five northern Lakota bands lived north of the Lower (in relation to the eastward flowing Platte) Brulés and populated the drainages of rivers flowing from the eastern Black Hills into the Missouri. Besides sharing the Black Hills and hunting grounds to the west with the southern Sioux, these Two Kettles, Miniconjous, Sihasapas, Sans Arcs, and Hunkpapas—all calling themselves *Lakotas*—also followed buffalo herds on broad swaths of prairie land east of the Missouri River where the Yanktonai and Yankton Sioux bands (Nakota) lived. Lakota, Nakota, and Dakota Sioux all frequented the Missouri River region to hunt and trade.[2]

ALTHOUGH HE WAS ONE OF MANY BAND CHIEFS (*WITASA ATANCAN*), the Hunkpapa Mato-cu-wi-hu, or Bear Rib, was a legend on the Upper Missouri when, in 1859, artist Carl Wimar portrayed him with a level, penetrating gaze, a somewhat flattened nose, a firm chin, and rather small mouth. His square, handsome face bore an expression of calm self-confidence. His hair, with no hint of gray, fell loose to his shoulders, hiding his ears but showing large brass hoop earrings. In one Wimar likeness, he wears three black-tipped eagle feathers stuck sideways into a topknot at the crown of his head. How Sioux men wore eagle feathers commemorated valorous deeds, such as coups (honors) earned by either killing or touching an enemy. Decorations on feathers—red dots for blood on Mato-cu-wi-hu's, for instance—detailed how they earned their honors. Mato-cu-wi-hu's adornments proclaimed him a courageous warrior and provider.[3]

[2]Ostler, *Plains Sioux and U.S. Colonialism*, 34–35; Unruh, *Plains Across*, 206; Gary Anderson, *Kinsmen*, 79–84, 87–91; Goetzmann, *Army Exploration*, 40–41; Maroukis, *Peyote and Yankton Sioux*, xvi–xxiv, 14, 5–41; Doane Robinson, "History of the Dakota," 24; Paulson, "Federal Indian Policy," 287; and Richard White, "Winning of the West," 319–43. Maroukis incorporated recent scholarship by Gary Anderson, by Herbert Hoover, and by Raymond DeMallie (see bibliography for some works by these authors) and others as well as oral history and oral tradition in describing Sioux origins and migration. No Lakota, Nakota, or Dakota called himself or herself *Sioux*, which is a French corruption of the Chippewas' derogatory name for them meaning "lesser adders." Today some Yanktons consider themselves Dakotas and say the designation of Yanktons/Yanktonais as Nakotas is in error. I use the Nakota designation as it was used during the 1854–68 period.

[3]Meyers, *Ten Years*, 78; Stewart, Ketner, and Miller, *Carl Wimar*, 17, 89, 120–21. See Bandel, *Frontier Life*, 95, Mallery, *Picture-Writing*, vol. 2, 266–328; and James Walker, *Lakota Belief*, 232, 270–81. I use the American Fur Company (AFC) designation of the Big Sioux River near Sioux City, Iowa, as the lower boundary of its "Upper Missouri Outfit" to define the "Upper Missouri." See Sunder, *Fur Trade*, 19.

Wimar's images of him project quiet power and, though they show only his head or torso, suggest height and physical strength. Stories, mostly embellished in the retelling, about his penchant for administering what one soldier called "terrible justice," abounded. One such tale recounted what happened after an Indian slaughtered a cow belonging to the American Fur Company (AFC). Such a deed called for punishment, but Honoré Picotte, the Fort Pierre trading post's bourgeois, or manager, did not want to jeopardize the lucrative profits made in trade with Indians by meting it out himself. The morning after the cow's demise, Picotte noticed Mato-cu-wi-hu watching repair work inside the fort and devised a way to solve his problem. In a staged manner, pacing back and forth near Mato-cu-wi-hu, Picotte lamented aloud how the time was past when brave men in the Sioux Nation would punish the guilty. Mato-cu-wi-hu's smile faded. Without comment, he left for his camp, where he learned the cow killer's name, entered the culprit's tipi, told him he had come to kill him, shot him dead, and then returned to the fort as if nothing remarkable had happened.[4]

Pierre Beauchamp, a hunter, trader, and Arikara interpreter for the AFC at Fort Berthold, related an incident that further illustrated the chief's character: After a Hunkpapa hunting party stole two of his horses in November 1858, Beauchamp risked going to their camp to reclaim them. Finding both animals near a tipi, he began saddling one when the thief saw him and yelled out. Beauchamp mounted and grabbed his rifle. As others ran to the thief's aid, Beauchamp sensed they might kill him, but they desisted when Mato-cu-wi-hu approached to learn what was causing the ruckus. However, Beauchamp and the thief continued to argue over the second horse. Finally, Mato-cu-wi-hu tied it up at his own tipi, but the thief cut the bridle and led the horse away. Mato-cu-wi-hu again took the horse and warned the young man not to touch it. Again, he did not listen. Finally, Mato-cu-wi-hu ended the dispute by killing the horse, chasing down the disobedient culprit, and thrashing him with his war club. Beauchamp took advantage of the confusion and fled.

Although this behavior might seem merely a manifestation of Mato-cu-wi-hu's own personality, a Two Kettle chief, when facing like circumstances at the same trading post, reacted in a similar fashion. When the bourgeois

---

[4]De Trobriand journal, 16 Oct. 1867, 93, State Historical Society of North Dakota (SHSND) Archives (hereafter cited as De Trobriand journal); De Trobriand, *Army Life*, 121 (cf. De Trobriand, *Military Life*); Schuler, *Fort Pierre Chouteau*, 56; Letellier, *Adventures*, 12, 15–16; Sunder, *Fur Trade*, 31–32; "Gazetteer of Pioneers in North Dakota," 356; and Mattison, *Henry A. Boller*, 70n52.

complained that one of Long Mandan's band had shot at the fort's bell and broken it, Long Mandan shot the bell-shooter dead. Although each man's personality may have been a factor, the argument can be made that their responses were based on the two chiefs' culturally based senses of justice.[5]

A third story involves no whites, although its chronicler, the adventurer Prince Maximilian of Wied, heard it from a white man. After some previously warring Ojibwa and Sioux warriors had smoked a peace pipe together, one Sioux warrior sneaked into the Ojibwa camp later and killed someone. When he brought home the man's scalp expecting praise, his chief instead ordered the Sioux man shot. The Sioux chief then called the Ojibwa to a council. Telling them "they must not believe that the Sioux could not uphold their treaties [or] that their word was not sacred," he handed over the Sioux man's body to them. While noting that perhaps the Sioux chief's purpose was to forestall the inevitable vengeance killing that would have otherwise followed, Maximilian found it a remarkable transaction. He commented in his journal that it demonstrated a Sioux chief's "power and love of justice, as well as their high regard for courage and determination."

Mato-cu-wi-hu, Long Mandan, and the anonymous Sioux chief, in choosing to eliminate what they considered the sources of present or potential conflict, jarred mid-nineteenth century American sensibilities about justice and seemed extreme to those telling the tales. Beginning with events taking place in southern Sioux country, the Sioux would face equally puzzling examples of what whites considered proper justice by the end of the 1854–68 period.[6]

STERN AS HE WAS WITH HIS OWN PEOPLE, MATO-CU-WI-HU HAD A reputation for friendship with and loyalty to whites, but events transpiring in southern Sioux country at mid-century would test that commitment.

In 1849, because of increased emigration to the California gold rush on the Oregon-California Trail, the army bought the old AFC trading

---

[5]Bell story from De Trobriand, *Army Life*, 119; "Council with the Sioux Indians at Fort Pierre" (hereafter cited as Harney Council); and *Report of Council Held at Fort Pierre* (hereafter cited as Council reprint).

[6]The story recorded in Maximilian's journal is from Witte and Gallagher, *North American Journals of Prince Maximilian of Wied*, vol. 2, 131. De Trobriand journal, 16 Oct. 1867, 92–94; De Trobriand, *Army Life*, 119, 121–23; and Mattison, *Henry A. Boller*, 70, 70n52, 156. De Trobriand retold these stories after Mato-cu-wi-hu's death.

post on the North Platte River known as Fort Laramie and converted it to military purposes. Several former fur traders working for the U.S. Indian Bureau convinced the commissioner of Indian affairs Luke Lea that the mere presence of soldiers would not prevent future clashes and suggested negotiating a treaty with the Plains Indians. Accordingly, Lea ordered the Indian superintendent David D. Mitchell and Indian agent Thomas Fitzpatrick to invite tribes from as far away as the Upper Missouri and northern Rocky Mountains to talks.

The resulting 1851 "Fort Laramie" treaty conference actually took place east of the post at Horse Creek. U.S. treaties with American Indians imitated the British practice during colonial times and, in effect, recognized Indian tribes as independent nations while at the same time demanding their loyalty to American authority. The Sioux, Cheyenne, Arapaho, and Shoshone delegations arrived in time to hear Mitchell's opening statement on September 8, 1851. The Mandans, Hidatsas (also known as Gros Ventres), Arikaras (Rees), and Assiniboines (called Hohe by Sioux) from the Upper Missouri River rode in that evening. The Crows came still later, and when the invited tribes had all gathered, 8,000 to 12,000 people congregated near Horse Creek.[7]

When Mitchell asked each nation to describe their territorial boundaries, the Upper Missouri Lakotas designated their home areas west of the Missouri with rivers and the so-called "Black Hills" as boundaries.[8] At mid-century, they lived south to north approximately as follows: Lower Brulés, Minconjous and Two Kettles, Hunkpapas and Sihasapas. Yanktonai Nakotas called a wedge roughly defined by the Missouri River and the Minnesota border home, whereas Yanktons lived south of the Upper and Lower Yanktonai bands. The Eastern Sioux—the four Dakota, or Santee, divisions—lived in Minnesota, with some few bands occupying land west of the Minnesota border. They signed separate treaties that same year and were not invited here.

The Horse Creek treaty required the remaining northern and the southern Sioux bands together to choose a head chief responsible for enforcing

[7]Prucha, *Great Father*, 7–8; Kvasnicka and Viola, *Commissioners*, 52; Wischmann, *Frontier Diplomats*, 191–92, 200; Morton and Watkins, *History of Nebraska*, 398; and A. B. Chambers, letter from the editor, *The Missouri Republican*, 24 Oct. 1851. These were not the Gros Ventres of the Blackfeet [Siksika] confederation.

[8]A 27 Aug. 1865 Indian Claims Commission decision redefined this western boundary because the Black Hills referred to in 1851 were not the same as the Black Hills of present-day South Dakota. See *Sioux et al. v. USA*, Indian Claims Commission, 15 (1865), Docket 74, "Findings of Fact," 584–98.

the treaty terms. This man must exert authority over all but the Dakota Sioux. Mitchell, a former trader familiar with Upper Missouri Indians, surely knew this was unrealistic. Because the Sioux roamed across thousands of miles, even counting the members of their nation seemed impossible. In 1850, an amateur scientist visiting Fort Pierre estimated that 30,000 Sioux lived along the Missouri River alone. Ethnographer Royal B. Hassrick halved that number, but whatever the population, it would be virtually impossible for one man to represent, and hold authority for, all seven Lakota and three Nakota tribes, or bands. Nevertheless, despite his own protestations and a warning from Conquering Bear's own band that this would not work, Mitchell appointed that Brulé to be witasa atancan (head chief) of all the Sioux. Besides its obvious impracticability, the concept that one man, even the most respected of chiefs, could speak for all in one band, never mind the entire nation, was foreign to people who made decisions by consensus after elders, headmen, and chiefs discussed issues in council. James R. Walker, a nineteenth-century army physician who immersed himself in a study of Lakota culture, explained how each band, as it broke off from the central band that existed "when the Lakotas came from the middle of the world," regarded other bands as friends (which is the translation of *Dakota*, *Lakota*, and *Nakota*). These autonomous friends considered themselves "allies against all others of mankind." By expecting individual band chiefs to sacrifice their autonomy to a central authority figure mandated to enforce the treaty, the whites sowed seeds of internal conflict among the Sioux. Thinking of their own convenience in dealing with so vast a nation, they ignored how such social upheaval might polarize the Sioux.[9]

When the Horse Creek council ended, the Indians, whether some realized it clearly or not, had agreed to allow Americans to build roads and establish military posts in their territories. They had promised to maintain peace with whites and each other and to pay reparations for damages or losses they caused whites. For its part, the government initially agreed to pay the Indians a $50,000 indemnity for damage already done to their lands and annuities of $50,000 for fifty years. Three Yankton, one Sans

---

[9]Hassrick, *The Sioux*, 30; Walker, *Lakota Society*, 18; and Culbertson, *Expedition*, 135. For Mitchell, see Barbour, *Fort Union*, 17, 33. Other Sioux culture sources include Gary Anderson, *Kinsmen*; Hyde, *Spotted Tails's Folk*, *Sioux Chronicle*, and *Red Cloud's Folk*; James Walker, *Lakota Belief*; Deloria, *Waterlily* (in which anthropologist Deloria presents a Lakota woman's cultural life as a novel); and Meyer, *History of the Santee Sioux*. For Sioux population, see Kingsley Bray, "Teton Sioux Population History," 165–88.

Arc, one Miniconjou, five Oglala, and five Brulé Sioux chiefs "touched the pen" to sign the treaty with their marks. However, before ratifying the treaty on May 25, 1852, the U.S. Senate reduced the annuity period from fifty to ten years and gave the president the option to renew it for five more. Five Upper Missouri Sioux chiefs—Smutty Bear, Struck-by-the-Ree, and Standing Medicine Cow (Yanktons); Red Fish (Miniconjou); and Crow Feather (Sans Arc)—made their marks of approval on the amended version that their agent circulated during the summer of 1853. Ten Platte River Sioux band chiefs, including Conquering Bear, also each drew an *X* on the amended document their interpreter read to them.[10]

The government, expecting all Lakota and Nakota bands to honor the treaty, sent treaty goods even to those who had not attended the Horse Creek conference. The Hunkpapas, Sihasapas, and Yanktonais who had approved neither the original nor the amended treaty continued to war with their traditional Crow, Assiniboine, and Arikara enemies. In time, Sioux resentment of the treaty's stipulations, which essentially required them to give up their warrior culture, festered. Some bands either refused to accept annuities or did so under protest when threatened by a growing faction of Sioux who wanted nothing more to do with whites. In Sioux culture, refusing a gift terminates an established kinship tie.[11]

The year of the treaty was important among the Hunkpapas, nonetheless. It was when Four Horns, Red Horn, Loud-Voiced-Hawk, and Running Antelope became tribal "shirt-wearers." Wearing colorful clothing as badges of honor, shirt-wearers were chief tribal council executives who helped make and implement decisions affecting the tribe. Aided by *akicita*, or soldiers who functioned as a police force, they also served as protectors. For this lifetime service, their bands expected shirt wearers to maintain the impeccable qualities and morals that inspired their appointments.[12] Mato-cu-wi-hu, though not a shirt-wearer, was influential enough among his tribesmen that whites singled him out as an authoritative leader. However, because he had always been friendly to

---

[10]Harry Anderson, "Controversial Sioux Amendment," 201–202, 204, 206, 206n10. The other Platte Sioux signers were Yellow Ears, Standing Bear, Burnt Man, Eagle Body, Smoke, Bad Wound, Medicine Eagle, Man-Afraid, and The Big Crow.

[11]Vaughan to Cumming, 19 Oct. 1854, "Report of the Secretary of the Interior," 296–97, in Annual Report of Commissioner of Indian Affairs (CIA), U.S. Department of the Interior, *Annual Report*, 1854 (hereafter cited as CIA annual report). Regarding the meaning of gifts, see Price, *Oglala People*, 50, 60–61.

[12]Utley, *Lance*, 9; Larson, *Gall, Lakota War Chief*, 36; and Running Antelope, pictographic autobiography, SDSHS Archives.

traders and other whites who trickled into the Upper Missouri country, he was by mid-century a man apart from other more traditionalist Hunkpapa authority figures.

Before any military forts lined the Missouri River above present Nebraska, some Sioux bands had come to depend on French, British, and, more recently, AFC traders and their competitors for blankets, cloth, metal utensils, guns, ammunition, and other items. Fort Pierre, the main post northern Sioux patronized, stood on the west bank of the Missouri a few miles upriver from the mouth of the Teton, or Bad, River. Named for the AFC's Pierre Chouteau, Jr., and completed in 1832, it succeeded older, smaller trading structures operating in the area since 1822.[13] A mile-wide plain surrounding the fort accommodated large encampments. Fur company personnel could peer out of bastions on the southeast and northwest corners of the twenty-four-foot-high log picket enclosure to watch their Indian trading partners approach. In 1849, Indian Commissioner Orlando Brown reported Indians exchanged about 75,000 buffalo robes annually at Upper Missouri posts like Pierre. Each robe purchased $3 worth of goods, making trade worthwhile for the Indians. River travelers would often see Indian people of all ages and both sexes passing time outside the trading post gates. Some, like Mato-cu-wi-hu's *tiospaye*, or extended family group, lingered near the fort for weeks. Thus, at mid-century, Mato-cu-wi-hu's band interacted often with white traders and visitors.[14] In 1854, they and other Upper Missouri Sioux bands were waging war against the Crows, pushing them farther west, raiding their Assiniboine, Arikara, Hidatsa, Mandan, and Ponca neighbors, but generally tolerating white traders. Many had strong kinship ties with whites who were married to Sioux women and with their mixed-blood offspring.

Since the Lewis and Clark Expedition passed through the area bringing a new American presence to the Upper Missouri, social interactions, though not without conflict, had been trending toward equilibrium between Americans—non-Indian fur traders, trappers, boatmen, and government agents—and the Sioux and other Upper Missouri tribes.

---

[13]After John Jacob Astor sold the AFC in 1834, the firm became Pratte, Chouteau & Co. When Pratte left in 1838, it became Pierre Chouteau, Jr., & Co. The old name, however, continued in use. See Sunder, *Fur Trade*, 4–7. Whether Plains Indians depended on trade goods or regarded them as luxuries is debatable. See Swagerty, "Uncle Sam Is a Weak Old Fellow," 93–94, and Sunder, *Fur Trade*, 4–7.

[14]Culbertson, *Expedition*, 76; and CIA annual report, 1849, 1021–23. See Hyde, *Red Cloud's Folk*, chaps. 1–4; and Hassrick, *The Sioux*, ix–xi.

However, by mid-century, the fur-trade era and the relative stability it had fostered was waning.[15]

In August 1854, an incident over a cow, though occurring far away on the North Platte near Fort Laramie, initiated armed conflict that would profoundly affect the Upper Missouri Sioux. The trouble began when some 1,500 Plains Indians were camped near the fort while waiting for their government agent to distribute their Laramie Treaty annuities. High Forehead, a Miniconjou visiting the Brulé camp near James Bordeaux's trading post, waited with them. When an ostensibly lame cow from a passing wagon train strayed into their midst, High Forehead killed it, butchered it, and presumably shared it with his Brulé hosts.

No one can know if High Forehead entertained any thought of retaliation for an incident that had occurred a year earlier at a North Platte River ferry crossing near Fort Laramie. When soldiers operating the ferry in June 1853 for emigrants refused some Miniconjous access to it, warriors commandeered it. The soldiers regained it, but a Miniconjou man fired on them. Later that day, Second Lieutenant H. B. Fleming led a detachment to the Indian camp to arrest him, but he refused to go. Someone opened fire. In the end, at least four Indians died. Sioux bands camped near Fort Laramie demanded retaliatory justice, but the influential Oglala chief, Man-Afraid-of-His-Horse, restrained them. In September 1853, when the new version of the 1851 treaty circulated for signing, anger about it spurred new calls for vengeance for the killed Miniconjous, but when warriors threatened Fort Laramie's destruction, moderate leaders once again managed to prevent violence.[16]

Now, a year later, when the immigrants whose cow High Forehead killed reached Fort Laramie, they complained about their loss. In contrast to how Mato-cu-wi-hu handled the cow-killer at Fort Pierre, Conquering Bear approached Lieutenant Fleming at Fort Laramie to offer up High Forehead, who was not of his band, if soldiers would "send for" him. At first, Fleming, perhaps recalling the ramifications of his own experience during the ferry incident, demurred; ultimately, though, he ordered recent West Point graduate Brevet Second Lieutenant John L. Grattan to go to the Brulé camp to "receive" the Miniconjou.

Once again, the Oglala headman Man-Afraid was in a position to argue for moderation. He happened to be at Fort Laramie and accompanied Grattan when he left for Conquering Bear's camp the next day

[15]Denig, *Five Indian Tribes*, 26–27; and Ostler, *Plains Sioux and U.S. Colonialism*, 31–32.

[16]Ostler, *Lakotas and the Black Hills*, 42; and Paul, *Blue Water*, 15–16.

with twenty-seven privates, one sergeant, a corporal, and an interpreter. Dragging two field cannons and hauling some men in a wagon, Grattan was ready to demand High Forehead's surrender. Man-Afraid warned against confronting so many Indians with so few soldiers, and trader Bordeaux, the Brulé chief Big Partisan's son-in-law, also warned against proceeding. However, even after seeing what a large force the adjacent Oglala and Brulé camps could produce, Grattan soldiered on, leading his men straight into the Brulé camp. Big Partisan, Conquering Bear, and another Brulé leader, Little Thunder, came forward to plead with Grattan to let the tardy Indian agent handle the matter. By one account, Grattan answered by vowing to "have [High Forehead] or die." What each side heard may have been altogether different because Grattan's interpreter, Lucien Auguste, was drunk.[17] Ultimately, Man-Afraid went to High Forehead's lodge. Inside, he found six warriors stripped to their breechcloths, ready for battle, because High Forehead was unwilling to surrender. Someone called for Bordeaux, watching from the roof of his trade house, to translate, but events cascaded too quickly.

When the six Miniconjous stepped out of their tipi to load their guns, soldiers flanked their cannons to face them. Grattan rode back and forth speaking to his men, dismounted, and stood with Man-Afraid, who saw Conquering Bear walk off, looking behind him. The Miniconjous fired, and the officer, according to Man-Afraid, "pointed towards the Bear and talked a great deal." The soldiers shot Conquering Bear, then fired the cannon at the Miniconjous' tipi but missed.

Obridge Allen, a civilian with Grattan's party, watching from Bordeaux's roof, saw both cannons fire less than a minute after the shooting started. Bordeaux said Grattan fell after personally firing one cannon. After that, Indians surrounded the wagonload of soldiers trying to get away. In the end, the Brulés and Oglalas killed Grattan and all his men, the last dying from wounds two days later. Conquering Bear lingered six days, but when he died, those close to him did not consider the soldiers' deaths enough justice.[18]

Every winter, the Sioux marked hides with glyphs depicting the main event of the past year—a record called a winter count. Even northern

---

[17]Obridge Allen and Paul Carrey testified to Auguste's intoxication. See *Engagement Between Troops and Sioux*, 10, 16–17, 20.

[18]Paul, *Blue Water Creek*, 18–24; and *Engagement between Troops and Sioux*, 1–27. Fleming counted twenty privates in a 20 Aug. 1854 letter to Thomas, but corrected the number to twenty-seven in a 1 Sept. 1854 letter to Winship.

bands marked 1854–55 as the year Conquering Bear died. In the face of such a debacle as the annihilation of an entire army unit, small as it was, subsequent army correspondence showed that the whites failed to comprehend how important Conquering Bear's death was to the Sioux. Reports focused on military justifications and the need to punish the Indians. One can only guess at the Indians' complicated reaction to the fact that whites had shot down the very man they had three summers ago so esteemed that they virtually forced him to represent the Sioux Nation.[19]

Reactions of Washington politicos to the so-called Grattan Massacre were diverse. Secretary of War and future Confederate president Jefferson Davis termed it the outcome of a deliberately planned attack by the Sioux. Representative Thomas Hart Benton (Mo.), a former Senate military affairs committee chairman and staunch manifest destiny advocate, nevertheless called it "a heavy penalty for a nation to pay for a lame runaway Mormon cow, and for the folly and juvenile ambition of a West Point fledgling."[20]

Possibly anticipating retaliation, a group of Oglalas sent a message to Brevet Lieutenant Colonel William Hoffman, then commanding at Fort Laramie, blaming the Brulés for the Grattan affair, saying Oglalas had only a small part in it. The Brulés, however, soon avenged Conquering Bear. According to Little Thunder, Conquering Bear's tiospaye of about ten lodges, or households, joined Big Partisan and his five lodges in the Sand Hills. From there, Red Leaf and Big (or Long) Chin—who were half-brothers to one another and were both brothers of the slain chief— joined with their two other brothers and their nephew Spotted Tail and headed out to Fort Laramie. On November 13, they were opposite a Platte River mail station when a mail wagon rumbled toward them. Big Chin dared a reluctant Red Leaf, wounded during the Grattan fight, to attack it to avenge both himself and Conquering Bear. In Sioux culture, bravery was all-important, and retribution—though in this case it was sure to escalate conflict with whites—was an accepted way to obtain justice. To prove he was no coward, Red Leaf started the attack and killed two white men. Big Chin killed a third. They rode away with a mailbag

---

[19]Candace Greene and Thornton, *Year the Stars Fell*, 235–37. Also cf. the American Horse (also known as [a.k.a.] Black Shield), Battiste Good, Cloud Shield, Flame, Lone Dog, Long Soldier, Swan, Major Bush, and No Ears counts. See also Cheney, *Sioux Winter Count*, 30–31; White Bull, *Lakota Warrior*, 19; and Karol, *Red Horse Owner's Winter Count*, 35, 61.

[20]Utley, *Frontiersman in Blue*, 114–15; see Sides, *Blood and Thunder*, 47. Benton served from 1853–55 in the U.S. House.

containing considerable money along with other mail. The robbery was important enough to one Brulé winter-count keeper to mark his buffalo hide calendar with a glyph for 1854–55 meaning "plenty of money winter." Lieutenant Colonel Hoffman, following his own culture's path to justice, demanded the mail robbers' immediate surrender.[21]

AFTER STAYING THE WINTER OF 1853–54 AMONG THE UPPER Missouri Indians, Indian Agent Alfred J. Vaughan could report to Superintendent Alfred Cumming in St. Louis that peace prevailed among the several tribes in his jurisdiction, except among the Sihasapas and Hunkpapas. Instead of accepting annuities, Vaughan wrote, they preferred to sustain themselves by war and horse stealing. Hunkpapa animosity to government gifts was not new. Chief Little Bear, Mato-cu-wi-hu's predecessor, had expressed it in a speech recorded in 1849: "Are we dogs, that they throw to us the scraps they no longer want? If our grandfather [the president] is so rich and so powerful, let him send us a hundred boats loaded with merchandise and munitions for we need powder and bullets in great quantity, and what you give to us could be held in the hollow of our hand."[22]

According to fur trader and amateur anthropologist Edwin Thompson Denig, writing in 1854, Little Bear's chieftainship began when he murdered an AFC trader, who was married to a Hunkpapa woman, in the trader's Grand River home. Little Bear's war with traders was at least a year old by then. In 1853, he sent his akicita to destroy carts, kill horses, and flog traders trying to set up a winter trade house in Hunkpapa territory. Before the 1851 Laramie Treaty, the Hunkpapas, along with the Sihasapas and Sans Arcs who often hunted and lived near them, "could be dealt with although not without some trouble," Denig said, but afterward, they declared war on the government and all whites, threatened forts, and produced only enough buffalo robes for their own use. Denig

---

[21]"Big Missouri Winter Count," in Cheney, *Sioux Winter Count*, 10, 12, 30. Brulé medicine man Kills Two's interpretation for 1855 states, "The Sioux robbed a guarded stagecoach carrying the payroll for a western fort and took all the money. Spotted Tail, the leader, was later arrested and imprisoned" (Little Thunder, 8 Dec. 1854 statement, quoted in Paul, *Blue Water Creek*, 78). Usually five to eight people occupied a lodge. See Denig, *Five Indian Tribes*, 15; and chart in Warren, *Explorer on the Northern Plains* (hereafter cited as Warren reprint), 48.

[22]De Girardin, "Trip to the Bad Lands," 66. Cumming succeeded Mitchell after Whigs lost the 1854 election.

could not fathom why they wanted to "return to their primitive mode of life." He attributed their conduct to the "bad council and example of their rulers."[23]

In February 1854 about sixty Sihasapas and Hunkpapas smoked a peace pipe with a mixed-blood hunter at Fort William, a trading fort opposite the confluence of the Yellowstone and Missouri Rivers, before murdering him and moving on to Fort Union, the large AFC post three miles upstream on the Missouri, to steal some fifty horses. Agent Vaughan feared that only military action would stop such behavior.[24]

When Vaughan returned to the Upper Missouri that summer to distribute annuities, Yanktons at a camp thirty miles above the Niobrara River's mouth greeted him joyfully. Vaughan may already have been their kinsman; sometime during his Upper Missouri years he married a Yankton woman. Brulés, Two Kettles, and Sans Arcs at Fort Pierre also received him kindly, and the band of Yanktonais 250 miles upriver was obviously pleased with what he delivered. As the steamboat chugged toward Fort Union, non-Sioux tribes offered similar receptions.[25]

However, on his return trip during September and October, a hundred lodges of Hunkpapas and Sihasapas—approximately 800 people—had grown impatient waiting a month for him at Fort Clark, a trading post near the Arikaras' earth lodge village. In council, a headman told Vaughan to do what he liked with their share of annuities because they "preferred the liberty to take scalps, and commit whatever depredations they pleased." The normally jovial agent warned them the president would chastise them for their bad behavior and insults.[26]

Proceeding on downriver, Vaughan counseled with the Cuthead Sioux band, who, he reported, also disregarded the Laramie treaty. After Vaughan spoke, Red Leaf, a prominent chief of this mixed band of Santees (Dakotas) and Yanktonais (probably not the Brulé chief who attacked the mail wagon), rose to his feet, knife in hand.[27] Vaughan

---

[23]Denig, *Five Indian Tribes*, 27.

[24]Vaughan to Cumming, 6 March 1854, quoted in Vaughan, *Colonel Alfred Jefferson Vaughan*, in *Yankton Sioux Tribe et al. v. United States*; and Denig, *Five Indian Tribes*, xxiii, 25–28.

[25]Larpenteur, *Forty Years*, 346. Vaughan to Cumming, 30 Sept. 1854, CIA annual report, no. 27, 287–95.

[26]Vaughan to Cumming, 19 Oct. 1854, CIA annual report, no. 28, 287–97 (quote on p. 297). Fort Clark is near present Washburn, N.Dak. Hassrick, *The Sioux*, 90.

[27]Denig, *Five Indian Tribes*, 31, 34, 34n41. In 1855–56, Red Leaf headed the *Tete Coupees,* or Cutheads. Denig called him a "chief variable in temper and action as regards whites but possessing great influence in his band." See Jacobson, "History of the Yanktonai and Hunkpatina Sioux," 4–24.

watched, stunned, as Red Leaf "cut all the bags containing the provisions to pieces, scattering their contents on the prairie, then threw the keg of gunpowder in the river." Some fifty Indians shot at it, eliciting predictable results. Vaughan did not hide his panic from Cumming: "I assure you that my situation here, as well as that of all the traders and their men, at present is perilous in the extreme."[28]

Red Leaf's behavior may have been a response to Conquering Bear's August killing, just as was the other (Brulé) Red Leaf's attack with Spotted Tail and the others on the mail wagon far to the south. Alternatively—although Vaughan seemed sure of his identification of the bag-cutter as a Cuthead—he may have been that Brulé chief. In October 1854, Vaughan reported Oglala and Brulé bands within 150 miles of Fort Pierre trying to recruit Upper Missouri Indians to "join them in a general war on the whites." The southern Sioux warned that they would monitor the Laramie to Pierre and Platte River trails and kill any whites they encountered.[29]

In March 1855, after a winter of vexing reports and discussion concerning the killing of Grattan and his men, Secretary of War Davis acted. To him the Grattan affair was the result of a deliberate Sioux attack. He ordered Brevet Brigadier General William S. Harney to the Platte River country to punish them. With both the Sioux and the military choosing retribution in meting out justice, the conflict between them was on a path to alienation that would preclude both cultures from taking a middle ground with each other.

Harney had a long history with Indians. He had fought Sacs and Foxes during the Black Hawk War, Seminoles in Florida, Comanches and Lipans in Texas, and while building forts in Wisconsin before the Black Hawk War had fathered a daughter by a Winnebago woman. Harney was also familiar with the Upper Missouri region. As a young lieutenant, he was with the Henry Atkinson and Benjamin O'Fallon expedition of 1824–25 meant to counter British fur companies' alleged incitement of Upper Missouri Indians to attack American traders and trappers. Because

---

[28]Vaughan to Cumming, 19 Oct. 1854, CIA annual report, no. 28, 296–97.

[29]Ibid., 287–97; Cumming to Harney, 30 Nov. 1855, frames (fr) 1083–4, reel 538, M567, Letters Received by Adj. General's Office (LR AGO), Sioux Expedition (SE), National Archives (NA); and Paul, *Autobiography of Red Cloud*, 107.

its goal was to win over Indians with so-called friendship treaties, the expedition's members met many Upper Missouri Sioux leaders.[30]

Now, thirty years later at Fort Leavenworth, Harney assembled 1,200 men—nearly 10 percent of the country's small standing army—from Sixth Infantry, Second Dragoon, Second Infantry, and Fourth Artillery units. In April, Secretary of the Interior Robert McClelland directed Superintendent Cumming, in charge of all but the Minnesota Sioux, to order any trader who had done business with Indians complicit in or "confederated with" the Grattan massacre or the mail robbery to leave the country. McClelland advised Cumming to withhold presents to bands hostile to the government and to inform Harney of anything that might facilitate military operations.[31]

Harney wanted to hire Delaware and Pottawatomie guides, but these Indians feared losing their annuities if they signed on. Their refusal angered Harney, who initiated a long-standing personal quarrel with the U.S. Indian Bureau by accusing their agents of deliberately thwarting him. Even without guides, however, Harney was confident he could take on "all the hostile Sioux combined . . . but a victory . . . is no victory at all in the eyes of the Indians, unless we destroy more of them than they do of us. . . . Savages must be crushed before they can be completely conquered." He sent part of his force on Missouri River steamboats to occupy Fort Pierre, which the army purchased that spring from the AFC. They would head off any Platte River Sioux escaping north. Harney considered Fort Pierre pivotal to his operations against the approximately 7,000 warriors he thought the Sioux Nation could muster.[32]

While Harney prepared the 600 troops under his personal command for war, the new Platte River Indian agent, Thomas S. Twiss, invited those Sioux who were seeking peace to come to talks at his agency near Fort Laramie. Among them were Oglalas who, Twiss said, tried to keep their young men from joining militant northern bands and were "constantly" recapturing and turning in horses the "marauding" Upper Missouri Miniconjous had stolen. Little Thunder, regarded as Conquering

---

[30]Adams, *Harney*, 31, 35–36; and Jensen and Hutchins, *Wheel Boats*, 1.

[31]CIA annual report, 1855, p. 331. Dragoons fought afoot or on horseback. In 1854, fewer than 11,000 men served in the army's five military districts. See Bandel, *Frontier Life*, 21, 72n42, and Sides, *Blood and Thunder*, 28.

[32]Harney to Thomas, 2 June 1855, "Official Correspondence Relating to Fort Pierre" (hereafter cited as OCRFP), 387–89; Cooper to Harney, 22 March 1855, fr356–8; Harney to Cooper, 14 July 1855, fr45; and Harney to Thomas, 3 Aug. 1855, fr115–17, all on reel 518, M567, LR AGO, SE, NA; Adams, *Harney*, 125.

Bear's successor by whites, and whose Wazhaza Brulé band included Spotted Tail and the other mail robbers, ignored Twiss's summons.

Harney's intelligence had Little Thunder's forty or so lodges camped opposite Ash Hollow on the North Platte at a small stream called Blue Water Creek. The hollow, on the south side of the river, was a popular stop on the California-Oregon Trail because of its springs and large shade trees. Intending to force Little Thunder to turn over the robbers and everyone responsible for the Grattan affair, Harney moved his troops to Fort Kearny, then in August set out with two companies of dragoons, two of mounted infantry, and five of regular infantry.[33] Arriving at Ash Hollow, Harney made his camp and staging ground.

First, he sent his dragoons and mounted infantry across the Platte at night to encircle the Indian camp and approach it from the north. Once they were in position, he planned to move five companies of infantry in from the south. Learning of the infantry's presence at Ash Hollow, but unaware of the threat to his north, Little Thunder sent a fur trapper to tell the general he "could have peace or war, whichever he wished." Harney wanted war, but he dispatched interpreter Colin Campbell to propose a parley in order to buy time for his mounted troops.[34]

Lieutenant Gouverneur Kemble Warren, the expedition's topographical engineer, recorded the substance of Little Thunder's and Harney's conversation: Harney, noticing Indians striking their lodges and moving up the valley, chided Little Thunder: "You sent for me to come and fight you or have a talk and now you are running away." Little Thunder, who was quite tall—some say six feet, six inches—and had an authoritative demeanor, admitted he did not want to fight and had done all he could to avoid it.[35] Harney accused the Brulés of camping near the busy trail in order to "steal and plunder" from passing whites and reminded him that, by the 1851 treaty, the president had "paid them to keep off this road and let his white children pass." When Little Thunder told Harney that Twiss

[33]Twiss to Manypenny, 20 Aug. and 3 Sept. 1855, CIA annual report, nos. 25 and 26, 398–99; Bandel, *Frontier Life*, 84n153; and Sweeny to "Barton," 10 Dec. 1855, SW 850 (99), Sweeny Papers, Henry E. Huntington Library. Targeting Indian villages was not a new U.S. Army tactic. See Paul, *Blue Water Creek*, 47. Indian captives counted 41 Brulé and 11 Oglala lodges at Blue Water Creek. Harney's companies averaged 50 men. Fort Kearny, Neb., named for Stephen Watts Kearny, should not be confused with Fort Phil Kearny, Wyo., named for Stephen's nephew. For alternate spellings, see Athearn, *Sherman*, 20n3.

[34]Todd, "Harney Expedition," 110; Adams, *Harney*, 129; Utley, *Frontiersmen*, 116; and Paul, *Blue Water Creek*, 90–107.

[35]Description from Hyde, *Spotted Tail's Folk*, 43, 288n4.

had called him in to talk peace, Harney snapped that he cared less about what the agent said than he cared about "the barking of a prairie dog."

When tumult in the camp indicated the Indians had discovered the mounted force behind them, Little Thunder "was off like an arrow." Even as the chief rejoined his people, Harney's troops were firing at them. The battle of Ash Hollow, or properly, Blue Water Creek, had begun. At nine that morning, Harney recalled his troops; by noon they had all returned. The Brulés and Oglalas had never experienced such a battle. Eighty-six of the 300 or 400 people in the Indian villages lay dead, and 70 were in captivity.[36]

Lieutenant Warren, surveying the scene from atop a hill, confided to his journal that the sight was heartrending. He saw "wounded women & children crying & moaning, horribly mangled by the bullets" meant for the warriors whose cover they sought to share. He rescued and tended as best he could two wounded women, a baby, two young girls, and two boys while the army surgeon and his assistants gave other rescued women and children "all the attention that skill and humanity could bestow." The Second Dragoon's commander, Mexican War veteran Lieutenant Colonel Philip St. George Cooke, acknowledged that "much slaughter" was involved in the fight. He seemed to anticipate censure when he reported that "in the pursuit, women, if recognized, were generally passed by my men, but . . . in some cases certainly these women discharged arrows at them."[37]

Altogether, Harney lost four men killed, seven wounded, and one missing. His soldiers buried their own dead, leaving Indian bodies for scavengers. When Harney ordered the Indians' possessions burned, Warren gathered as many artifacts as he could to send to the Smithsonian Institution. Scalps of two white females along with documents from the mail coach robbery were convenient, if after-the-fact, justification for Harney's military action.[38]

Harney had his men build earthworks at the mouth of Blue Water Creek—a makeshift Fort Grattan—meant to protect travelers and the

---

[36]Transcription of Warren's journals in James Hanson, *Little Chief's Gatherings*, 104–107; Paul, *Blue Water Creek*, 105. Warren's journals are preserved in N.Y. State Library and Archives, Albany.

[37]McLaird and Turchen, "Dacota Explorations of Warren," 362–63; Drum, "Reminiscences of Indian Fight," 147; and Cooke to Winship and Harney to Thomas, both 5 Sept. 1855, CIA annual report, no. 58, copied in Werner, *With Harney*, 50–87.

[38]Harney to Thomas, 5 Sept. 1855, CIA annual report, no. 58, in Werner, *With Harney*, 50. See photos in James Hanson, *Little Chief's Gatherings*.

monthly mail between Forts Kearny and Laramie. He left a Sixth Infantry company to garrison it and monitor prisoners while he led his troops upriver to Fort Laramie. On September 10, Agent Twiss informed Lieutenant Colonel Hoffman that Little Thunder intended to ask Harney for peace on behalf of the North Platte Sioux bands. Meanwhile, the chief and his akicita would apprehend the mail party murderers and bring them "dead or alive" to Harney.[39]

Five days later, Man-Afraid-of-His-Horse and several other Oglala and Brulé leaders set up camp near Fort Laramie with about 300 lodges housing perhaps 2,400 people. Harney described them as "beg[ging] piteously to be spared" at a September 22 council, but he made peace contingent on their turning over stolen animals and the mail coach robbers. Despite Little Thunder's avowals to Twiss, neither he nor any other Brulé or Oglala chief would or could bring them in. Harney warned peace seekers to remain south of the Platte no matter what might happen on the north side. Meanwhile, he sent some dragoons to close down Fort Grattan and ordered the company guarding the prisoners there to take them to Fort Kearny. Little Thunder's family would remain with Harney.[40]

Observing the Indians had plenty of ammunition, Harney ordered traders to operate only near military posts so the army could monitor and stem the gun trade. Agent Twiss protested to Superintendent Cumming that this order was "wrong and fraught with evil. It is the remote cause of all the present Sioux difficulties . . . [and of] bitter and angry feelings between the Indians and the whites." Therefore, he forbade Indians to visit military posts without him. However, Twiss admitted the Blue Water fight was a "thunder clap" to the Indians. Now they understood truths they "did not believe before that chastisement." He predicted the northern Sioux would "have no desire nor wish to fight or prolong the war" with Harney.[41]

Leaving some dragoons to garrison Fort Riley in Kansas, Harney set off on September 29 with four dragoon companies, six infantry companies, and a Fourth Artillery battery on the 325-mile trek to Fort Pierre. His route, along an existing traders' trail, cut directly through Sioux territory.

[39]Harney to Thomas, 25 Sept. 1855, fr475, reel 518, M567, LR AGO, SE, NA; "Dacota Explorations," 368; and Twiss to Hoffman, 10 Sept. 1855, fr1086–87, reel 538, M567, LR AGO, SE, NA.

[40]Hyde, *Spotted Tail's Folk*, 68–74; McLaird and Turchen, "Dacota Explorations of Warren," 368; and Harney to Thomas, 25 Sept. 1855, fr475–77, reel 518, M567, LR AGO, SE, NA.

[41]Order, 18 Sept. 1855, Fort Pierre post returns (PR), reel 920, M617, NA; Circular, fr85, reel 538, M567, LR AGO, SE, NA; Adams, *Harney*, 133–35; Harney to Thomas, 24 and 26 Sept. 1855, fr88–91, 477, reel 538, M567, LS AGO, SE, NA; and CIA annual report, 1855, no. 27, Twiss to Manypenny, 1 Oct. 1855, and no. 28, Twiss to Cumming, 10 Oct. 1855, 400–405.

Seeing no Indians during the first ten days' march, Harney sent the artillery and two Sixth Infantry companies back to Fort Laramie.

Sketchy reports of Harney's battle began appearing in newspapers about September 24. A St. Louis paper included the provocative assertion that "the Indian women fought furiously." On October 10, a complete account, closely following Harney's official correspondence and dated September 5 from the Camp on the Blue Water, appeared in the *St. Louis Missouri Democrat*. Signed by "A Spectator," it was widely copied by other papers. Although Harney's superiors praised him, many people judged Ash Hollow as much a massacre as the year-ago Grattan fight. Opinions differed, even at official levels. George Manypenny, Indian commissioner when both events happened, later contended Harney attacked "an innocent band of Sioux Indians" uninvolved in that "sad affair."[42]

A great shift in perception had grown out of the summer's events. Now that the Sioux had experienced the U.S. military's power and will to fight them, they could no longer disregard it. Furthermore, Harney's response to the Grattan affair was one they could understand. Just as they conducted their own retaliatory attacks on ranchers and travelers as justice for Conquering Bear's death, they could accept that Harney's retaliatory actions sought justice for Grattan's men. However, it is doubtful any Sioux chief or warrior expected this conflict over a cow to escalate toward war on a nation-to-nation level. Harney wanted war, and he was ready to wage it against all or any Sioux.

---

[42]Harney to Thomas, 25 Sept. 1855, reel 518, M567, LR AGO, SE, fr475-7, NA; "The Latest News," *St. Paul (Minn.) Daily Pioneer*, 1 Oct. 1855, and "Correspondence of the *Missouri Democrat*. Gen. Harney's Battle with the Sioux," 10 Oct. 1855; Harney to Thomas, 5 Sept. 1855, CIA annual report, no. 58, in Werner, *With Harney*, 50–53; and Manypenny, *Our Indian Wards*, 159.

Chapter 2

"He Makes Us Tremble"

IN JUST OVER A YEAR, A DISPUTE OVER A COW SPIRALED INTO
conflict that gave secretary of war Jefferson Davis an excuse, if not justification, for a military solution to the problem of Sioux standing in
the way of westward expansion. General Harney, having avenged the
thirty soldiers killed in the Gratton fight, was now poised to fight the
entire Sioux Nation.

Brevet Brigadier General William S. Harney was fifty-five in 1855.
His auburn hair, beard, and mustache had turned white, but his six-
foot-four, broad-chested frame was still imposing; his blue-eyed gaze
still penetrating. An observer noted that Harney stood "as straight and
erect as any Sioux chief." He was "brusque in manner, rough in mould
and mein, . . . harsh of speech, and in no way fastidious about his choice
of adjectives to emphasize his commands or displeasure."[1]

Because images of Mato-cu-wi-hu hint he was of typical male Sioux
stature—six feet, on average, and with "strong muscular frames"—he
and Harney probably stood eyeball to eyeball. In their intolerance for
insubordination, the two also might have seen eye-to-eye. In 1834, Harney beat a household slave so severely she died. Though he was indicted
for murder, a jury acquitted him. In 1844, at Fort Washita, he berated
a private who refused to dig a latrine, threw him on the ground by his
hair, and beat him with a walking stick, inflicting injuries that kept the
man hospitalized for a week. During Harney's time on the Upper Missouri, a witness saw him savagely beat a teamster who mistreated a mule.[2]

However, just as with Mato-cu-wi-hu, Harney's behavior may not have
been solely an expression of his personality. American military culture
tolerated what some contemporaries considered cruel treatment. In 1866,

[1]Adams, *Harney*, 3, 8, 134, 162; and George Miller, "Military Camp," 119–20. Throughout,
original materials are reproduced as written, without correcting spelling.

[2]"Report," Latta to Dole, 27 Aug. 1862, CIA annual report, 336–41; Adams, *Harney*, xvi, 8,
47–51, 80, 128, 139–40; George Miller, "Military Camp," 120; and Beam, "Reminiscence of Early
Days," 304–305.

Private William Murphy of the Eighteenth Infantry witnessed a soldier being punished for drunkenness by being made to lie on the ground under a hot summer sun with his arms and legs stretched and tied to four stakes. Flies swarmed around his face and entered his mouth, nose, and ears. This treatment, Murphy said, was called "spread-eagling."[3]

The six Second Infantry companies Harney sent ahead to begin converting Fort Pierre to a military installation were possibly the first American soldiers young Upper Missouri Sioux ever encountered. Three decades earlier, when Harney was with the Atkinson and O'Fallon expedition, their fathers or grandfathers signed treaties acknowledging they lived within the territorial limits of the United States, which would protect them and provide occasional "benefits and acts of kindness." They had agreed to trade only with Americans, whom they vowed to protect while turning over to American authorities any foreign traders who entered their country. Finally, the chiefs had agreed to surrender stolen property and anyone guilty of misconduct to government agents.[4] Those soldiers went home and, likely, out of the minds of most Upper Missouri Sioux.

Harney's vanguard soldiers soon discovered that its remote location in the vast, newly created, sparsely populated Nebraska Territory made Pierre a hardship station. Sioux City, in the state of Iowa, was only a few cabins at the Big Sioux and Missouri Rivers' confluence, but it was their nearest post office.[5] Between Sioux City and Fort Pierre—about 265 miles—only a few fur traders' cabins, seasonal Indian camps, and semi-permanent Indian villages dotted the Missouri's banks. From Fort Pierre upriver to the Missouri's source in the Rocky Mountains, only the fur forts Benton, Union, and Berthold; some smaller trade houses; and the Mandan, Hidatsa, and Arikara towns near Berthold supported any permanent population.

Transporting men, equipment, and supplies to Fort Pierre in what one soldier called "this wild region of the Far West," proved difficult. Because of abnormally low water, the troops had to lighten the steamboats by unloading stores at several points below the fort, leaving men behind

---

[3]Monnett, *Where a Hundred Soldiers Were Killed*, 43.

[4]Kappler, *Indian Affairs*, vol. 2, *Treaties*, 227–30. Talks took place 22 June, 5 and 16 July 1825. Harney signed as witness 22 June 1825.

[5]George Miller, "Fort Pierre," 110–11, 114; and Wessells to Thomas, 8 Jan. 1856, OCRFP. Iowa became a state in 1846. The Kansas–Nebraska Act became law 30 May 1854. Nebraska Territory stretched north to the international border from the fortieth parallel and west from the Missouri River to the Continental Divide and included parts of present-day N.Dak., S.Dak., Mont., Colo., and Wyo.

to guard them. Consequently, the six companies' arrival at Fort Pierre beginning July 7, 1855, was, according to temporary post commander Major W. R. Montgomery, "protracted and in detachments." Valuable supplies sank with one of the boats. On two boats, cholera became epidemic. At Omaha, quartermaster Parmenus T. Turnley hired the town's only physician, Dr. George L. Miller, to accompany the expedition to Fort Pierre.[6]

Dr. Miller's stay at the fort coincided with that of a large contingent of Sioux—he estimated 6,000—who probably remained to trade robes and furs after the AFC steamboat *St. Mary* brought them their Fort Laramie treaty goods. When that boat returned from its annual trip to upriver posts, Miller, still at Fort Pierre, observed Indians at council augment their speeches with graceful, eloquent sign language and sometimes-flamboyant gestures. The experience awed him. "A finer body of men in physical stature and dignity of personal bearing I never saw in my life than . . . these untutored Sioux Indians."[7]

Before trekking overland to join Harney in time for the Blue Water battle, Lieutenant Warren had set aside more than 310 square miles for the Fort Pierre military reservation, explaining that sparse resources required a large area. Indeed, the men found necessities—feed for livestock and fuel for themselves—hard to come by. Early in August, Montgomery had to send a detachment twelve miles below the fort for hay and wood. Despite hardships, several wives had come along or would soon join their husbands. When Mrs. William Harrison, wife of a private in Company D, Second Infantry, gave birth on board the steamboat *Genoa* on the way to Fort Pierre, the couple named their daughter after the boat. The sutler's wife and her baby boy along with Turnley's wife and their baby girl were curiosities to the local Indians, who would spend hours watching them through cottage windows.[8]

In June, agent Vaughan and supervisor Cumming delivered annuities to the Yanktons at Handy's Point, a favorite camp about thirty land miles above the Niobrara River's mouth. Vaughan reported them

---

[6]Coyer, "Wild Region," 232–54; Montgomery to Cooper, 31 July 1855, OCRFP, 389–90; and Turnley, *Reminiscences*, 135, 138. George Miller, "Fort Pierre," 112–13, reported one cholera death.

[7]George Miller, "Fort Pierre," 117–18.

[8]Warren to Winship, 7 Aug. 1855, OCRFP, 391–94; Fort Pierre PR, Aug. 1855, reel 518, M617, NA; Turnley, *Reminiscences*, 158–59, 161, 168–69; Coyer, "Wild Region," 247; Meyers, *Ten Years*, 66. Sweeny to wife, 9 May 1856, mentions Mrs. [Thomas C.] Madison, Mrs. Thomas Wright, and Mrs. Christopher S. Lovell. Dr. Miller's wife accompanied him to Fort Pierre (cited in George Miller, "Fort Pierre"). See also Van Vleit to Turnley, OCRFP, 401; and George Miller, "Fort Pierre," 121.

grateful that the president had sent soldiers. However, at Fort Pierre only twenty-seven lodges of Two Kettle Lakotas and a small contingent of Lower Yanktonai Nakotas accepted, but did not seem grateful for, the government presents. A hundred miles farther upstream, the Lower Yanktonai chief Little Soldier's twelve earth-lodge households seemed satisfied with their gifts. They were tending crops, but Vaughan feared a severe drought doomed their harvest.[9]

Next, 840 Arikaras who were crowded into sixty earth lodges at Fort Clark welcomed the two men but complained about Sioux "depredations and murders." The Sioux outnumbered them and were better armed, so the Arikaras hoped the soldiers would chastise treaty violators and protect its adherents. Although drought and an August frost damaged Arikara crops, Vaughan thought they would have enough for themselves but not enough to trade. Vaughan and Cumming found the Mandan population, which had been severely reduced by a smallpox epidemic during 1837–38, had increased to about 252 individuals living in twelve lodges.

While at Fort Clark, Cumming, who would continue upriver to make a treaty with the Blackfeet (Siksika) tribe, sent runners to the Hunkpapas and Sihasapas to meet him when he returned in the fall. The Sioux held the messengers captive twelve days before fifty-four chiefs and principal men arrived at Fort Clark. Cumming was gone, but a chief told Vaughan that, although he wanted to accept the annuities, if he did, the others would likely kill him, his companions, and their horses. The delegation left promising to bring part of their people to accept their annuities when Vaughan and Cumming returned from upriver.

Vaughan next visited the forty lodges of Hidatsas, a tribe related to the Crows and numbering about 760, who lived at Like-a-Fishhook Village, also known as Fort Berthold. They, too, complained about Sioux stealing horses and murdering their people and were pleased that soldiers were on the Upper Missouri. At his next stop, Fort Union, Vaughan gushed about the Assiniboines. He called these Sioux enemies—although linguistic relatives—"the best Indians on the continent" because they honored their Laramie treaty obligations. People living around Fort Union could not let down their guard, however. In May, a party of Hunkpapas and Sihasapas attacked seven Fort Union employees, wounding two and robbing them. Horses disappeared from Forts Union and William, and

---

[9]Jacobson, "History of the Yanktonai and Hunkpatina Sioux," 4–5, 13–14, 20, 22. Little Soldier's band was a subgroup of Two Bear's *Honcpatela* or Lower Yanktonai band. For Yanktonai earth lodges, see Hurt, "Additional Notes"; and "Wiciyela or Middle Dakota," 2–3.

a pair of hunters lost meat, horses, guns, and clothing to Sioux raiders. Because Sioux war parties were still in the Yellowstone country, Vaughan did not attempt to deliver the Crows' annuities, nor could he persuade fur company personnel to do it.

When fifteen Sans Arc and Miniconjou Sioux appeared on the hills near Fort Union, Vaughan invited them for a parley inside the fort. They admitted to Vaughan's interpreter, Zephyr Rencontre, that they were among 220 warriors intent on "hunting" Assiniboines. The tribes had been warring since the early 1700s, but this latest skirmish was important enough that a Brulé Sioux winter count—instead of depicting Conquering Bear's death—designated 1854–55 as when the Sioux killed five Assiniboines. Now, in late summer 1855, these warriors told Vaughan that before they left their villages, some Miniconjous had returned from stealing government mules and horses from Fort Laramie. After Vaughan lectured them about violating treaty stipulations, this group vowed to go home and depredate no more. During this time, Sioux also raided livestock from stage stations, forts, and private ranches along the Oregon and Mormon trails.[10]

A few days later, when Fort Union sent out its usual "outfit" to trade with the Crows, Vaughan tried again to deliver the annuities. Seven Crow hunters who had come to escort Vaughan pressed ahead up the Yellowstone, where Sioux, possibly those Vaughan had entertained, attacked them. The seven hunters considered their escape "miraculous." Vaughan left the goods at Fort Union and returned to Fort Clark to await the Hunkpapas and Sihasapas, said to be two days, or about a hundred miles, distant. He invited Yanktonais camped four days away also to come for their presents. Meanwhile, he began his report to Cumming, who was still upriver. The presence of troops had brought about "great change in the conduct" among the Hunkpapas and Yanktonais, and he suggested that Fort Pierre's commanding officer and a "formidable number" of soldiers show themselves at Sioux villages in order to reduce the number of murders and robberies they customarily committed. Besides, he advised, such an excursion would familiarize the officers with the country.

Game had been so scarce along the river during spring that, according to Vaughan, some inhabitants had to "subsist solely on the carcasses of

---

[10]Vaughan to Cumming, 12 Sept. 1855, CIA annual report, 1855, no. 24, 391–98 (quote about "best Indians on the continent" on p. 394); Werner, *With Harney*, 21–22; Hoffman to Pleasonton, 4 Nov. 1855, fr1077, reel 538, M567, LR AGO, SE, NA; and Utley, *Frontiersmen*, 115. Battiste Good glyphs depict warfare with Assiniboines beginning in 1709–10. See Candace Greene and Thornton, *Year the Stars Fell*, 75, 77–78, 86, 89, 91–92, 95, 97, 236.

drowned buffalo, which they find on the banks and sand-bars of the river; in the summer and fall upon roots. . . . Starvation must be the ultimate fate of most of the Sioux bands," he surmised, "and they plainly see it." Nevertheless, Sioux leaders, insisting their people had been "created for the chase," would not take up other work. Vaughan blamed destitution for Sioux aggression. In early September, a party of Hidatsas visited Vaughan at Fort Clark to return five horses they had stolen from the Sioux. They asked Vaughan to guarantee that, in return, the Hunkpapas would give up five horses they had stolen from them.[11] Vaughan knew nothing yet of the September 3 battle at Blue Water, but perhaps the Upper Missouri Sioux did. In any case, they continued to delay coming to Fort Clark.

EARLY DURING HIS MARCH TO FORT PIERRE, HARNEY SENT FOR the six Second Infantry companies there to meet him on the Pierre– Laramie trail. It took weeks for Harney's order to reach Pierre; it was September 16 before seven officers and 250 men started. Iron Horn (Miniconjou), Yellow Hawk (Sans Arc), and another chief, Rising Sun, together representing what Lieutenant Thomas W. Sweeny considered "two of the most warlike tribes of the Sioux nation," accompanied them, they said, in order to discuss peace terms with Harney.[12] Instead of meeting Harney, the Fort Pierre group met an expressman bearing news of the battle and Harney's orders for them to turn back. According to Sweeny, the three chiefs seemed "greatly alarmed" at the news. Taking advantage of this anxiety, the officers warned them that, in return for peace, they must surrender anyone who had murdered whites or stolen their property. A few days later, the chiefs hastened home ahead of the soldiers. Possibly, they spread word of the Blue Water battle to the Upper Missouri bands before Brulé and Oglala runners could do so. The Second Infantry soldiers reached Fort Pierre only a few days before Harney, who arrived during a sleet storm with his four Second Dragoon and four Sixth Infantry companies.

Harney learned later that on October 18, just as he and his men were in sight of Fort Pierre, the mail robbers from Little Thunder's Brulé

---

[11]Vaughan to Cumming, 12 Sept. 1855, CIA annual report, no. 24, 391–98 (direct quotes of Vaughn on p. 396). Boller, *Among the Indians*, 95, also mentions Indians eating drowned buffalo.

[12]Charles Hanson, "Fort Pierre–Fort Laramie Trail," 3–7. Band affiliations of Iron Horn and Yellow Hawk (Rising Sun not listed) from Harney Council and from Council reprint, 24–26.

band—Red Leaf, Long Chin, and Spotted Tail—fearing for their captive families—surrendered at Fort Laramie. One boy who was in on the
mail robbery was too sick to leave his lodge, but the other surrendered
then escaped. The chiefs returned him to Hoffman at Fort Laramie, but
the sick youth remained ill. Finally, Hoffman accepted as substitutes the
warriors Standing Elk and Red Plume. When the escort led the prisoners
away to Fort Leavenworth, several family members accompanied them.[13]

General Harney was appalled at the ramshackle collection of buildings
that comprised Fort Pierre and for which the army paid $45,000. He
was also furious that his men had not even constructed proper "sinks"
(latrines) or made the place livable. The soldiers had erected some portable
prefabricated barracks that their inventor, the expedition's quartermaster,
Captain Turnley, had intended for southern posts. Painted red inside and
out, they perched on stilts two feet above ground. The men would find
these rickety, uninsulated three-quarter-inch board structures inadequate
during Upper Missouri thunderstorms and blizzards.[14]

Recognizing that not all his nearly 900 men could be housed near the
fort, even crowded thirty to each building, Harney dispersed them to
temporary winter quarters. Two Second Infantry companies remained
near the stockade, but three others dug in at camps a few miles upriver;
another set up below on Farm Island. The four Sixth Infantry companies
settled in on the Missouri's east bank twelve miles above the fort near
where a Yanktonai band was spending the winter. The exiled soldiers
built log houses and fared better than those living in the prefabricated
barracks. Only Harney and his staff stayed inside the fort walls.[15]

In addition to redistributing his infantrymen, Harney sent some dragoons to a location near Fort Lookout trading post. He ordered Major
Marshall S. Howe farther downriver with another dragoon squadron
and some Second Infantry privates to help unload supplies from the *Grey
Cloud*, stalled above the Niobrara's mouth at Ponca Island. Howe was also
to establish a cantonment, or temporary camp, suitable for a permanent

---

[13]Fort Pierre PR, Oct. 1855; Hoffman to Pleasonton, 9 Feb. 1856, fr22–28, reel 539, M567; affidavits by Jarvis, 7 Feb. 1856, fr35; Bordeau, fr38; and Ward, fr53, reel 539, M567, all from LR AGO,
SE, NA. Also, Hoffman to Winship, 4, 6, and 8 Nov. 1855; Hoffman to Pleasonton, 13 Dec. 1855;
Howe to Hoffman, 4 Jan. 1856; Hoffman to Pleasonton, 6 Jan. 1856, 11 Feb. 1856, and 12 Feb. 1856,
all from reel 536, M567, LR AGO, SE, NA; and Hyde, *Spotted Tail's Folk*, 76.

[14]Meyers, *Ten Years*, 72–73, 90–93; Nowak, "From Fort Pierre to Fort Randall"; Athearn, *Forts
of the Upper Missouri*, 40; Turnley, *Reminiscences*, 127–29; Todd, "Harney Expedition," 117–25;
Adams, *Harney*, 135–40; Utley, *Frontiersmen*, 117; and Paul, *Blue Water Creek*, 73.

[15]Fort Pierre PR, Jan.–June 1856, reel 920, M617, NA; and Sweeny to wife, 26 Feb. 1856, SW 850
(103), Sweeny Papers, Henry E. Huntington Library.

military post somewhere between the White and Niobrara Rivers. To relay communications among his far-flung troops, Harney employed local mixed-bloods and Indians as expressmen. "They are willing," he reported, and "will be useful and economical agents." Even Mato-cu-wi-hu's brother, Running Antelope, a noted orator, served as courier.[16]

In early November, Iron Horn, Yellow Hawk, and Rising Sun, with some twenty warriors, came to Fort Pierre under a white flag. Harney reported that these Sans Arcs, Hunkpapas, Miniconjous, Two Kettles, Yanktonais, Yanktons, Oglalas, and Santees claimed to be "in a pitiable condition, suffering for everything," and "only want[ed] to live." To prove their sincerity, they brought in stolen horses and mules and a warrior who had killed a white man. Harney distributed provisions and let them keep the prisoner in custody. According to Sweeny, "In the morning they were missing, all except Iron Horn, who surrendered himself, expecting, no doubt, to be shot or hung instantly." The old man, as Sweeny described him, "said he saw no hope of making peace after what happened; so he made up his mind to die . . . and he seemed to be much surprised that he was not thus disposed of." In his report, Harney remarked that Indians viewed imprisonment "with so much dread and detestation, as frequently to attempt their own lives."[17] Sweeny believed Iron Horn and all the old chiefs sincerely wanted peace, but young warriors "almost to a man, oppose them." When no one pursued them and Iron Horn remained alive, a larger contingent of Sioux returned under a white flag to talk with Harney.[18]

Before Harney's November meeting with the chiefs, Secretary Davis had suggested that if Harney found it appropriate, he should hold a convention with submissive Sioux leaders. In an October 10, 1855, letter, Adjutant General Samuel Cooper authorized Harney to tell the Indians that his convention would be "preliminary to a treaty made with them by the Department having charge of Indian Affairs." Despite that a military-sponsored treaty would impinge on U.S. Indian Bureau

---

[16]Fort Pierre post returns for Oct. 1855 say Howe took Companies E and K, not one as in Harney's Order no. 19, 1 Nov. 1855, Fort Pierre. For more on Howe and the other dragoons, see OCRFP, 405, and Harney to Cooper, 21 Feb. 1856, fr994-8, reel 538, M567, SE, LR AGO, NA. Fort Lookout was near present Chamberlain, S.Dak. "They are willing" quote is from 8 March 1856 letter to Secretary of War Davis in Harney Council, 1–2. Running Antelope's work for Harney in De Trobriand, *Army Life*, 16 Oct. 1867, 124.

[17]Bandel, *Frontier Life*, 38; and Harney to Davis, 10 Nov. 1855, fr646-59, reel 518, M567, and Harney to Thomas, 9 May 1856, fr365-6, reel 539, M567, both in LR AGO, SE, NA.

[18]Sweeny to "Barton," 10 Dec. 1855, SW 850 (99), and 15 Dec. 1855 addendum, Sweeny Papers, Henry E. Huntington Library.

jurisdiction and exacerbate animosity building between the two bureau-
cracies, Davis directed Harney in December 1855 to go ahead with his
March 1856 "convention or treaty." Accordingly, Harney sent directives
like the following one dated November 9, 1855, to the main chiefs of
nine Sioux bands:

> To the Two Bears, Yanktonais.
> I wish to see ten men of your Band—the men whom your people most
> trust—men whom I can rely upon and believe all they say. I want them to
> come on the 1st of March; or one hundred days after this time. I will then
> tell them what I expect and require them to do. All those who wish the
> war to continue, must not come in. The Chiefs must come and the men
> with them and these must be such as can answer for their Band. All who
> come in under this invitation, shall be free to go when they please. If they
> comply with my demands, it may end the war.[19]

Harney's animosity toward the Indian Bureau found another outlet
when Superintendent Cumming and his party stopped at Fort Pierre on
their return from the Siksika (non-Sioux Blackfeet tribe) treaty negotiations upriver. Blaming Big Head's Yanktonai band for stealing their
mules and horses, they asked Harney for replacements. The story, perhaps
apocryphal, was that the trim, fit, towering Harney informed the 300-
pound Cumming that he had plenty of mules, "but you can't have one; and
I only regret that when the Indians got your mules they didn't get your
scalp also. . . . Here all summer I and my men have suffered and boiled to
chastise these wretches while you have been patching up another of your
sham treaties to be broken tomorrow and give us more work." Ultimately,
Charles Galpin, the AFC trader who had helped negotiate the sale of
Fort Pierre to the army and who was building a new AFC trading post a
few miles above Fort Pierre, provided the mules.[20] Lieutenant Colonel
Hoffman at Fort Laramie kept the feud alive over the winter when he
wrote Harney that Agent Twiss had been "pursuing a course calculated
to thwart" Harney's policy of allowing Indians to trade only near military

[19]Cooper to Harney, 10 Oct. 1855, fr646-59; Davis to Harney, 26 Dec. 1855, fr661-5, reel 518, M567, and Circular, 9 Nov. 1855, fr673, reel 518, M567, all in LR AGO, SE, NA; Harney Council, pp. 4–5, Adams, and Two Bear letter, Frank Zahn Collection, SHSND Archives. For a discussion of Harney's lack of authority to conduct a treaty, see Adams, *Harney*, 136–38.

[20]Harney to Cooper, 21 Nov. 1855, LR AGO, SE, fr667 and fr700-03, RG 94, NA; Cumming to Harney, 19 Nov. 1855, LR AGO, SE, fr1080-1, and Vaughan to Harney, 2 March 1856, fr1096-7, RG 94, NA; Vaughan to Cumming, 15 Feb. 1856, reel 539, M567, LR AGO, SE, fr57, NA; and Sunder, *Fur Trade*, 172. For difficulties over pricing Fort Pierre, see Turnley, *Reminiscences*, 145–48, 153–55. Cumming story in Chittenden, *Steamboat Navigation*, 356n.

posts. Furthermore, Hoffman collected affidavits from traders and others accusing Twiss of trading Indian annuity goods for personal gain.[21]

Soon after Harney rebuffed Cumming, Big Head and his principal men visited Fort Clark to see what annuity goods Vaughan, who remained there after Cumming left for St. Louis, set aside for their band. Examining the goods, Big Head, whose band represented perhaps one-fourth of all Yanktonais, told Vaughan that because of bad weather and the "destitute condition of his people" he would take as many blankets, knives, and fabric with him now that his few pack animals could carry. A few weeks later he returned with his principal men well armed and, as Vaughan reported, "showing . . . unmistakeable signs of hostility." They accepted Vaughan's invitation to a feast, but with "cold independent indifference."

Big Head opened discussions "by deliberately lifting [Vaughan's] spectacles from [his] eyes and remarking[,] in a passion, that he wished to see the presents he had left." Vaughan led Big Head and five of his companions, all armed, into the storeroom while those left outdoors in the 22-below-zero weather began a barrage of gunfire. "Nothing was indiscreet enough to cross their path but a cat and seven chickens," Vaughan told Cumming. Only the cat survived the three-hour-long shooting spree, during which Vaughan remained in the storeroom as the Indians vilified him and the president. Someone had told them their share of the annuities should be $2,000; they judged these worth less than half that. Where, they asked, were the powder, balls, guns, and rice? When Vaughan denied he had those things, they accused him of hiding goods somewhere in the fort. The more Vaughan talked, "the more furious they became." Fearfully, he eased away to his quarters. On the following day, all the Indians stormed into the fort, shooting. They placed lookouts at each gate before "twenty rushed into my room and closed the door." Guards stood outside his and other rooms where employees holed up. The men in his room "furiously struck the butts of their Guns on the floor, drawing the balls, putting them into their Mouths, then dropping them into their hands and rubbing them dry, and placing

---

[21]Bordeau, Jarvis, Ward, and Guerrier affidavits in Pleasonton 27 Feb. 1856 letter and Hoffman to Pleasonton, 9 Feb. 1856, fr22–27, 31, 36, 40, 41, reel 539, M567, and Vaughan's 22 March 1856 interview with Twiss's interpreter, fr1042-8, reel 539, M567, all in LR AGO, SE, NA. The Twiss–Harney quarrel is further documented in fr168, 170–71, 173, 175, 178–79, 181, 183–84, 186, reel 539, M567, LR AGO, SE, NA. See also Manypenny, *Our Indian Wards*, 156–59; Kvasnicka and Viola, *Commissioners*, 61; Utley, *Frontiersmen*, 119; Hyde, *Spotted Tail's Folk*, 76, 76n4, 130; and Snowden, "Journal, 27 June–15 November 1857," pp. 64–66, folder 6, box 9, Warren Papers, New York State Library and Archives (hereafter cited as Snowden's Warren Expedition journal).

them back into their guns." Vaughan interpreted these actions to mean they were ready to kill him. Although his report does not explain how this scene played out, he survived to blame unnamed "designing White men" for the incident. Vaughan probably did not know how the general had treated his boss when he reported to Cumming how gratified he was that a "new era is about to dawn" because "there is a 'Harney' upon the watch tower" to usher it in.[22]

Cold had enveloped the Indian camps and the men at Fort Pierre and its cantonments well before the winter of 1855–56 officially began. On December 9 Harney ordered that shoes issued to his men be "large enough to permit grass or hay to be worn on [the] inside," presumably for insulation. Worried because he had heard nothing from Howe's dragoons, Harney set out five days before Christmas with a detachment to find them but also to scout a more accessible, more easily supplied location for a permanent fort to replace Pierre. The group marched through deep snow and below-zero weather. Several men, including the general, suffered frostbite. Three animals died. After marching 230 miles in eighteen days in these conditions, they arrived at Ponca Island January 7. Concern for Howe turned to anger when Harney found him sharing comfortable quarters with the steamboat's captain on the *Grey Cloud* while his men camped on the open prairie instead of sheltering in woods a mile distant. Howe's surviving animals, Harney reported, "are pitiable objects." He declared Howe unfit for command and arrested him.[23]

Harney learned of a likely location for a post on the Big Sioux River some 130 land miles from the Ponca Island camp that was already the winter rendezvous for Yanktons, Santees, and Poncas. (Because the Poncas lived near the Yanktons, Harney mistook these offshoots of the Omaha tribe for Sioux.) Five hundred Santees, whom he described as Indians who "have annuities and supplies, and who divide their ammunition with the others when bent on mischief," were currently camped on the Big Sioux. Because it was their habit in spring "to rob and maraud upon the settlers," Harney would install six companies on the west bank in order to deter them, protect the Nebraska frontier, control Indians on

[22]Vaughan to Cumming, 15 Feb. 1856, SE, fr57-63, reel 539, M567, LR AGO, SE, NA. See also Holley, *Once Their Home*, 64–65.

[23]Sweeny to wife, 10 Feb. 1856 and 26 Feb. 1856, SW 850(102) and SW 850(103), Sweeny Papers, Henry E. Huntington Library; Harney to Thomas, 11 Jan. 1856, fr740-745, and Harney to Cooper, 20 Feb. 1856, fr994-8, reel 539, M567, LR AGO, SE, NA; Coyer, "Wild Region," 243; Wessells to Cooper, 8 Jan. 1856, OCRFP, 415; and Clow, "Mad Bear," 145.

the Iowa frontier, and keep the Minnesota Sioux away from the Missouri River. A Big Sioux garrison could "flank and check" Sioux bands north or east of the Missouri and keep communication open with Fort Pierre, where Harney would leave two infantry companies.[24]

Despite the brutal weather and threat of attack from Indians who were desperate because of cold and starvation, enlisted men tried to escape from Fort Pierre. During their Ponca Island trip, Harney and his escort captured two deserters who, Lieutenant Sweeny wrote his wife, "were in rather a bad condition; four of their comrades were frozen to death, and they had been living off the bodies for several weeks." Harney returned to Pierre too late to campaign against Big Head, who, after bullying Vaughan, had joined Sihasapas and Hunkpapas west of the Missouri.[25]

When Vaughan arrived at Fort Pierre February 2 from Fort Clark, ten Sioux chiefs were already awaiting Harney's March 1 conference. Vaughan wrote Cumming that his "heart was moved . . . at the solemn appeals that the heads of this once powerful nation made." Their unnamed spokesman was contrite: Instead of believing those who warned that soldiers would come, "we closed our ears and would not listen, but our eyes are open and we now see." He apologized for Big Head's treatment of Vaughan, adding that the agent's "heart must be good for we never saw you angry, neither did we ever come with empty hands but what you filled them." The spokesman asked Vaughan to plead their cause to Harney, saying that "the Big Chief of the Soldiers is an awful man, when he speaks to us he makes us tremble."

Vaughan rejoiced in his report that Harney had "produced more terror and dismay among those hostile Sioux and renegade White men . . . than any one could have imagined or dreamed of." To end war with the Sioux, "it is only necessary now to exterminate Big Head's party, and one-third of the Blackfeet Sioux [Sihasapa] and Uncpapa [Hunkpapa] Bands." After that, "peace, happiness and prosperity will be restored to those different tribes disposed to do right."[26]

---

[24]Lee to Stoker et al., 9 March 1857, fr59l, Fort Randall Letters Sent (LS), 1856–67, RG98, NA; Harney to Thomas, 11 Jan. 1856, fr994–98, and Harney to Cooper, 21 Feb. 1856, fr740–45, reel 539, M567, LR AGO, SE; and Harney to Cooper, 20 Jan. 1856, OCRFP, 416–18.

[25]Sweeny to wife, 10 Feb. 1856 and 26 Feb. 1856, SW 850(102) and SW 850(103), Sweeny Papers, Henry E. Huntington Library; Harney to Thomas, 11 Jan. 1856, fr740–45, Harney to Cooper, 24 Feb. 1856, fr2, and Vaughan to Cumming, 15 Feb. 1856, fr57, all three on reel 539, M567, LR AGO, SE, NA; and Clow, "Mad Bear," 145.

[26]Vaughan to Cumming, 15 Feb. 1856, fr57-63, reel 539, M567, LR AGO, SE, NA. All quotes are on frames 60 and 61.

As the winter of 1855–56 dragged on at Fort Pierre, some Second Infantry soldiers found company and warm buffalo robes in the Yanktonai camp of about twenty lodges near Cantonment Miller. They learned Indian games and tried to teach the Indians to play poker, despairing of that when they failed to convince them that the queens were more important than the jacks, whose pictures they so admired. Fifteen-year-old Augustus Meyers, a musician in Company D, visited his Indian acquaintances almost daily. He found the old generally "austere and dignified" and the young, particularly young women, "droll." Enthralled by them all, Meyers attempted to learn the Sioux language. Off duty, he and other young soldiers dressed in blankets, painted their faces, and did war dances around "council fires."[27]

The Indians surrounding Fort Pierre suffered through this harsh winter as they had many before it. Pemmican's vitamin C–rich berries protected them from scurvy while the soldiers' lack of fruits and vegetables became life threatening. Joints swelled, gums bled, and teeth loosened. To prevent frozen feet and hands, Harney recommended soldiers wear buffalo skin moccasins and gloves instead of government-issued clothing. In an apparently serious communication to the adjutant general in Washington, he reported that two civilian employees lost frozen penises to amputation. Nerves frayed. The Farm Island commander, often drunk and abusive, argued with a private, then later sought him out in his tent and shot him. According to Private Meyers, the murder was hushed up and called an accident.[28]

Harney assumed he would stay in the Upper Missouri River country through the following winter and, in February, planned accordingly. He would buy corn from the Arikaras, Mandans, and Hidatsas who farmed near Fort Clark, paying with the Indians' preferred currency of sugar, molasses, and coffee. He would be "more liberal than the traders," who charged too much for what he considered the "contemptible price of a cup of sugar for each bushel." He would also buy a hundred skin lodges because, after using one on his trip to find Howe, he found them superior to tents and easy to transport Indian fashion.[29]

[27]Meyers, *Ten Years*, 76–90.

[28]Athearn, *Forts of the Upper Missouri*, 40–47; Meyers, "Dakota in the Fifties," 154–65; Harney to Cooper, 21 Feb. 1856, fr994–98, LR AGO, SE, RG 94, NA; and Clow, "Mad Bear," 145.

[29]Harney to Cooper, 21 and 22 Feb. 1856, 9 March 1856, fr969–73, 994–98, 999–1005, reel 539, M567, LR AGO, SE, NA.

Chapter 3

"Justice Hereafter"

ON HIS MARCH FROM PONCA ISLAND BACK TO FORT PIERRE IN EARLY 1856, Harney encountered no military resistance; thus, he and his superiors assumed he had cowed all Sioux into submission. As he prepared over the 1855–56 winter for his conference, he intended to intimidate, not persuade, the Upper Missouri Sioux into doing his bidding. Indeed, his aggression against the southern Sioux and his invasion northward had already done that. A few days before his conference was to begin, with more than a hundred Sioux present, Harney's adjutant, Lieutenant Sweeny, wrote his wife that some chiefs had asked him to "intercede as they seem to have an awful fear" of this man they called 'Mad Bear.'[1]

On March 1, representatives of nine bands—Hunkpapas, Yanktonais, Yanktons, Two Kettles, Sihasapas, Sans Arcs, Miniconjous, Brulés, and a lone Oglala—crowded around Fort Pierre. The Yanktonai chief Big Head, famous in his nation for having counted more coups—touched more enemies in battle—than any other warrior, stayed away. The Brulé leader Little Thunder came on foot through deep snow, bringing Antoine Jarvis, Agent Twiss's Sioux interpreter. Twiss belatedly notified the Oglalas about the meeting, evidently in order to sabotage Harney's plans. The Brulés invited the Oglala headman Man-Afraid-of-His-Horse to go with them, but only the one Oglala chief, coincidentally named Big Head, traveled with them.[2]

A stir of nervous anticipation must have arisen among the Indians as Harney, his interpreters, officers, clerks, orderlies, and a few soldiers acting as guards climbed the hill near the post and filed into two large

---

[1]Adams, *Harney*, 62–63, 140; Sweeny to Bodge, 10 Feb., 1856, and Sweeny to Ellen Sweeny, 26 Feb. 1856, SW 850(102) and SW 850(103), resp., Sweeny Papers, Henry E. Huntington Library. Quotes are from Harney to Davis, 8 March 1856, in Harney Council.

[2]Transcripts and letters in Harney Council and Council reprint are the main sources for this chapter; notes cite additional sources. Clow, "Mad Bear," 145; Coyer, "Wild Region," 244; Harney to Davis, 8 March 1856; Twiss to Harney, 15 Dec. 1855, fr1090–91, reel 538, M567; Harney to Thomas, 28 Feb. 1856, fr19–20, reel 538, M567; and Hoffman to Pleasonton, 9 Feb. 1856, 11 Feb. and 12 Feb. 1856, fr22–28, reel 539, M567, reel 539, M567, 67–69, 71, all in LR AGO, SE, NA.

hospital tents attached to one of Turnley's larger portable cottages. This provided a 1,200-square-foot sheltered space, open enough for soldiers at a distance to see the speakers. On the dais, Harney sat in the middle flanked by officers with others behind them. Mrs. Turnley and Mrs. Atkinson also took seats. Vaughan, these Indians' agent since 1853, sat with Harney and his attendants.[3]

Harney, through Vaughan's interpreter, Zephyr Rencontre, welcomed the Indians and remarked that Big Head, whose band had "insulted" Vaughan, "has not come, but I did not expect him; I suppose him to be too busy."[4] With no preamble, he listed the president's demands: Chiefs must surrender stolen property and all Indians who murdered or "outraged" whites to authorities at the nearest military post. Indians must not "lurk" near roads whites traveled and must not molest, but rather should protect, whites traveling through Indian country by permission of "proper authorities." The president expected obedient bands to shun any band not meeting these requirements.

In return, the United States would protect them from "impositions" by whites and punish offenders according to white man's law. It would restore annuities to Sioux that had been denied them since the Grattan affair, delivering them at the most convenient military post. Finally, it would free Indians imprisoned after the Blue Water fight who were innocent of "murder, robbery, or other high crime" against whites.

Harney complimented Little Thunder's Brulés for their recent conduct, then he told the crowd that the Indians need only give up "'the man who killed the cow,' and 'the one who killed Gibson'" for him to release the Brulé prisoners. Because both High Forehead, who had killed the Grattan-affair cow, and the man who in June 1855 had killed Gibson (a wagon train boss from Missouri) both belonged to Lone Horn's Miniconjou band, Harney intensified the pressure on Lone Horn: "The women and children of the Brulés are crying to go home, and as soon as these two men are delivered up, then these women and children can go with the Brulés."[5]

Next, Harney ticked off his own demands: The Indians must select men they recognize as chiefs in order that the general would know "whom they are to obey." A chief who could not "make his band obey him" must report his failure to the nearest military officer, who would enforce

[3]Adams, *Harney*, 142; and Turnley, *Reminiscences*, 170.

[4]Joseph Jewett (or Jouett), Colin Campbell, and Frank La Framboise also interpreted for Harney. See Doane Robinson, ed., "Fort Tecumseh and Fort Pierre Journals," 235, 237.

[5]Werner, *With Harney*, 21; Bandel, *Frontier Life*, 28; and Paul, *Blue Water Creek*, 83.

obedience for him. The Sioux must make peace with the Pawnees. They should raise stock and grow crops such as pumpkins and corn to avoid "killing so many buffalo, which will soon be killed off." Those wanting to farm should select a place near a military post. The government would then plow land, advise them, and assist them.

His last few rules were a miscellany: The Sioux should stop all trade in horses and mules because "it encourages their young men to steal and lose their lives." Buffalo robes would no longer compensate for depredations and murders. Instead, chiefs must turn over perpetrators to a military officer or Indian agent for punishment. The Hunkpapas, Yanktonais, and Sihasapas who "are for war" must join Big Head's band, whom the others must shun. From now on, neither he nor Vaughan would recognize chiefs not of the peace party. The recording clerk described Harney as standing to "very emphatically" proclaim, Indian fashion: "Big Head's band shall not live upon the face of the earth, as a band!"

Harney sat before praising Mato-cu-wi-hu and Fire Heart, whom Vaughan had commended to him for wanting to obey the president if only their "bad people" would let them.[6] Harney would help them if they ordered their "bad people to leave them. Let them join Big Head's band and meet me if they dare!" If the two chiefs complied, Harney would be "the best friend they ever had." If not, "they will find me the worst enemy they ever had."

The Sioux deliberated the next morning and, when talks resumed that afternoon, identified their head chiefs. Of the six Lakota bands, Mato-cu-wi-hu would represent the Hunkpapas; Fire Heart, the Sihasapas; Little Thunder, the Brulés; Long Mandan, the Two Kettles; Lone Horn, the Miniconjous; and Crow Feather, the Sans Arcs. Of the Nakotas, Two Bear would speak for his Honcpatela, or Lower Yanktonai, band, whereas Black Catfish would lead the Upper Yanktonais, who called themselves "The-Band that-Wishes-the-Life." Struck-by-the-Ree would head the Yanktons. Also among the Indian dignitaries were the Yankton chiefs Medicine Cow and Smutty Bear, who, along with Struck-by-the-Ree and Crow Feather, had signed the amended Laramie Treaty. Harney seated all these men in front of the other Indians and opposite himself and his officers.

Little Thunder spoke first. He was glad to know all the women and children from his own lodge held captive since the Ash Hollow (Blue Water Creek) battle were alive. "I don't wish to fight you; what I want

---

[6]James Hanson, *Little Chief's Gatherings*, 162. Nevertheless, Fire Heart may have been among those accosting Vaughan. See Foster, *Strange Genius*, 73, 153, 169, 171, 327.

with you is to shake hands." (He and others who spoke probably meant to include his own band, if not the entire Sioux Nation. According to anthropologist Ella Deloria, who was part Yankton Sioux, "A spokesman speaking for a great group, generally says 'I' as for each one individually.")[7]

Little Thunder emphasized that, because he had turned in stolen horses and the mail robbers had surrendered at Fort Laramie, his people expected him to bring home the Ash Hollow prisoners. "You have asked us to be friendly. I have tried." He knew Harney wanted the two Miniconjou men. He wished he could bring them in.

Harney was conciliatory: "From what we had heard I expected to fight [Little Thunder's Brulés] everywhere. . . . I don't find them as expected. There are a great many good men among them, but some bad ones, like other people." He acknowledged they seemed intent on friendship and peace. Even so, Harney would not shake hands with Little Thunder. "I have no doubt in a few days, when those [Miniconjou] men are brought in, I shall be able to do it." Then Harney said to the interpreter, "Tell Little Thunder he can have his people that are here to take back with him." At that, the Indians applauded.

Perhaps it was Harney's concession or simply the peer pressure Harney had engineered against him that inspired Lone Horn to rise to say he would bring in High Forehead and the man who had killed Gibson, as well as the stolen horses and property Harney asked for. "I take pity on my friend, Little Thunder. I wish his people to go with him."[8]

The Sans Arc Crow Feather spoke next. He had never asked the president for troops, considering them a "bad thing," yet the Great Father had sent them. "If you force me to fight you . . . you can do it, but I do not want to fight you." Harney acknowledged that Crow Feather had not asked for soldiers. However, some of his people had asked Vaughan "for one thousand women, but the Great Father thought one thousand men would do much better." Crow Feather might have recognized Harney's reference to what seemed a set piece of Sioux oratory. In council at Fort Pierre in 1849, the Hunkpapa chief Little Bear, now an elder in Harney's audience, had refused government presents in what an observer recalled as a long and vehement speech to his Indian Bureau agent. He said whites had "lived with the women of our tribe long enough; we want in our turn a thousand young girls, virgin and of white skin."[9]

---

[7]Paul, *Blue Water Creek*, 77–78; and Deloria, "Dakota Texts," 208n2.

[8]See Council reprint, 6, 7, 17, and 27, for Little Thunder's kinsmen's presence at Pierre.

[9]De Girardin, "Trip to the Bad Lands," 66; and Athearn, *Forts of the Upper Missouri*, 29.

Now, at Harney's conference, Fire Heart said he was glad to see soldiers, but his father had told him he "should fight with the whites." [It is
unclear if he meant beside or against them.] Harney said he remembered
meeting the elder Fire Heart when he was with the 1825 expedition. He
called the son "a good man and his father was before him." Nevertheless,
the son "must separate the good from the bad."

Mato-cu-wi-hu, speaking next, drew on his own legend: "My brother,
if you will look around this fort, you will see some dry bones, which show
my nation how to behave well towards the whites." The translator added
parenthetically, "meaning the bones of an Indian he had killed for mis-
behaving towards the traders."[10] Mato-cu-wi-hu continued, "I think the
whites very good. I am not going to fight." However, he wanted traders
to stay where they were, and he did not like Harney's directive to "throw
a part of my nation away" by exiling Big Head. He claimed no part in
"things that happened out in the country. I didn't wish them so. . . . If I
wanted to fight you or insult you, I would have gone below into the settlements." As for cultivating the ground, that was for "women and old men
that have no wings." However, he did agree to surrender stolen horses.

Harney answered Mato-cu-wi-hu through Rencontre: "I know he is
a good man, and I know there's a great many good men in his band."
Harney would be satisfied if the two chiefs "pick out the bad men and
bring them to me." Vaughan interjected, "I believe Bear Rib [sic] is a
good man, but he has some people who are bad. He came to me several
times and said he could not control his people." Harney warned that if
Mato-cu-wi-hu could not bring the bad men in, "I must go after them.
But I don't want to do that, for our friends are mixed up with them."
Mato-cu-wi-hu said he would see what he could do.

Next morning, Big Head, the Oglala who had come in with Little
Thunder, took a seat with the principal chiefs. Medicine Cow, of the
Yanktons, sat in for Struck-by-the-Ree, whom Harney had mysteriously
sent away "on business for his people." The general began the session with
a compromise. He told Mato-cu-wi-hu and Fire Heart that, although
the bad men in the Hunkpapa and Sihisapa bands must be punished,
Vaughan had convinced him to require each to bring in just five of the
worst men. Fire Heart rose and stretched out his arms in gratitude.

Mato-cu-wi-hu said to Rencontre, "My brother has asked me for five
men. If I can get them, I will do so." Harney snapped at Rencontre, "His

---

[10]Letellier, "Louis D. Letellier," 226; and Letellier, *Adventures*, 16.

answer will not do. I must know positively whether he can get them or not." Mato-cu-wi-hu acquiesced, "I will bring them to you; the balance will then live." Fire Heart said he, too, would bring in five men.

That settled, Two Bear, the short, stocky, fierce-looking chief of the Honcpatela, or Lower Yanktonai, band, took his turn. After some pleasantries, Two Bear set his piercing gaze on Harney: "Your manners are very hard, very severe; but the way I was raised they are the same thing." Because his brother, who had been witasa atancan, had recently been killed, he asked if he should "be in his place?" Harney answered yes. "From this day I see you have made me a chief. If I ask you to help me, will you do it?" Harney's answer had to wait for translation, but Two Bear went on to say he commanded 300 lodges and that when he speaks to them, they listen. Although "some winters we are obliged to eat our own horses," he claimed never to have "hurt or robbed a white man." He made peace with "all our friends on the river," as Vaughan advised, and even when recently Rees and Hidatsas killed two in his band, he "took no notice of it." He vowed that, from now on, "if anything shall happen through my young men," he would report it to Vaughan.[11] He told Harney, "from this day, if you want anything from me, or anything to be done," he would do it. Two Bear ended by asking Harney to treat Big Head as he had Mato-cu-wi-hu and Fire Heart.

Harney replied to Rencontre, "He says my manner is rough, maybe it don't agree with my heart; I can't follow my heart always, I must follow my head; a man who follows his heart only is no chief, sometimes he is too good, and sometimes too bad. As to what he said about Big Head, perhaps I will take the news to him myself. I want nothing more said about Big Head . . . he has picked out his own trail, and he must keep it."

Black Catfish of the Upper Yanktonai "Band-that-Wishes-the-Life" told how his father, dead thirty-three years, had gone several times to Washington, D.C.[12] "He staid there three winters, and called himself half-white man. Half of his body was a chief, and the other half was a soldier." Black Catfish's father had predicted soldiers would come to their country and had advised his son to treat them well. "I have always done

---

[11]Two Bear description from Tucker-Butts, *Galvanized Yankees: Face of Loyalty*, 83. Using 8 people per lodge, his band had some 2,400 people. See Denig, *Five Indian Tribes*, 15; and Warren, "Preliminary Report of Explorations of Nebraska and Dakota, 1855–1857," reprint of 1875, p. 48, folder 8, box 19, Warren Papers, New York State Library and Archives (hereafter cited as Warren report). Brackets in the transcript indicate Two Bear called Vaughan "father."

[12]Sioux delegations went to Washington, D.C., in 1812 and 1824. See Viola, *Diplomats in Buckskin*, 22–23, and Gary Anderson, *Kinsmen*, 121.

so, and never hurt anybody." He, too, was concerned about Big Head, whom he lived near. "I don't know which way to take to keep away from him." After Harney acknowledged Black Catfish, Two Bear spoke up again to request that Vaughan remain their agent. Vaughan said he would, but given that he served at the pleasure of whatever administration was in power, as did all Indian agents, this was a rash promise.

Long Mandan, the stern Two Kettle chief, was making preliminary remarks when, on this cold, rainy day, the Yankton chief Struck-by-the-Ree arrived, saying he had been twenty-five days getting to the council, and for the past five had gone without food. Until his belly was full, he could not talk. When Harney told him to go get something to eat, Mrs. Turnley took him to her kitchen and served him coffee and hot rolls.[13]

After this interruption, the Two Kettle chief resumed his speech. Long Mandan said that after the agent told him to try farming, he and some young men he had chosen had begun. "I am fifty years old, and . . . have never misbehaved to the whites." Since he had become chief, another "chief stepped up and killed two of my people for insulting the whites . . . I was not able to stop my young men from drunkenness and insulting the whites until I had two of my people down; should you see any bones around, they are theirs." Like Mato-cu-wi-hu, Long Mandan drew on his reputation. "Again, at this fort, a man shot at a bell and broke it, but I saw it was wrong, so I killed the man who did it; . . . you can see by this whether I like your white people or not."[14] He did not want whites farther up the river, but he wanted the Fort Pierre traders to remain.

Harney, not above using Sioux ideas of justice when advantageous to him, praised Long Mandan: "He has shown himself a great chief in killing those men; that is the reason the whites like him so much, . . . he punished the bad men and made the rest behave themselves."[15] But he said the Great Father's soldier would "go where they please and take what they please, but they will always be just to his red children."

Little Thunder asked Harney to allow traders to serve his band again and begged "permission to go through my own country as I used to, to run buffalo as I used to. My children are now all on foot, and are obliged to walk." Harney granted Little Thunder permission to travel and told

---

[13]Turnley, *Reminiscences*, 171.

[14]See De Trobriand, *Army Life*, 119; and De Trobriand, "Vie Militaire Dans le Dakota," typescript translated by Will, De Trobriand Papers, SHSND Archives, 93. De Trobriand mistakenly attributes this story to Mato-cu-wi-hu.

[15]Harney apparently misunderstood in thinking Long Mandan had killed all three.

him "he shall have his traders," but they must locate at military posts. This way, Harney explained, Indians would get more in trade for their robes and other goods. If they behaved, Indians would have "justice hereafter." Officers and soldiers would be their friends, even assimilate them. "I hope it will not be long before we will all be like one people."

Bone Necklace, the other Lower Yanktonai band chief, changed the subject: "You have given these men a talk about cultivating the ground; they said nothing about it. . . . I heard all you said and I wish to do what you want." He requested grain and a white man to show him "how to plant, [so] that my women and children may learn it and eat and have a life." He wanted to do this near "where the traders are." Harney said he would help. "If they have fields they can have all the old men, women, and children at home, without the trouble of taking them about when they go after buffalo."

Little Thunder, impatient for the release of prisoners, asked Harney again when he would get them. When Lone Horn brings in High Forehead and the man who killed Gibson, Harney said. Only then would he notify Fort Kearny to release them. Little Thunder pressed him: "When will this be?" Harney: "I expect . . . when the weather is good."

Mato-cu-wi-hu summed up the Indian side for that day's talks: "We have all heard what our brother [Harney] has said and we all agree to it." Harney replied that he was so far "well satisfied with everything that has been done and said. My heart feels good."

Of all the Sioux spokesmen, Struck-by-the-Ree was probably the best informed about the United States and its people. He had been to Washington, D.C., as part of an 1837 delegation, and, if only because they lived farthest downstream, he and his band had more dealings with whites than other northern Sioux. Indeed, if oral tradition was true, American soldiers had played a part in Struck-by-the-Ree's life from his birth. He was proud that Meriwether Lewis had wrapped him, when an infant, in an American flag and predicted that he would grow up to be a great chief and a friend to the white man.

On March 4, after remarking on the beautiful day, the chief, probably wearing his customary otter-skin turban, saluted Harney: "The man who calls himself a man and is not afraid to die is yourself. I am one also."[16]

---

[16]Struck-by-the-Ree's name apparently dated from when, after a battle, he was left for dead with a Ree's arrow point piercing his body. By extracting it, his brother-in-law, Fort Pierre bourgeois Picotte, possibly saved his life. For Picotte, see Holley, *Once Their Home*, 94, 284–85; Gray, "Honoré Picotte," 189, 191–93; and Doane Robinson, ed., "Fort Tecumseh and Fort Pierre Journals," 237. Yankton tradition has Struck-by-the-Ree, who died in 1888, newborn during the 1804 Calumet Bluff (Gavin's Point) encounter. Nakota men often wore otter skin turbans. See "Wiciyela or Middle Dakota," 4.

But, he said, "if you starve you will take what you meet with and live," explaining why his band had stolen livestock. "I see you here, and your manners and situation are enough to scare any of us; but if I was afraid I would squat down, but I don't. If I do what you tell me, I know I will be well off and well treated."

Why Harney had sent the chief away earlier was revealed during some repartee between them about who in his band had eaten how many cattle and how many horses would compensate for them. Struck-by-the-Ree suggested how whites might remove such temptations in the future: "When the men in charge of [livestock] . . . get to the Big Sioux [River], they get liquor and stay drunk for several days; they don't take care of their animals, and lose them, . . . whenever it happens that animals give out, it is better to kill them than leave them on the prairie." He complained how much liquor was available near the settlements. Whites who hired Santees as hunters paid them with liquor. The Santees got drunk "and the whites beat them, and the Santees turn round and steal hogs, &c.; and all that comes on my back."

Struck-by-the-Ree turned his attention to agents. "When an agent comes here he is poor, but he gets rich, and after he gets rich he goes away and another poor one comes." Vaughan, however, was not like that. He "is the only one who has been a father to us. . . . We have always seen fathers before this put by everything that was sent here for us, and we only got a handful; but he gives us everything." He also praised traders Charles Galpin and Charles Primeau and said of interpreters Colin Campbell and Zephyr Rencontre, "We like them, and want to give them a present, but you won't let us."[17]

Struck-by-the-Ree brought up a long-standing issue of money he believed was due the Yanktons from an 1830 land cession that would not be settled until the 1970s. Yanktons, though invited, had not attended talks where Dakotas, Otoes, Omahas, Sacs, and Foxes ceded a forty by two-hundred-mile strip of land stretching from the Mississippi River in northeast Iowa to the upper Des Moines River.[18] "I should like to-day

---

[17]Holley, *Once Their Home*, 179–82. Trader Charles Primeau was born in 1814 in St. Louis. Campbell, interpreter for Harney at Ash Hollow, came to the Upper Missouri about 1832; his mother was Mdewakanton. See Doane Robinson, ed., "Fort Tecumseh and Fort Pierre Journals," 237; Gary Anderson, *Kinsmen*, 68, 117; and Gary Anderson, *Little Crow*, 21. Rencontre came to the Upper Missouri about 1828 and married a Yanktonai woman. Pattee, "Reminiscences," 288, 288n46.

[18]Hoover, "Yankton Sioux Tribal Claims," 127–42, examined Yankton claims made in U.S. Court of Claims Docket 332A, B, C, and D in the 1960s and 1970s. See "Neutral Ground," *Iowa Journal of History and Politics* 13, no. 3 (July 1915): 311–48, and *History of Western Iowa*, 35–36. (Treaty signed 15 July 1830; proclaimed 24 Feb. 1831.)

to have this part of my money," Struck-by-the-Ree insisted, in vain, as before.

Apparently, Harney left soap and warm water for Indians to use. Struck-by-the-Ree seemed affronted: "Now this warm water; if you want to clean me out, I would be the same thing after rubbing and rubbing that I am now." He suspected more than his unwashed flesh offended whites, including the president, who, he understood, "thinks great of me, and likes me; but I think that when I am dead [he] will be glad."[19] He praised his friend, Little Thunder. "We were once close together and he gave me horses; now we are apart, we are poor enough all but to die."

Struck-by-the-Ree, probably meaning personal pronouns collectively, said he would not beg for his life. "If you want me to die of poorness, I'll do it. You came here and whipped me, and after that you starved me." He stepped forward and handed some affidavits of his good behavior to the general, adding testimony that he, too, had killed one of his young men who had killed a white man. Harney looked them over, then explained to his audience: "He says a great deal about the beef and the ponies. I told him he must return a good horse for each beef he had taken." The president "don't care for a few old horses; he don't want them; but it is to let the Indians see they must not do anything bad." Harney had heard enough about the animals. "That is all settled. I know what it is to be hungry; and I can [overlook] a great deal."

When Struck-by-the-Ree admitted his young men had traveled to the Platte to war with the Pawnees, Harney insisted he make peace with that tribe "as it is for the benefit of all of us; and if any violate it, they will have me on their backs, and they will find me a hard load to carry." Harney expressed his wish for a return to the peaceful conditions that he remembered from thirty-one years ago. "I would like to see all the bands of the Missouri have their villages on the river, with big fields of corn, where they can live and be happy. . . . Many of their men are ashamed to work, but they are very foolish; the whites are brave good warriors, and they are rich, because they cultivate the soil." However, Harney did not want Sioux to cross the Big Sioux River. "If they go among the whites[,] there will always be trouble and that must be stopped."

Struck-by-the-Ree, Harney said, "had done nothing for which to beg his life." Punishing his own people was "very good conduct," because "it may have saved the lives of a great many good men." It was better if

---

[19]Struck-by-the-Ree met President Andrew Jackson in 1837. Franklin Pierce was currently president.

a few bad men died "to preserve peace than for their sake a great many should afterwards suffer." Rhetorically, he asked who was the "cause of all this trouble now? Just one bad man. 'The man who killed the cow.' The Great Father does not care about a cow; but that fellow was a bad fellow, and was not given up, this caused all the difficulty. It was a very little thing, yet see how it spread over the whole Sioux nation from one bad fellow. I hope all the red people will remember this."

The Yankton Smutty Bear reminded Harney that the white chief at the Horse Creek conference assured him he soon would be like a white man and have a big house. "But he told me a lie, for I am not like a white man yet." He had "worn all the nails off my fingers trying" to raise corn as the white man advised, but when he was planting, Pawnees came and stole his horses. Vaughan restrained him from retaliating, and "they stole them again." Furthermore, last fall a white man stole his horse and brought it to Pierre. He wanted that horse back, packed "in case you give me something to eat." Harney assured Smutty Bear he would get his horse, but the white man at Horse Creek had promised too much. "Perhaps his children's children may be like the whites, and I want him to commence, that they may have our habits, &c." He could not promise them houses, but if they settled "where we can get at them," he would help them with farming.

Harney asked each head chief to choose several subordinate chiefs and "soldiers" to police each camp. The army would uniform and feed these 700 or so sub-chiefs and soldiers. On March 5, chiefs who had not submitted names did so. When the Hunkpapas' turn came, Little Bear stood to explain his absence from the list: "I have been the chief of the Oncpapas [sic], but now I am an old man and cannot do it. I have children. I tell my young men this is a hard matter what you tell them, and that they should be very careful." He handed the general a copy of the 1825 treaty signed with his mark. Harney answered: "The Little Bear was a good chief, and governed his people well. His son will do well if he acts as his father did before him."[20]

Two Bear expressed unease about the new social order Harney was imposing: "I think that from this day you want to raise me, and make a new nation out of an old one." He beseeched the Great Spirit, the president, and Harney: "I want you to take pity on me and wish me what

---

[20]Mato-cu-wi-hu was in Little Bear's *tiwahe* (immediate family) and possibly his biological son. See Standing Rock Tribal Tourism Office web page. For Sioux kinship, see Deloria, *Speaking of Indians*, 24–27.

is good, so that I can tell my nation when I get back to them." Harney assured Two Bear that Indians "need not expect any harm from me unless they are bad themselves. Everything I tell them is for their good, and must be done. They cannot see it now, but . . . in a year from now I am sure that they will receive twice as much for a robe as they do now; . . . Tell them not to fear, I shall be here with them and will assist them, but they must do what I tell them."

Harney then, absurdly, asked his audience to help catch deserters. "You shall be paid for it," he told them—$30 for every deserter brought in to a military post. Struck-by-the-Ree was skeptical: "If I were to catch one of your men maybe he would shoot me." Harney: "You must shoot him first, and if you kill him you shall have the reward by telling me where he lays."

After Mato-cu-wi-hu, Lone Horn, and Fire Heart agreed they could deliver the five men Harney required of each by May 15, Harney turned to Little Thunder: "You have met with a severe blow; I am sorry it did not fall upon some one less friendly to us." He shook hands with him, saying, "I will always be your friend hereafter." What must have been more gratifying to Little Thunder than the handshake was Harney's promise to send the Brulé prisoners from Fort Kearny to Fort Laramie, where Little Thunder could collect them. However, Harney did not promise release for the Fort Leavenworth prisoners. He did not know that as soon as Spotted Tail, Red Leaf, and Long Chin surrendered at Fort Laramie, Agent Twiss urged Superintendent Cumming to ask President Franklin Pierce to pardon them. Pierce did so on January 16, 1856, but the prisoners, lacking transportation, remained at Fort Leavenworth through the winter. When the other Brulé prisoners were freed at Fort Kearny in May, Spotted Tail and the others were among them.[21]

With council business concluded, Harney ceremoniously distributed documents to chiefs and sub-chiefs to serve as proof to whites of their friendship. The document given to The-One-Who-Uses-His-Heart-for-All appointed him a sub-chief of Mato-cu-wi-hu's Hunkpapa band for as long as he would "obey and respect him."[22]

Adjourning the conference, Harney said, "I hope the Great Spirit will take care of you, and that He will put good into your hearts, and that you all may have plenty, and keep your hands and hearts clean, that you

[21]Todd, "Harney Expedition," 112; Ward affidavit, 7 Feb. 1856, fr53, reel 539, M567, LR AGO, SE, NA; and Hyde, *Spotted Tail's Folk*, 76–80.

[22]Mattison, *Henry A. Boller*, 146.

may not be afraid to meet that Great Spirit hereafter." The Indians gave Harney "tremendous" applause.

Vaughan enthused to Lieutenant Sweeny: this was the "best Treaty ever made with the Sioux Nation." After trading furs and buffalo robes at Galpin's new AFC post a few miles upriver from Fort Pierre, most Indians left the area. Even the Yanktonais who lived semi-permanently near Fort Pierre departed. That summer, the steamboat *St. Mary* returned to St. Louis with 22,000 buffalo robes gleaned from all the AFC's Missouri River posts—only one-third the company's annual 1840s average of some 75,000 robes.[23]

On April 19, the Oglalas finally arrived at Fort Pierre. Harney accepted Mischief Maker as the representative chief and Man-Afraid-of-His-Horse as one of his chosen sub-chiefs. Harney spoke at length the first day, outlining the same terms the others had agreed to but tailoring his comments to their proximity to the Oregon Trail. He told them he had heard, but was not certain, of the Leavenworth prisoners' presidential pardon. On the second day, Mischief Maker and Wounded-in-the-Face spoke briefly before signing the document.[24]

Several 1855–56 winter counts—Flame's (Two Kettle), Lone Dog's (Yanktonai), and Swan's (Miniconjou), for example—depict the Harney conference with a soldier shaking hands with an Indian. The Hunkpapa Long Soldier's count shows the soldier holding out his arms without hands; the anonymously rendered Rosebud winter count shows a Lakota woman shaking hands with a soldier. Two winter counts surviving only as texts—an anonymous one called the Major Bush winter count after its collector and the John No Ears (Oglala) winter count—also mention the peace agreement, calling Harney "Hornet."[25]

Hornets stir things up; they disrupt things.

---

[23]W. H. Hutton, "Report of Yellowstone Expedition," 1856, pp., 23–24, folder 3, box 9, Warren Papers, New York State Library and Archives (hereafter cited as Hutton's 1856 journal); Meyers, *Ten Years*, 106; Way, *Way's Packet Directory*, 412; and CIA annual report, 1849, 1021–23. Partners Daniel Marsh Frost and Edward G. Atkinson were official expedition sutlers (suppliers on an army post). Meyers, *Ten Years*, 104–105; and Coyer, "Wild Region," 244. Vaughan left March 8.

[24]Harney to Secretary of War, 22 April 1856, fr328, 330–43, reel 539, M567, LR AGO, SE, NA. See also Davis to F. Pierce, 31 May 1856, in Council reprint; and Coyer, "Wild Region," 253n68.

[25]Candace Greene and Thornton, *Year the Stars Fell*, 237–39.

Chapter 4

"A New Era Will Dawn"

WHAT DID HARNEY'S AUDIENCE AT THE MARCH 1856 PEACE conference think (if Rencontre was so bold as to translate accurately) when he said the president's soldiers would "go where they please and take what they please"? What did they make of his sending Struck-by-the-Ree on an arduous journey after horses only to teach Indians how to behave? Struck-by-the-Ree's apt response to Harney's suggestion that Sioux act as bounty hunters for deserting soldiers indicated he well knew to comply would be folly. Nevertheless, Harney's insults, condescension, and niggling pettiness were less consequential than his attempt to segregate those preferring appeasement from the bands ready to fight to preserve their social order.

In a letter to Secretary of War Davis accompanying the treaty transcript, Harney maintained that, because they recognized the reality of their situation, the Indians had come to the "irresistible conclusion, that to live hereafter they must work. They . . . have already, in some instances, commenced—but they have not been able to succeed. . . . They have asked our government to help them with a beginning, in raising corn and other simple grains and vegetables; to give them hoes and seed, and to have their land ploughed." Harney was aware of the effects of white culture on indigenous people: "It is not yet too late for us to requite, in some degree, this unfortunate race for their many sufferings, consequent to the domain of our people on the soil of this continent." He added, "These Indians, heretofore proud, stern, and unyielding, now ask of us that assistance which all nations have conceded to each other when ever it has been sought. With proper management a new era will dawn upon such of the Indians as yet remain." He acknowledged, also, broken promises: "The Sioux seek [the new era] and look forward to it with a hope which I trust may not be blighted. They have been deceived so often by the whites that they would never again give them their confidence."[1]

---

[1] Harney to Davis, 8 March 1856, in Harney Council, pp. 1–4. Minnesota became a state in 1858.

Struck-by-the-Ree's Yanktons may have been receptive to a settled life of farming, but before all Sioux would be willing to change their lives so drastically, Harney believed the government needed to control them. In the letter to Secretary Davis, Harney pondered how the army might extend its authority over the Minnesota Sioux bands who "pass into this portion of the country to commit depredations on the whites, [and] trespass on the bands of their own nation living here," and he advocated treating all Sioux as one nation. To manage them, he suggested establishing a single command that would be central to the region bounded in the west by the Rocky Mountains, in the north by the international border, in the east by the Mississippi River, and in the south by the state of Iowa and the Platte River. Harney suggested to Davis that a large force should go through Sioux country that very summer to demonstrate the "ability and intention of the government to enforce obedience to its commands, whenever occasion shall require it."

Harney's immediate concern, however, was replacing Fort Pierre. His interpreter Colin Campbell had operated Fort Lookout for the AFC for years and recommended that site near the mouth of Crow Creek. So did Zephyr Rencontre. Struck-by-the-Ree, whose sub-chief, Smutty Bear, camped there often, also recommended it. Harney agreed it would be an ideal central command location. Meanwhile, he ordered the squadron of Second Dragoons in Kansas to the other promising site near Sioux City.[2]

After Lieutenant Warren spent the winter in Washington, D.C., drafting maps and writing his report for Harney's 1855 Sioux Expedition, Harney had new orders for him. Over the 1856 summer, he was to "obtain reliable information of the Missouri River, from Fort Pierre to some point above the mouth of the Yellowstone." Returning to the Upper Missouri in May, Warren found some 5,000 Sioux assembled at Fort Pierre for the council at which they were to surrender their "bad men."

On May 21, Harney hosted a feast for Mato-cu-wi-hu, Fire Heart, Lone Horn, Crow Feather, and Long Mandan, the first to arrive.[3] Lieutenant Sweeny wrote that, because of rumors of an intended attack while the council was in session, "we had everything prepared in case of

[2]Fort Pierre PR, Jan. 1856, reel 920, M617, NA. See Sunder, *Fur Trade*, 48, 117, 175; Harney Council; Kurz, *Journal*, 103; and Harney to Thomas, 28 April 1856, fr357–58, reel 539, M567, LR AGO, SE, NA. See also Kurz, *On the Upper Missouri*, 40; and Harney to Thomas, 12 March 1856, OCRFP, 424–26.

[3]Foster, *Strange Genius*, 74; Warren report, xvi, 13; Fort Pierre PR, June 1856, Special Order (SO) 26, RG 94, NA (Harney's order to Warren); Jordan, "Happiness," 15, 21–22; Hutton's 1856 journal, 24–26; and G. K. Warren's 1856 journal, 17–25 May 1855, folder 5, box 19, Warren Papers, New York State Library and Archives (hereafter cited as G. K. Warren's 1856 journal).

treachery." During dinner, Mato-cu-wi-hu told of his dream predicting that the young men he surrendered would live. Previous to this dream, Mato-cu-wi-hu said, he had "wished the prisoners to die[;] they deserve it," but now he hoped General Harney would pity them. Thanking the Indians for gifts they presented to him, the general remarked that he was poor and had nothing to give in return. Perhaps, he added, he would soon be as poor as Long Mandan, who, because he had given Harney the robe right from his back, wore only a breechcloth. The others laughed a little, according to Warren, with Long Mandan joining in and commenting that he was born naked, raised naked, and was proud to be naked now.[4]

The main council began the following day with the chiefs begging leniency for the prisoners. It went well, Sweeny wrote his brother, until it came time for Mato-cu-wi-hu and Fire Heart to turn over their men and stolen animals. "Things looked so squally" as the guard seized the prisoners that Sweeny involuntarily grasped his hidden pistol. But nothing happened, and Harney, who had also secreted two pistols in his breast pockets, later praised the Indians' good conduct since March and their promptness in attending this meeting. Furthermore, he wrote Secretary Davis, the Indians' "earnest and evidently sincere professions of good conduct in future and their entreaties for the pardon of the prisoners" impressed him. "With strong admonitions as to their behavior hereafter," he released the Hunkpapa and Sihasapa men.[5]

He was not so benevolent to the two Miniconjou prisoners, making a show of arresting High Forehead and Gibson's murderer at council in front of their peers. In the letter to Secretary Davis, Harney wrote that for three days afterward, five Miniconjou chiefs "in the name of their people, most respectfully but earnestly, sought to excite my pity and obtain a pardon for these two persons." Lone Horn even pledged that he, his soldiers, and sub-chiefs would "kill these men on the first provocation offered to the whites" if Harney would let them go. The prisoners themselves promised, if spared, to "prove by their conduct they were worthy of such clemency."

[4]Sweeny to "Dear Bodge," 5 June 1856, SW 850(110), Sweeny Papers, Henry E. Huntington Library; and G.K. Warren to brother Will, 24 May 1856, and G.K. Warren's 1856 journal, (undated remarks in the front of the 1856 journal where dated entries begin 6 Jun 1856), both in G.K. Warren Papers, New York State Library and Archives; Harney to Secretary of War, 23 May 1856, fr412-14, reel 539, M567, LR AGO, SE, NA. In his letter to his brother Will, Warren identifies Lone Horn as Long Horn and Long Mandan as Big Mandan.

[5]Sweeny to "Dear Bodge," 5 June 1856, SW 850(110), Sweeny Papers, Henry E. Huntington Library; and Harney to Secretary of War, 23 May 1856, fr412-14, reel 539, M567, LR AGO, SE, NA.

"Mitigating circumstances" and "the manners, customs and views of this people . . . so different from our own," together with the two prisoners' lack of hostility and "the great suffering the Sioux had already experienced," elicited Harney's mercy. On May 23, in front of all the Sioux chiefs and headmen, he ordered the two prisoners brought from the guardhouse. Telling them "how great has been the intercession in their behalf, and how much indebted they should be to their chiefs," he freed them. "They appeared very grateful," Harney said, "and their people embraced them with joy."[6]

The following day, Harney introduced Warren to the Indians, warning them not to impede his party as it traveled through their country. Five feet six and weighing little more than 125 pounds, the twenty-six-year-old lieutenant probably did not impress the Indians as he stood next to the towering Harney, but the dark-haired officer stood erect and was said to be "poised and striking in appearance." He had graduated second in his West Point class and was already a rising star in the topographical corps.[7]

Another important bit of business was completed when Fire Heart and Mato-cu-wi-hu confirmed that Big Head and eight lodges of his Yanktonai relatives now lived far upriver at Apple Creek near present Bismarck, North Dakota. Harney sent word to Big Head that no one would harm him if he came to hear the treaty conditions, but Big Head declined the invitation.[8]

Young Augustus Meyers, with other soldiers, watched the conference from a distance. "We could observe the dramatic gestures of the Indian orators and hear the grunts of approval," he wrote. "What the great talk was all about, we did not know." The warriors "were painted, and their lustrous dark skins glistened in the bright sunlight when they had cast off their robes and blankets. It was a sight long to be remembered." On the last night, he could "hear the tom-toms, and the voices of the bucks and squaws until early morning." The next day, 2,000 Sioux approached Harney's headquarters inside the stockade. When Harney appeared, Indian women beat drums while men played willow flutes in salute. Meyers said the "curious noise could be heard for miles around."[9]

---

[6]Harney to Secretary of War, 23 May 1856, fr412–14, reel 539, M567, LR AGO, SE, NA.

[7]G.K. Warren to brother Will, 24 May 1856, Warren Papers, New York State Library and Archives. Descriptions of Warren from Goetzmann, *Army Exploration*, 407; Chittenden, *Steamboat Navigation*, 208–209; and Foster, *Strange Genius*, 74.

[8]Harney to Secretary of War, 23 May 1856, fr412–14, reel 539, M567, LR AGO, SE, NA; Clow, "Mad Bear," 147; and Sweeny to Bodge, 5 June 1856, SW 850 (110), Sweeny Papers, Henry E. Huntington Library.

[9]Meyers, *Ten Years*, 104–105; and Meyers, "Dakota in the Fifties," 168. The monograph's editor erroneously doubted Meyers's May dates; see 167n22.

ON MAY 25, HARNEY LEFT FORT PIERRE WITH A TEN-MAN ESCORT to visit the dragoon camps and, as it turned out, for good. Despite his promise to the Sioux that he would remain in their country, Harney's superiors decided otherwise. Given that he had apparently cowed the Sioux, the War Department deemed further military action against them unnecessary. A June 20, 1856, order told Harney to report to Fort Leavenworth for reassignment.[10]

On May 31, Colonel Francis Lee arrived to command the six companies of Second Infantry left at Pierre and its cantonments. Sweeny, who served with Lee in the Mexican War, called him "a fine old fellow, a brave and skillful soldier, and accomplished gentleman." Lee was familiar with the Dakota Sioux; he had commanded for a time at Fort Snelling and in 1854 oversaw construction of Fort Ridgely near the Santee reservations. Although the majority of Sioux had left the Pierre area before Lee arrived, Mato-cu-wi-hu's band remained nearby at least until mid-June, when post returns show that Lee authorized rations for "Indian Chief 'Bear Rib' &c."[11]

WARREN CONSIDERED THE PART OF SIOUX COUNTRY HE HAD explored suitable only for the "powerful tribes of roving savages" who occupied it. Consequently, he recommended Forts Pierre and Laramie be permanently occupied, if only as power symbols, and he urged prompt exploration of "this vast territory." Harney agreed. After helping to lay out Fort Lookout, Warren and topographer Hutton returned to Fort Pierre. On June 28, they, geologist and medical doctor Ferdinand V. Hayden, and meteorologist J. Hudson Snowden boarded the AFC's steamboat *St. Mary* to explore upriver. Hayden, a small, energetic young man, had been scouring this region for fossils since 1853. When he joined Warren's 1856 expedition, he was famous in scientific circles for his Upper Missouri discoveries.[12]

A seventeen-man Second Infantry escort accompanied the scientists. Vaughan, also aboard, distributed annuities at Two Bear's camp near Fort

---

[10]Harney to Cooper, 9 March 1856, and Cooper to Harney, 20 June 1856, OCRFP, 422, 426–27; and Fort Pierre PR, July 1856, Order no. 17, 17 July 1856, reel 920, M617, NA.

[11]Sweeny to Bodge, 5 June 1856, SW 850 (110), Sweeny Papers, Henry E. Huntington Library; and Gary Anderson, *Kinsmen*, 190, 207. The army built Fort Snelling at the Minnesota and Mississippi River confluence (St. Paul) in 1819.

[12]G. K. Warren to brother Will, 24 May 1856, quoted in Goetzmann, *Army Exploration*, 411; Fort Pierre PR, June 1856, Order no. 12, 17 June, reel 920, M617, NA; Foster, *Strange Genius*, xi, 7, 62–66, 74; Warren report, xvi, 13; Fort Pierre PR, June 1856, SO 26, reel 920, M617, NA; Jordan, *Happiness*, 21–22; Hutton's 1856 journal, 25–26; and Chittenden, *Steamboat Navigation*, 208–209. See also Chaky, "Fossils and the Fur Trade," 28–31.

Pierre, where, Hutton recorded, "we were received with a most clamorous and ear piercing chant of exultation." While warriors saluted them with celebratory gunfire, families watched from a steep hillside. The Indians "presented a lively contrast of red, white & blue" and were the "best-looking and best-dressed band" Hutton had seen. Perhaps mistaking them for Big Head's band, he identified these Lower Yanktonais as "outlaws from their tribe and grand scamps generally." In council Two Bear complained about having to move his entire camp to Fort Pierre to claim annuities. If he left his women, children, and old men behind, his enemies would kill them.[13]

Near Fort Clark, Little Soldier's Yanktonais greeted the boat, also with gunfire and chanting. They seemed to Hutton much poorer than Two Bear's people even though they regarded their annuities as hardly worth sacrificing a buffalo hunt. Beyond Fort Clark, the Arikara chief Black Bear said he needed protection from Sioux who were "continually robbing him and doing as they pleased." Mandans they met later that day begged Vaughan "to keep sick white men from coming up the river," a reference to smallpox breaking out along the river. Warren judged Hidatsas near Fort Berthold contented and the trading post a "snug place."[14]

Using the view from the steamboat's pilothouse, Snowden and Hutton sketched the Missouri's course from Fort Pierre to its confluence with the Yellowstone River. Lieutenant Warren took positional observations en route and, after arriving at Fort Union on July 10, made further determinations during a "whole lunation." When the boat continued eighty-five miles farther up the Missouri, Hutton went along to continue mapping. Famous frontiersman Jim Bridger had just returned to Fort Union from conducting Sir George Gore, a flamboyant Irish lord, on a long sports adventure in the Yellowstone and Powder River country. Although Gore continued adventuring, Warren hired Bridger to guide his expedition up the Yellowstone valley.

Bridger led Warren and the scientists away from Fort Union on July 25, 1856. Accompanying them (besides the military escort) were a hunter, a cook, laborers, mule drivers, and the scientists' assistants—a total of thirty-four armed and well-supplied men.[15] Along with Vaughan and his companions, who were on the way to distribute annuities to the Crows, they stayed the first night at Gore's camp about eight miles upstream.

---

[13]Hutton's 1856 journal, 38, 40, 73; and G. K. Warren's 1856 journal.

[14]Hurt, "Additional Notes"; "Wiciyela or Middle Dakota"; Hutton's 1856 journal, 40; and G. K. Warren's 1856 journal.

[15]See "Michael DeSomet," 24–37; Paul, *Blue Water*, 98; and James Hanson, *Little Chief's Gatherings*, 116.

By then, Gore and his forty-three men had killed more than 100 bears, 2,000 buffalo, and some 1,600 elk and deer. Vaughan told Superintendent Cumming, who had granted the nobleman a passport to enter Indian country in spring 1854, that this was "more than they had any use for[,] having killed it purely for sport."[16] Warren bought wagons, mules, and horses from Gore to use during the summer as they explored the Yellowstone River to the mouth of the Powder River. They collected mineral and fossil specimens, made astronomical and meteorological observations, and described the flora and fauna before returning downstream in September to a changed world.[17]

Smallpox had devastated the Mandans, Hidatsas, and Arikaras, but Yanktonais at Little Soldier's village remained unscathed and in good spirits. At Fort Pierre, only two Second Infantry companies remained to guard army property. Newly built but already abandoned, Fort Lookout would have offered quarters with wood floors, shingled roofs, and sturdy doors, but Harney had orders, issued July 20, to instead establish a post, Fort Randall, thirty miles upriver from the confluence of the Niobrara with the Missouri. This was, indeed, his own idea. Although his focus had been on the Big Sioux River site for his new fort, after exploring near Howe's Missouri River camp, Harney had changed his mind. He wrote Adjutant General Cooper that he was "fully satisfied" that the Howe-camp's neighborhood offered "the best position for a depot of supplies on the [Missouri] river to furnish the country back in the interior to the Black Hills." It also presented the "nearest practicable point of the Missouri to Fort Laramie." Private Meyers was among those tearing down what they had just built at Fort Lookout and shipping the materials by steamboat to the new site. With its unwalled, open layout, Fort Randall was now Lee's Second Infantry headquarters, housing five officers commanding 245 men.[18]

Lieutenant Warren led another military exploration through Lakota territory in the summer of 1857. He and topographer P. M. Engel met their Second Infantry escort, commanded by Lieutenant James McMillan, at

---

[16]G. K. Warren's 1856 journal; Spence, "Celtic Nimrod," 61–62, 64; and guide's 24 July journal entry quoted in Jack Roberts, *Amazing Adventures of Lord Gore*, 141, 162–66.

[17]G. K. Warren's 1856 journal; Spence, "Celtic Nimrod," 65; and Sunder, *Fur Trade*, 181–82.

[18]Hutton's 1856 journal, 122; Jerome Greene, *Fort Randall*, 11, 13; Fort Pierre PR, July 1856, reel 920, M617, NA; Abercrombie to Cooper, 3 Oct. 1856, OCRFP, 437–38; Fort Pierre PR, May and June 1856, reel 920, M617, NA; Meyers, *Ten Years*, 116–25; Hart, *Old Forts*, 53–54; Fort Pierre PR, July and August 1856, SO no. 37, 16 July, reel 920, M617, NA; Slaughter, "Fort Randall," 425; Stanley, *Personal Memoirs*, 38; Harney to Cooper, 30 June 1856, and quotes from Harney to Cooper, 22 Feb. 1856, fr1001, reel 538, M567, both in LR AGO, SE, NA; Harney to Thomas, 28 Feb. 1856, fr515–16, reel 539, M567, NA; and 31 Oct. 1856, OCRFP, 434. Recruits arrived 26 June 1856, by 22 May 1856 post order no. 53.

Sioux City and left there July 6. Geologist Hayden, meteorologist W. P. C. Carrington, and Dr. Samuel H. Moffitt had already departed Omaha. Within two weeks, they all converged and explored their way toward Fort Laramie. Pestering mosquitoes, persistent rainy weather, and illness made their trip grueling.

They saw no Indians for a month. Then, on August 13, their hunter brought a Brulé Indian to their camp who seemed frightened at seeing the soldiers—possibly, Snowden thought, because of "recollections of Blue Water." This man reported sixty lodges of his band less than ten miles away and abundant buffalo along the Niobrara River. He also told of a battle between U.S. troops and some Cheyennes after which the Indians had made tracks to the Black Hills. The next day, the explorers saw several Indians fleeing, but the same man brought two others to them. Without an interpreter, they could learn little from one another, and after Snowden gave them shirts and knives, the Indians "went upon their way rejoicing." The travelers passed three Indian lodges—not the sixty the Brulé had predicted.[19]

On August 19, the expedition arrived at Fort Laramie, where Brevet Lieutenant Colonel Hoffman, commanding, explained that on June 29, Colonel Edwin V. Sumner fought Cheyennes on the south fork of the Solomon River. Seven warriors and two soldiers had died. The Second Infantry subsequently captured three Cheyennes at Rawhide Butte where some Oglalas and Brulés were waiting for annuities. The capture, according to Snowden, "created a stampede amongst the Sioux," who, he surmised, also feared an attack.[20]

While resting and refitting at Fort Laramie, Warren obtained maps from men who knew the back country and consulted with Twiss, who advised that the Sioux probably would not hinder his explorations into the Black Hills. In September, Warren sent Lieutenant McMillan's escort off with Snowden and Dr. Moffitt to explore the White and Niobrara Rivers. Warren's own group—Hayden, Carrington, Engel, their guide and interpreter (Edward de Morin), and seventeen hired men—approached the Black Hills along a fork of Beaver Creek.[21] Near the volcanic peak

[19]Snowden's Warren Expedition journal, 38–48.

[20]Utley, *Frontiersmen*, 121–24. See also Paul, *Blue Water Creek*, 150; and Snowden's Warren Expedition journal, 48.

[21]Manypenny to McClelland, 25 June 1856; Twiss to Manypenny, 24 June 1856; McClelland to President Pierce, 26 June 1856; President Pierce to Senate and House, 24 July 1856; all in Harney Council. See also Adams, *Harney*, 137, 144; Kvasnicka & Viola, *Commissioners*, 61; Utley, *Frontiersmen*, 118–19; and Warren report, 18. For Morin, see Hafen, "Edward de Morin," in *Mountain Men*, ed. by Hafen, vol. 9, 134. This Beaver Creek is in western S.Dak.

the Indians called *Inyan Kara Sapa,* or "the hill that makes the rocks," they came upon some forty-five lodges of Oglalas whose headman was The Bird's Down (a.k.a. White Feather). Warren explained that the president sent him to "look at the country and tell him what was here." The Indians gave Warren's party some meat but requested that he not continue along the stream they were on because he would scare away the "few buffalo on it." Mato-cu-wi-hu later explained to Warren that Indian soldiers would summarily kill anyone who frightened off buffalo during a hunt. These Oglalas asked Warren to "take pity on them and not make them starve," and instead go down "the next branch of the Belle Fouche [River] to the east." Warren invited Bird's Down to bring ten warriors to their camp for something to eat. Warren's younger brother, Edgar, along for the trip, commented in his journal that the Indians had some very pretty horses. Lieutenant Warren recognized one as Sir George Gore's and concluded they were the Indians who had barred the sportsman from the Black Hills the previous year.[22]

After Warren's party had left Gore's camp, the Irish nobleman continued to sport about near the Black Hills. Gossip that Sihasapas and Hunkpapas had murdered Gore and the twelve men with him alarmed Vaughan, who was concerned that the sportsmen, by "killing and scattering the small quantity of game which is [the Indians'] only means of subsistence," might have driven the Sioux to "acts of desperation." By Christmas, Vaughan could inform Cumming that Gore survived, although the Hunkpapas and Sihasapas had robbed him. Gore's party had struggled for days toward the mouth of the Little Missouri River until Hidatsa hunters from Like-a-Fishhook Village rescued them and helped them survive the winter. Commissioner Manypenny recommended to the secretary of the interior McClelland that all Gore's skins, pelts, and elk horns be confiscated and sold, with the money to benefit the Indians. The secretary wondered, however, if a more tactful approach might be better than resorting to the law "as justice is all that is demanded." He assigned the job of confiscation to Cumming and Vaughan, but when Gore stopped at Fort Lookout in the spring, his large mackinaw boat was laden with furs and pelts.[23]

---

[22]G. K. Warren's 1857 journal; Edgar Warren's 1857 journal, 9 Sept. 1857; and Warren report, 18–19.

[23]G. K. Warren's 1857 journal; and Jordan, *Happiness,* 22. Jack Roberts, *Amazing Adventures of Lord Gore,* reproduces Vaughan's letters, 190–91, 193–96; Mattison, *Henry A. Boller,* 44n42; and Meyers, *Ten Years,* 122–23. The 1845 Hidatsa earth lodge village 25 miles south of present Mandan has been restored. See Bowers, *Hidatsa Social and Ceremonial Organization,* 464–65. For Gore and the Hidatsas, see Manypenny's and 13 Jan. and 20 Jan. 1857 letters, both in Jack Roberts, *Amazing Adventures of Lord Gore,* 193–209, 197, 199.

Warren might not have understood how angry the Indians he met now still were over Gore's slaughter. He may not have understood that the Black Hills were a source of spiritual, as well as physical, sustenance for Lakotas, nor realized how fearful they were of losing them to whites. When one of Harney's Blue Water Brulé captives, Brown Hat (Battiste Good), made a pilgrimage to the Black Hills in the "many sacrificial flags winter" (1855–56 of his winter count), a bird who spoke as a woman appeared to him. She said the Creator had given the Hills to the Sioux and made her sentry over them. She would not allow "the pouring of blood" on them.[24] Nevertheless, the men confronting Warren in September 1857 seemed willing to do battle to keep his party out of this sanctuary. Forty or more Lakota headmen arrived despite rain and blasting wind determined to persuade Warren to turn back. Half were from a camp of Miniconjous and Sihasapas who had learned of Warren's party from the Oglalas. Among the leaders crowding into a makeshift shelter to show Warren their papers were Lone Horn's sub-chief The-Elk-That-Hollows-Walking (Miniconjou); Black Shield, who was either Fire Heart's Sihasapa sub-chief or, more likely, the Miniconjou chief of that name; and Black Buffalo, who produced his father's paper signed by Meriwether Lewis. Warren explained he wanted to follow the Cheyenne River's north fork to Bear Butte, northeast of present Sturgis, South Dakota, then proceed to the Niobrara River.[25]

Black Shield's answering speech was impassioned: Harney had told them if they found whites traveling in this part of the country, they should tell them to leave, and, if they did not, "they should take all they had . . . whip them, and turn them back by force." Warren said he knew they "could do so to traders" without papers, but the president's paper ordering him here was better than other papers. Black Shield did not believe Warren's denial that he was here to build a road. Already, he said, the president "had asked them for a road along the Platte," one along White River (the Pierre–Laramie Trail), and passage on the Missouri River. They could not give up this "last spot." Warren insisted he had come "only to see what was in their country" and warned that, if they

[24]Candace Greene and Thornton, *Year the Stars Fell*, 4, 292–93; and Mallery, *Picture Writing*, vol. 1, vi, 287–90.

[25]Warren translates A-hag-a-hoo-man-ie as "The Elk that Hollows when he runs" and as the Elk-that-Bellows-Walking. Harney's clerk used both "Hollows" and "Hollos." Candace Greene and Thornton, *The Year the Stars Fell*, 247, also discuss the name. See Ronda, *Lewis & Clark among the Indians*, 27, 30–40. Visitor center materials at Bear Butte State Park explain its religious significance.

stopped him, the president would send many soldiers to force them to yield. Others spoke, one chief foreseeing a time when Sioux "would again have to fight the whites." Therefore, if they let Warren pass through their country now, whites "would know how to fight them." In a journal aside, Warren admitted that the "only security these [I]ndians can have in the possession of their country would be in its utter worthlessness to the whites."[26]

The Miniconjou headmen stayed with Warren's party all night. On the following snowy morning, the standoff held until both parties agreed more talking was futile. Warren ordered the Indians away to a separate fire, but ten headmen stubbornly remained the night. A Brulé returning to Warren's camp after visiting the Oglalas tied his horse on the opposite side of the creek, explaining to Warren that others had confided that if he wished to live he should keep his horse away from the explorers' horses. An alarmed Morin, translating, deduced that "the head men staying with us . . . feared the young men might attack us and they wished by their presence to avoid a collision."[27] The chiefs confirmed the threat.

Warren, undeterred, requested a guide to the large Miniconjou camp where Mato-cu-wi-hu was supposed to be. Only if Mato-cu-wi-hu, whom Warren believed Harney had made the "great chief" among all the Sioux, insisted, would he turn back.[28] No one would go as guide; instead, they sent for Mato-cu-wi-hu. Some chiefs left, but Black Shield and four others stayed to sleep, again, beside Warren's fire.

Better weather the next day allowed Warren to move to a more defensible position, and that night the self-appointed guardians left. When Mato-cu-wi-hu did not arrive after three days, Warren considered it proof of the Hunkpapa band's hostile intent and backtracked on Beaver Creek some forty miles in order to take another route. Warren had given up seeing Mato-cu-wi-hu when he and a Miniconjou sub-chief, The-One-Who-Shoots-the-Bear-Running (later known as Lame Deer), appeared on the trail. When Warren insisted on going to Bear Butte by his originally planned route, Mato-cu-wi-hu asked why Warren wanted so badly to go to this place, *Mato Paha*, which the Sioux believed was spirit-filled. Because it was high and he could see a lot of country from

---

[26]Hayden lists no gold among the expedition's mineral discoveries (Warren, *Explorer on the Northern Plains*, 46, 81–83), but rumors of gold had circulated for years. See Donald Jackson, *Custer's Gold*, 3–7, and Meyers, *Ten Years*, 133–34.

[27] G. K. Warren's 1857 journal, 17 Sept. 1857.

[28]I found no documentary evidence that Harney considered Mato-cu-wi-hu more than a band chief.

its summit, Warren responded. Mato-cu-wi-hu said he would tell him his decision tomorrow.

In the morning, Mato-cu-wi-hu stood firm with what the others had told Warren, explaining that at a meeting the previous summer, the Lakotas had agreed "to hereafter let no one" come into their country.[29] Warren snapped back that, in that case, he had better let them risk going ahead. He had not come to harm the Sioux. All he wanted was for the Indians not to keep them from their work. Mato-cu-wi-hu said he wanted to help, but if he did, the others might kill him. He was not afraid to die, but he did fear that, with him dead, they would impoverish his family by killing his horse and destroying all he had. Warren reminded Mato-cu-wi-hu that Harney expected all his sub-chiefs and soldiers to obey Mato-cu-wi-hu, and chided him that "if he could not do what he wished then he was no chief." Mato-cu-wi-hu retorted that he "did not care to be chief," because white men did not "listen to what he said." He pointed out that if he went to Warren's country and did as he pleased, whites would stop him. Likewise, Warren had no right to do as he pleased in Sioux country. Warren cited the president's orders. Mato-cu-wi-hu said the president had no more right here than Warren. The heated exchange ended with Warren stomping off to "look around the country." Mato-cu-wi-hu and Lame Deer also "went out by themselves."[30]

Toward evening, Mato-cu-wi-hu returned. At dinner, he admitted that if any other white man besides Warren had come here, he would have had his akicita strip them of their belongings. However, Warren impressed the chief when Harney introduced him at Fort Pierre. Therefore, if they would only go as far as Elk Creek, the chief would alert his people not to harm them. Warren said he could not promise to halt there. After supper, Mato-cu-wi-hu told Warren he could go where he pleased this time but must not come again. Warren assured him that his people "would never be worse" for letting them go, but he would convey Mato-cu-wi-hu's wish to the president that he not send more whites.

When Mato-cu-wi-hu and Lame Deer departed Warren's camp on September 24, Warren had few provisions left. Nevertheless, he gave them what he could. Mato-cu-wi-hu accepted the gifts, saying he believed Warren was poor because he "gave away so much." In his culture, "good

[29]Mato-cu-wi-hu appeared 23 Sept. 1857. For Lame Deer, see James Hanson, *Little Chief's Gatherings*, 191n46. Handwritten pages 20 and 22, and G. K. Warren's 1857 journal, both in Warren Papers, New York State Library and Archives.

[30] G. K. Warren's 1857 journal, 23 Sept. 1857.

hearted men always were poor"; he was very poor himself. Warren and his men explored eastward along the northern perimeter of the Black Hills to Bear Butte. They climbed it, drew their maps, and, on the way back to the Missouri, camped on Wounded Knee Creek.[31]

In his report, Warren acknowledged what a difficult position Mato-cu-wi-hu was in. With "whites to fear on one hand[,] his own people on the other[,] he can not well please both. He has my warmest sympathies." Warren conceded the Indians' objections to his traveling through their country made sense. He understood their need to "retain the buffalo in their neighborhood till their skins would answer for robes." If the explorers had continued, "we might have deflected the whole range of the buffalo . . . and prevented the Indians from laying in their winter stock of provisions and skins, on which their comfort if not even their lives depended." Their willingness to defend their position with violence was "not unlike what we should feel toward a person who should insist upon setting fire to our barns."[32]

Warren admitted he and his men were breaking Harney's treaty, which according to Sioux interpretation forbade white people to travel in the interior of their country. (Perhaps neither he nor the Indians knew Congress would never ratify it.) Furthermore, the Miniconjous accused Warren's party of exactly what it was doing, "examining the country to ascertain if it was of value to the whites, and to discover roads through it, and places for military posts." To allow the encounter to escalate to violence, he reasoned, aside from being dangerous to his own expedition, might have driven the Indians to commit a "desperate act" requiring "government chastisement."[33] Despite his condescension, it is clear Warren had come to respect Mato-cu-wi-hu and knew Mato-cu-wi-hu also respected him. He recorded Mato-cu-wi-hu's observation that he, Warren, treated his men well. "I gave them all plenty to eat. . . . I was a small man but he knew that small men would be listened to as well as large ones. He did not think it was necessary to be tall to be great."[34]

During their time together, Warren and Mato-cu-wi-hu had occasionally set weightier matters aside to engage in less formal conversation.

[31] G. K. Warren's 1857 journal, 24 Sept. 1857.

[32] Ibid.; and Warren, *Explorer on the Northern Plains*, 19.

[33] Warren, *Explorer on the Northern Plains*, 19; G. K. Warren's 1857 journal, 21 Sept. 1857, and Edgar Warren's 1857 journal, 21 Sept. 1857. See also Milligan, *Dakota Twilight*, 6; and Hasselstrom, *Roadside History*, 327–28.

[34] G. K. Warren's 1857 journal, 24 Sept. 1857. Also quoted in McLaird and Turchen, "Dacota Explorations of Warren," 379.

Warren (and his brother Edgar) recorded some of these exchanges, providing rare examples of a soldier trying to understand a Sioux chief and learn his concerns.

The accounts show Mato-cu-wi-hu an intelligent, dignified man with certain gaps in his knowledge. He had never been part of a Washington delegation and did not believe white men were as numerous as people said they were. Therefore, since Harney "had only whipped one little band" of Sioux at Blue Water, he believed it would be different if whites engaged the entire Sioux Nation. In other respects, Mato-cu-wi-hu was well informed. He knew that when Harney left the Upper Missouri in 1856 he had gone to fight Indians in Florida and afterward campaigned against Mormons in Utah. He pointed out Harney's hypocrisy in telling them not to go to war while "he was all the time going to war himself." He also knew Yanktons had recently sold a swath of land claimed also by other Sioux and agreed to live on a reservation. Consequently, Yanktons were as unwelcome in this country as whites.

If annuities were meant to purchase entry to this country, Mato-cu-wi-hu said his people did not want them. Furthermore, the goods were not worth the trouble of a trip to claim them, and, if they were not present when the goods arrived, they got nothing. With two buffalo robes buying one blanket, trade was satisfactory. Harney had promised that competition would lower prices, but new traders only brought smallpox. Mato-cu-wi-hu and his people wanted no bribes to avoid war with their traditional enemies because war for them was both a pastime and a necessity.[35]

SNOWDEN'S GROUP, EXPLORING THE WHITE AND NIOBRARA RIVERS, also met some Sioux. On a rainy, windy, mid-September day, they saw a white tipi in the distance with people scurrying around it. "At our approach," Snowden recounted, "the women and children fled to the hills," but one man—the papers he produced identified him as Big Bull, a Little Thunder sub-chief—approached on "a splendid white [I]ndian horse." When Snowden's men told him to send back those who fled—they would not harm them—Big Bull explained that "only the women . . . were frightened, not being accustomed to seeing Soldiers."[36]

[35]Edgar Warren's 1857 journal; McLaird and Turchen, "Dacota Explorations of Warren," 158–61; Warren report, 20; and Adams, *Harney*, 165, 168–73. Harney headed the Utah expedition from 29 June to 29 Aug. 1857.
    [36]"The Bull Man" in Council reprint, 24.

A few days later, Snowden returned from a side trip into the hills and found Little Thunder and forty others at his camp. The Brulé chief wanted to know "the meaning of our presence in their country," but the mixed-blood Cree interpreting for both sides knew little English. He discerned, however, that the Sioux were exasperated at whites scaring away their game. Little Thunder reminded the interlopers about Harney's promise "that no white man should come into their country without a licence from him." Little Thunder and the others warned that the road ahead was bad, and besides, many Brulés were in the vicinity. They pointed out a better way, but the explorers insisted on continuing as planned. Little Thunder volunteered escorts, he said, to keep his tribesmen from stealing horses. The travelers bid farewell to Little Thunder's party with some tobacco, powder, and lead.[37]

Because rain delayed departure the following day, a few old Indian women from Little Thunder's group ventured into the explorers' camp to sell moccasins and other items. Once underway, Snowden's party soon came to the lodges of the four men Little Thunder delegated to accompany them. They were Standing Elk and three old chiefs. Snowden described Standing Elk as "fine looking," very intelligent, and considered an expert on whites because of his Leavenworth experience. One of the old men, Snowden wrote, never tired of talking about his visit to Washington several years earlier.[38]

As they neared the Nebraska sand hills, the guides suggested the party make an alternate river crossing instead of taking a likely looking trail. Snowden and his men ignored the advice and became mired in quicksand and thwarted by deep ravines. With the Missouri River only four or five days distant, the chiefs declared there was little danger of horse theft. Three left, but Standing Elk accompanied Snowden's party a few miles farther in order to argue that although he knew "the country through which we were travelling belonged to the 'Great Father' . . . the game, grass, wood, etc.,"[39] all belonged to the Brulés. Before departing, he asked them if they could spare some ammunition.

That afternoon, the explorers camped near two tipis situated below some bluffs. The Brulés whom the tipis belonged to had been hunting buffalo, and they came to Snowden's expedition to sell fresh meat. A day later, a mule that had escaped from its herder turned up in an Indian

---

[37]Snowden's 1857 journal, 56, 59–62.

[38]Ibid., 64–66; and Hyde, *Spotted Tail's Folk*, 76n4. Sioux visited Washington in 1851 during Fillmore's presidency.

[39] Snowden's 1857 journal, 24 Sept. 1857.

camp about twelve miles away. Its owner recovered it and everything it was carrying except a Colt's pistol, which, according to Snowden, "the Indians said was not in the holster when they found the mule." About a week later, while the explorers waited at the same camp for Warren's party to join them, two more mules disappeared.[40]

According to Snowden's October 11 journal entry, "twenty-two Brulé Indians crossed the river and charged into the camp with their bows shining and arrows in their hands." Instead of drawing a weapon, Snowden grabbed his notebook and described the encounter. After calm returned, the Brulé claimed to have mistaken the explorers for French traders. After learning their identity, they wanted a toll for passage given that, as Snowden wrote, "we were eating all their plums & wild fruit and burning their wood [and] . . . our horses were eating & destroying all the grass along the river." When they accused the party of "killing & scaring away all the game," Snowden dismissed their complaints. They left only when he threatened to fire on them. After using up all the grass in the area and saying so in his journal, Snowden moved his group down the river. At one point, Lieutenant McMillan's men used picks and shovels to make a ford across White Earth River and "improve" the hill on the opposite side.

On October 15, 1857, the group heard shots and "a whoop" from the hills. It was a vanguard of Warren's party. After a few days of reorganizing, Warren sent some men to follow the Niobrara to its confluence with the Missouri to determine if the area was suitable for a road. He and Snowden continued with the main party to Fort Randall.[41]

During both Warren expeditions, smallpox had been a worry on the Upper Missouri. By Christmas Day, 1856, Agent Vaughan could report that the smallpox outbreak among the Arikaras and Mandans had abated. For Warren, Mato-cu-wi-hu tallied Sioux smallpox fatalities at 134 Sihasapas and 30 of Big Head's Yanktonais. Warren estimated casualties for all the Upper Missouri tribes at possibly 3,000. He tabulated the total population of the nine western Sioux bands at 3,000 lodges, or about 24,000 persons, including 2,880 Yanktons, 6,400 Yanktonais, 2,920 Hunkpapas, 1,320 Sihasapas, 1,320 Sans Arcs, 1,600 Miniconjous, 3,680 Oglalas, 3,040 Brulés, and 800 Two Kettles.[42]

---

[40]Snowden's 1857 journal, 25 Sept. 1857, 66–73; Warren report, xxiv and xxv, 16–22.

[41]McLaird and Turchen, "Dacota Explorations of Warren," 163; and Warren report, 21.

[42]Jack Roberts, *Amazing Adventures of Lord Gore*, reproduces Vaughan's letter, 195–96; Warren report, 48, 54; Coyer, "Wild Region," 241. For Sioux population, see Kingsley Bray, "Teton Sioux Population History," 165–88.

After three years among the Upper Missouri Sioux, Warren deduced they had the strength and will for "prolonged and able resistance to further encroachment of the western settlers." He believed displacing them would be necessary and that war pressure to do it was increasing. Indeed, he regarded "the knowledge of the proper routes by which to invade their country and conquer them" the greatest value of his explorations. He understood his own complicity. "I almost feel guilty of crime in being a pioneer to the white men who will ere long drive the red man from his last niche of hunting ground." He was sympathetic to the challenge Sioux leaders faced. Mato-cu-wi-hu was "a great friend to peace with the whites and the most influential warrior in his nation." He had "fine mental powers" and risked his life by trying to control his own people.[43] Many Sioux overestimated their strength and numbers compared with Americans. Although Mato-cu-wi-hu foresaw "the inability of his nation to withstand the troops" and therefore tried "to avert a collision," he would have difficulty convincing other Sioux of it. "His position is an embarrassing one, for if as a friend to the whites he yields to their wishes, he loses friends at home and if he joins in with the prevailing wishes of his people he leads them to certain destruction."[44]

---

[43]Warren's handwritten p. 20 and his 27 Jan. 1858 letter in Warren Papers, New York State Library and Archives; Warren report, xxvi–xxvii, 51–53.

[44]Handwritten pp. 20 and 22, Warren Papers, New York State Library and Archives.

Chapter 5

Losing Ground

Like the Lakotas Mato-cu-wi-hu represented, Nakotas and Dakotas east of the Missouri experienced unprecedented upheaval during the last three years of the 1850s. Minnesota licensed dozens of land speculation companies eager to stake claims in, and win separate territorial status for, what people were already calling "Dakota." Captain John B. S. Todd, a Sixth Infantry captain and Ash Hollow veteran, passing through Sioux City in November 1855 on furlough, surmised it might be "destined to be of some importance." During his army career, Todd had observed how lucrative the fur trade could be. Before joining Harney's expedition, he commanded Minnesota's Fort Snelling, where traders for decades had become wealthy doing business with Chippewas, Winnebagos, and Dakotas. Accordingly, Todd resigned his commission shortly after returning to duty in June 1856 to become Daniel Marsh Frost's business partner. His timing was propitious. In mid-May 1857, the two infantry companies at Fort Pierre abandoned it, as ordered, for Fort Randall, where Todd was sutler. A month later, the army authorized D. M. Frost and Company to take over the buildings and public property left at Forts Lookout and Pierre. In addition, the partners began to establish licensed trading posts in unceded land east of the Missouri that showed promise as future town sites. Simultaneously, they worked politically to open Indian land to settlement and obtain territorial status for Dakota.[1]

The men at Fort Randall were considerably more comfortable during the 1856–57 winter than they had been at Fort Pierre the winter before. The challenges were different here, too. By March 1857, Colonel Lee had to cope with whites squatting on Ponca tribal land near the new post. At first, like Harney, Lee mistook the Poncas for a band of Sioux. He

[1]Todd, "Harney Expedition," 129; Paul, *Blue Water Creek*, 4; Fort Pierre PR, July 1856, SO no. 80, 2 July 1856, reel 920, M617, NA; McLaird and Turchen, "Dacota Explorations of Warren," 150n29; Fort Pierre PR, Dec. 1855–May 1856, reel 920, M617, NA; Paige to Frost & Co., 17 July 1857 and 18 July 1857, OCRFP, 429–30; and Lamar, *Dakota Territory*, 65–73.

warned the squatters that if they did not leave their claims, he would first send soldiers to compel them to leave, and if they still did not go, he would let "Old Bear" [Smutty Bear] and his Yanktons have a free hand in chasing them off.[2]

However, events taking place some 300 miles to the east in Minnesota and Iowa involving the Santee Sioux soon replaced the squatter problem as Lee's main concern. In March, Inkpaduta, a Wahpekute chief opposed to white settlement in the country near Okoboji and Spirit Lakes in northwestern Iowa, struck at settlers there. Word of some thirty-eight killings and kidnappings—Inkpaduta and his followers had captured thirteen-year-old Abbie Gardner and three other white women—soon reached Fort Ridgely near the two Dakota reservations. When Tenth Infantry soldiers failed to rescue the kidnap victims, the onus fell on the reservation Dakotas to bring Inkpaduta to justice.[3] If they did not bring him in, their agent threatened to withhold the Dakotas' annuities. The Dakotas on their reservations along the Minnesota River—the Sissetons and Wahpetons lived northwest of where the Yellow Medicine River flows into the Minnesota; the Wahpekutes and Mdewakantons, southeast of that confluence—wondered what Inkpaduta's crimes against whites had to do with them. But the winter had been hard, people were nearly starving, and the agent's threat was compelling. They sent out search parties. Militia groups from Iowa and Minnesota also tried to rescue Inkpaduta's captives, but all failed.[4]

Lee did not receive the May 5 letter ordering him to send troops to Spirit Lake until May 26, and the detachment of infantry, dragoons, and teamsters did not get underway until the first week in June. By then, the Indians had murdered two captives and another was ransomed to two reservation Dakotas. In June, a party of Yanktonais bought Abbie Gardner from Inkpaduta and turned her over to three Dakota men who had come to rescue her.[5]

---

[2]McLean to unidentified "Captain," 24 Dec. 1856, Fort Randall LS, 1856–67, RG 393, NA; Lee to Stoker et al., 9 March 1857, Fort Randall LS, 1856–67, RG 393, NA; and Athearn, *Forts of the Upper Missouri*, 58.

[3]Oehler, *Great Sioux Uprising*, 251n4; Gary Anderson and Woolworth, *Through Dakota Eyes*, 20; Beck, *Inkpaduta*, 27–29, 50–51; and "The Spirit Lake Massacre," *St. Paul Daily Pioneer and Democrat*, 26 March 1857. See also Van Nuys, *Inkpaduta*.

[4]Beck, *Inkpaduta*, 65–99.

[5]Lee to Day, 31 May 1857, 2 June 1857, 7 June 1857, and 15 June 1857; and Lee to Cooper, 23 June 1857, Fort Randall LS, 1856–1867, RG 393, NA; and Bakeman, *Legends, Letters and Lies*, 6. See Lee, *History of the Spirit Lake Massacre*.

This predicament occurred during a spate of transfers at Fort Randall. Colonel Lee ordered the dragoons back there in order to transfer them to Fort Leavenworth, while the infantry companies, whose transfer was to Fort Ridgely, continued to that post. Meanwhile, Lee heard Spirit Lake marauders were camped northeast of Fort Pierre on the James River. Instead of taking action, he asked his superiors if he should apprehend them, requesting that an answer be sent by telegraph "as high up the Missouri as possible," which at the time was probably St. Joseph, Missouri. When the transfer chaos ended, six Second Infantry companies remained to garrison Randall. Inkpaduta found safe haven across the international border, and although reservation Dakotas did not bring him in, their agent relented and distributed annuities. Resentment over the incident festered, however.[6]

EVEN AS WARREN'S PARTY EXPLORED LAKOTA TERRITORY, NAKOTAS and Dakotas contended with a road-building incursion into their country. During the California gold rush, Minnesota engineer William H. Nobles pioneered a pass through the Sierra Mountains. Afterward, he sought support for a wagon road from Minnesota to South Pass, the Oregon-California Trail's passage across the Rocky Mountains. In 1856, his group of speculators, the Dakota Land Company, wheedled a $50,000 appropriation from Congress. By spring 1857, Nobles was building the Fort Ridgely to Fort Lookout portion of his road.

Smutty Bear's large band of Yanktons had been six days on a futile hunt through deep snow for buffalo before confronting Nobles near Lake Benton, northwest of Lake Shetek.[7] Their horses were starving, and because gophers had destroyed their corn crop, they were desperately hungry. Even so, they promised a fight if Nobles crossed the Big Sioux River. Furthermore, messengers from the Sisseton and Wahpeton agency at Yellow Medicine warned the road-builders about Inkpaduta's

[6]Lee to Cooper, 23 and 30 June 1857, 88 left, Fort Randall LS, 1856–67, RG 393, NA; Fort Randall PR, June and July 1857, reel 988, M617, NA; and Bristow, "Inkpaduta's Revenge." By 1851, the St. Louis & Missouri River Telegraph Co. served Weston and St. Joseph. Service from Omaha began about 1860.

[7]Doane Robinson, "History of the Dakota," 245. Robinson names Smutty Bear as leading the Yanktons; Nobles names no one. "From Nobles' Expedition," *St. Paul Daily Pioneer and Democrat*, 23 March 1857.

activities. Fearing all-out war between whites and the Sioux, Nobles left his men bridging the Cottonwood River while he backtracked to Yellow Medicine for more and better ammunition. Presents appeased the Yanktons, and by September Nobles's crews finished the roadbed to the Missouri. Because the army had abandoned Fort Lookout in July for Fort Randall, the road was now a 254-mile-long road to nowhere. Despite his own experience, Nobles reported he had "no reason to believe that the Indians in that country will ever interfere with travellers" over his new road. His engineer, Samuel A. Medary, Jr., made it as straight as possible in order to accommodate a future railroad route. "At the terminus of the road are dense forests of good timber," Medary reported, "and the land along the entire route is such as will invite the early attention of the emigrant." Despite the hype, financial and political trouble consequent to a financial panic in August 1857 permanently terminated Nobles's road.[8]

WHEN DEMOCRAT JAMES BUCHANAN BECAME PRESIDENT IN March 1857, staid, straight-laced, white-haired A. H. Redfield replaced Vaughan as Upper Missouri Indian agent. Redfield's initial meeting with Struck-by-the-Ree and his sub-chiefs was cordial, but the Yanktons immediately (and again unsuccessfully) broached their 1830 land dispute with the Omahas.[9]

At Fort Pierre a large delegation of Two Kettles, Miniconjous, Hunkpapas, Brulés, Sihasapas, Sans Arcs, and Yanktonais greeted their new agent. Through Zephyr Rencontre, whom Redfield judged "a sensible, well informed and good man," the Indians told him they were trying to abide by the treaty but were disappointed Harney did not send the promised uniforms for their soldiers. In his report, Redfield urged Congress to do so. "The government will suffer much in the estimate of the Indians if a promise made by an officer so high in rank and character as General Harney is left unfulfilled." Despite hearing orators' complaints about trespassers, hunters, and trappers, Redfield deemed these talks satisfactory. "Their language, and manner indicated, I think, a sincere friendship and a strong desire for peace and quiet, and to observe the

    [8]Lee to Patten, 28 May 1857, Fort Randall LS, 1856–67, RG 393, NA; Campbell, *Report upon the Pacific Wagon Roads*, 4, 13–15, 22, 23; and Helen White, *Ho!* 4–5. Fort Lookout was abandoned 17 July 1857, reel 988 (see OCRFP, 430–32).
    [9]Sunder, *Fur Trade*, 178, 192; Wischmann, *Frontier Diplomats*, 289; and Redfield to Haverty, 9 Sept. 1857, CIA annual report, no. 56, 123–40. Vaughan became the Blackfeet (Siksika) tribe's agent.

stipulations of the treaty." Of the chiefs he met, Redfield found Mato-cu-wi-hu, Two Bear, and the Brulé chief Iron Nation the "most able and influential." He distributed treaty goods and collected receipts, then visited Two Bear's Yanktonai camp, where he "held a good talk" and "a pleasant, friendly interview." As his steamboat, *Twilight*, pulled away, Redfield believed he had "left [these Sioux] . . . better and happier than I found them."[10]

Although Big Head stayed away from Fort Pierre, Redfield stopped at his camp of sixty-seven lodges to find these Upper Yanktonais "in an uneasy and disturbed state of mind." He had given away their share and only had some tobacco and a little food for them. They begged for his pity and professed friendship but insisted he deliver next year's annuities to their camp, not the fort. Redfield said he could not do that, but he assured them safety at Pierre "if they behaved well." After the council, he entertained some headmen on the boat with bread and sugared coffee. When they promised good behavior, Redfield gave them coats and pants for the chiefs and more provisions to take home. The new agent deemed his interaction with Big Head's band "very fortunate" and hoped they would "reform their habits."[11]

In council between Hidatsas and Mandans near Fort Berthold, the Hidatsa orator Long Hair told Redfield that, while some Sioux were "telling you many good words," others "stole eight [horses] from us and killed one of our best young men." He explained that Hidatsa country extended from Heart River to the Yellowstone's mouth, "yet I cannot send my young men just across the river here to kill a buffalo . . . without their being attacked and killed." Even Minnesota Sioux had come to steal horses, "thus reducing four of my young men to poverty and their wives and children to starvation." Warriors caught one Sioux horse thief and asked him "why he had ears if not to hear, but he said nothing; so they cut off one of his ears; then cut off one of his hands, and they took off his scalp and sent him back to his people to learn sense." Another time, Long Hair said, Sioux smoked the peace pipe with him, "then turned away and immediately stole our horses and killed our people." Meanwhile, Sioux tried to convince the Berthold tribes that accepting annuities caused their poverty, deaths, and sickness. Long Hair figured "the Sioux wish to be the strongest and most powerful people on the earth."[12]

---

[10]Redfield to Haverty, 25 June 1857, CIA annual report, no. 56, 123–26.

[11]Ibid.

[12]Hassrick, *The Sioux*, 90; Long Hair's speech, 1 July 1857, CIA annual report, no. 58, 138–39; and Sunder, *Fur Trade*, 192.

At Fort Union, Redfield heard more about Sioux aggression. Bourgeois Frederick G. Riter told Redfield that in November Sioux robbed a trading party of their carts, killed a white man and his Assiniboine companion, and severely wounded another. While Redfield listened, twenty-five mounted warriors appeared on the prairie to the north, just out of gunshot range. When they ventured within yelling distance, Redfield invited their leaders inside for a parley. Five Sans Arcs who came admitted their band stole horses from neighboring Fort William.[13]

Congress appropriated funds for a new Upper Missouri Indian agency, but Redfield argued in his report that no agent could safely live in an ordinary house "unless it is built under the protection of some fortified post." He emphasized how dependent he was on the fur traders' hospitality, protection, and help in distributing annuities and recommended building more military posts rather than an independent agency. Redfield also found it impractical to make roving tribes practice agriculture even though buffalo were rapidly disappearing. He predicted even skilled farmers would fail.

On his return trip, Redfield arrived at Fort Berthold during a Sioux assault on the nearby Hidatsa and Mandan villages. The mounted Yanktonais drove off horses and killed oxen then assailed the fort. The local Indians reclaimed some horses but lost four men killed and several injured during the chase.

Sixty-five miles downriver, an astonished Redfield found some 600 tipis housing more than a thousand Sihasapas, Hunkpapas, Sans Arcs, Miniconjous, Yanktonais, Yanktons, and others. They claimed to have convened to buy corn from the Arikaras, but Redfield was skeptical. "The real object no doubt was to agree upon a course of extensive winter operations against the Assiniboines and Crow and perhaps, even the Upper Blackfeet [the Siksika tribe]." The Sioux lodges looked new, Redfield observed, "and the men were all well mounted, clothed, [and] armed." He convened leaders to try to persuade them to cease war, horse theft, and "all other depredations," not only with whites, but also with other Indians. They listened politely, but in their speeches they demanded no more white men enter or pass through their country, and they wanted no soldiers or government goods. In short, Redfield reported, "they wanted to be let alone to do as they pleased."[14]

The Arikaras told Redfield that Yanktonais had a few days earlier

---

[13]Redfield to Haverty, 9 Sept. 1857, CIA annual report; and Sunder, *Riter, Fur Trade*, 157–69.
[14]Redfield to Haverty, 9 Nov. 1857, CIA annual report, no. 57, 136–37.

killed several of their men. In his report, Redfield appealed for troops, particularly for Fort Berthold, and opined that troops should have stayed at Fort Pierre, especially given that Indians thought the soldiers had left out of fear. Having troops in the area would be "for the good of the Sioux as well as for the protection of the poor nations." It would be easier to control and pacify the Sioux now, he contended, than if they were left alone to commit more "outrages" that would "demand severe chastisement and the destruction of many lives."[15]

At Fort Pierre, Redfield found a number of Yanktons and Yanktonais eager to talk. Although they seemed peaceful and were grateful for small gifts he presented, the Yankton White Medicine Cow petitioned anew for the 1830 land dispute money and protested about Nobles's road through their country. Redfield was possibly less optimistic after meeting the 28,248 "souls" he represented on Upper Missouri.[16]

IN THE FALL, FORT RANDALL SUTLER JOHN TODD CALLED A meeting at Struck-by-the-Ree's village to ask the Yanktons to sell most of their land. They summarily rejected the idea, but Todd persisted. To help present his case, he sent to Fort Pierre for his business partner, Charles Picotte. Because Charles's mother was Struck-by-the-Ree's sister, the younger Picotte was kin to many and had their confidence. He also had a reputation for good character among whites. A contemporary described him as "over six feet tall, broad-shouldered, straight as an arrow, and a most perfect gentleman."[17] Photographs show him in maturity dressed in city clothes, sporting a luxuriant mustache. Picotte agreed to represent the Yanktons at a new council, but when Todd insisted on talking to the Indians without him, he walked out and the Yanktons followed. With their champion back at Fort Pierre, no Indian would speak to Todd, so Todd ate crow and sent once more for Picotte. Ultimately, Picotte and Zephyr Rencontre advised the Yanktons to go with Todd to Washington to discuss a land deal with the president.

Tall and slender, Todd stood straight and dressed elegantly, appearing the dignified Kentucky patrician and West Point graduate that he was. His delegation of fifteen Yankton chiefs and headmen, including Picotte,

---

[15]Ibid.

[16]Ibid., 135–38.

[17]Gray, "Honoré Picotte," 191–93; and Holley, *Once Their Home*, 61–62.

Struck-by-the-Ree, and Smutty Bear, left for Washington December 11, 1857. Picotte recalled Todd, "fearing that the Indians might get sick by changing water," kept a full keg of whiskey handy on the stagecoach ride to Iowa City, where they boarded a train.[18] Arriving in Washington on New Year's Day, 1858, they began the usual rounds intended to impress Indians with America's power. Struck-by-the-Ree had been so regaled in 1837, but for some Yankton leaders this was an eye-opening experience. On their excursion to the Navy Yard, the Washington Arsenal, and the Marine Barracks, the Sioux joined delegations of Pawnees, Poncas, Potawatomis, and Sacs and Foxes also in town. At the Marine Barracks, the band played as four battalions performed a mock battle with blank cartridges. Throughout the trip, Todd used "discretion, care, and cunning" to persuade Struck-by-the-Ree that a sale would benefit his people. The chief, once convinced, sold the others, telling them "white men are coming like maggots. It is useless to resist them." If they did try, "many of our brave warriors would be killed, our women and children left in sorrow." Therefore, he said, "We must accept it, get the best terms we can get and try to adopt their ways."[19]

Ultimately, the Yanktons sold some 14 million acres of land between the Big Sioux and Missouri Rivers for $1.6 million, or about 12¢ an acre. This sale included land Lakotas had given the Yanktons stewardship over when the Iowa and Fox tribes had forced the Nakota bands west onto the prairie. By the April 19, 1858, document, the tribe agreed to move to a 400,000-acre reservation on the Missouri's east bank. The Yanktons retained control over the Minnesota pipestone quarry their ancestors had mined for centuries to make sacred pipes, and they granted 640 acres each to Picotte and Rencontre, plus 120 acres each to three of Picotte's mixed-blood widowed sisters and to a friend of the tribe, Paul Dorion.[20]

When the chiefs arrived home in May, they learned many of their people opposed the treaty. Almost immediately, Smutty Bear recanted and tried to prevent its acceptance and ratification. Struck-by-the-Ree

---

[18]Lamar, *Dakota Territory*, 65–66; Holley, *Once Their Home*, 56, 66–67; and Doane Robinson, "History of the Dakota," 246.

[19]Viola, *Diplomats in Buckskin*, 137, cites a 28 Jan. 1858 article in the *Washington Union*. Obituary of John Blair Smith Todd, *Yankton (Dakota Territory) Press*, reproduced in "General John Blair Smith Todd," 498; and Hasselstrom, *Roadside History*, 194–95.

[20]Kappler, *Indian Affairs*, vol. 2, *Treaties*, 776–81. The reservation extended thirty miles up the river nearly to Chouteau Creek. The quarry is at modern Pipestone, Minn. For Dorion, see Hafen, *Mountain Men*, vol. 8 (1971), 107–12, and Doane Robinson, ed., "Fort Tecumseh and Fort Pierre Journals," 237.

remained stalwart, but he and Picotte, along with others who supported the treaty, received death threats.[21]

Meanwhile, that same spring Frost, Todd, and Company, who had won the government contract to deliver the 1858 annuities, leased the steamboat *Twilight* to transport them, their trade goods, and employees to its Upper Missouri posts. Redfield was also aboard, and even before the boat arrived at Struck-by-the-Ree's village on June 5, several Yankton chiefs boarded to express their anger about squatters. Whites had staked out claims before the land sale was final, and Struck-by-the-Ree threatened that if Redfield did nothing about the trespassers he would use force to remove them himself. Observing this contentious onboard council was twenty-two-year-old Henry A. Boller, hired as clerk at Fort Atkinson, a new post that would compete with the AFC's Fort Berthold for Mandan, Hidatsa, and Arikara business. In his journal, Boller wrote that some warriors on shore "were for scalping all of the whites, but presents judiciously given calmed them down for the *time*." The *Twilight* resumed its journey without bloodletting and arrived at Fort Randall with its calliope screeching. When Redfield reported Struck-by-the-Ree's concerns to the commanding officer, the dignified, white-haired Major Hannibal Day assured him he would remove the squatters. However, as Boller noticed, "the Mormon War having drawn off the other companies," only eighty men from two companies remained as garrison. Despite that, Captain Henry Walton Wessells boarded the *Twilight* with forty enlisted men to escort Redfield to Fort Union.[22]

Boller described the band playing a quickstep as it led the troops to the boat. The escort filed on board to a lively reel and cheers from the crowd. As the boat churned away, the band played a patriotic tune and the boat's scaled-down twelve-pounder cannon, called a "mountain" howitzer, fired a thunderous farewell. According to Boller, those watching were "bedizened and astonished." Boller realized Redfield requested the military escort because "Indians everywhere are highly exasperated, and an attack on us is not improbable." Nevertheless, some on board regarded the soldiers as "too few to overawe the Indians, and of little or

---

[21]Doane Robinson, "History of the Dakota," 246–49; and Lamar, *Dakota Territory*, 27–64.

[22]Mattison, *Henry A. Boller*, 14 June 1858 letter to mother, 34–35; Boller, *Among the Indians*, xi, 18–19; Meyers, *Ten Years*, 135–45, 165; Larpenteur, *Forty Years*, 264–68; Adams, *Harney*, 159, 164–81; and Fort Randall PR, May, June, July, Sept. 1858, reel 988, M617, NA. See also Athearn, *Forts of the Upper Missouri*, 61; and Sunder, *Fur Trade*, 192, 216–17. The four companies that left in May returned by September.

no account if we are attacked."[23] Redfield's reception at Smutty Bear's village near Fort Lookout did, in fact, nearly turn violent. Not only were the Indians angry that Redfield had left their annuities at the lower village, they were also incensed about squatters' blatant violations.

Even before taking the Yanktons to Washington, D.C., Todd and his cronies had anticipated success in obtaining territorial status for Dakota. They were not alone in this belief. The Dakota Land Company, chartered by the state of Minnesota, had established a community at the falls of the Big Sioux River knowing that, until treaty ratification (which would happen on February 16, 1859), this town, Sioux Falls, was on Yankton land. In addition to Sioux Falls squatters, Sam Medary, Jr. (the engineer for Nobles's road) and some of his Dakota Land Company partners had illegally spent the winter of 1857–58 at a place he envisioned as a town site. When Smutty Bear and a large group of Yanktons, Yanktonais, and Santees set out to confront both these groups, the Medary squatters near present Brookings, South Dakota, skedaddled, leaving the Indians to loot and raze the abandoned buildings and take the abandoned livestock. At Sioux Falls, where squatters had constructed a stockade and stayed to defend it, Smutty Bear and his warriors backed down.[24]

Smutty Bear's supporters were not the only Sioux riled by the Yanktons' land deal. At Fort Pierre, Redfield's "long and tedious and disagreeable talk" with Sioux chiefs and head men mostly concerned their objections to it. These Sioux, who wanted Redfield to write the president to stop it from going through, were "in a most disturbed and irritated state of mind," he told his new St. Louis superintendent, A. M. Robinson. In the end, Redfield persuaded them to accept their annuities, although "they growled also at the small amount of presents sent them." Redfield agreed: "The presents given the Indians in this agency under the treaty of Laramie are really so small, and the Indians so numerous, that it is quite doubtful whether in many cases there is not more injury than good produced thereby."[25]

When the *Twilight* tied up at Big Head's Yanktonai village, the fur company employees, sensing trouble, stayed on the boat. That proved prudent. According to Boller, when St. Louis artist Carl Wimar asked

[23]Mattison, *Henry A. Boller*, Boller to mother, 14 June 1858, 34–35.

[24]Lounsberry, *Early History*, 216; Lamar, *Dakota Territory*, 40–43. Minnesota Admission Bill, 11 May 1858, Congressional Globe, vol. 43, appendix, p. 402; Doane Robinson, "History of the Dakota," 248–49.

[25]Redfield to Robinson, 1 Sept. 1858, CIA annual report, no. 24, 437.

one warrior if he would sell some of his arrows, he armed his bow with one, saying he would "sooner put one thro' Wimar."[26] As Redfield headed home after visiting other tribes, the Sioux at Fort Pierre again refused their presents for fear other Sioux would injure them and their property. Redfield described the tribes' majority as "haughty, proud, self-willed, and hostile." They were "determined to be free from restraint and to do as they please."[27]

At Fort Randall, Redfield spoke again with Smutty Bear's band, who still would not accept presents. At Struck-by-the-Ree's village, he gave away what the other Sioux had refused. These numerous Lower Yanktons, Redfield reported, "know best what is for the true interest of their tribe. They are all much in favor of the treaty, and will be greatly disappointed and offended if it is not carried out." Smutty Bear's Upper Yanktons, he believed, would eventually be "satisfied when they see and feel" the treaty's benefits. Redfield acknowledged, however, that without his military escort, he might not have passed safely through Sioux country to deliver goods to upriver tribes.[28]

Redfield was disappointed that Major Day had done nothing about the increasing number of squatters. Redfield continued to Sioux City, but on September 29, Major Wessells, in command now at Randall, sent for him. Wessells had received orders "to furnish . . . the requisite force to expel trespassers" and needed Redfield to accompany troops to specify what he wanted done. Accordingly, on October 5, he joined Captain C. S. Lovell's march. The squatters were gone, but the expedition burned hay and yanked claim stakes from patches of plowed land. Redfield had mixed feelings about what he had set in motion. He told Robinson these "trespasses, though illegal and a great wrong to the Indians, were made by our bold class of hardy, enterprising, and intelligent *pioneers*, by whom, in a great degree, our nation has become great, rich, extended, and powerful." He believed it "useless and wrong unnecessarily to resist this class. All our great public domain *fit for settlement and cultivation* must be opened" to the thousands awaiting "permission to enter upon the Yancton country."[29]

---

[26]Mattison, *Henry A. Boller*, 21 June 1858 letter to father, 38; Boller, *Among the Indians*, 24–27; and Athearn, *Forts of the Upper Missouri*, 61. Wimar's letter in Hodges, *Carl Wimar*, 17–23, has inaccuracies but conveys the sense of danger. Wimar made likenesses of Mato-cu-wi-hu on this trip.

[27]Redfield to Robinson, 12 Oct. 1858, CIA annual report, no. 25, 444–45.

[28]Redfield to Robinson, 1 Sept. and 12 Oct. 1858, CIA annual report, nos. 24 & 25, 435–46.

[29]Redfield to Robinson, 12 Oct. 1858, CIA annual report, no. 25, 444–45 (Redfield's italics).

Smutty Bear's raiders who had chased off the Medary squatters sold the cattle they had confiscated to traders serving the Arikaras the following January. This would be their only recompense from squatters, but by some twisted perception of justice, the government deducted money from the Yanktons' funds to compensate the illegal Medary squatters for property losses.[30]

IN OCTOBER 1858, TRADER HENRY BOLLER WAS HEADING HOME TO Fort Atkinson after a trading expedition. His Hidatsa traveling companions were accustomed to the aurora borealis shimmering in the sky, but another wondrous sight—a comet—made everyone uneasy. All he had read about comets "being the heralds of wars and tumults" had Boller sharing "superstitious fears of the Indians and wondering what it boded." His companions predicted their village would be attacked. Sure enough, near there, riders raced toward them to inform Chief Four Bears that a Sioux war party fired on hunters the previous day. Hidatsas killed all nine Sioux but lost four of their own. Two wounded Hidatsas later died.[31]

Only days afterward, some Hidatsas returned from the Ree village downriver with news. Hunkpapas and Sihasapas were in the area and wanted to trade. Hunkpapa chief Black Moon had already visited the Rees with an advance party. On October 22, Mato-cu-wi-hu's brother, Running Antelope, came in to bargain heatedly with Berthold's interpreter, Pierre Garreau, and the Fort Atkinson interpreter, Charles Patineau. Tempers eventually cooled enough to establish price parameters.[32]

Three days later, the approach of thirty Sioux warriors inspired Boller's literary talent. He observed "the gleaming of their polished lances and the glitter of the small mirrors . . . suspended from their necks." While they "boldly galloped down the bluffs that separated the high rolling prairie from the timbered bottom," the village buzzed with activity. Emerging from the timber, the Sioux cantered onto a sandbar, dismounted, and

[30]Mattison, *Henry A. Boller*, letter, 25 Jan. 1859, 84; and Doane Robinson, "History of the Dakota," 248–49. Boller claimed Santees sold the cattle.

[31]Boller, *Among the Indians*, 148n46, 148–49. Hidatsas adopted this Four Bears, born Assiniboine, who won leadership through war against the Sioux and died in 1861. See De Trobriand, *Army Life* (Lakeside Press edition), 270, 270n31. Italian astronomer Giovanni Donati discovered the comet 2 June 1858.

[32]Patineau (a.k.a. Pacquenade) et al. Running Antelope (Tatokainyanka), a.k.a. *Cabria qui Cour*.

"shouted to their individual friends or comrades, declaring who they were and asking to be crossed over."[33] Mandan and Hidatsa women helped ferry the visitors over in bullboats—simple round tubs made from single buffalo hides stretched around willow frames. The Hidatsas greeted the party warmly.

Boller admired these "tall, noble-looking men of symmetrical form" and described how "their long black hair was carefully combed and gathered into a plait on each side of the head, bound with scarlet cloth, while the neatly-braided scalp-lock was adorned with a strip of otter-skin." They wore "finely-dressed deerskin shirts, beautifully worked with stained porcupine quills of various colors, and fringed with scalp-locks and dyed horsehair." Their "wild and game appearance," Boller thought, "told of a lordly spirit unsubdued." He noticed that "each one wore a white blanket, and was completely armed with bow and arrows, fusee [musket], tomahawk, and scalping-knife." Many carried lances. "The war-eagle feathers on their heads danced and fluttered in the wind and the hawk-bells and dried antelope-hoofs, with which their shirts and leggings were lavishly hung, tinkled and rattled with every motion as they stalked proudly about, literally monarchs of all they surveyed." Several wore Navaho blankets. When the Fort Atkinson traders invited these "elegant and dashing strangers" to a feast, the visitors seemed delighted with the blue and scarlet cloth, mirrors, and knives given to them as presents. The Sans Arc chief Crow Feather remarked on the traders' new buildings. "These whites used to dwell in a dirty brown lodge full of holes, but now they have a fine, large white one."

According to Boller, the Sioux believed the comet "to be a forerunner of wars and troubles." They claimed not to know about the nine Sioux the Hidatsa killed, speculating that the dead men belonged to Two Bear's or Big Head's Yanktonai bands. The Sioux socialized for three days before leaving for the forks of the Knife River some sixty miles away, where more than a thousand lodges of Miniconjous, Yanktonais, Sans Arcs, Sihasapas, and Hunkpapas camped for the winter.[34]

The year 1859 opened with Sioux all along the Upper Missouri anxious about whites. In January, Boller wrote, war parties were everywhere.

---

[33]All quotes by Boller are from Boller, *Among the Indians*, 156–59.

[34]Mattison, *Henry A. Boller*, 137–47; Boller, *Among the Indians*, 154–61; and James Walker, *Lakota Belief*, 104, 120, 127, 204. For Navaho blankets, see winter counts in Candace Greene and Thornton, *Year the Stars Fell*, 233–34.

Scarcity of buffalo caused great suffering among Nakota bands wintering near Long Lake and Lakotas along Heart River. Nakotas living at Painted Woods south of present Washburn, North Dakota, ate their horses. The part Mandan Yanktonai chief Medicine Bear made peace with Rees and Hidatsas in order to buy corn from them.[35]

By spring, Sioux and Rees were again at war. Lower on the river, Struck-by-the-Ree's and Smutty Bear's Yankton factions continued to argue about the land-sale treaty. In July 1859, when all Yanktons had to move to their reservation, Smutty Bear and his followers disrupted an outdoor meeting by riding their horses amongst the attendees. Smutty Bear was in mid-lecture about how wrong it was to give up lands where their fathers had died when the steamboat arrived carrying Redfield and their treaty goods. Redfield defused the situation by offering the Indians a great feast if they would all go immediately to their reservation.[36]

Fourth Artillery recruits who had replaced the Second Infantry at Fort Randall maintained order until the move was complete the first week in August. Surveyors marked off 166 lots on either side of Redfield's headquarters for Indians to live on in individual family units, like whites. Struck-by-the-Ree and eight other chiefs helped people settle in, and an agency farmer started them in their new occupation. Soon 2,000 Yanktons lived near the agency, which Redfield named Greenwood after Alfred Burton Greenwood, commissioner of Indian affairs.[37]

Upriver, intertribal war persisted. In a July 27 battle near Fort Atkinson between Arikara hunters and several hundred Miniconjous, Sans Arcs, Two Kettles, Cuthead Yanktonais, and Santees, the Rees lost ten dead and thirty-four wounded, and the Sioux left thirty-three dead on the field after carrying off a number of both dead and wounded.[38]

Spread Eagle passenger Dr. Elias J. Marsh recorded in his journal that only about thirty lodges of Sioux—Mato-cu-wi-hu's Hunkpapas, Two Bear's Yanktonais, and Fire Heart's Sihasapas—were at Fort Pierre to welcome new Upper Missouri agent Bernard S. Schoonover, who replaced

[35]Mattison, *Henry A. Boller*, 24 Jan. 1859 letter to brother, 84–86. For Medicine Bear lineage, see "Wiciyela of Middle Dakota," 7.

[36]Boller, *Among the Indians*, 215–17, 265–66, 274–77, 279–80, 292–96, 314–17, 321–22; and Doane Robinson, "History of the Dakota," 244–53.

[37]Fort Randall PR, July and Aug. 1859, reel 988, M617, NA. Hoover, "Yankton Sioux Tribal Land History," in *Yanktons v. Gaffey*.

[38]Albers and Tweton, *Native People*, 45–47. Robert Little Bird identifies Big Head as head of a Cuthead band. Waneta's Cuthead band lived at Lake Traverse. See Diedrich, *Odyssey*, 9, 11. Mattison, *Henry A. Boller*, 99–100.

Redfield, now exclusive agent to the Yanktons. Also on board was West Point topographical engineer Captain William Franklin Raynolds, who was planning to embark from Pierre on a new overland exploration of the Yellowstone and Missouri Rivers. When Sioux leaders boarded the boat that night, Captain Raynolds found Mato-cu-wi-hu reticent. Perhaps he regarded the new explorers as proof that his friend Lieutenant Warren had been unable or, worse, had not bothered to articulate Sioux concerns to the president. "Hardly know what to make of them," Raynolds confided to his journal.[39]

Indians squatted on the ground in a semi-circle while whites sat on chairs the morning of the council. Sioux spokesmen voiced their main concern—opposition to the 1858 Yankton land sale. Mato-cu-wi-hu explained his view that Yankton chiefs ceded land belonging to all Sioux. He also protested whites coming to Sioux country, which he defined as stretching from the Mississippi River to the Missouri, including both sides of the Missouri, and where they traveled between the Yellowstone and the Platte. Mato-cu-wi-hu asked if he could assume what he said would go to the president, adding that he doubted it would. He believed that in transit, people substituted other words for his.[40]

Two Bear also appealed to Raynolds not to trespass. Before replying, Raynolds had to review Schoonover's copy of the Yankton treaty. He had no orders concerning it but, noticing that Harney's 1856 treaty stipulated authorized travelers should not be mistreated, Raynolds claimed "the privilege of transit as a right and not as a favor." Confirming Indian suspicions about annuities being bribes, he said he would give them their promised goods only if they would "carry out that agreement." Neither Raynolds nor the agents seemed to know Congress never ratified the Harney agreement as a treaty.[41]

One chief asked Raynolds who would be accountable if their young men attacked his party despite the chiefs' efforts to prevent them from doing so. The president, he answered, would hold all Sioux responsible and "send soldiers and wipe the entire nation from existence." Ultimately,

---

[39]Marsh, "Trip up the Missouri River"; Sunder, *Fur Trade*, 223; Athearn, *Forts of the Upper Missouri*, 63; and William Franklin Raynolds, "Yellowstone and Missouri Exploring Expedition, 18 June 1859–4 October 1860" (hereafter cited as Raynolds journal), William Robertson Coe Collection, Yale Collection of Western Americana, Beinecke Rare Book and Manuscript Library (hereafter cited as Yale Beinecke Library).

[40]Speech in Doane Robinson, "History of the Dakota," 248–49, and in "Exploring the Black Hills," 28–29.

[41]Council reprint, 3, 31; and Denver to Robinson, 10 Nov. 1858, BIA LS, reel 50, M298, NA.

the chiefs agreed not to interfere with Raynolds and his men. They also accepted their Laramie Treaty annuities but refused to sign receipts for them because, as passenger Dr. Marsh heard someone say, "whenever they put their name to paper they afterwards regretted it and found themselves in trouble."[42]

Seeing the chiefs at ease later inside the large apartment of the trading house where they were staying banished "all ideas of dignity in the Indian character," leaving Raynolds "vividly realizing . . . that the red men are savages." Without their "gaudy vestments and barbaric trappings," they were, he told his diary, lacking any glory. "A filthy cloth about their loins, a worn buffalo robe, or a greasy blanket, constituted the only covering to nakedness." As they lay about smoking, what Raynolds saw as "dirt and degradation" repelled him.[43]

The starchy captain had a more positive encounter with Little Thunder's sub-chief Medicine Cap, also known as The Frog, who arrived at Fort Pierre on June 23 to trade. He impressed Raynolds with the authority he held over his warriors and with his looks: "About 35 years of age, straight as an arrow, over six feet in height, possessed of striking features, a keen black eye, and an expressive face, he is physically one of nature's noblemen." After engaging in a long conversation at the trading house, Raynolds invited the Brulé chief to visit him at his camp. Medicine Cap brought an interpreter, and again the two men spoke at length. The chief remarked that, although he had come to trade, he had only a small party with him. He explained they had to leave their families behind because to bring them would have required many horses to haul all the tipi poles. Raynolds showed the chief one of the army's new Sibley tents, explaining how a white man had improved on the Indian design. Medicine Cap remarked that the tent must need many poles. No, Raynolds answered, "only one." Surprised, Medicine Cap saw that Henry Hopkins Sibley had used the cone shape, vent flaps, and doors of Indian lodges but used only one center pole tethered by guy wires. "Ah, that is iron; we cannot have it." Raynolds asked why a pole of similar strength could not be made of wood. Medicine Cap replied, "I have a man in my tribe . . . [who] can make an excellent axe helve[;] . . . I will have him try." Raynolds noted that the "interest and eagerness for improvement exhibited by this Indian

---

[42]Marsh, "Account of a Journey," Historical Society of Missouri, St. Louis (hereafter cited as Marsh journal); and C. P. Chouteau to Floyd, 1 Nov. 1859, in Choteau, "Report to Secretary of War John B. Floyd, 1859," sc 532, Montana State Historical Society Archives Collections.

[43]"Exploring the Black Hills," 31.

was wholly in contradiction to the usually received opinion that they are indifferent or lack curiosity. I should not be surprised to learn that he had extemporized Sibley tents for his band."[44]

The Raynolds party left Fort Pierre June 28, 1859, with interpreter Zephyr Rencontre and an unnamed Sioux guide. Jim Bridger, the official guide, would join them at Fort Union. Lieutenant Caleb B. Smith, Second Infantry, commanded the escort. Taking a northwest course, they proceeded without interference to the northern edge of the Black Hills, where they stopped to climb Bear Butte. As they neared Crow country, their Sioux guide deserted, taking as his pay his army mule, its saddle, and bridle. Perhaps he knew the uneasy truce the 1851 Horse Creek treaty had mandated was over. When Crows, during a raid, killed the Miniconjou chief Black Shield's sons in the spring of 1859, Black Shield called together Lakotas for a war council in the Black Hills. On June 12, his sons' avengers attacked Crow warriors near Fort Sarpy, a new but short-lived trading post near the mouth of the Bighorn River. The war apparently had started earlier when, according to 1857–58 winter counts, a Sioux killed a woman during a Crow raid.

Raynolds reached the Powder and Yellowstone Rivers' confluence in July and explored south of the Yellowstone and along the Big Horn mountains.[45] In October, he established his 1859–60 winter camp near Twiss's Upper Platte Indian Agency at Deer Creek, about a hundred miles west of Fort Laramie. In February, Little Thunder and several of his sub-chiefs stopped by. Raynolds "made them a little feast and gave them some tobacco," which "seemed to satisfy them," but the next day it was obvious traders had given them liquor. Raynolds told the Brulé chief his annuity goods were stored at Fort Pierre. However, given that Little Thunder's band usually ranged between the Platte and Niobrara Rivers, he seems to have depended on Twiss's agency for sustenance. Later that year, he complained to the adventurer Sir Richard Burton, passing through on the Oregon Trail, that Twiss stole from Indians and gave his pet bear more sugar, coffee, and flour than he gave the Sioux for whom such commodities were intended.[46]

---

[44]Ibid., 32–33. Tent inventor Henry Hopkins Sibley should not be confused with Minnesota's Henry Hastings Sibley.

[45]Sunder, *Fur Trade*, 162; Kinglsey Bray, *Crazy Horse*, 63; winter counts in Candace Greene and Thornton, *Year the Stars Fell*, 241–42; Raynolds journal, 21 July 1859; Marsh journal, 31 July 1859; and Goetzmann, *Army Exploration*, 420.

[46]Hyde, *Red Cloud's Folk*, 93; Raynolds journal, 7 Feb. 1860; and Hyde, *Spotted Tail's Folk*, 89.

In March 1860, several Sioux bands wintering about 200 miles to the north of Raynolds's winter camp sent Miniconjou Chief Lone Horn as emissary to warn the explorers not to pass through their country. Raynolds said he must obey the president's orders. "We cannot restrain our young men," Lone Horn warned, "They will kill you." Raynolds countered: "Then, your tribe will be held responsible." Lone Horn asked where the expedition intended going that summer and seemed surprised when Raynolds drew a map showing them heading west to explore Yellowstone and Missouri headwaters, respectively in present Yellowstone National Park and southwestern Montana.[47] Raynolds made it clear, though, that they intended to return down the Yellowstone to its Missouri confluence, then cross Sioux country to Fort Randall. Lone Horn demanded Raynolds travel along the Missouri's north bank instead. Raynolds responded: "It will be nearly winter; my horses will be broken down. I will be in danger of being unable to get out of the country. I must take the shortest route."

Lone Horn asked if any more parties of whites would be coming. Raynolds said he did not know of any, "unless my party does not get home at the right time. You know there are soldiers at Fort Randall . . . If you want soldiers in your country . . . kill my party and then you will have enough." Lone Horn was slow to reply: "It may be that they will not hurt you; we will try to restrain our young men." Raynolds said his men were well-armed and would defend themselves. He believed Lone Horn left "satisfied that the best course for them to pursue was to allow us to proceed quietly on our journey."[48]

Raynolds's assistant, Lieutenant Henry E. Maynadier, was in charge of a smaller party traveling overland down the Yellowstone valley. When his party's work was completed, he traveled to Fort Union, arriving on August 1, 1860. Maynadier bought provisions and camped near the confluence to wait for Raynolds's contingent to arrive in boats from Fort Benton. When he learned Sioux had recently shot a Fort Union employee, Maynadier crossed the Missouri to a protected spot near the fort.[49]

Raynolds arrived August 7, and the expedition hastened on. Maynadier's two mackinaw boats reached Fort Berthold on August 20 just as

---

[47]Raynolds journal, Oct. 1859 through March 1860. Lone Horn arrived 14 March 1860.

[48]"Exploring the Black Hills," 26–57.

[49]Journal of Henry E. Maynadier (hereafter cited as Maynadier journal), chap. 2, William Robertson Coe Collection, Yale Beinecke Library; Snowden journal, 1 Aug. to 15 Aug. 1860; and Raynolds journal, 7 Aug. 1860.

some Hunkpapas and Sihasapas arrived to trade at the Mandan and Hidatsa villages. As Maynadier put it, these Sioux "were disposed not to be very polite towards my small party." He was thankful when, that same afternoon, Lieutenant James L. White and a large number of soldiers who had been helping to build the Mullan road across the Rockies, also heading home, came ashore. (In June 1859, John Mullan had begun building a government road connecting Fort Benton to Walla Walla, Washington Territory.)[50]

When the Sihasapa chief Little Elk requested a council with Maynadier, White agreed to wait so the soldiers could travel downriver together, making, Maynadier said, "our united force equal to any the Sioux could bring against us."[51] Accordingly, thirty Indians gathered in a room with Lieutenants White and Maynadier and Fred Riter, now the Berthold bourgeois. Pierre Garreau translated as an old Indian opened with a speech Maynadier characterized as stereotyped, including complaints about whites killing and driving away game and building roads through their country. The old man added, "I love my children as you white men love yours, and when I see them starving, it makes my heart black, and I am angry. We are glad to have the traders, but we don't want you soldiers, and road-makers."[52]

Little Elk asked Maynadier to tell the president that agents had cheated Hunkpapas and Sihasapas and whites had driven them from their lands. They would continue to refuse treaty goods. They did not want any more steamboats on the Missouri River because they believed goods they brought made them sick with smallpox and other diseases. He was probably also reacting to the dramatic increase in river traffic after the *Chippewa* pushed the head of navigation to within twelve miles of Fort Benton in July 1859 and, in 1860, along with the *Key West*, reached that post.

Little Elk turned to the Hidatsa chief Four Bears. "You, friend Matotopa . . . you and your people have dwindled to a handful, because you live near the whites and raise corn." The remark elicited an angry outcry among the Hidatsas that Garreau refused to translate. When the excitement subsided, Little Elk boasted that Sihasapas and Hunkpapas could

[50]Kautz, "From Missouri to Oregon," 12 May and 9 June 1860, 199, 199n25, 203–204, 206; Vaughn to Greenwood, 31 Aug. 1860 (Report no. 29) in CIA annual report.

[51]Maynadier journal, chap. 2; Snowden journal, 15 Aug. to 23 Aug. 1860; Watkins, "Oregon Recruit Expedition," 127–28, 140; and Kautz, "From Missouri to Oregon," 219.

[52]Maynadier journal, chap. 3, p. 77.

kill any white soldiers sent against them. Then, after expressing outrage at Riter for trading through a post window instead of allowing them entry inside the fort, the chief, "streaming with perspiration," sat down, "and commenced to fan himself cool."[53]

Maynadier began his talk by chastising Hunkpapas and Sihasapas for spreading rumors they had killed all the explorers. He explained his mission—"to see what [the country] looks like and how the Indians are." Because he heard complaints against Hunkpapas and Sihasapas everywhere he had been, he would have to tell the president they were "very bad." The president might send soldiers. Maynadier further warned that if Sioux wanted to stop him as he continued downriver, "they may call to me, but if they fire I will land and fight them."

As Maynadier moved to leave the room, an old man rose, took his hand "as if he had been my grandfather," and said, "My son, you and Little Elk are too young; your heads are hot, and your tongues work too easily." He claimed that "we never make wars unless we are imposed upon," and he begged Maynadier to tell the president "a good story of us." When he asked for food to take home to their families, Maynadier responded with sarcasm: "Friend, my flour and sugar and bacon will make you sick, and I have too much regard for you to put temptation in your way and send you home ill." The old man was expressionless.[54]

In his report, Maynadier concluded complaints against the Sihasapas and Hunkpapas were "universal and well founded. They rob and murder indiscriminately, regarding only the size of a party and taking good care of their own precious scalps." However, he now had useful intelligence about them. They normally lived in the game-rich wooded valleys of three Missouri tributaries—the Heart, Knife, and Cannonball Rivers—and used the badlands between the Little Missouri and Powder Rivers as refuge from enemies. Maynadier predicted the military would eventually have to enter these areas to "chastise these bands."[55]

Raynolds arrived at Fort Berthold on August 22, just as the Sioux were leaving. The united expedition and White's Mullan-road-building party left together the next day, Raynolds by land and Maynadier and the road builders by boat. In council at the Arikara village near Fort Clark three

---

[53]Lass, *History of Steamboating*, 18–19; Way, *Way's Packet Directory*, no. 1018, 86; Sunder, "Frederick G. Riter," 157–69; see Mattison, *Henry A. Boller*, 139, 139n4, 149; Maynadier's journal, chap. 3. See Elmer Ellis, "Journal of H. E. Maynadier," 45; and Goetzmann, *Army Exploration*, 45.

[54]Maynadier journal, chap. 3, p. 83.

[55]Ibid., 85.

days later, an elderly Ree chief complained about the Sioux and requested the president's protection. Maynadier contrasted this old chief's "languid and despondent air" with Little Elk's "fiery manner and clear ringing vowels," believing it indicated their people's respective conditions. He assured the Arikara chief he would deliver the message and advised him that the president did not object to Rees defending themselves, and "if they were not strong enough he would help them."[56]

On September 2, 1860, Maynadier's group surprised the AFC traders at the new Fort Pierre, who had believed rumors of their demise. The expedition departed a few days later after Raynolds and his land party caught up. At Fort Randall, Maynadier was "gladdened by the sight of familiar faces, and the hospitable attentions of the officers of the post." The "delicate refinement" of their hosts seemed to Maynadier "like magic." When Raynolds arrived, he, too, was impressed with signs of civilization at the post, marveling at its garden produce.[57]

As the 1860s began, the Sioux world was in turmoil. Many Upper Missouri Sioux had become surly and distrustful of whites. Some bands saw war as the only way to keep whites out of Indian country, yet they seemed to be taking out their frustrations on the Assiniboines, Rees, Mandans, and Hidatsas. Perhaps by warring on their neighbors, the militants were falling back on old enemies as a reaction to indecision about how to handle new ones. Even the most remote Lakota bands could foresee that Harney, Warren, Raynolds, and the soldiers at Fort Randall were only the vanguard of continuing invasions; certainly, Mato-cu-wi-hu's, Lone Horn's, and others' diplomatic efforts had failed to deter trespassers. Most of all, the Yanktons' land deal appeared to frighten as well as anger even peace-minded bands who feared inadvertently bartering away their homeland by accepting annuities.

---

[56]Ibid., 94–95.

[57]Ibid., 97–99; and Raynolds, Raynolds expedition official reports, 147–49. See also Snowden journal through 25 Sept. 1860; Elmer Ellis, "Journal of H. E. Maynadier," 41–51; and Sunder, *Fur Trade*, 172n29. Galpin built the new trading post in 1859 on the west bank of the Missouri a few miles above the old one. See Mattison, "Report on Historical Aspects," 30, cited in Smith, "Fort Pierre II," 108.

Chapter 6

Giving Bear Rib Ears

FOR YEARS YANKTONAIS SOUGHT, SOMETIMES BY VIOLENT DEMON-
strations, compensation for vast tracts of land the Santees sold by treaty in
1851—lands that they, the Yanktonais, also claimed.[1] The Santees' agents
tried to effect a peaceful solution, but by 1859, Northern Superintendent
William J. Cullen, based in St. Paul, despaired of reaching one. Lately,
Yanktonais were also angry at the presence of a new military post, Fort
Abercrombie, on the Red River near Lake Traverse. "Further friendly
measures toward them seem to be useless," Cullen reported, "and if they
persist in their lawless and reprehensible course, it will become necessary
to chastise them into submission."[2]

Adding to his frustration, this year the Indian department sent annuities meant for two Lakota bands and two Yanktonai bands to St. Paul
instead of to St. Louis. Therefore, Cullen, whom Sisseton and Wahpeton
agent Joseph R. Brown characterized as caring little about understanding Indians as people, had the responsibility of distributing these treaty
goods as well as those for the Santees. In April 1859, Cullen invited the
Yanktonais to a council at the Kettle Lakes in their own country west
of the Minnesota border in today's southeastern North Dakota. He
would bring them special presents and "adjust differences and preserve
peace" between them and the Sissetons, whom they especially blamed
for selling lands held in common.[3]

Cullen paid the Mdwakanton and Wahpekute Santees at the Lower
(Redwood) Agency first. Because the Upper (Yellow Medicine) Agency
census rolls were not prepared, he refused to distribute Wahpeton and

---

[1] Gary Anderson, *Kinsmen*, examines cultural pressures on Dakotas in chap. 9, "The Treaties of 1851," 175–202.

[2] Greenwood to Thompson, 26 Nov. 1859, CIA annual report, p. 14; and Gary Anderson, *Kinsmen*, 238–39.

[3] Cullen to Greenwood, 15 Aug. 1859, CIA annual report, no. 14, 59–60; Gary Anderson, *Kinsmen*, 223; Council reprint, 3, 31; Denver to Robinson, 10 Nov. 1858, BIA LS, Dakota Conflict of 1862 Manuscript Collection, Minnesota Historical Society (MNHS) Archives (hereafter cited as Dakota Conflict of 1862 MSS). The Sans Arc, Two Kettle (both Lakota), Honcpatela, and Band-that-Wishes-the-Life (both Nakota) annuities were misdirected.

Sisseton annuities until after his trip to the lakes.[4] When angry Sissetons tried to prevent him from departing, the confrontation grew ugly. Finally, with an escort from Fort Ridgely and Agent Brown along, the expedition proceeded. On July 10, on the Whetstone River, Cullen met He-Who-Pursues-the-Grizzly-Bear, a Yanktonai chief from Two Bear's band, who said he could not tell Cullen where the rest of the Yanktonais were or if they intended to meet him. When the expedition reached its destination four days later, no Yanktonais were in sight. Cullen was flummoxed.

Learning Black Catfish's Band-that-Wishes-the-Life was nearby, Cullen summoned them. When these Lower Yanktonais arrived, their appearance shocked him. "They were literally half starved, their faces pinched with famine, and their bodies exhibiting extreme emaciation, with but shreds of blankets hanging about them." The only food they had was some wild turnips. Cullen gave them twenty-four sacks of flour and a barrel of pork. When scouts returned without intelligence about the missing bands, who, these Yanktonais said, were probably hunting buffalo, Cullen, Brown, and Major Thomas Sherman, commanding the escort, admitted failure. Cullen offered the goods intended for other Yanktonais to Black Catfish's people. They eagerly accepted the food, Sherman reported, "but unhesitatingly and peremptorily refused to receive anything else," saying no responsible chief was with them and they feared consequences from accepting government presents.[5]

On the return trip, Cullen's entourage stopped at Standing Buffalo's Sisseton village at Big Stone Lake, and Major Sherman took captive a man who earlier impeded Cullen's wagon train. Cullen suspected another man of being with Inkpaduta during the 1857 Spirit Lake murders. When threatening to withhold annuities unless the band surrendered him failed, Sherman took hostages to use as barter and called out a Second Infantry company from nearby Fort Ridgely to support him and intensify the pressure. The soldiers eventually delivered the impugned Spirit Lake accomplice to civil authorities for trial. In his report, Cullen said although he wanted the other people he had taken hostage "whipped and their heads shaved, [to] disgrace them before all their people," the chiefs pledged the prisoners' good conduct to prevent this. Cullen, "upon more mature reflection . . . apprehended that men so degraded might be rendered desperate, become outlaws . . . and . . . commit murder or outrage upon some

---

[4]Meyer, *History of the Santee Sioux*, 106; and Cullen to Greenwood, 15 Aug. 1859, CIA annual report, no. 14, 62.

[5]Cullen to Greenwood, 15 Aug. 1859, CIA annual report, 62–63; and Sherman to Abercrombie, 5 Aug. 1859, hereafter cited as Fort Ridgely docs, MNHS Archives.

unprotected settler, to redeem themselves in the opinions of their people."
Besides, he was withholding their annuities, from which he deducted
enough to "cover the expense of [the man's] detention." Satisfied Standing
Buffalo's band was now "thoroughly humbled," he released the hostages.[6]

Cullen was confident the "unusual number of troops passing from
opposite points through the country" gave Sioux "a wholesome sense
of the power of the United States, and of the promptness with which
offenders may be punished." This show of force, he surmised, "struck
them with a panic," and he was pleased the Indians "have been taught
to feel their own inferiority" and exhibited "a sense of humiliation . . .
in all their intercourse." He was confident even "a single unarmed man
may pass unquestioned and unmolested, hereafter, over every portion of
the prairies." Minnesota and Dakota settlers no longer need fear "Indian
molestation." Cullen congratulated himself for averting "an Indian war,
fatal to the peace and prosperity of this portion of our country." On July
29, he finally gave the Sissetons and Wahpetons their annuity payment.
At Mankato a week later, he paid claims to non-Indian volunteers who
had attempted to rescue 1857 Spirit Lake captives.[7]

In August 1860, He-Who-Pursues-the-Grizzly-Bear, who met Cullen on his failed trip, along with Bone Necklace, brought a delegation
representing Yanktonais holding council near the Missouri to Yellow
Medicine to explain their absence the previous year. The Missouri River
Sioux bands, they told Agent Brown, feared the government would negotiate for all their land east of the Missouri. Therefore, they "threatened
eternal enmity" to any Yanktonais who met Cullen's party. A rumor also
circulated saying the government would use the Kettle Lakes gathering simply to destroy the Indians. Why else would such a large body of
troops accompany the presents? Despite such threats and rumors, some
Yanktonais had intended to meet Cullen. However, they needed to follow
the ever-dwindling buffalo west of Devil's Lake or starve. Bone Necklace
insisted Yanktonais sought friendly relations with the government, along
with its protection and support.[8]

---

[6]Sherman to Abercrombie, 5 Aug. 1859, Fort Ridgely docs, MNHS Archives; and Cullen to
Greenwood, 15 Aug. 1859, CIA annual report, no 14, 58–69.

[7]Cullen to Greenwood, 15 Aug. 1859, CIA annual report, no 14, 67–68; and "From Redwood,"
29 July 1859, "Payment of Volunteers in Minnesota," 6 July 1859, and "Our Own State," 10 Aug.
1859, all in *St. Paul (Minn.) Daily Pioneer and Democrat*. Congress appropriated $20,000 by a 14
June 1858 act. Cullen approved approximately $25,000 of the roughly $46,000 claimed. Commissioner Greenwood authorized Cullen to make partial payment of about $19,000; the balance was
to defray investigation expenses.

[8]Brown to Cullen, 25 Oct. 1860, CIA annual report, no. 18, 285–86.

ON MARCH 2, 1861, PRESIDENT JAMES BUCHANAN SIGNED DAKOTA
Territory into being two days before Abraham Lincoln took office, entitling
it to a governor, secretary, and three judges, all federally appointed. This
event came at a time when sedition rumors were rampant. Iowa railroad
surveyor Granville M. Dodge wrote a friend on April 2 (four days before
the attack on Fort Sumter) that secessionists at Saint Joseph planned to
capture the steamboat *Omaha*, which was carrying two companies of the
Fourth Artillery transferring from Fort Randall to Fort Leavenworth. No
one attacked the boat, but the artillerymen's departure left only a hundred
or so men at Fort Randall under a captain, John A. Brown. In July, Brown
left with six other officers to fight for the Confederacy. By then, Second
Lieutenant Thomas R. Tannatt was Fort Randall's highest ranking officer.[9]

During 1861 Upper Missouri Yanktonais kept contact with friends and
relatives on the Minnesota reservations, but when they visited the Santees
at annuity time, their land dispute caused heated arguments. Northern
district Indian superintendent Clark Thompson complained that Yanktonais and Santees were so interrelated it was hard to tell who deserved
the goods. The daring, warlike Yanktonais, he said, tended to "overawe
the peaceably disposed and animate and encourage the vicious among the
other bands." Their "audacity renders troops necessary at the payments."
Thompson also accused them of "constantly committing depredations" on
defenseless Minnesota, Iowa, and Dakota settlers. By contrast, on an 1861
trip to the Santees' reservations, Thompson was surprised to find many
"wearing the garb of civilization . . . living in frame or brick houses . . .
with stables and out-buildings, and their fields indicating considerable
knowledge of agriculture." He thought it possible to "entirely revolutionize
their tribal character, and convert them into good citizens."[10]

From what Indian Commissioner William P. Dole could tell by
November 1861, "Indian affairs in Dakota for the year past have been
satisfactory." Nonetheless, he believed it "would be good policy to locate
these Indians on reservations at an early day." Dole downplayed reports of
Indian depredations in northwestern Iowa, calling them "comparatively
unimportant." The only hostile Indians there, he claimed, were a "few

---

[9]Dodge to Kasson, 2 April 1861, 661; Harney to Asst. Adj. Gen. Townsend, 8 and 11 April 1861,
662, 665; and Miles to Townsend, 30 April 1861, 676–77, all in *War of Rebellion: Official Records of
Union and Confederate Armies* (hereafter cited as OR), series 1, vol. 1, pt. 1; Pattee, "Reminiscences,"
278. Dakota Territory's 350,000 square miles included all of Montana, both modern Dakotas, and
eastern Idaho from the international border south along the Continental Divide to the 43rd parallel.
The Turtle Hill and Niobrara Rivers bounded it on the south to include part of present Wyoming.

[10]Thompson to Dole, 30 Oct. 1861, CIA annual report, no. 22, 679–83.

bands of Santees, who do not participate in the distribution of annuities" to the reservation Indians. Of the Missouri River Sioux, Dole was happiest with the Yanktons who had cultivated about 800 acres. Although settlers feared Upper Missouri Indians, his St. Louis supervisor assured Dole there would be no attacks.[11]

The reservation Yanktons' new agent was President Lincoln's appointee, Walter A. Burleigh. According to one historian, the tall, energetic doctor and lawyer "slammed, slashed, cajoled, bought, and argued his way through Dakota politics." Graft, nepotism, and payroll irregularities were only some of his alleged offences. An investigator who looked into Burleigh's activities as Indian agent concluded "it took a superior imagination to be able to perpetrate so many frauds at one time." Burleigh's reports revealed none of this. In his first, he expressed disappointment that the reservation's 1861 crops "suffered . . . in consequence of the miserable manner in which they were attended to." However, the Indians promised that the following spring "the whole male population of the tribe" would "plant and sow for themselves." Three Upper Yankton band chiefs, Medicine Cow, Pretty Boy, and Little Swan (a.k.a. Little White Swan), recently had given up their free lifestyle to live in houses on the reservation.[12]

With Congress preoccupied by the American Civil War, the Yanktons' 1861 annuity money had not arrived even by October, and the few provisions Burleigh distributed seemed so insufficient that many suspected him of secretly unloading the shipment and storing most of it. After a contentious council, 150 warriors "painted, armed, and equipped in fighting style" surrounded the office and warehouse. They piled hay against buildings preparatory to burning them and demanded tribal-owned powder from the magazine. If they wanted a fight, Burleigh blustered; they should call for reinforcements from Indians upriver. Instead of attacking, however, the malcontents held another council. Burleigh kept guards on duty overnight, but next morning, when he noticed women and children leaving while the men remained, he sent to Fort Randall for help. Lieutenant Tannatt arrived at the agency with one company just as the Indians began war dances. According to Burleigh, the "disappointed Indians and their evil advisers became frightened and left by daylight the following morning."[13] Later, when three companies of the Fourteenth Iowa Volunteer Infantry Regiment passed through the Yankton reservation en route to garrison

[11]Dole to Smith, 27 Nov. 1861, CIA annual report, no. 22, 626–36.

[12]Lamar, *Dakota Territory*, 109–110; and Maroukis, *Peyote and the Yankton Sioux*, 44–45.

[13]Burleigh quotes from Burleigh to Branch, 24 Oct. 1861, CIA annual report, no. 45, 730.

Fort Randall, many residents were away on a buffalo hunt. An interpreter told Sergeant Amos Cherry that the absent hunters who had threatened to burn the agency when they returned might muster 8,000 warriors. Cherry sensed discontent among those who stayed behind. They were "all well armed and equiped but are in a state of starvation allmost."[14]

By "evil advisers," Burleigh meant whites and mixed-bloods who "stick to the Indians like so many 'blood-suckers,' as long as there is the least possibility of swindling them out of . . . their furs, provisions, or annuity goods." He also complained of "unprincipled men" who squatted on government land just outside the reservation to give Indians whiskey and tobacco in return for trade items. Later investigations proved he should have included himself in both categories. In his report Burleigh seemed genuinely concerned, predicting dire conditions for Yanktons should their cash payment not soon arrive. They needed food, clothing, and winter supplies, and many were sick from every "disease which suffering humanity is heir to."[15]

THE FOURTEENTH IOWA ARRIVED AT FORT RANDALL SICK AND exhausted on a gray December day. Their forty-year-old elected captain, John Pattee, a former Iowa state auditor, had marched his 300 volunteer soldiers, mostly newly recruited farmers, 540 miles from Iowa City. Because Lieutenant Tannatt, whom Pattee described as a "bright and agreeable gentleman," and the regulars still occupied the fort, the Iowans camped in their tents for a few days.[16]

Meanwhile, Abraham Lincoln appointed his friend and family physician, William A. Jayne, Dakota Territory's first governor. Military matters were on Jayne's mind from the start. In April, recruiters in Yankton, the town that sprouted from the 120-acre plot the Indians had given Charles Picotte, and two other new towns, Vermillion and Bon Homme, formed the first of what would be two companies of Dakota Cavalry.[17]

---

[14]Shambaugh, "Iowa Troops," 408.

[15]Burleigh to Branch, 24 Oct. 1861, CIA annual report, no. 45, 728–31.

[16]Shambaugh, "Iowa Troops," 374, 408–11. Weather from Robrock, "Seventh Iowa Cavalry," 2; Pattee, "Reminiscences," 273–78; Athearn, *Forts of the Upper Missouri*, 72–74; and Lounsberry, *Early History*, 218. Cherry letter dated Jan. 1862.

[17]Richard Ellis, *General Pope*, 6; Doane Robinson, "History of the Dakota," 246–48; Lamar, *Dakota Territory*, 27–64; Athearn, *Forts of the Upper Missouri*, 75–79; Josephy, *Civil War in the American West*, 131; and Dyer, *Compendium*. Company A, Dakota Volunteers, First Battalion Cavalry, was formed at Yankton in April 1862.

Consequent to Dakota's new territorial status, the Upper Missouri's spurt of change accelerated after President Lincoln signed the Homestead Act into law, offering, for a small registration fee, 160 acres to adult family heads who were U.S. citizens or intended to become citizens. If settlers remained on their claims for five years and improved them, they would own them free and clear. Many soldiers at Fort Randall took advantage of this offer, as did some Missouri River travelers. Indians did not qualify; as a group, they could not become citizens.[18]

Also in 1862, Lincoln signed the Pacific Railway Act to facilitate construction of the nation's first transcontinental railroad; the act granted loans to the Union Pacific and Central Pacific companies as well as twenty sections of land per mile of railroad track laid. (In 1864, Lincoln signed the Northern Pacific Railroad Act into law for a northern route.) Southern Sioux would feel the effects of this railroad legislation before the northern Sioux, but railroads were never far from the minds of whites negotiating with any Sioux.[19]

Upper Missouri denizens witnessed even more change when gold discoveries lured prospectors to the northern Rocky Mountains. The 1862 influx began even before prospectors discovered gold on Grasshopper Creek in Idaho (soon to be Montana) Territory that summer.[20] Would-be miners could take steamboats up the Missouri to Fort Benton, then branch off the newly completed Mullan Road at a spot convenient to the gold country. Even with the Civil War on the lower river and Indians on the upper river making steamboat travel perilous, vessels did not want for passengers.

On May 27, 1862, another new Upper Missouri agent, Samuel N. Latta, arrived at Fort Pierre on the *Spread Eagle*, where, as always, a crowd of Sioux—between 2,000 and 3,000 this time—waited. Among them, for once, was the infamous Yanktonai Big Head, who boarded the boat before it landed to demand immediate payment from Latta for the previous six years of what he called Harney Treaty annuities he considered due him. If he did not get those accumulated annuities, he told Latta, he would not accept those now offered. Latta refused to accommodate him.

---

[18] Fort Randall LS, 1856–67, RG 393, NA. In an 18 March 1863 letter, two Dakota Cavalry men requested leave to see to their "land claims near Vermillion." On 2 June 1924, Congress granted citizenship to all U.S.-born Native Americans, but because state law governed the right to vote, some states barred voting until 1948. Individual Indians found ways to become citizens before 1924. See Standing Bear, *My People the Sioux*, 279–81, and for a citizenship plan never enacted see Gary Anderson, *Kinsmen*, 163–64. Article 6, Fort Laramie Treaty of 1868, grants citizenship to Indians holding land patents.

[19] Larson, "Chief Gall and Abe Lincoln's Railroad" 17–18.

[20] Burlingame, *Montana Frontier*, 84.

As Latta had men stack goods on shore in seven separate bundles, one each for the Brulé, Sihasapas, Sans Arcs, Miniconjous, Hunkpapas, Two Kettles, and Yanktonais, *Spread Eagle* passenger A. H. Wilcox observed that the 500 or 600 warriors congregated near the landing were "in a surly mood," and their families were not with them. When the council on the riverbank began, Indians gathered around the agent and other white men, including Wilcox. "A peculiar sensation came over me on being surrounded by them that I had never experienced before," he wrote. "They were all large powerful men, straight as arrows and nearly naked."[21]

According to Wilcox, Latta congratulated the Indians for "having so good a father as the President" and pointed out the "great pains and expense he had gone to in sending them their annuities."[22] The chiefs' responses were "stunners," taking "the starch all out of the agent and all the rest of us." They "did not at all appreciate the guardianship of the Great Father." They told Latta "they did not want his goods and would not take them[;] that they considered the whites as trespassers and invaders of their country[;] and that the time was close at hand when they would put a stop to our travelling up and down the Missouri river." The Brulé chief Standing Elk added that whites had been killing their buffalo and cutting their timber for a long time. It was time, now, "to stop all intercourse with them and drive them out of the country." Standing Elk directly addressed the *Spread Eagle*'s owner, Charles Chouteau, son of AFC partner Pierre Chouteau, reminding him that their fathers had traded together just as they had. However, "things are not going to be as they have been[. W]e are not going to have any more to do with the whites and from this [*sic*] on you may consider us your enemies." He accused Chouteau of furnishing Mandans, Hidatsas, and Arikaras with guns and ammunition. "Only last week they came down here and killed one of our chiefs." Standing Elk demanded Chouteau give him guns and ammunition he suspected were aboard the boat. Otherwise, he warned, the boat would not leave. Chouteau made some remarks in French, after which the council ended abruptly with loud talk from the Sioux. Wilcox and the others, "expecting a row of no small dimensions," boarded the boat and loaded their weapons. As the crew hastened to get up enough steam to depart, armed Indians positioned themselves on the opposite bank "three ranks deep . . . more than twice the length of the steamboat." They fired in unison but hit no one. When some Indians boarded and

---

[21]Athearn, *Forts of the Upper Missouri*, 79; Latta to Dole, 27 Aug. 1862, CIA annual report, 1862, 336–41; and Wilcox, "Up the Missouri," Montana State Historical Society Archives Collections.

[22]Sunder, *Fur Trade*, 222. Wilcox apparently mistook Blackfeet [Siksika] agent Reed for Latta.

attempted to extinguish the engine fires, Chouteau ordered guns still in boxes and kegs of powder and balls brought up from the boat's hold and set ashore with some additional tobacco. The engine was not yet at full steam when the boat left the bank, its passengers, Wilcox wrote, "glad to get out of the hands of these freebooters."[23]

In his report, Latta called the Fort Pierre council contentious. He said Mato-cu-wi-hu, "a brave and good man," had protested that, although he had been a friend of the government's for eleven years, he too was disappointed that the troops Harney had promised for protection against the hostiles had not materialized. He would accept the goods this time but assured Latta that in doing so he would endanger his own life as well as those present. The other chiefs left without their shares.[24]

On June 5 a group of traditional-minded Miniconjou and Sans Arc warriors arrived at Fort Pierre saying they intended to kill not only Mato-cu-wi-hu, but also five of his principal men. At this time Mato-cu-wi-hu's band—who stood ready to defend the fur post whenever other Indians, even of their own nation, threatened it—comprised about a hundred lodges housing Miniconjou, Sans Arc, Two Kettle, and Hunkpapa peace factions. The next day's events became legend. Comparing contemporary accounts with reminiscences produces a plausible version:[25]

When Mato-cu-wi-hu heard the newcomers meant to kill him, he "just laughed," saying he did not believe they were brave enough to do it. Mato-cu-wi-hu's son and another headman wanted to go with him to see these men, but the chief insisted on going alone. Tying his mule to a post near the hostiles' camp, he went first to see the bourgeois, Charles Primeau.[26] Primeau's wife offered coffee and bread, but Mato-cu-wi-hu refused it, saying he had bad news. A gun discharged outside, and a man rushed in to tell Mato-cu-wi-hu that someone had shot his mule. Mato-cu-wi-hu grabbed his double-barreled shotgun and went to investigate, but all in the hostile camp were inside their lodges, the nearest about thirty steps away.

[23]Wilcox, "Up the Missouri," 5–6, Montana State Historical Society Archives Collections.

[24]Latta to Dole, 27 Aug. 1862, CIA annual report, 336–37.

[25]I used the following accounts of events: Will Robinson, "Digest of Reports, 1853–1869," 288–89, 299–300; Primeau to Chouteau, 20 June 1862, forwarded to Dole, 305–306; and Latta to Dole, 27 Aug. 1862, 336–41. AFC employee David Gallineaux told AFC employee Joseph Wandel an account that Wandel told Charles E. DeLand in 1901. See Frederick Wilson, "Old Fort Pierre and its Neighbors," 296–97, and DeLand, "Addenda," 366n68. DeLand called Wandel's version a "characteristic narrative." Some accounts incorrectly put Mato-cu-wi-hu's murder at Fort La Framboise.

[26]It is unclear if this was the first of two of Mato-cu-wi-hu's sons to succeed him. De Trobriand, *Army Life*, 120–21, writes of a son who died of disease soon after succeeding Mato-cu-wi-hu. Primeau worked for the AFC after it bought out his firm.

About twenty feet south of the southeast bastion, near where post employees Louis La Plant and Basil Clément were making coffee over a campfire, Mato-cu-wi-hu found his dead mule. "This is the third time that such a thing has happened," the chief complained. As he spoke, a Sans Arc Sioux named Ousta fired at him from a nearby tipi. As Mato-cu-wi-hu fell back into La Plant's arms, dying, he fired back, killing his own assassin. Other accounts have Mato-cu-wi-hu shooting twice, also wounding Ousta's accomplice, another Sans Arc named Tonkalla (Mouse). Although he did not witness the assassination, Primeau reported that Mato-cu-wi-hu was "traitorously shot down by the Sans Arcs. Before dying he killed the Indian who shot him and another of them was shot down by his young men who had remained here."[27] Amidst the subsequent confusion, the attacking Indians and their families rushed in the fort's open gate to plunder and vandalize. One of Mato-cu-wi-hu's faithful ran to the chief's camp on the Bad River with the stunning news. According to one retelling, Mato-cu-wi-hu's warriors discarded their clothing and prepared for battle within fifteen minutes, but the interlopers inside the fort had already closed the gate. In frustration, Mato-cu-wi-hu's followers "killed every dog and every horse outside," according to chief Martin Charger. Charger's wife, Eliza, later recalled how "an old squaw had a travois and a mule in front of it[. S]he run up towards the hills, and they headed her off and found that there was a man sitting in there . . . it was Mouse." Yellow Hawk (Sans Arc), Crow Feather's "Harney" sub-chief, killed the mule and shot Mouse "right through the head." Another account has Mouse's cousin Red Dog killing Mouse, and Stirs-the-Bear (a.k.a The-One-Who-Runs-the-Bear), a Sihasapa, finishing off a wounded Ousta.

Primeau, apparently not knowing (if true) that Mouse was also dead, finally persuaded the Indians inside the fort that—because only one man was lost to each side—the best way to end the matter would be to "pay big" for the murder. They agreed to pay Mato-cu-wi-hu's son in horses. That settled, Primeau regained control of the fort and persuaded Mato-cu-wi-hu's people to give the aggressors a two-hour head start to leave the area. Nevertheless, one witness said the war party "never stopped to camp anywhere for three days afterwards, they was so scared at the party behind them."[28]

---

[27]Will Robinson, "Digest of Reports, 1853–1869," Primeau to Chouteau, 20 June 1862, forwarded to Dole, 305–306. Clément's name, with a French pronunciation, sounds like and is sometimes spelled "Claymore." DeLand, "Addenda," 329n16; "Biography of Old Settlers," 341–43.

[28]Eliza Charger, "Reminiscence" (Martin Charger's widow's reminiscence, as told to her son, Samuel Charger, 23 July 1923), folder 58, Doane Robinson Collection 1856–1946, SDSHS Archives (hereafter cited as Eliza Charger reminiscence). Wilson, "Old Fort Pierre," 296–97; and DeLand, "Addenda," 366–67n68. Some versions have Mato-cu-wi-hu's eldest son away hunting at the time.

Meanwhile, fort personnel and members of his band buried Mato-cu-wi-hu, a Christian, in the ground near the post. A few weeks later, anthropologist Lewis Henry Morgan, who had attended the contentious council on his way up the Missouri, returned downriver and visited the grave, surrounded by wooden pickets and marked with an American flag on a staff.[29]

Shortly before Mato-cu-wi-hu died, he let Primeau know he never wanted soldiers in Sioux country before, but now he hoped they would come. He wanted the president to "take his people and protect them." For a time after his death, his 250 or so followers became "wandering outcasts," according to Latta, but they continued to ask for military protection. Latta recommended a cavalry regiment come to help defend them and other "small tribes and the emigrants." He thought a new treaty should be made with all the Upper Missouri tribes.[30]

On June 20, 1862, Primeau wrote Charles Chouteau from Fort Pierre that "in all likelihood, all our troubles with these Indians will be this fall or winter or next spring, in steamboats passing up the river to Ft. Benton." The Hunkpapas, Sihasapas, and Upper Yanktonais already had been acting "as tho at war with us. When they met a white man they ill-treated and abused him." Primeau blamed a band of Upper Yanktonais and Hunkpapas, led by Black Moon, Medicine Bear, Red Horse, and the Santee Inkpaduta for robbing him of some 4,000 buffalo robes. Remembering the reward offered for Inkpaduta after the 1857 Spirit Lake Massacre, Primeau commented to his bosses in St. Louis that providing military assistance where needed that summer should be easy since "there are at [Fort] Randall 400 men who are of no earthly use there." The recipients forwarded his letter to Commissioner Dole.[31]

Six weeks after the assassination, ten chiefs from the traditionalist Hunkpapa faction sent a letter to Latta in care of Fort Berthold trader and interpreter Pierre Garreau: First, they wanted Charles Galpin's boat sent back. They apparently knew he and his Sioux wife, Eagle-Woman-Whom-All-Look-At, were on a trading trip to Fort Benton. Claiming both sides of the Missouri, they acknowledged that they had "given

---

[29]Warren, "Explorations in Nebraska and Dakota," 160n37; "Biography of Martin Charger" (10 Sept. 1899 interview with Mrs. Pelagie Sarpe Charger Narcelle and her son Samuel Charger), Charles E. Deland Papers, 1890–1935, SDSHS Archives (hereafter cited as Martin Charger biography; Larson, Gall, 247n24; and Morgan, Indian Journals, 229.

[30]Will Robinson, "Digest of Reports, 1853–1869," Latta to Dole, 27 Aug. 1862, 319–22, and "Report," Jayne to Dole, 8 Oct. 1862, 336–41.

[31]Will Robinson, "Digest of Reports, 1853–1869," Primeau to Chouteau, 20 June 1862, forwarded to Dole, 305–306; and Sunder, Fur Trade, 171–72.

permission to travel by water but not by land. Boats carrying passengers we will not allow." They apparently meant that they would allow boats to ply the Upper Missouri with cargo but would not allow them to bring whites who might stay and take their land. If these demands were not met, they promised war. "We notified Bear's Rib not to receive presents. He had no ears, and we gave him ears by killing him. If other people take your presents we will give them ears like Bear Rib's. We have told other agents the same thing. . . . If you don't stop the whites from traveling through our country we will." If the whites send soldiers, "all we ask of you is to bring men, not women dressed in soldiers clothing." They mistrusted Latta; perhaps he would tear up their letter and tell the president "we are all quiet and receive your presents," thereby keeping his job and filling his "pockets with money," while the president "knows nothing of what is going on, but is like a blind old woman who cannot see." They begged him, "for once" to tell the president "what we say and tell him the truth." Little Bear was among the signatories. If he was the old man Harney assumed in 1856 was Mato-cu-wi-hu's biological father, the rift within the Hunkpapas was wide indeed.[32]

Mato-cu-wi-hu's intelligence, wisdom, and courageous leadership commanded respect from whites and his peace-minded followers even as he incurred the wrath of his traditionalist kinsmen. Whether his was the right way for his people or not, he influenced Sioux history as much, if not more, than his better-known contemporaries. What might have transpired had he not protected Warren's expedition, for example? It is easy to imagine devastating outcomes for all concerned.

[32]Will Robinson, "Digest of Reports, 1853–1869," Chouteau to Dole, 2 Dec. 1862, 304; and Utley, *Lance*, 49, 49n17. Garreau probably wrote the chiefs' 25 July letter for them. Chouteau sent a copy to Dole. The letter was sent by Feather-Tied-to-His-Hair, Bald Eagle, Red Hair, The-One-that-Shouts, Little Bear, Crow-that-Looks, Bear Heart, Little Knife, and White-at-Both-Ends.

(*left*) William S. Harney, 1850s.
Courtesy Nebraska Historical Society.

(*below*) Geologist Ferdinand V.
Hayden's 1854 sketch of Fort Pierre.
Courtesy New York State Library,
James Hall Papers, 1830–1930
(*sc16478 box 49, folder 1442*).

"Bear Rib, One [Lone] Horn, Iron Horn"
in a pencil sketch on paper, done ca. June 7, 1858.
*Courtesy Saint Louis Art Museum, Gift of Mrs. M. F. Hahn,
Object no. 61:1941.*

Struck by the Ree, Yankton Nakota.
*Courtesy State Archives of the South Dakota
State Historical Society.*

(*left*) Long Mandan, Two Kettle
Lakota. *Courtesy State Archives of the
South Dakota State Historical Society.*

(*below*) Gouverneur Kemble
Warren. *Courtesy New York State
Library, Gouverneur Kemble Warren,
Papers, 1848–1882 (SC10668, box 62)*

(*above*) Bear Butte. *Author's photo.*

(*below*) Fort Randall, Dakota Territory, in the 1860s.
Courtesy State Archives of the South Dakota State Historical Society.

John B. S. Todd.
*Courtesy State Archives of the South Dakota
State Historical Society.*

SIOUX DELEGATION
top row, left to right, Medicine Cow, Charles Picotte,
and Louis Dewitt; *lower row, left to right,* Strike the Ree,
Zephier [Zephyr]Rencontre, and The Pretty Boy.
*Courtesy State Archives of the South Dakota
State Historical Society.*

(*left*) William Franklin Raynolds. *Courtesy State Archives of the South Dakota State Historical Society.*

(*below*) Mrs. Charles E. Galpin— Eagle Woman. *Courtesy State Historical Society of North Dakota, no. 1952457.*

PART II

Consolidation in Conflict

1862–1865

Legend:
- – – – Sibley and Sully 1863
- —— Sully 1864
- ■ Military forts
- ▲ Trading forts
- ● Towns

0 25 50 mi

MINNESOTA

IOWA

NEBRASKA

MONTANA

WYOMING

INTERNATIONAL BORDER

Mississippi R.

Ft. Snelling
Ft. Ridgely
Ft. Abercrombie
Red R.
Lake Traverse
Big Stone Lake
Minnesota R.
LOWER DAKOTA RES.
UPPER DAKOTA RES.
Spirit Lake
Pipestone Quarry
Sioux City
Vermillion
Sioux Falls
Big Sioux R.
Ft. Wadsworth
Kettle Lakes
Whetstone R.
James R.
Sheyenne R.
Pembina
Devil's Lake
Ft. Totten
Turtle Mtns
Mouse R.
White Earth R.
Whitestone Hill
Dead Buffalo Lake Battle
Long Lake
Big Mound Battle
Stony Lake Battle
Beaver Cr.
Ft. Pierre II
Ft. Thompson
CROW CREEK RES.
Ft. Randall
NEW CROW CREEK RES.
Missouri R.
Ft. Sully
Ft. Sully II
Ft. La Framboise
Whetstone Agency
Bad R.
White R.
Wounded Knee Cr.
Niobara R.
Ft. Stevenson
Ft. Berthold
Killdeer Battle
Knife R.
Ft. Rice
Heart R.
Cannonball R.
Missouri R.
GREAT SIOUX RES.
Grand R.
Moreau R.
Cheyenne R.
BADLANDS
Bear Butte
BLACK HILLS
Little Missouri R.
Battle of the Badlands
Ft. Buford
Ft. Union
Little Muddy R.
Poplar R.
Milk R.
Missouri R.
Yellowstone R.
Cole-Walker Battles
Musselshell R.
Big Horn R.
Rosebud R.
Tongue R.
Powder R.
Belle Fourche R.
N. Platte R.
Ft. Laramie
Bozeman Trail
Ft. Reno
Ft. Phil Kearny
Ft. C. F. Smith
N. Platte R.

N

Sioux Country 1862–1868. *Map by Bill Nelson.*

Chapter 7

Necessity His Justification

IN THE SUMMER OF 1862, TENSIONS CONTINUED TO ESCALATE OVER whites' unceasing incursions into Sioux territory and Mato-cu-wi-hu's murder—war was almost inevitable. When it came, though, it was from an unexpected corner of Sioux country. Hundreds of miles from the Upper Missouri, resentment simmering among the Minnesota Sioux would soon explode, overshadow Mato-cu-wi-hu's assassination, and involve the entire Sioux Nation. It would begin in the east and, during more than four years, spread west and eventually south. Were it not for the inconvenience of it being concurrent with the Civil War, white America, judging by its frequent use of the word "extermination" in pleas for military action, would have welcomed a Sioux war as a means to accomplish it.

On the two Santee Sioux reservations in Minnesota, the summer of 1862 brought dissension and worry. The so-called blanket Indians—those who wanted to maintain their traditional ways—remained in the majority, but their agent and other whites favored the growing number of "civilized" Indians who had planted crops and become Christians. Yet even those who lived in brick houses, farmed, and dressed like whites resented the traders who had cheated and deceived them over the years. Kinship ties cultivated during the fur trade era when whites made some effort to assimilate into Sioux culture, if only to increase profits, had atrophied. Now whites living on or near the reservation did not value the reciprocal generosity, support, and protection Sioux kinship provided. Some settlers, especially those who were European-born, perceived class and race distinctions that prohibited basic understanding, let alone assimilation, of another culture.[1] By August 1862, all four Santee tribes—Mdewakantons, Wahpekutes, Wahpetons, and Sissetons—had grown restive. As settlers crowded into Minnesota, traditional Indians could no longer find enough

---

[1] The Sioux kinship system engendered complicated relationships among themselves and with outsiders. See Deloria, *Speaking of Indians*; Gary Anderson, *Kinsmen*, xxvi–xxix; and Gary Anderson, *Little Crow*, 16.

game to live on. All waited eagerly, desperately, for their annuity payment, which was due July 1 but still had not been delivered in mid-August.

Anticipating that traders would try to cheat them once their annuity money from an 1851 treaty arrived, some young Indian men living near the Lower (Mdewakanton and Wahpekute) Agency at Redwood formed a soldiers' lodge to present a united front in seeking fair treatment. U.S. army regulars were serving in the Civil War, leaving only Company B, Fifth Minnesota Volunteer Infantry Regiment, to garrison nearby Fort Ridgely. Lodge members asked post commander Captain John Marsh if he intended to help collect money traders claimed Indians owed them. Marsh assured them his men were not collection agents for traders. When the traders heard that, they colluded to deny credit to Indians until the overdue payment was available to settle Indian debts. Someone commented that without credit until the annuities arrived, Indians would surely starve. "So far as I'm concerned," storekeeper Andrew Myrick supposedly retorted, "if they are hungry let them eat grass."

Word spread about Myrick's remark. Despite their anger, the Lower Agency soldiers' lodge, meeting August 17 to decide what to do, could reach no consensus on a course of action. That day four young hunters from Shakopee's (Little Six's) Mdewakanton village at Rice Creek ended the indecision when a dare to steal eggs led first to a shooting contest with some settlers, then to their murdering all five people, including two women.[2] The young men rode into the Rice Creek village that night on stolen horses yelling for men to get their guns because they had begun the war with the whites.

At an early morning council, the Mdewakanton and Wahpekute Lower Agency chiefs saw that the majority of their band members wanted nothing less than to take back their traditional tribal lands and expel or kill all whites living there. Mdewakanton Chief Taoyateduta (Little Crow) agreed, reluctantly at first, to lead this war of desperation. With war proponents clamoring for action, he ordered a raid that day on the Lower Agency compound at Redwood. Warriors broke into the warehouse and attacked any whites they came upon. Andrew Myrick was among the first to die. The Indians who killed him and mutilated

---

[2]Gary Anderson, *Kinsmen*, 251 (including quote by Myrick about eating grass). Anderson clarifies time, place, and context of this remark and discusses kinship breakdown as one cause of the conflict. See also Wakefield, *Six Weeks*, 5–7, and Oehler, *Great Sioux Uprising*, 24–27. Many letters, diaries, reminiscences, and other documents are archived in the Dakota Conflict of 1862 MSS (M582), MNHS Archives. Accounts differ; there may have been six Indian men.

his body stuffed a symbolic handful of dry grass in his dead mouth. Small bands of Sioux fanned out to kill, rape, and capture white people and mixed-bloods unsympathetic to their cause and to loot and destroy property in a twenty-six-county swath of Minnesota.[3]

After a private from Fort Ridgely rode furiously into Fort Snelling with the news, Governor Alexander Ramsey hurriedly assigned troops recruited for the Civil War to the conflict. To lead this force of mostly infantry, he appointed former fur trader Henry Hastings Sibley, resident since 1834 and Minnesota's first governor. Partly because of kinship ties through his father-in-law, the influential Mdewakanton chief Bad Hail, Sibley had profited enormously from the 1851 Sioux treaty.[4]

Sibley was too far away to be of immediate help. Fort Ridgely commander Captain Marsh left nineteen-year-old Lieutenant Thomas P. Gere in command and, with forty men, headed to Redwood Agency, encountering fleeing refugees along the way. At a ferry crossing, Indians ambushed the small force, killing twenty-four and wounding five. Marsh also died, drowning when his leg cramped as he tried to cross the river. The Indians lost one man. On August 20, Taoyateduta led 400 Sioux against Fort Ridgely, where only seventy-six men and two officers remained to protect civilians seeking safety at this jumble of mostly wooden buildings with no protective walls. Soldiers built earthworks and fended off attacks from all directions with cannon fire. Refugees kept arriving. Taoyateduta attacked two days later with double the force, but artillery again repulsed attackers.[5]

Taoyateduta had little luck convincing the Upper (Sisseton and Wahpeton) Agency leaders to join his war, but he did recruit two Sisseton chiefs, White Lodge and Lean Bear, whose villages were located near the Dakota border northwest of Lake Shetek. The two chiefs had been uneasy about the fifty or so white people living in their home country (present Murray County, Minnesota) and welcomed the commission to attack settlers there and along the Big Sioux River.[6]

---

[3]Big Eagle's account in Gary Anderson and Woolworth, *Through Dakota Eyes*, 56; Oehler, *Great Sioux Uprising*, 37–38, 56; Schultz, *Over the Earth*, 48, 55, 60, 80–83, 139; and Gary Anderson, *Little Crow*, 121–30, 136. Sioux mutilated enemy dead to disable them in the next world. See contemporary accounts in the Dakota Conflict of 1862 MSS.

[4]Gary Anderson, *Kinsmen*, 93, 180, 190–99; and Josephy, *Civil War in the American West*, 101–105.

[5]Carley, *Dakota War*, 15–16; Josephy, *Civil War in the American West*, 112–13; and Sheehan's and Jones's reports nos. 1 and 2, 26 Aug. 1862, OR, vol. 13, 248–50.

[6]In 1852 Lean Bear spoke to Governor Ramsay of whites' injustice to Dakotas. See Helen Jackson, *Century*, 321.

While Taoyateduta was making his August 20 assault on Fort Ridgely, the two Sisseton chiefs saw to their small arena of the wider war. The Duleys, Wrights, Everetts, Eastlicks, and Irelands were neighbors on the prairie east of Lake Shetek. Sioux they regarded as friends warned them that some 300 "bad Indians" were prowling around, threatening to burn cabins and kill everyone in them. Consequently, these families—with only five guns among them—holed up in John and Julia Wright's sturdy, two-story log home until an Indian friend, Pawn, persuaded them to leave the house to hide instead in the swampy forest. This seemed like a good idea until Lean Bear rode toward them, obviously intent on mayhem. William Duley and Thomas Ireland aimed and fired almost simultaneously. As Lean Bear fell dead from his horse, Indians quickly surrounded the settlers, killing John Eastlick and Billy Everett and injuring both of Billy's parents.

Pawn, now clearly siding with White Lodge, insisted that Mrs. Wright and Mrs. Everett, who was bleeding from a neck wound, come with him as his wives. He assured them no one would harm them or their children. With no other options, Julia Wright and Almira Everett crawled to the base of the ridge where Pawn and White Lodge waited. William Duley urged the other women to go with Pawn as well and take their children. With her husband dead, Lavina Eastlick also decided to trust Pawn. As they approached the ridge, Lavina's four-year old son, Freddy, lagged behind. An Indian woman picked up a tree branch and beat the boy severely. Lavina could only watch as another woman clubbed her older son, Frank, until blood spurted from his mouth. Meanwhile, the men killed Mrs. Ireland and another woman. Almira Everett also died of her wounds.

Two of White Lodge's companions took the oldest Ireland girls, Rosa and Ellen, aged nine and seven. When Lavina said something that angered Pawn, he loaded his gun and shot her. The ball entered her back and exited her hip before passing through her right arm. When she did not die, someone beat her about the head and shoulders with a gun. She lost consciousness, and they left her for dead. After regaining consciousness, she crawled for three days to a road and safety. By then, more than two dozen Lake Shetek residents were dead.[7]

With Lean Bear dead, White Lodge assumed leadership and took the captives to his camp near the Yellow Medicine River's source. From there

[7]Carley, *Dakota War*, 23–24; Gary Anderson and Woolworth, *Through Dakota Eyes*, 14; Schultz, *Over the Earth I Come*, 109–111; and Oehler, *Great Sioux Uprising*, 114–16. See Eastlick's account in Drimmer, *Captured*, 314–29.

he sent a party to Sioux Falls, where, outside of town, they killed judge Joseph B. Amidon and his son (or grandson). Because the settlement was fortified, the Indians did not invade. However, when frightened inhabitants learned the scope of what Governor Jayne (Dakota Territory) was calling a "terrible and appalling massacre," they abandoned the town.[8] Once these Indians rejoined White Lodge, they all set out for the Missouri River. White Lodge offered the Lake Shetek captives to some Yanktonais along Elm River, but they declined them. The Sissetons continued westward.

In New Ulm, Minnesota, residents twice repulsed Taoyateduta's warriors. Since August 26, Colonel Sibley had been moving his ill-equipped force toward Fort Ridgely, but newspapers oozed derision about his incredibly slow progress. As violence spread, Governor Ramsey wrote newly promoted General-in-Chief Henry W. Halleck asking that General Harney, who had so successfully cowed the Lakota and Nakota six years earlier, come to chastise the rampaging Dakotas. The Civil War, in its second bloody year, necessarily claimed both Halleck's and President Lincoln's attention. However, Lincoln's secretary, John G. Nicolay, who had come to Minnesota with Commissioner Dole to observe treaty negotiations with the Chippewas, wrote Secretary of War Stanton August 27 that the "Indian war grows more extensive" and insisted that retaliation against the Sioux "be a war of extermination."[9]

On September 2, some 500 warriors under Mdewakanton chiefs Taoyateduta and Big Eagle defeated 150 Sixth Minnesota Cavalry volunteers at Birch Coulee, killing or wounding approximately half the men and eighty-five cavalry horses. The next day, the same Indians scattered a detachment of soldiers at Acton.

Fearing the war would spill into Dakota, Governor Jayne alerted Brigadier General James G. Blunt, commanding the Department of Kansas at Leavenworth, that "family after family are leaving our Territory. . . . We must have immediate aid and assistance from you or else our Territory will be depopulated." Jayne worried Upper Missouri Lakotas and Nakotas would ally with Dakotas, leaving "a few thousand people at the mercy of 50,000 Indians." Because the territorial militia had no arms, he

[8]Goodspeed, *Province and the States*, vol. 6, 230–31; and Jayne to Dole, 8 Oct. 1862, no. 35, in CIA annual report, 320.

[9]Ramsey to Halleck, 25 Aug. 1862, 597; Halleck to Ramsey, 29 Aug. 1862, 605; Jayne to Blunt, 613; Wilkinson, Dole, and Nicolay to Lincoln, 27 Aug. 1862, 599; and Nicolay to Stanton, 27 Aug. 1862, 599–600, all in OR, vol. 13; and Carley, *Dakota War*, 54–55. (Henry Hastings Sibley should not be confused with tent inventor Henry Hopkins Sibley.)

urged Blunt to send immediately 300 muskets, with ammunition, three cavalry units, and three six-pounder artillery pieces to equip a blockhouse under construction at Yankton.[10]

On September 8, Iowa's governor Samuel J. Kirkwood wrote Secretary Stanton that the Yanktons had (but they actually had not) joined the Santees to "threaten our whole northwestern frontier. The settlers are flying by hundreds." He believed rumors that British traders were encouraging the Indians and that the whole Sioux Nation was poised for a "war of extermination against the frontier." Everyone from Saint Paul to New Mexico might be in danger. Kirkwood called out 500 mounted volunteers, but the Iowans, too, lacked arms and equipment. Only prompt action, he believed, could prevent a massacre. "General Harney is just the man we need for this service."[11]

On September 9, Minnesota's governor advised an emergency state legislature session that "nothing which the brutal lust and wanton cruelty of these savages could wreak upon their helpless and innocent victims, was omitted from the category of their crimes." He chose egregious examples:

> Infants hewn into bloody chips of flesh, or nailed alive to door posts to linger out their little life in mortal agony, or torn untimely from the womb of the murdered mother and in cruel mockery cast in fragments on her pulseless and bleeding breast; rape joined to murder in one awful tragedy; young girls, even children of tender years, outraged by their brutal ravishers till death ended their shame and suffering; women held in captivity to undergo the horrors of a living death; whole families burned alive; and, as if their devilish fury could not glut itself with outrages on the living, its last efforts exhausted in mutilating the bodies of the dead. Such are the spectacles, and a thousand nameless horrors besides, which their first experience of Indian war has burned into the brains and hearts of our frontier people; and such the enemy with whom we have to deal.

The governor insisted Sioux be "exterminated or driven forever beyond" Minnesota's borders.[12]

Harney commanded the Department of the West at St. Louis from 1860 until May 1861, when Secretary of War Simon Cameron and President Lincoln, partly because they doubted his loyalty, replaced him with

---

[10]Jayne to Blunt, 3 Sept. 1862, OR, vol. 13, 613.

[11]Nutt to Kirkwood, 15 Sept. 1862, 638–40; Kirkwood to Stanton, 8 Sept. 1862, 620; and Pope to Halleck, 16 Sept. 1862, 642, all in OR, vol. 13; Chittenden, *Steamboat Navigation*, 288–89, 369; and Adams, *Harney*, 240, 341n44.

[12]Ramsay, *Message of Ramsay to Legislature of Minnesota.*

Nathaniel Lyon. Harney would reenter the Sioux's lives later, but General John Pope, who had performed badly during the Second Battle of Bull Run, would deal with the present crisis.[13] Pope graduated West Point a topographical engineer in 1842 and, like Harney, served in Florida and in the Mexican War. He had alienated many with his braggadocio and political machinations, but Pope knew Minnesota. In 1849, he led an expedition to examine the border region and scout locations for forts along the Red River. His report scolded the government for "failing as yet to extinguish the title of the Indians, and to throw open to the industry of the American people a country so well adapted to their genius and their enterprise." His map, however, so closely resembled explorer Joseph N. Nicollet's 1838 map that his commanding officer accused him of plagiarism and refused Pope's request for another Minnesota posting.

Now Pope saw Stanton's order to head the new Department of the Northwest for the banishment it was but also as an opportunity to restore his reputation. Arriving in St. Paul on September 16, Pope wrote Halleck: "You have no idea of the terrible destruction already done and of the panic everywhere in Wisconsin and Minnesota. . . . Crops are all left standing and the whole population are fleeing." He was pleased to find Sibley—who, when he was Minnesota's first territorial representative in Congress, had helped Pope promote his Minnesota report, published in book form in 1850—in charge of what few military forces existed.[14]

THE INDIANS WERE GONE WHEN SIBLEY REACHED FORT RIDGELY three days after Pope arrived in St. Paul. His 1,500 volunteers set out to find Taoyateduta, but four days later the chief, with as many as 1,500 warriors, found them instead. Sibley lost thirty-seven men in the ambush near Wood Lake but administered heavy casualties and earned promotion to brigadier general.[15]

---

[13]Adams, *Harney*, discusses the loyalty issue, 226–41; Thomas to Harney, 669, 669n, Thomas to Lyon, 21 April 1861, 670, and Miles to Townsend, 30 April 1861, 676–67, all in OR, vol. 1; and Williams to Thomas, 29 April, 489–90, and Harney General Order (GO) no. 11, 30 May 1861, 493, both in OR, vol. 53.

[14]Cozzens, *General John Pope*, 206; Goetzmann, *Army Exploration*, 16–19, 75; and Pope, "Report of an Exploration," 1850. Stanton to Pope, 6 Sept. 1862, 617; and Pope to Halleck, 16 Sept. 1862, 642, both in OR, vol. 13.

[15]"Skirmish with Indians at Wood Lake," reports 1 and 2, 23 Sept. 1862, 278–81; and Halleck to Pope, 29 Sept. 1862, 688, both in OR, vol. 13. Sibley mistook Wood Lake for one nearby. See Carley, *Dakota War*, 62–63.

Meanwhile, another front opened when a mixed band of Sissetons and Wahpetons surrounded Fort Abercrombie, the Red River post isolated on the edge of Dakota and garrisoned by a single Fifth Minnesota company. Captain John Vander Horck did not learn how widespread the violence was until August 23 when his scouts found five mutilated bodies in a Breckinridge hotel. Ammunition stored at Abercrombie did not fit his command's muskets and he had not received any that did when on August 30 Indians raided the livestock. Twice—on September 3 and 6—they attacked the fort. Eighty men and a hundred or so women and children held off attackers until Governor Ramsey's four-company rescue party arrived in time to defend against two more attacks, the last on September 29. Five soldiers died; the Indians lost many more.[16]

Taoyateduta fled north after the Wood Lake battle, and by the end of September fighting was over. Militant Santees had slaughtered perhaps 800 settlers, by some estimates, and were holding hundreds captive. Most afterward withdrew across the international border or to Devil's Lake in northern Dakota Territory to hunt. White Lodge and the other Lake Shetek marauders eventually camped at Beaver Creek on the Missouri's east bank in present Emmons County, North Dakota, where eighty to a hundred tipis sheltered perhaps 800 people, including about a hundred fighting men.[17]

Pope wrote Sibley that he agreed "the horrible massacres of women and children and the outrageous abuse of female prisoners, still alive, call for punishment beyond human power to inflict. . . . It is my purpose utterly to exterminate the Sioux." Sibley should "destroy everything belonging to them and force them out to the plains" unless he could capture them. "They are to be treated as maniacs or wild beasts, and by no means as people with whom treaties or compromises can be made." However, Sibley was stymied. He had too few rations, it was too late for livestock to find grass on the prairie, and he could not legally cross the international border. Instead, he began interrogating his own prisoners and those who had since surrendered.[18]

Many Indians and mixed-bloods who had rescued or sheltered captives released them to Sibley. By September 28, he had about ninety white

---

[16]Ramsey to Halleck, 8 Sept. 1862, OR, vol. 13, 620; Carley, *Dakota War*, 56–58; Paxson, "Diary," 103–104; Diedrich, *Odyssey*, 42; and Doane Robinson, "History of the Dakota," 296. Robinson has Taoyateduta present at the 26 Sept. Abercrombie skirmish.

[17]Doane Robinson, "History of the Dakota," 305. See Sibley to Pope, 5 Oct. 1862, 711–12, OR, vol. 13.

[18]Pope to Sibley, 28 Sept. 1856, OR, vol. 13, 685–86; and Carley, *Dakota War*, 64–70.

women and children and more than a hundred mixed-blood former captives at his "Camp Release." The officers in his military commission would try suspects. Sibley told Pope he would execute those found guilty "although perhaps it will be a stretch of my authority. If so, necessity must be my justification."[19]

All fall, Taoyateduta's followers dribbled into Camp Release, hoping, Sibley conjectured, for leniency. Sibley wrote four Sisseton chiefs he knew as friends, assuring them troops sent after Taoyateduta and his followers would not injure them or any innocent bands. Nevertheless, he advised them to stay in their villages. Because militants had killed so many of his soldiers' family members, "they might not be able to distinguish you from the guilty bands and [might] fire upon you." In his note to the Mdewakanton and Wahpeton leaders, Sibley promised no injury to the innocent who surrendered immediately under a white flag. Otherwise, his troops would "treat them as enemies," and if they attacked more white settlers he would "destroy every camp of the lower Indians I can find without mercy."[20]

Although Sibley commended Standing Buffalo's, Wanata's, and Red Feather's followers for "their decided refusal to receive or countenance Little Crow and his devilish crew," these benign bands still, he contended, required "sifting and purging in order to discover the guilty individuals among them." Sibley assured Pope that although the military commission's proceedings might "not be exactly in form in all the details," he would "probably approve them, and hang the villains." In summarizing Sibley's reports for Halleck, Pope agreed executions would be necessary and would "have a crushing effect" on the others.[21]

Sibley's and Pope's reports alarmed President Lincoln. He weighed Nicolay's, Governor Jayne's, and congressional representative John Todd's advice and reports against Halleck's cousin Bishop Henry B. Whipple's opinion that the conflict could be blamed on whites as much as on

---

[19]Sibley to Flandreau, 28 Sept. 1862, 687, and Halleck to Pope, 29 Sept. 1862, 688, OR, vol. 13. See also Oehler, *Great Sioux Uprising*, 203; Sibley's adjutant, Lt. R. C. Olin, was judge advocate, assisted by Col. William Crooks, Lt. Col. Marshall (briefly), Maj. George Bradley, and Capts. Grant and Hiram S. Bailey. Lawyer Isaac Heard was recorder. Missionary Stephen R. Riggs, who knew most of the Indians and spoke Sioux, acted as interrogator. Antoine D. Frenière, a mixed-blood, interpreted. (See Carley, *Dakota War*, 68.)

[20]Sibley to Wanatua, Standing Buffalo, Tah-ton-ka-nangee, and Wa-mun-dee-on-pe-du-tah and an unaddressed note, 3 Oct. 1862, OR, vol. 13, 708–709.

[21]Sibley to Pope, 5 Oct. 1862, 711–12, and Pope to Halleck, 7 and 10 Oct. 1862, 716, 724, both in OR, vol. 13. Red Feather was also known as Scarlet Plume, and Waneta's name was variously spelled.

Indians. The Episcopal cleric had begun championing Indian causes after arriving in Minnesota in 1859.[22] While Lincoln contemplated the situation, Pope ordered Sibley not to execute prisoners at Camp Release. Instead, he should send them to Fort Snelling.

When fresh mounted troops arrived at Camp Release, Sibley ordered them west to search for stragglers on the prairie and, if possible, "find and exterminate" White Lodge and the other Lake Shetek murderers. He cautioned Lieutenant Colonel Marshall, who was commanding the troops, against "using any undue or unnecessary violence toward the Indians . . . and especially do not permit any insult to the females." Soldiers had scalped Indians; Sibley wanted no more of that. "The bodies of the dead, even of a savage enemy, shall not be subjected to indignities by civilized and Christian men." Scalping enemies had ritualistic meaning for the Sioux; whites had no such justification. (Ethnologist Royal B. Hassrick, explained: A scalp was "a badge of honor, a sign of victory, and a symbol of life . . . Scalping was no mere bloodthirsty act of the savage mind but a ritualistic necessity for men who believed that the human spirit was somehow in and of human hair.") Marshall's detachment captured thirty-nine men and about a hundred women and children, among whom, Sibley told Pope, were "several murderers and rascals, who will of course be made to pay the penalty of their crimes." Lack of grass and low rations prevented Marshall from pursuing other Sissetons and Yanktonais farther west. Sibley, however, told Pope he doubted "whether [Yanktonais] have harbored or even seen Little Crow and his small band of refugees."[23]

By the time Sibley ended the trials on November 3, his commission found 303 guilty and sentenced them all to hang. Pope telegraphed the condemned list to the president, but Lincoln wanted "a full and complete record of their convictions" and "a careful statement" of "the more guilty and influential of the culprits." Pope complied but urged Lincoln to authorize all 303 executions in order to avoid mob violence. Governor Ramsey concurred.[24]

Sibley's improvised military court had interviewed, with no defense counsel present, nearly 400 Indians and mixed-bloods, taking, in some cases, only five minutes per interview. The panel comprised soldiers

---

[22]Nicolay, "Sioux War"; and Josephy, *Civil War in the American West*, 137.

[23]Sibley to Pope, 7 Oct. 1862, 717–18, and 15 Oct. 1862, 739–40; Sibley to Marshall, 13 Oct. 1862, 735; and Sibley to Pope, 21 Oct. 1862, 756–58, all in OR, vol. 13; James Walker, *Lakota Belief*, 232; and Hassrick, *The Sioux*, 90.

[24]Lincoln to Pope and Ramsey to Lincoln, 10 Nov. 1862, OR, vol. 13, 787.

who had fought those they were judging and whose families and friends may have been victims. One commissioner admitted his "mind was not in a condition to give the men a fair trial." Furthermore, the commission condemned to death anyone who had "fired in battles, or brought ammunition, or acted as a commissary in supplying provisions to the combattants, or had committed some separate murder." Because Sioux traditionally told victory stories after success in battle, so-called confessions were easy to elicit. Furthermore, the Camp Release trials baffled most defendants. One educated mixed-blood who spoke English fluently thought his interview would only determine if he would face trial later in a civilian court. Most white Minnesota residents, however, agreed with Senator Morton W. Wilkinson's petition to President Lincoln: "These Indians are called by some prisoners of war. There was no war about it. It was wholesale robbery, rape, murder." Separating those who had killed during battle from those who had murdered, raped, and pillaged, Lincoln determined that thirty-nine deserved death. One man convicted on the strength of testimony from two boys was later pardoned.[25]

On November 7, Sibley began moving the non-condemned Indians to Fort Snelling and those with death sentences to a camp near Mankato. Along their route, whites assembled to assail the Indians, some pummeling them with their bare hands or even attacking them with pitchforks and axes. Many of the Indians suffered serious injuries; a few died. One white woman grabbed a baby from an Indian woman's arms and smashed it to the ground. The infant died soon after.[26]

On the day after Christmas 1862 in Mankato, William Duley, whose wife, Laura, had been captured by White Lodge, pulled the rope causing the floor of a massive scaffold to fall. All thirty-eight condemned men dropped at once. Local doctors took the unprecedented opportunity of what remains the largest multiparty legal execution in the United States to obtain cadavers for study. By night, they dug up bodies buried four feet deep in a common grave. Dr. William W. Mayo, whose sons founded the Mayo Clinic, was among the grave robbers.[27]

[25]Carley, *Dakota War*, 68–75; Sibley to Pope, 21 Oct. 1862, OR, vol. 13, 756–58; and Gary Anderson and Woolworth, *Through Dakota Eyes*, 15.

[26]Carley, *Dakota War*, 70; George Crooks's and Good Star Woman's accounts in Gary Anderson and Woolworth, *Through Dakota Eyes*, 261–67; and Diane Wilson, *Spirit Car*, 41–42, 184–199. Wilson's well-researched memoir offers a vivid account of the historic march and a personal account of a 2002 commemoration march.

[27]Josephy, *Civil War in the American West*, 138; and Oehler, *Great Sioux Uprising*, 114–16, 223. See also Buck, *Indian Outbreaks*, 271–71.

The army sent the condemned Indians whose lives Lincoln saved to serve one- to three-year sentences at Davenport, Iowa. Innocent Santees or those who had risked their own lives to save settlers remained at Fort Snelling. Their annuity money paid these families' expenses over the winter. In February 1863, as punishment for the previous summer's violence, the government abrogated all treaties with the Santee Sioux, taking away their Minnesota reservations. As soon as navigation was possible, steamboats took those not imprisoned at Davenport to a new reservation named Crow Creek on the Missouri's east bank opposite the old Fort Lookout site. Although some Sioux had implicated Winnebagos in the Fort Ridgely and New Ulm fighting, the commission convicted none. However, to calm its citizens' fears and answer anti-Indian demands for "extermination or removal," Minnesota also exiled Winnebagos to Crow Creek.[28]

The total breakdown of white and Indian relations in Minnesota over time would unite far-flung Sioux bands whose different Lakota, Nakota, and Dakota dialects offer proof of centuries-old separation. However, external and internal turmoil would complicate that unity. Sioux winter counts avoid the 1862 conflict and any mention of the aftermath. Dakotas did not keep such pictographic histories, but several Nakota winter counts record 1862 only as a time when buffalo were unusually abundant. Garrick Mallery, first to head the Bureau of Ethnology, founded in 1879, collected his first winter count while an army colonel stationed in Dakota in 1876. "Perhaps the reason for the omission of any character to designate the massacre was the terrible retribution which followed," he wrote. Indeed, with Sioux all but eradicated from Minnesota, Pope planned a military campaign into Dakota to punish Santee fugitives living on the prairie and to push any survivors west of the Missouri, away from settlers and travelers.[29]

---

[28]Gary Anderson, *Kinsmen*, 278; Sibley to Pope, 30 Sept. 1862, 694–95, and 21 Oct. 1862, 716; Pope to Halleck, 7 Oct. 1862, 755, and 20 Oct. 1862, 756–58, all in OR, vol. 13; Lass, "Removal," 361–63; and Big Eagle's account in Anderson and Woolworth, *Through Dakota Eyes*, 149. See Helen Jackson, *Century*, 322–24; and "The Indian Murderers at Post McClellan," *Davenport (Iowa) Democrat*, 27 Apr. 1863.

[29]Mallery, *Picture-Writing*, vol. 1, 285; Candace Greene and Thornton, *Year the Stars Fell*, 251; James Howard, "Dakota Winter Counts," 387–88; Karol, *Red Horse Owner's Winter Count*, 37, 61; White Bull, *Lakota Warrior*, 20; Halleck to Stanton, 25 Nov. 1863, OR, vol. 22, pt. 1, p. 12; Wilson, "Old Fort Pierre," 302; Pattee "Reminiscences," 288–89; and Fort Randall PR, Jan. 1863, reel 988, M617, NA.

Chapter 8

An Injudicious, Outrageous Act

MATO-CU-WI-HU'S ASSASSINATION AND THE SANTEE WAR PROMPTED Lower Yanktonai chief Two Bear to complain that the United States had not kept its promise to protect peaceable Indians. Never had the Sioux Nation been so polarized, and now came confirmation in 1862 of a northern Rocky Mountain gold strike. The attendant increase in river traffic through Sioux country to what would soon be Montana Territory would surely further perturb the Sioux. Governor Jayne feared a costly, disastrous war unless the government addressed Sioux fears of losing their hunting grounds.

When Santees "invited, urged and threatened" the Yanktons to join their war against whites, the Yanktons instead pledged loyalty to the president and the United States, vowing, according to Agent Burleigh, to "stand by it while they lived and die under its protection." Struck-by-the-Ree, Mad Bull, and Smutty Bear planted crops and, according to Jayne in his role as U.S. Indian Bureau superintendent, were teaching their people "the advantages of a settled life." Even bands led by Pretty Boy, Medicine Cow, Little Swan, and Feather-in-the-Ear had reluctantly "settled down and are planting." Burleigh credited "gentlemanly" Iowa officers and soldiers at Randall for being on hand to quell potentially unruly behavior when he distributed cash annuities in late June. All the same, Burleigh fortified Greenwood agency with a blockhouse. At first, the Yanktons were suspicious of the two-story structure defended by a six-pounder Dahlgren gun and two smaller cannons. Now, with Santees threatening them and killing reservation livestock and their Upper Missouri kinsmen also angry, they valued its protection.[1]

ON OCTOBER 10, INDIANS SOME 150 MILES DOWN THE MISSOURI from Fort Berthold—possibly White Lodge's group—hailed miners

[1]Jayne to Dole, 8 Oct. 1862, in CIA annual report, no. 35, 319–22; and Burleigh, 25 Oct. 1862, in Will Robinson, "Digest of Reports, 1853–1869," 308–10. See also Lounsberry, *Early History*, 288.

heading home in a large wooden mackinaw boat. When the whites ignored them, the Indians shot into the air, then showered them with bullets at a narrow place on the river. With Indians insistently motioning them to land, the helmsman indicated he would comply. More warriors emerged from hiding places, and when they stopped firing, the steersman abruptly swung the boat around broadside while the miners "poured a volley, which tumbled Mr. Redskin right and left . . . making them skedaddle in every direction." Indians pursuing on the riverbank wounded four miners.[2]

Later in autumn, another boatload of miners descended the river as paying passengers of trader Charles Galpin, now a partner in the AFC's competitor, La Barge, Harkness, and Company. He and his Sioux wife, Eagle-Woman-Whom-All-Look-At, were coming home from the Upper Missouri trading posts he supervised when, at Beaver Creek, Indians on the riverbank gestured for them to stop.[3] Despite sensing hostility, Galpin got out of the boat and tethered it to a tree. Eagle Woman recognized a young Santee, who told her three Yanktonais friendly to whites were in White Lodge's camp about four miles below. The Galpins requested to see them. Tension increased, and as they waited, Eagle Woman heard someone yell, "Kill them, kill them." She was incensed by the unfriendly reception: "I have traveled a long distance, have come clear through the enemy's country in safety and unmolested; and now, when almost home, I am surprised to be treated in this unfriendly manner!"[4]

Stormy Goose and two other Yanktonais finally arrived from below to tell Eagle Woman that White Lodge's people would have no mercy on her. One of the three warned the menacing group gathered around that they would have to kill him in order to harm her. Eagle Woman had been sitting so still in the boat that one warrior suspected her of hiding something. The Galpins' four-year-old son had died upriver, and Eagle Woman had insisted on bringing his body home for burial. She "admitted" concealing a present for White Lodge. Accepting that

[2]"From the Upper Missouri/A Desperate Fight with Indians," *Mineral Point (Wis.) Weekly Tribune*, 19 Nov. 1862. (Reprinted from 1 Nov. 1862, *Sioux City (Iowa) Register*.)

[3]Sunder, *Fur Trade*, 234. The Galpins probably knew about the Santee war. See Harkness, "Diary of James Harkness," 5 Sept. 1862 entry, 348.

[4]Gray, "Story of Mrs. Picotte-Galpin," 10–11; Chouteau to Dole, 2 Dec. 1862, in Will Robinson, "Digest of Reports, 1853–1869," 304; and Holley, *Once Their Home*, 289–91. Cf., Pattee, "Reminiscences," 283–84, and Doane Robinson, "History of the Dakota," 304–305, 305n501. Chouteau's account, though contemporary, is secondhand. Robinson and Holley interviewed participants, but it was years later. This is a plausible version based on conflicting accounts.

explanation, the Indians towed the boat, with its passengers, along the shore toward White Lodge's camp. Once there, Galpin disembarked, but Eagle Woman spotted warriors preparing an ambush and called out. As soon as her husband jumped back into the boat, she cut the mooring rope with a hatchet. All aboard lay flat on the boat's bottom and, as it drifted out into the main channel under fire, they heard a woman yell in English that she was a captive and other white prisoners were in the camp. Knowing they could do nothing themselves, the Galpins hurried on to tell others. On November 3, they stopped briefly to bury their son at Fort La Framboise—the La Barge, Harkness, and Company fort that Frank La Framboise managed a few miles upriver from the new Fort Pierre.[5] At Fort Pierre, a mixed-blood man who had escaped from the Santees with his family confirmed that they still held many white and mixed-blood prisoners.[6]

Meanwhile, La Framboise devised a plan for freeing White Lodge's hostages. When the Minnesota trouble erupted in August, Taoyateduta had invited the Two Kettle band staying near the two trading posts to join the war. Some few did, but others, horrified at the atrocities, wanted nothing to do with the Santees. Among them were eleven idealistic young men who formed a soldier lodge devoted to charitable endeavors. Taunted as fools, the name stuck; they became "Fool Soldiers," a name that soon extended to the mixed band of peaceable Sioux who frequented the trading posts. La Framboise pointed out that a rescue mission would offer them an opportunity to practice their principles, and he offered to give them provisions, expense money, and horses to use as ransom.[7]

The young men left Fort La Framboise on November 10. At Swan Lake Creek, the peaceable Lower Yanktonai chief Bone Necklace told

[5]Gray, "Story of Mrs. Picotte-Galpin," 10–11; Holley, *Once Their Home*, 289–90; Doane Robinson, "History of the Dakota," 305–306; G. Hubert Smith, "Fort Pierre II," 92–93, 108; Pattee, "Reminiscences," 288; Doane Robinson, "Fort Tecumseh and Fort Pierre Journals," 217n287; Gary Anderson, *Kinsmen*, 66–67, 106; and Drips, *Three Years*, 25.

[6]"Digest of Indian Commission Reports," 308; and Pattee to Smith, 17 May 1863, Fort Randall LS, 1856–67, RG 98, NA

[7]Soldiers' lodges or warrior societies were exclusive fraternal associations with their own rules and rituals. Members, who generally did not include chiefs, influenced councils, policed the camp, and enforced discipline. See, e.g., James Walker, *Lakota Society*, 62–65, and *Lakota Belief*, 264. Pattee credited Primeau with impelling the Fool Soldiers, but La Framboise wrote the *Sioux City Register* a year later claiming that distinction. Gray, "Santee Sioux," 49, 49nn11–12, 50, 50nn14–17, corrects errors in various accounts. See also Barbier, "Recollections of Ft. La Framboise," 232–42, and Doane Robinson, "History of the Dakota," 308–14. The accounts given by Charger (a.k.a. Martin Charger) and another Fool Soldier mention no outside influence.

them White Lodge and his Sissetons had moved farther downriver. The Fool Soldiers traveled four more days to reach the camp, where they laid out a feast and explained why they had come. At council, White Lodge advised the youths, "These white captives we have taken after killing many of the people. We will not again be friends to the whites. We have done a bad thing and now we will keep on doing bad things. We will not give up the captives. We will fight until we drop dead."[8]

The Indians had been trading the captives among themselves for various items of value. Julia Wright belonged now to White Lodge, who told the Fool Soldiers he wanted to keep her because he was an old man and she took good care of him. The Fool Soldiers persisted, finally enlisting the old chief's sons, Chase-the-Ree and Black Hawk, to wrest Julia free. Black Hawk also released his own young captive. After much talk and payment of all the horses and provisions, White Lodge surrendered Laura Duley and her five-year-old niece, Julia's five-year-old daughter, the Ireland girls, and Almira Everett's daughter. The Fool Soldiers moved them a safe distance away, and by morning, two young men from Bone Necklace's band arrived with a horse to help. They rigged a travois to carry the children and Laura, who was lame. Noticing Julia's bare feet, Charger gave her his moccasins, wrapping his own feet in old clothing. As they moved on, White Lodge came after them, limping with rheumatism, intent on taking back his prisoners. With six guns among them, the young men guarded the rear ready to kill White Lodge if he made any trouble, but after awhile, he gave up. Bone Necklace's band gave them food and a cart to carry the children.[9]

At Fort La Framboise, Frank's Sioux wife Bright Eyes and other women provided the former captives with clothing and such amenities as soap. On November 26, leaving notes of thanks commending the Fool

---

[8]Diedrich, *Dakota Oratory*, 80; and Doane Robinson, "History of the Dakota," 309, 313n508. The speech is as Martin Charger remembered it years later. Swan Lake Creek is a Missouri tributary in northern S.Dak. "Proceedings of a Board Appointed to Negotiate a Treaty," (listed under "Misc. Military Papers" [Misc. MP] in the bibliography), 29, named Two Kettle band members Two Lance, One-that-Runs-After, Runs-Amongst-Them, Flying Bird, His-Horse-Runs, Watchful Dog, Fast Hawk, Two Tails, Good Bear, One-that-Runs-the-Enemy, Four Bears, One Rib, The-One-that-They-Laugh-at-While-Flying, and Small Cloud "for their efficient service in obtaining from the Santee Indians and bringing into the settlements, [by 1866] eight white prisoners."

[9]Lounsberry, *Early History*, 289; Oehler, *Great Sioux Uprising*, 113; Doane Robinson, "History of the Dakota," 308–14; and Buck, *Indian Outbreaks*, 99–112. Chase-the-Ree should not be confused with Chased-by-the-Ree (Yankton). For Black Hawk, see Holley, *Once Their Home*, 60. Robinson identifies the Yanktonais as Don't-Know-How and Fast Walker.

Soldiers, the rescued captives continued their journey escorted by two post employees. The mixed-blood escapee and his family joined them.[10]

ON NOVEMBER 25, ON POPE'S ORDERS, CAPTAIN ANDREW J. Millard brought his Sioux City Cavalry volunteers to Fort Randall to join John Pattee's Fourteenth Iowa troops. Because other companies of the Fourteenth had been decimated in the Civil War Battle of Shiloh in Tennessee, those at Randall would form part of a new Forty-first Iowa Volunteer Infantry Regiment. When the Galpins brought news of captives, Pattee, now a major, left Millard in command at Fort Randall and headed north to the rescue with one company and a small artillery contingent. Two days out, Pattee's force met the former captives and their escorts. Because Pattee had orders to station troops at Fort Pierre, he proceeded on, but he sent letters back to newspapers in Cedar Falls and Sioux City describing the former captives' ordeals. Continuing to St. Louis and then east, Galpin also talked to reporters. Eagle Woman remained at Fort Randall, where her stepdaughter, Louise Picotte De Grey, the post interpreter's wife, was caring for the Galpins' two daughters. They and other women at the post nursed the refugees waiting to rejoin their families.[11]

Near the trading posts, Pattee learned from the Fool Soldier band—in flux but now comprising 500 or so Two Kettles, Yanktonais, Hunkpapas, and even a few Santees—that White Lodge and his followers were camped about 200 miles upriver at Painted Woods Creek near present Wilton, North Dakota. Instead of pursuing them, Pattee left Company B, Captain Bradley Mahana commanding, at Fort Pierre to protect the traders and prevent Santees from "encroching upon the settlers below." Hiring Zephyr Rencontre's grown son, Alex, to carry mail between Company B and Fort Randall, Pattee trundled his seventeen-man artillery battery home.[12]

[10]Gray, "Santee Sioux," 51; Cf. Doane Robinson, "History of the Dakota," 308–14; Eliza Charger reminiscence; Martin Charger biography, 11–13; Pattee, "Reminiscences," 285; Kingsbury, *History of Dakota Territory*, 255–57; U.S. Bureau of the Census, 1860 unorganized Dakota Territory census, family 1220, p. 123; and Hal Porter, "Battle of Whitestone Hill: A Pictorial and Historic Record," Porter scrapbook vol. 2, SHSND Archives (hereafter cited as Porter scrapbook).

[11]Fort Randall PR, Jan. 1863, reel 988, M617, NA; Wieneke narrative, in Shambaugh, "Iowa Troops," 367, 381n34; and Gray, "Story of Mrs. Picotte-Galpin," 10–11, 14.

[12]Pattee, "Reminiscences," 284–89.

At the Yankton agency, Burleigh urged Commissioner Dole to procure President Lincoln's authorization to form a regiment to march against White Lodge and the others. With soldiers, he boasted, he would free all white captives by April 1 and take "enough scalps to carpet Pennsylvania avenue from the White House to the Capitol, if desired."[13]

Two days before the mass execution at Mankato, Burleigh and Jayne telegraphed Lincoln that Santee leaders Taoyateduta, White Lodge, Sleepy Eyes, and Pawn, along with the Upper Yanktonai chief, Big Head, were wintering on the Missouri and "murdering all the whites in that region." They urged Lincoln to encourage Pope to act quickly "if they are to be captured." In addition, James McFetridge, a legislator on his way to Yankton from Pembina, a settlement in the far northeast corner of Dakota, reported 1,200 Sioux warriors wintering at Devil's Lake. They had access to ammunition and supplies at the Red River settlements, and he thought they likely would join Taoyateduta's forces to attack Americans come spring. In January, Pope placed John Cook, a newly promoted brigadier general, in charge of organizing a summer campaign.[14]

IN JANUARY 1863, A FRIGHTENED FUR TRADER CAME TO FORT Randall to alert Major Pattee that some Santee families camped near him had several pieces of white people's clothing. Pattee took action on his own, justifying himself to General Cook on his return. The settlers, he wrote, "both white and half-breeds" felt insecure while these starving Indians were "camped in the neighborhood." Because "these Ih-santees claimed to be Yanktons and were thus approaching the settlements for no good purpose," Pattee told Cook he "concieved it my duty to capture them." Accordingly, he sent food as an enticement with his invitation for the Santees to meet him. With Second Lieutenant James M. Bacon, a sergeant, two corporals, and fifteen Dakota Cavalry privates, Pattee suffered through a January snowstorm to reach the trader's cabin, where they found seven lodges of Indians, all claiming to be Yanktons or Yanktonais. The trader gave them the location of several more tipis and, after six days in the field, the detachment returned to Fort Randall with thirty-one prisoners—nine men and twenty-two women and children.

[13]Burleigh to Dole, 17 Nov. 1862, "Digest of Indian Commissioner Reports," 307.

[14]Williams, Burleigh, and Jayne to Lincoln, 24 Dec. 1862, OR, vol. 22, pt. 1, p. 867; Wilson, "Old Fort Pierre," 302; Pattee "Reminiscences," 288–89; Fort Randall PR, Jan. 1863, reel 988, M617, NA; and McFetridge report, 23 Nov. 1862, in "Digest of Indian Commission Reports," 307–308.

Believing more Santees might be camped in the area, Pattee sent Bacon with a detail to find them.[15]

When one of his prisoners—perhaps the one whose feet were frozen when he was arrested—died in the Fort Randall guardhouse, Pattee announced the death to General Cook this way: "I have the honor to report that I have been relieved of the care and custody of one of the Ihsantee prisoners just captured. Last night at Retreat he received orders from the Commander in chief of the universe to take up the line of march for the 'happy hunting ground' and obeyed with great reluctance." Pattee "had positive proof" that this man, one of Yankton chief Medicine Cow's brothers, had been "engaged in the massacre at Yellow Medicine." What the proof was, he did not say. Three Dakota Cavalry troopers claimed to know some of Pattee's prisoners and declared them "notorious thieves and cut throats" belonging to Inkpaduta's outlaw band blamed for the 1857 Spirit Lake massacre. Someone identified White Lodge's son, Buffalo Ghost, who had "three times been a prisoner in Minnesota and three times escaped unpunished."

Because some captives claimed to be Yanktons, Pattee sent for Struck-by-the-Ree and interpreter Colin Campbell. After they and other chiefs questioned each prisoner individually, Pattee released four men for lack of evidence, along with the women and children, among whom were children of Yankton chiefs Pretty Boy and Feather-in-the-Ear. Ultimately, Pattee kept seven men of mixed Santee and Yankton parentage, who, he explained to Cook, "convicted themselves of having participated in the massacre in Minnesota" or admitted they were there during it. "So the Yankton chiefs decided." No one heeded Pattee's recommendation that they be tried in Minnesota. They remained in his guardhouse.[16]

THE IOWA COMPANY AT FORT PIERRE SINCE DECEMBER FOUND quarters there cramped; therefore, Captain Mahana sent some men to

---

[15]Pattee, "Reminiscences," 290n48; Pattee to Cook, 28 and 31 Jan. 1863, Fort Randall LS, 1856–67, RG 393, NA; and Fort Randall PR, Feb. 1863, reel 988, M617, NA.

[16]Pattee "Reminiscences," 290–91 (includes "So the Yankton" quote); Diedrich, *Odyssey*, 67; Fort Randall PR, Jan. and Feb. 1863, including SO 6, 1st Mil. Dist., Dept. NW, 8 Feb., RG 94, NA; and Pattee to Cook, 28 Jan. (includes "notorious" and "three times" quotes), 31 Jan. (includes "I have the honor" and "Yellow Medicine" quotes), and 24 Feb. 1863, Fort Randall LS, 1856–67, RG 98, NA. Pattee received the order to free the children 21 Feb. The adult prisoners were Lightning, The-One-that-Runs-Twice, Good Elk, Crazy Wind, Bursted Rock, The-One-that-Throws-His-Medicine, and The Grandfather.

make camp near Fort La Framboise, where they constructed their own dirt-roofed cabins from logs they cut and dragged across the frozen river. Their neighbor, Frank La Framboise, whose mother was a Sisseton chief's daughter, was under suspicion of selling ammunition to Santees. In early February Pattee ordered Lieutenant Marvin R. Luce, commanding the cantonment, to investigate and arrest La Framboise and shut down his business if Luce found evidence against him. Although either Zephyr or Alex Rencontre also accused La Framboise of mistranslating details of Yankton chief White Crane's report of some Santees' location and intentions, La Framboise apparently withstood the scrutiny.[17]

The real worry as spring approached was the likelihood Santees would attack Fort Pierre. When Bone Necklace's Yanktonais and the remnants of Bear Rib's mixed band returned from winter quarters, the soldiers welcomed them as protectors. As Sergeant Amos Cherry, aware of the Yanktonais' bad reputation, assured friends back home, these particular Indians "have allways befrended the whites and are treated very kind by them in turn." He told how soldiers prepared a feast to thank the Fool Soldier society for rescuing the Minnesota captives and served it "with as much gusto as could be expected of an Astor House" waiter.[18]

Cherry thought young chief Bear Rib—called Son of Bear Rib by those who remembered Mato-cu-wi-hu by that name—a "noble" young man. He especially admired Crazy Dog or Fool Dog (Tashunka-witko), a tall, commanding man with fine features, who that winter traveled with Eagle Woman's brothers White Hawk and Two Lance hundreds of miles to rescue eleven-year-old Melvina Ingalls from Santees at Painted Woods Creek. They were unable to rescue two captive white boys, and White Lodge vowed to have his remaining prisoners' scalps "in his belt when he fights the white men next spring," according to Sergeant Lambert A. Martin. Nonetheless, Cherry told his friend that Crazy Dog was always welcome "to our quarters and our table" for rescuing Melvina.

---

[17]Wieneke narrative, "Iowa Troops," 367, 381n34; Porter scrapbook, vol. 2; Gary Anderson, *Kinsmen*, 106; G. Hubert Smith, "Fort Pierre II," 92–93, 108; Pattee, "Reminiscences," 288; Doane Robinson, ed., "Fort Tecumseh and Fort Pierre Journals," 217n287; Gary Anderson, *Kinsmen*, 66–67, 106; Drips, *Three Years*, 25; and Pattee to Luce, 4 Feb. 1863 and Pattee to Cook, 18 Feb. 1863, Fort Randall LS, RG 393.

[18]Pattee to Mahana, 4 Feb. 1863, Fort Randall LS, 1856–67, RG 393, NA; and Cherry letter, 7 May 1863, in Shambaugh, "Iowa Troops," 412–16. White Crane and Mrs. Galpin's brothers, White Hawk and Two Lance or Drags-the-Stone, were among those feted, as were Bone Necklace, Red Dog, Red Vine, Fool Dog, and Scratch, "a noted chief of the tribe." Accounts of the second rescue effort differ, but Cherry's is contemporary.

Even General Cook rewarded Crazy Dog with ponies confiscated from other Indians.[19]

Early during the August war, the Mdewakantons Cut Nose and Shakopee had captured Melvina and killed her father, Jedediah H. Ingalls. By the time Crazy Dog rescued her, Cut Nose was in U.S. custody but Shakopee was in exile north of the border. Melvina is "most all the daytime with the soldiers and they pet her beyond description," Martin wrote his sister.[20]

Meanwhile, Bear Rib brought word that some militant Hunkpapas, Sans Arcs, and Sihasapas were coming to Forts La Framboise and Pierre to trade. Cherry acknowledged the soldiers feared trouble but felt sure they could hold out "against any odds." At the Fool Soldier dinner, Bone Necklace and Eagle Woman's brother Drag-the-Stone or Two Lance vowed to fight alongside their hosts. Unlike Cherry, Sergeant Martin worried the fort could only muster "a handful . . . We are at the mercy of the red men, if they only knew it."[21]

When militant Indians heard General Cook's troops were coming, some 1,200 to 1,300 lodges from most Sioux bands met in March in the Black Hills to decide what to do. Two Sihasapas from Bear Rib's peace band attended, leaving friends to worry the Hunkpapas would hold them captive. "We are anxious to know our future career, whether it is to combat these Indians or receive them as friendly," Martin told his brother.[22]

As winter gave way, sutler Charles P. Booge brought badly needed supplies to the camps between the fur posts and news that, with the river so low, General Cook would allow no boats up until the expedition set out sometime in June. Consequently, Mahana confiscated for his soldiers the provisions Booge had brought to trade to Indians. According to Martin,

[19]Description from Custer, *Boots and Saddles*, 36. Samuel Brown's recollections, Gary Anderson and Woolworth, *Through Dakota Eyes*, 74–79; Pattee, "Reminiscences," 316; Gray, "Story of Mrs. Picotte-Galpin," pt. 1, 11; and Martin to sister Mary, 23 Feb. 1863, Martin Papers, Yale Beinecke Library. Fool Dog later signed with Lower Yanktonais on one treaty and with Hunkpapas on another. Cherry letter, 7 May 1863, in Shambaugh, "Iowa Troops," 412–16; Gary Anderson and Woolworth, *Through Dakota Eyes*, 70–79.

[20]Martin to sister Mary, 23 Feb. 1863, Martin Papers, Yale Beinecke Library; and Myers, *Soldiering*, 6. Age from Gray, "Story of Mrs. Picotte-Galpin," pt. 1, 11–12; Pattee "Reminiscences," 304–305, 305n65 (note 65 is out of place). See also Brown's account, Gary Anderson and Woolworth, *Through Dakota Eyes*, 73, 75–76. A Sioux City physician's family took Melvina Ingalls (variously spelled) in.

[21]Cherry letter, 7 May 1863, in Shambaugh, "Iowa Troops," 412–16. Two Lance as Drag the Stone is from Gray, "Story of Mrs. Picotte-Galpin," pt. 1, 11; Martin to "Dear friends at home," 12 May 1863, Martin Papers, Yale Beinecke Library.

[22]Martin to brother, 28 March 1863, and Martin to "Dear Friends at home," 12 May 1863, Martin Papers, Yale Beinecke Library.

when Booge was unable to offer a traditional feast, the Indians "killed one of his oxen, made a feast and told him to leave this country for they would trade no more with him."

Even some in the Fool Soldier band were "getting most confounded bold and troublesome," Martin grumbled. Nevertheless, he was learning to speak Sioux and told his brother how "gay and festive" the Indians looked when they came inside the fort to dance. On one occasion, La Framboise rewarded the dancers with tobacco, brass rings, and paint, and Lieutenant Luce gave them thirty pounds of flour. Martin told his family he was smitten with "a young lady of 16 . . . superior in looks and intellect, yes[,] who far excels any eastern damosel in any manner you may suggest. Be not surprised if I should either tary in the Territory or take a damosel of the forest with me to the east."[23]

At Fort Randall, Pattee learned through Yankton informers that White Lodge planned to come south to steal horses from whites. Had not an alarming number of his men—fifty-four—been sick, Pattee would have relished the opportunity to apprehend them. Instead, he asked Cook to send a company of cavalry to Fort Randall. A few days later, the Yanktonai chief Big Head surprised Pattee with a visit. "He talks but little but I understand that he gives himself up to the Whites and is willing to follow their advice." Pattee allowed him to return to Fort Pierre, "where large numbers of Indians are now collecting." Pattee also learned Santees were "dividing into small parties for gurilla warfare," and "are receiving aid and Council constantly from the British above Pembina."[24]

The dreaded visit from some 800 lodges of militant Hunkpapas and Sihasapas to Fort Pierre worried Pattee enough that he asked Cook's permission to take another company of soldiers there by the first boat. However, the actual visit happened first, and Sergeant Cherry described it as peaceable. At least, they "gave no insult sufficient to bring on a fight." With the Iowans already on half rations and in danger of running out in ten days, had the Indians demanded food, Cherry believed "every man of us would have died at once" rather than give up his meager provisions. Instead, the visitors, who seemed to have plenty to eat, laid out a feast for the resident band and tried to persuade them to "leave here and make those fellows with the blue coats leave allso." In council, Bone Necklace

[23]Martin to "Dear Friends at home," 12 May and 17 Apr. 1863, Martin Papers, Yale Beinecke Library. For Booge, see Wolfe to Smith, 13 May 1863, Fort Randall LS, 1856–67, RG 393, NA; and Levering, "Recollections."

[24]Pattee to Smith, 1 April 1863, Fort Randall LS, 1856–67, RG 393, NA.

told them his band would "stand by the traders" who had provided for them all winter.

After the Hunkpapa group left Fort Pierre, a relieved Pattee turned his attention to longstanding accusations post sutler John B. S. Todd and others had made against him. In a very long letter dated March 18, Pattee had defended himself, but on that same day, he received conflicting reports concerning hundreds of lodges of Brulé Sioux camped three days' distant from Fort Randall. Pattee requested to go to regimental headquarters in Sioux City, and in early May, he left Captain George Wolfe of Company G in charge of the post to contend with the Brulés. Wolfe had other alarming news for Cook. He had received reliable intelligence that five war parties Taoyateduta sent out to investigate Cook's expedition's progress were set to attack settlers between Fort Randall and Sioux Falls.[25]

Pattee's prisoners claiming to be Yanktons were still in the guardhouse. Wolfe asked a Hunkpapa mail carrier, Antoine LeClare, down from Fort Pierre, to identify them. LeClare accused Lone Grandfather, a son of White Lodge, of capturing his in-laws at Yellow Medicine during the war, and he identified two Yanktons as horse thieves. LeClare added his indictment against La Framboise, saying he had refused to feed Indians friendly to whites in favor of four lodges of Santees that winter. Wolfe vouched for mixed-blood LeClare's verity, telling Cook he "comes well recommended from Fort Pierre and seems to be much more intelligent than the average of his class of being."[26]

Daily reports of small numbers of Santees near Randall never came in time for Wolfe to do anything about them. When the Brulés moved to within a mile of the post, ostensibly to trade, Wolfe, calling them "impudent and sassy," ordered them farther from the garrison in order to preserve grass for his own stock. Because they came mounted with no old people accompanying them, leaving their lodges some twenty miles away, they looked like a war party. They refused to go, saying the land was theirs. When Wolfe denied them food unless they moved, they did, but Wolfe feared they would return with reinforcements. General Cook complicated matters by ordering that a detachment of Dakota Cavalry be sent to investigate an attack on two white men sleeping in their freight wagon five miles from Vermillion. While the forty cavalrymen were

[25]Cherry letter, 7 May 1863, in Shambaugh, "Iowa Troops," 413; Pattee to Smith, 5 April and 3 May 1863; and Wolfe to Smith, 13 May 1863, all in Fort Randall LS, 1856–67, RG 393, NA. Cherry's 7 May letter is on pp. 412–416.

[26]Wolfe to Smith, 17 May 1863, Fort Randall LS, 1856–67, RG 393, NA.

gone, Wolfe would have only fifty men at Randall. Reinforcements, Wolfe told Cook, were an "imperative necessity."[27]

Once the river thawed, prospectors began descending the Missouri in mackinaw boats. At Fort Pierre, Sergeant Martin heard of one group supposedly carrying "350 pounds of dust or $60,000 worth of gold" from the mines. With little snow in the mountains, the river was low enough to ford in many locations. If the usual June "rise" did not come, steamboat navigation might be impossible.[28]

Nevertheless, General Cook began readying his forces for the summer's campaign in earnest after the Sixth Iowa Volunteer Cavalry arrived at Sioux City and the Second Nebraska Cavalry joined them at a camp on Big Sioux River bottomland. The former Fourteenth, now the Forty-first, merged with the Sioux City Cavalry to form four companies—a battalion—of the Seventh Iowa Volunteer Cavalry Regiment. Cook answered Wolfe's plea by ordering a Sixth Iowa battalion under Major Edward P. Ten Broeck to Fort Randall; they would accompany Pattee in pursuit of the same Hunkpapas, Sans Arcs, and Sihasapas who had visited Pierre and who supposedly now were moving toward Randall. Another Sixth Iowa battalion would garrison Fort Randall under Lieutenant Colonel Samuel McLean Pollock.[29]

Pattee and Ten Broeck were away when Pollock arrived, and while he was waiting to cross to Fort Randall, Pollock noticed Seventh Iowa men ferrying Indians and demanded an explanation. The corporal in charge said he was following Pattee's order. Pollock, carping that "if Iowa boys are here only to cross Indians, they had better go home," immediately countermanded it. Cook had told him to treat all Indians above Fort Randall as hostile. Furthermore, Cook advised, the best way to tell if Indians were friendly or hostile was to "examine their livers." A delegation of Yankton chiefs soon called on Pollock, expecting the customary hospitality of a modest meal. Instead, Pollock told them "he had come to give them a feast of cold lead and was prepared to issue it at once." They had five minutes to break camp and one day to move six miles from the fort.[30]

---

[27]English, "Dakota's First Soldiers," 267–68; and Wolfe to Smith, 17 May 1863, Fort Randall LS, 1856–67, RG 393, NA. See also Doane Robinson, "History of the Dakota," 329.

[28]Martin to "Dear friends at home," 17 April 1863, Martin Papers, Yale Beinecke Library.

[29]Pope to Halleck, 18 May 1863, OR, vol. 22, pt. 2, p. 288; Pattee, "Reminiscences," 292–98, 297n61, 301n63; and Fort Randall PR, July 1863, reel 988, M617, NA.

[30]Martin to "Dear friends at home," 21 June 1863, Martin Papers, Yale Beinecke; Cook's 26 May 1863 GO 14; Pollock's orders in "To Whom it May Concern," 6 June 1863; and Pollock's 8 Feb. 1864 testimony, all in "Proceedings of a Board of Investigation," Abraham Moreland service records, box 8263, RG 94, NA; Pattee "Reminiscences," 294.

Pollock heard rumors of a large body of Indians rendezvousing near the earth lodge village on the James River known as the "Dirt Lodges," where the Drifting Goose and Sweating Lips Yanktonai bands lived. Thinking it a war council, he sent Captain T. W. Burdick with sixty men to engage any Indians there. They found only seven, who opened fire, then attempted to flee, but ultimately surrendered. Burdick learned other Indians had planted corn at the dirt lodges earlier, then headed west to the Missouri. Under threat, the prisoners revealed the trail these others had taken to Medicine Lake, some fifty miles distant. No one was there, and at Fort Randall, his prisoners "gave such an account of themselves" that Pollock released them. (While Ten Broeck and Pattee were away at Fort Pierre, Pattee's prisoners escaped.)[31]

ABRUPTLY, THE MILITARY CAMPAIGN HAD A NEW LEADER. IN MID-May, General-in-Chief Halleck telegraphed Pope that Brigadier General Alfred Sully "had better take General Cook's place." During Harney's Sioux Expedition, Captain Sully had commanded one of the two Second Infantry companies that wintered at Fort Pierre during 1856–57. Therefore, he knew the country and probably a number of Upper Missouri Sioux leaders. From his stints at Fort Ridgely before and after his Pierre posting, he also knew some Santees. Furthermore, Sully had earned his general's star commanding the First Minnesota Volunteer Infantry at such major Civil War battles as Antietam and Fredericksburg. During the same Second Bull Run Battle that Pope had bungled, Sully had performed superbly. After Sully arrived in Minnesota, Pope, who wanted his own man, warned that Sully's "health [is] not strong enough for active campaign." Halleck was insistent. "Sully is the man for that place."[32]

Receiving Pope's order to take charge of the Iowa District and the expedition on May 21, Sully immediately set about undoing Cook's and Pollock's disastrous Indian policy. On June 6 he instructed his officers and men that not all Indians should be treated as enemies. He, Sully, would "designate what tribes, and in what sections of the country the

---

[31]Drips, "To the Dirt Lodges," in *Three Years*, 28–29; and "Wičíyela of Middle Dakota," 3. They were located near present Ashton, S.Dak.

[32]Pope to Halleck, 18 and 19 May 1863 and Halleck to Pope, 19 May 1863, OR, vol. 22, pt. 2, p. 288; SO 69, Dept. of NW, 21 May 1864, OR, vol. 53 (supplement), p. 558; Fort Randall PR, June 1863, reel 988, M617, NA; Cozzens and Girardi, *Military Memoirs*, xix, xx; and Gary Anderson, *Little Crow*, 117. For Sully's Civil War record, see Moe, *Last Full Measure*.

Indians are to be considered hostile and so treated." However, on June 14, 1863, a cavalry detachment acting under Pollock's old order added kindling to an already red-hot situation. In a letter home, Sixth Iowa Private Milton Spencer remarked that the "truth, as near as we can get at it puts the conduct of our men in rather bad light."[33]

The incident began when Sergeant William Newman, looking for his straying horse, came upon some Indians. Although he later admitted an antelope was also running away in the same direction he was, he returned to Fort Randall accusing Indians of shooting at him. Next morning, Pollock detailed Captain A. B. Moreland and nine men to investigate. They found Indians along Ponca Creek, which originates in present Tripp County, South Dakota. By most accounts, the Indians neither resisted nor tried to escape and willingly gave up their arms. The elderly Two Kettle chief Puffy Eyes (also called Pouting Eye) showed the soldiers General Harney's note vouching for his good character. Then, apparently believing the soldiers released them all, the Indians started to walk away. The soldiers fired, killing seven, including Puffy Eyes. Galpin later identified the victims as belonging "partly to the Two Kettle band, partly to the Brulés and partly to the Yanktons," and deemed them all friendly to whites.[34]

Pattee learned of the debacle from the lone survivor who fled, wounded, to the Sioux camp near Fort Pierre. On his return to Randall, Pattee played the diplomat: "I went out to the camp alone without arms of any kind and . . . told them I was sorry for what had been done and asked them to wait until the general came up and I would try and get him to make some suitable arrangement with the families . . . I stayed in the camp for hours to show them that I was willing to trust to their good judgment. This I thought was the only way to avoid trouble." Acting Dakota governor John Hutchinson called the killing of the seven "an unfortunate affair" and commended the victims' friends for making no "hostile demonstrations" afterward.[35]

---

[33]Sully's GO 22, 6 June 1863, quoted in Farb, "Military Career," 34; Spencer's quote from Goodwin, "Letters of Spencer," 244–45.

[34]"Proceedings of the Board of Investigation," Jan. and Feb. 1864, in Abraham Moreland service record, box 8263, RG 94, NA. Witnesses were Pollock, Newman, Moreland, Sgts. Eben M. Jones and Charles F. Hobbs, Prvts. Ely W. Townsend and Ezriah Herrington, Charles Galpin, and Capt. Miner. See also Drips, *Three Years,* 33; English, "Dakota's First Soldiers," 265; Goodwin, Spencer to Father and Sister, 5 July 1863, in "Letters of Spencer," 245–46; and Holley, *Once Their Home,* 292–93.

[35]Pattee, "Reminiscences," 292–95; Hutchinson to Dole, 23 Sept. 1863, no. 67, and Latta to Dole, 27 Aug. 1863, no. 80, CIA annual report, 270–73, 288–89.

Sully was incensed about the affair. From Sioux City on June 17, he raged at Pollock, whose report had mysteriously not reached him. Sully told him to arrest the guilty parties and await his arrival. In defending himself to Sully, Pollock cited Cook's order—which deemed it "a fair representation" that "every Indian met is our enemy." Sully arrested Pollock, and Captain George H. Wolfe took command. Newly promoted Lieutenant Colonel Pattee would command the District of Iowa at Sioux City while Sully took the field. Because Sully was taking almost all the troops with him, he worried the killings might incite "Indians we leave in our rear, to revenge." Settlers might pay "perhaps with their lives, for this injudicious, outrageous act."[36]

Later, when the Sully-appointed board of investigation looked into the seven murders, Captain Moreland, a lawyer in civilian life, was the accused. Military justice did not call on the lone survivor to testify; neither civil nor military justice allowed Indians to testify against whites. The version that emerged was that while some men searched for the missing horse, Moreland and Sergeants Charles F. Hobbs and Eben M. Jones herded the prisoners toward Fort Randall. They had not gone far when Moreland ordered Hobbs and Jones to shoot them. The board decided to require "no further action on the subject."[37]

LOW WATER AND HIGH WINDS DELAYED UPPER MISSOURI steamboat travel and, consequently, Sully's 1863 campaign. With the Fort Pierre landing out of reach, the *Shreveport* discharged its welcome freight at Fort La Framboise May 27, and by early June, the area between the posts metamorphosed into a supply depot.

Private Spencer, arriving with Ten Broeck's Sixth Iowans, was shocked to find the Fool Soldier band so hungry they would exchange moccasins worth $1 in Sioux City for a few hard crackers. Fifty pounds of flour would buy an $8 or $10 buffalo robe. Rations for the Iowans who were now Company L of the Seventh also were dangerously low, and with two

---

[36]Cook's 26 May 1863 GO 14; Pollock to "To Whom it May Concern," 6 June 1863; Burleigh to Sully, 15 June 1863; Sully to Pollock, 11 and 17 June 1863; Pollock to Sully 19 June 1863; Moreland to Pollock, 14 June 1863, all in the "Proceedings of the Board of Investigation" in Abraham Moreland service record, box 8263, RG 94, NA; Fort Randall PR, June through November 1863, reel 988, M617, NA.

[37]Pattee "Reminiscences," 293; and Sully's GO 9, Dist. of Iowa, 26 Jan. 1864, in Abraham Moreland service records, box 8263, RG 94, NA. The inquiry ended 18 Feb. 1864. See also Scott and Kempcke, "Journey," 6–7.

soldiers suffering from scurvy, the garrison particularly needed fruits and vegetables. Animals also suffered. When someone set the already drought-dry prairie afire, burning thirty or forty miles of grassland between the Bad and Missouri Rivers, area Indians, traders, and soldiers were all outraged, some blaming bumbling Sixth Iowa soldiers; others, militant Sioux.[38]

As more troops and supplies arrived, the Sioux grew increasingly defiant. When the *Shreveport* tried to pull away from Fort La Framboise on June 9, some 400 to 500 gathered on shore and some grabbed the lines to hold the boat. The *Shreveport* did not have their annuities; this year the *Robert Campbell* would bring them.

Pattee and Ten Broeck, just arriving at the new fort's construction site with their men, were the ranking officers. When they chose not to punish the Indians, many Iowa soldiers, Minnesota events fresh in their minds, believed their commanders forfeited an opportunity for a fight. The boat's log, however, records only that people at Fort La Framboise "informed us that the Indians were getting very saucy and that we had better keep a sharp lookout for them."[39]

All along the Upper Missouri, people waited for Sully. Near deserted Fort Clark the crew picked up some Arikaras and Hidatsas who had harvested corn at the nearby abandoned Arikara village. However, a hard frost had killed most other vegetation. They said they were starving and would have to abandon their own country unless soldiers came to protect them from the Sioux. Hidatsas, Arikaras, and Mandans fought Sioux several times during the winter and spring near a new Fort Berthold—actually deserted Fort Atkinson, which the AFC bought after Sioux burned the original Berthold in 1862. The three tribes rejoiced to know the president was sending enough soldiers to potentially "whipp the whole Sioux nation."[40]

According to the *Shreveport*'s log, game was abundant near the mouth of the Yellowstone. On June 8 "buffalo could only be counted by acres." Yet at Fort Union, meat supplies were low because hunters feared attack. At Fort William—the La Barge, Harkness, & Company post—Sioux had killed two employees and stolen all the livestock.[41]

The *Campbell*, carrying Indian agents and annuities, did not leave St.

[38]Cherry letter, 7 May 1863, in Shambaugh, "Iowa Troops," 412–16; Goodwin, "Letters of Spencer," 244; and Pattee, "Reminiscences," 294.

[39]Drips, *Three Years*, 25–26; "Log of the *Shreveport*," 27 May 1863, Montana State Historical Society Archives Collections (hereafter cited as *Shreveport's* log); "Log of Steamer Robert Campbell," 275 (hereafter cited as *Campbell's* log).

[40]*Shreveport's* log, 1, 3, and 6 June 1863 (quote in 6 June entry).

[41]*Shreveport's* log, 4, 8 and 9 June 1863; and Sunder, *Fur Trade*, 235, 240, 244, 251–52.

Louis until the *Shreveport* was past Fort Union. Knowing the army's plans and dreading this 1863 trip, Agent Latta appealed to Dole to take seriously the Sioux threats made at Fort Pierre before Mato-cu-wi-hu's murder. He reminded Dole the only way the *Shreveport*'s captain had been able to navigate through Sioux country the previous August was by planking the boat's pilothouse and bow against attack. Some 600 emigrants—including two large overland parties leaving Minnesota well before August 1862—had traveled by wagon to Fort Benton. Latta expected more river and overland travel this summer and feared Indians would attack emigrants and try to confiscate government property.

The Blackfeet [Siksika] tribe's agent, Henry Reed, complained to Dole that even with some $70,000 worth of goods between them on board and with women and children among the thirty or so passengers, he and Latta were not "allowed even thirty soldiers to go along to help to protect *us* or our goods." The campaign was about to start; Sully insisted he could spare no soldiers. Like Harney, Sully disparaged the Indian Bureau. If they were afraid, he told Reed and Latta, they could "travel behind him to Fort Berthold." Reed scoffed, "At the rate they [the soldiers] have already come, [Berthold] could be reached probably next August."[42] Not since Harney's time on the Upper Missouri were the military and the Indian Bureau at such cross-purposes there.

When the *Campbell* reached the trading posts on June 25, Latta found the non-reservation Indians waiting for him "in a suffering condition." They accepted their goods with gratitude but expressed exasperation about the Randall killings. To compensate for the seven, some of whom he knew "had periled their lives in procuring the release of Minnesota prisoners from the Santees," Latta distributed special gifts.[43]

The *Campbell*'s log caught the mood. "The savages sit around on the earth in silent groups that brooks evil to the white man. All are painted and armed." A crewmember noticed several women with their legs cut to express grief for the seven killed men. Decades later, Eagle Woman Galpin remembered the Two Kettle chief, Long Mandan, asking the agent for monetary compensation for what he termed a massacre. This chief whom Harney had praised for killing the man who shot the bell at old Fort Pierre was not so eager now to please whites. When cash

---

[42]Pope to Halleck, 18 May 1863, OR, vol. 22, pt. 2, p. 288; Pattee "Reminiscences," 296–98, 297n61. Latta to Dole, 7 March 1863, no. 73; Stanton to Secretary of the Interior, 24 March 1863, no. 77; Dole to Usher, 19 June 1863, no. 78; and Reed to Dole, 11 June 1863, no. 79, all in CIA annual report, 284–88.

[43]Latta to Dole, 27 Aug. 1863, no. 80, CIA annual report, 288–89.

reparation was not forthcoming, Long Mandan shook his fist in the agent's face, vowing, "I'll get pay for them."[44]

Private Spencer learned that some of these Indians planned now to leave for the Platte River country to hunt buffalo.[45] Perhaps another purpose of the trip was to solicit Oglala and Brulé aid against Sully.

Upriver, the agents learned that only days earlier several hundred Sioux attacked Fort Berthold and the Arikara, Mandan, and Hidatsa villages, driving off all the horses. When the *Campbell*'s captain, Joseph La Barge, noticed a large Sioux war party following the boat, Latta distributed guns designated for Indians to unarmed passengers. (A crewman later said Latta traded the best Indian goods to passengers for his own profit.)[46]

On July 2, the *Campbell* met the *Shreveport*, captained by Joseph La Barge's brother John, coming downstream. Because Sioux had stopped the *Shreveport* upriver from Berthold, John intended to escort his brother upstream. Three days later, while the crew chopped and loaded wood, Indians on the south side of the river fired at the *Campbell* and tried to board her. About fifty miles below the Yellowstone's mouth at a place known as Tobacco Gardens, several hundred Indians again threatened the *Campbell*. That night, with Sioux on both banks, the brothers anchored their boats near one another in the middle of the river. On July 7, the Indians, identifying themselves as Hunkpapas, Miniconjous, and Sihasapas, demanded that the boats land. Former Frost and Todd employee Henry Boller, who was aboard the *Campbell* on his way to the mining districts, understood enough Sioux to translate what they were chanting—whites were dogs fit to kill, and they intended to kill them. A few in the band wore new blankets, coats, and pants that were part of annuity distributions just made at Pierre. The Two Kettle chief Long Mandan was probably among them. According to Eagle Woman, he led a group far upriver to intercept the agents' steamboat and avenge the seven Sioux killed at Randall.

Hoping presents of coffee, sugar, and tobacco would appease them, Latta asked Joseph La Barge to send out the *Campbell*'s rowboat to bring some chiefs and headmen aboard for talks.[47] Passenger Alexander Culbertson's Blackfeet wife warned against it. Nevertheless, six unarmed men

---

[44]Ibid.; Boller, *Among the Indians*, 359, 357–75; and *Campbell*'s log, 26 June 1863, 275, 275n2. See also Chittenden, *Steamboat Navigation*, 298–314; Sunder, *Fur Trade*, 244–48; Holley, *Once Their Home*, 291–93; and Goodwin, "Letters of Spencer," 248. *Campbell* pilot C.J. Atkins annotated the log later for publication.

[45]Goodwin, "Letters of Spencer," 248.

[46]*Campbell*'s log, 27 June 1863, 275, 275n3. The AFC bought Fort Atkinson in 1862.

[47]Boller, *Among the Indians*, xxix; and Holley, *Once Their Home*, 291–93.

boarded the yawl and paddled to shore. As Latta told it, "the moment the yawl touched the shore several Indians seized it; others ran up, shook hands with the men, sprang back and commenced the slaughter by shooting and stabbing." Reed took up the story: "[The Indians] rushed on the men and killed three, and severely wounded the fourth, so that but two men escaped . . . by one falling down in the boat and the other throwing himself over the side." Like Latta on the *Campbell*, Reed had dispersed guns to unarmed men on the *Shreveport*. Under fire from about 300 rifles, double-barreled shotguns, and the boats' three cannons, the Indians disappeared into the thick brush. Later, someone told Latta the Indians lost thirty-eight killed, forty wounded, and five dead horses during the three-hour fight called the "Tobacco Gardens Massacre."[48]

After burying the dead, the *Shreveport* and *Campbell* continued upriver without further incident. On the way down, they stayed together, passing Tobacco Gardens again on July 14. The *Campbell*'s log reported "no foe" there and the three graves undisturbed. After its crew stockpiled wood at Berthold and the boat was under way, two Indians fired from the bank but vanished when those aboard returned fire. The crew kept a double guard at night and only stopped once at the mouth of Grand River to bury a chambermaid. Both boats reached the Forts La Framboise and Pierre area on July 22.

Relief was short-lived. At Crow Creek Reservation, where Sully had halted his army, soldiers fired across the *Campbell*'s bow, ordering her to stop or be sunk. Joseph La Barge convinced Sully his boat could not carry the loads required, but Sully impressed the *Shreveport* to serve with other boats engaged for the expedition. Refusing, John exchanged boats with Joseph, who complied.[49]

Pollock's outright hatred, Pattee's ambivalence, and an ordinary soldier's fascination are examples of the gamut of regard white soldiers gearing up for the campaign had for the Sioux. Such attitudes seemed both cause and effect of incidents between them over the months following the Minnesota conflict and certainly contributed to the growing belief among all Sioux that they could not trust white soldiers to distinguish between peaceable and war-minded people. The summer's military expedition would further strain any equilibrium that persisted.

[48] *Shreveport*'s log, 7 July 1863; and Holley, *Once Their Home*, 291–93.

[49] Latta to Dole, 27 Aug. 1863, no. 80, and Reed to Dole, 16 Aug. 1863, no. 81, CIA annual report, 288–90; Athearn, *Forts of the Upper Missouri*, 104–106; *Shreveport*'s log for dates given; *Campbell*'s log, 277–84; Wolfe to Courtwright, 5 Aug. 1863, and Wolfe to Pell, 8 Aug. 1863, Fort Randall LS, 1856–67, RG 393, NA. See also Sunder, *Fur Trade*, 246–48, and Chittenden, *Steamboat Navigation*, 304–19.

Chapter 9

Babies on the Battlefield

GENERAL POPE'S CAMPAIGN PLAN CALLED FOR SULLY, WITH HIS predominantly cavalry force, to ascend the Missouri in order to simultaneously cut off any Sioux that Sibley's Minnesotans forced toward the river. Accordingly, on June 16, 1863, General Sibley started west with a five-mile-long column comprising 2,000 infantry, 800 cavalry, and a light artillery battery. More than 200 wagons carried ninety days' rations for the 3,300 soldiers, teamsters, and other non-combatants along with supplementary feed for thousands of head of livestock. His was not an army of disinterested mercenaries: many had lost friends, family, and property during the Minnesota violence and had fought Sioux during 1862.[1]

At Fort Abercrombie Sibley weeded his command, leaving behind twenty-nine invalids. He left another third of his force entrenched at a camp they named "Atchison" between the Sheyenne and James Rivers. On July 21, with Pierre Bottineau and former Indian agent Joseph Brown guiding, his culled army of 1,400 infantry and 500 cavalry crossed the James River onto the *couteau*, or hilly country, bordering the Missouri River. Some Red River mixed-blood hunters told them of Sioux camped west of Devil's Lake. Sibley headed there, and around noon on July 24, scouts galloped in with news of a large body of Indians on the move less than three miles away. Sibley ordered his men to throw up earthworks and make camp beside a nearby lake. Soon, clusters of Indians showed themselves on hilltops.[2]

A scout recognized a relative among one of the groups, the Sisseton chief Scarlet Plume, who had opposed Taoyateduta's war, and went to meet him. Scarlet Plume warned that others planned to invite Sibley

---

[1]Pope to Kelton, 30 March, 303–304, and 1 June 1863, 304–305, OR, vol. 22, pt. 2; and Kudelka, *March*, 59.

[2]Fort Abercrombie PR, Aug. and Sept. 1863, reel 694, M617, NA. Other sources for the events come from OR, vol. 22, pt. 1, as follows: Report no. 1 by Sibley, 7 Aug. 1863, 352–59; Report no. 2 by McPhaill, 5 Aug. 1863, 359–60; Report no. 3 by Crooks, 5 Aug. 1863, 361–64; Report no. 4 by Marshall, 25 July 1863, 364–66; and Report nos. 4 and 5 by Baker, 5 Aug. 1863, 366–72. These reports are cited by author's name in the notes (e.g., "Sibley's report").

and his officers to a council and ambush them. Surgeon Josiah S. Weiser, wearing his officer's uniform, approached the Indians who were talking to the scout, and immediately a young man from Inkpaduta's band, perhaps mistaking Weiser for Sibley, came forward and shot him. Sibley's scouts retaliated as warriors emerged from behind low hills to surround the army on all but the lakeside.[3]

When Sibley ordered Colonel Samuel McPhaill of the First Minnesota Mounted Rangers to recover Weiser's body, a full-scale engagement began. Leaving three companies of Rangers dismounted to skirmish with Indians materializing out of the surrounding hills, McPhaill ordered Captain E. M. Wilson to advance on foot with three other Ranger companies, supported by three more mounted companies, to fire on the main body of Sioux. Two mounted companies drove the Sioux about two miles away, where McPhaill, with Lieutenant Colonel Marshall's Seventh Minnesota Infantry protecting his flanks, charged those holding the highest hill, called Big Mound. Meanwhile, part of the Sixth Minnesota Infantry under Colonel William Crooks held off a large number of warriors threatening the camp.

Sergeant J. W. Burnham, Tenth Minnesota Infantry, described the scene: "The lonely lake, the rocky hills, the naked, yelling Indians, soon discomfited and flying, the battery of four guns all doing their best, the charging cavalry with sabers drawn, the infantry following, while over all was the darkened sky, the heavy rolling thunder and the incessant lightning with but little rain."[4] Sibley, on high ground with the battery, watched Indian families file away on distant hills while his soldiers engaged between 1,000 and 1,500 warriors. McPhaill's charge pushed them from the hills and ravines onto the plains. During the downhill part of this action, lightning struck and killed Private John Murphy of the Rangers, seriously injured another man, and knocked McPhaill's saber from his hand. Despite this, McPhaill rallied four companies for a forward push at the Indians who, by then, were dug in near their own camp. The soldiers soon dislodged them, and a running fight ensued. Two shots from a six-pounder cannon confirmed the Indians' decision to flee.

Sibley sent the Rangers after them with companies of the Seventh and Tenth regiments commanded by Marshall marching double-quick

[3]Beck, *Inkpaduta*, 121; Gary Anderson and Woolworth, *Through Dakota Eyes*, 273–78; and Van Nuys, *Inkpaduta*, 277.

[4]Sibley's report, 352–53; Burnham diary, 24 July 1863, quoted in Lounsberry, *Early History*, 297–98. Lounsberry erroneously puts Burnham in the 6th Minn. Inf. See Kudelka, *March*, 103.

behind in support. Captain John Jones, with one six-pounder cannon and a section of howitzers, accompanied them. The Rangers chased the Indians some fifteen miles, killing and wounding many before darkness ended the fighting. Instead of setting up camp where they were, as Sibley remembered ordering him to do, McPhaill, obeying what he thought were his orders, led his exhausted men back to the main camp, arriving at 5:00 A.M. Including the previous morning's march, they had covered some forty miles.

Four men were wounded, one seriously, and three cavalrymen died during the nine-hour Battle of Big Mound—Murphy from lightning, Lieutenant Ambrose Freeman by an Indian attack while he was hunting, but only one, Gustav Stark, from combat.[5] Next day, Sibley sent fresh men to pursue the Indians from where the Rangers left their trail the night before. Soldiers buried their own dead, then burned and destroyed equipment and household effects left in the abandoned Indian camp and strewn across the prairie. Early on July 26, Sibley pushed his army after the Indians. Before the soldiers were finished establishing camp near Dead Buffalo Lake, some eighteen miles from Big Mound in present Kidder County, North Dakota, warriors appeared. At first, fighting was long-range. Captain Jones drove them off with his field pieces, but they returned in greater force in a flanking maneuver. The Rangers and two Sixth Minnesota companies held off those attempting to stampede the mule herd grazing on the lakeshore. A battalion of Sixth and Ninth men, supported by a battery section, fiercely fought other warriors until they retreated, uncharacteristically leaving some dead behind.[6]

On July 28, while on the march near Stony Lake, the soldiers discerned a large force of perhaps 2,000 Indians moving rapidly toward them. Sibley took immediate steps to protect his long wagon train while Colonel J. H. Baker's Tenth Minnesota checked the Indians' frontal advance. At one point, Baker heard an Indian on a hill yell to another, "We are too late; they are ready for us." Another answered, "But remember our children and families; we must not let them get them." The Seventh and the Rangers defended the wagons' left side while artillery fended off attackers elsewhere. The number of warriors was sufficient to enclose the army in about a five- or six-mile, 240-degree arc. Intense firing on both sides ceased when Sibley pulled his men into formation and closed

---

[5]McPhaill's report, 359–60; Sibley's report, 354; and Kudelka, *March*, 74–75.

[6]Patch, diary, 26 July 1863, A.P294, MNHS Archives (hereafter cited as Patch diary); and Crooks's report, 361–62.

up his wagon train. Warriors fired some parting volleys and, "with yells of disappointment and rage," quickly retreated. Sibley considered Stony Lake the most significant of the three fights. Baker declared it "numerically, the greatest effort the Indians had yet made upon the forces of the expedition."[7]

Sibley had to admire his foe, calling the engagement a "last desperate effort of the combined Dakota bands to prevent a farther advance on our part toward their families. . . . No such concentration of force has, so far as my information extends, ever been made by the savages of the American continent." Sibley guessed nearly 10,000 men, women, and children had comprised their camp. Estimates of Indian casualties varied from soldier to soldier. A scout named Edward Patch counted nine dead men and two dead women at Big Mound. McPhaill's Rangers killed some thirty-one at Big Mound and Dead Buffalo Lake. Although artillery must have killed and wounded a considerable number, Baker's men saw only three Indians fall.[8]

From his scouts' conversations with the Indians, Sibley learned he had fought Sissetons, Wahpetons, Cutheads, and Yanktonais. He judged the latter the most powerful Sioux band. Because of the Indians' individualistic mode of fighting, the Sisseton chief Standing Buffalo, the Wahpekute chief Inkpaduta, and the Lower Yanktonai chief Two Bear all were credited with generalship. Standing Buffalo tried to stay out of the conflict, but his warriors' only option at Big Mound was to fight. Among other leaders thought to have fought Sibley in 1863—willingly or not—were the Sissetons Pretty Lodge, Standing Buffalo's brother Handsome Boy, Sweet Corn, White Lodge, and Young Sleepy Eyes; the Mdewakanton chief Little Six (Shakopee); and Medicine Bear of Black Catfish's Upper Yanktonai Band-that-Wishes-the-Life. Some Hunkpapas and Sihasapas who crossed the Missouri to hunt joined the fighting at some point.[9]

By the time Sibley reached the Missouri, Indian families were on the west bank. As the warriors crossed, Sibley turned his six-pounder cannons on them but did not attempt further pursuit. From bluffs on the

[7]Sibley's report, 353–59.

[8]Patch diary, 24 July 1863; McPhaill's report, 360; Kudelka, *March*, 74; and Baker's report, 369–72. John Platt, Co. L, wounded at Dead Buffalo Lake, died 28 July.

[9]Sibley to Meline, 2 Sept. 1863, OR, vol. 22, pt. 1, p. 910; Beck, *Inkpaduta*, 119–22; and Josephy, *Civil War in the American West*, 142–44. Band affiliations deduced from Council reprint and from Diedrich, *Odyssey*, 51–52.

west bank Indians taunted the soldiers by flashing sunlight at them with mirrors. One yelled across that the Indians did not want to fight the whites. Nevertheless, they shot at soldiers trying to fill their canteens. Their bows, arrows, and old guns, however, were no match for the soldiers' better weapons.[10]

Making camp near Apple Creek, Sibley ordered destroyed some 130 to 150 abandoned Indian wagons and carts. A few Sioux still lurked on the east side of the river. Sibley's aide, Lieutenant F. J. H. Beaver, whom Colonel Crooks described as "an English gentleman, of qualities worthy of the best, a fellow of Oxford University," disappeared after delivering an order to the Sixth Minnesotans to stop scouring the woods. Sibley sent up rockets as signals, but neither the lieutenant nor a missing Sixth Infantry soldier responded. The next day, a detachment found them both. Beaver had been shot with three arrows. "Like most of the army [Beaver] wore his hair short," one soldier remarked, "and the Indians had cut around his head endeavoring to scalp him, but were unable to pull it loose." Instead, they "scalped the long whiskers from one of his cheeks. The soldier, having longer hair, was scalped in the usual manner." Sibley's men also did some scalping. "We have 40 of their topknots in our possession," one man boasted in a letter home. A Seventh Minnesota man later told of a camp rumor that, after Indians set a grass fire and tried to stampede the army cattle, someone left "messes of beans seasoned with strychnine" for Indians to find. Theodore Carter, Seventh Minnesota Infantry, had no proof but "little doubt as to its having been done, for there [were] many men in our command who had lost friends by the hands of the savages, and some had been rendered frantic from the abuse of their wives, daughters or sisters."[11]

When Sully did not show up after a week, Sibley knew that the planned coordinated effort against the Indians was a failure. He started his army back to Minnesota. A detachment he sent to sweep the prairie near Devil's Lake came upon a half-dead boy who, to their amazement, turned out to be Taoyateduta's son, Wowinape. A Seventh Minnesota man in the detail wrote home that "when we found him he was hard up . . . his thyes isent larger than my arms." Wowinape confirmed that Taoyateduta had

[10]Patch diary, 28 July 1863. See also Capt. J. W. Burnham's diary, 29 July and 31 Aug. 1863, p. 300, as excerpted in Lounsberry, *Early History*, 297–302 (hereafter cited as Burnham diary).

[11]Crooks's report, 361–64; Burnham diary, 30 July 1863, 300; Herb Watson to father, 16 Aug. 1863, in Charles Herbert Watson Papers, MNHS Archives; and Carter, "Reminiscence," in "Theodore G. Carter manuscript," p. 28, MSS 20007, SHSND Archives (hereafter cited as Carter reminiscence).

been to the Missouri that spring trying to recruit Mandans, Arikaras, and Hidatsas to join his war against the whites. Those tribes not only rebuffed the Santees, they attacked them. His efforts thwarted, Taoyateduta headed for the Turtle Mountains and the international border. Early in summer, however, the chief and a small party returned to Minnesota on a horse raid. While Taoyateduta and Wowinape were picking berries near Henderson, a farmer who did not know the chief shot him. Wowinape prepared his father's body as best he could, then wandered on the prairie some twenty-eight days until Sibley's forces found him.[12] Later, Wowinape was tried and found guilty of horse theft, murder, and complicity in the 1862 conflict. Although sentenced to hang, he was ultimately released and lived to age eighty-eight.

Instead of giving Chief Taoyateduta the burial Wowinape prepared him for, whites brought his body into Henderson and deposited it in the street. Among other defilements, boys lighted firecrackers in the decapitated head's ears and nostrils. At some point, adults dismembered the body in order to prove Taoyateduta's identity by some anatomical peculiarities and then disposed of the rest of it on a garbage heap. The Minnesota Historical Society displayed a few of Taoyateduta's body parts until 1971, when it turned over his meager remains to his family to bury during a private ceremony at Flandreau, South Dakota. Wowinape's son attended that belated burial.[13]

Sibley's battle dead totaled two, with one killed outright and another dying later from his wound. His expedition, however, suffered four murders by Indians, one suicide, seven deaths from fever, one of a wound unrelated to battle, and one by lightning. On the way home, Chaska, one of Sibley's thirty-two Santee and mixed-blood scouts, became sick and died within an hour. Theodore Carter suspected friends of teamster George Brackett of poisoning Chaska because they suspected him of murdering Brackett when he disappeared during the early part of the march. However, Brackett turned up alive at Camp Atchison in "pitiable" condition after five days alone on the prairie. Carter commented, "Chaska was exonerated, but just the suspicion of treachery had cost him his life."[14]

Sibley considered the campaign "highly satisfactory." It routed "vigilant," "powerful," "confident" enemies, inflicting perhaps 150 casualties,

---

[12]King, "Private Morton," 16. Wowinape's account and Brown's recollection are in Gary Anderson and Woolworth, *Through Dakota Eyes*, 279–82, 272–73.

[13]Sibley to Meline, 23 Aug. 1863, OR, vol. 22, pt. 1, pp. 908–909; and Carley, *Dakota War*, 83–86.

[14]Carter reminiscence, 27, 29–30.

then drove them in "confusion and dismay, with the sacrifice of vast quantities of subsistence, clothing, and means of transportation, across the Missouri River . . . to perish miserably in their utter destitution during the coming fall and winter." Now the Sioux knew from experience, first, government soldiers could reach them in their own country and second, warriors were "utterly powerless to resist the attacks of a disciplined force." Without the Missouri as impediment, Sibley contended, "the utter destruction of a great camp containing all their strength was certain." Despite his victories and low casualties, Sibley regretted not extirpating all those responsible for 1862 violence. Yet it gratified him that "the bodies of many of the most guilty have been left unburied on the prairies, to be devoured by wolves and foxes." The scout Edward Patch thought they achieved little. "We all feel disheartened and that the Indians have outwitted us though we have drove them from Minnesota."[15]

On September 2, Sibley, still marching homeward, received a message from Standing Buffalo, whose band had left the others after the battle at Big Mound. Standing Buffalo said that some Indians had recrossed the Missouri, intending to winter at Devil's Lake. He described survivors as frightened and utterly destitute. In addition, many Sioux had drowned crossing the Missouri. He said seven chiefs were willing to exchange murderers who had attacked some miners in a mackinaw boat in return for peace. Sibley knew nothing about the miners and was amused the Sioux claimed no more than thirteen warriors killed at Big Mound, Dead Buffalo Lake, and Stony Lake when his command found forty-six dead on those battlefields. He believed their reluctance to acknowledge casualties was "characteristic of the race." Standing Buffalo would wait in the Dogden country near present Butte, North Dakota, for Sibley's answer to his offer to surrender on condition he would not be "sent a great distance nor held prisoner." Ultimately, instead of surrendering, he wandered indecisively over the prairie north and south of the border for years.[16]

BACK ON THE MISSOURI, FOUR COMPANIES OF THE THIRTIETH Wisconsin Volunteer Infantry Regiment guarded Sully's fleet of charter steamboats transporting men and supplies to the staging area known

---

[15]Sibley's report, 352–59; and Patch diary, 29 July 1863. See also McPhaill's, Crooks's, Marshall's, and Baker's reports, 359–72.

[16]Sibley to Meline, 2 Sept. 1863, OR, vol. 22, pt. 1, p. 910; and Diedrich, *Odyssey*, 53–54.

as Peoria Bottoms between Forts Pierre and La Framboise. When Dr. Burleigh noticed abundant food on these transports and demanded some for his starving Yanktons, George Rust, in charge of the army subsistence stores on board, not only refused, he persuaded the lieutenant commanding troops on the boat to put Burleigh under guard. Burleigh, who blamed Sully for the incident, later brought charges against the general for "habitual drunkenness rendering him unfit to perform his duties in a proper manner." Sully's soldiers also had antagonized Burleigh. With Yankton men away hunting when the expedition was at the reservation, some Second Nebraska cavalrymen had rummaged through empty lodges and disturbed the dead on their scaffolds to take away souveniers.[17]

Arriving at Peoria Bottoms the last week in July, Sully sent Sergeant Martin's Company L of the new Seventh Iowa Cavalry to Fort Thompson, the agency on the Crow Creek reservation.[18] A few other Iowa and Nebraska companies, Wisconsin infantrymen on loan from Sibley's district, and the Dakota Cavalry would stay behind to garrison Randall and Thompson, patrol the river, and build and defend a new military post near Fort Pierre.

Finally, on August 21, when Sibley's troops were well on their way home, Sully began marching his army north. He had 1,200 cavalry and a four-gun battery, along with wagons and drivers enough to haul ninety days of rations for the men and forage for 4,000 horses and mules. Although the expedition's quartermaster hired Galpin, back from his trip east, as Sully's chief guide and interpreter, La Framboise apparently replaced him.[19]

After a few days, this cumbersome army, traveling in four side-by-side columns with wagons and extra horses enclosed by horsemen, intersected a buffalo herd. Sully sanctioned a hunt, but called it off when he noticed the men "disabled more horses than buffaloes." On August 26, scouts discovered Indian women and children who claimed they were trying to find the Crow Creek reservation although they were heading north,

[17] Regimental Muster and Descriptive Rolls 1861–65, 30th Wisc. Vol. Inf. Rgt., Wisconsin Historical Society Archives; Martin to parents, 21 July 1863, Martin Papers, Yale Beinecke Library; Rust military papers, Reel 3, Dakota Conflict of 1862 MSS, MNHS Archives; and Pierce 5 July 1863 diary entry in Rowan, "Second Nebraska's Campaign," 29.

[18] Martin to parents, 4 July 1863 and 6 July addition to it, Martin Papers, Yale Beinecke Library.

[19] Sully's 1863 campaign is detailed in OR, vol. 22, pt. 1, pp. 565–68: See Report no. 1 by Sully, 11 Sept. 1863, 555–61; Report no. 2 by Wilson, 3 Sept., 561–64; Report no. 3 by House, n.d., 564–65; and Report no. 4 by Furnas, 6 Sept. 1863, 565–68. These reports are cited by author's name in the notes (e.g., "Sully report").

not south. Sully sent two Nebraska cavalry companies under Captain Dominick La Boo to capture anyone else on the trail. From the women, Sully learned Sibley had fought Indians somewhere near the head of Long Lake.[20] On the way there, in an area where numerous Indians had recently passed, the main army discovered an old man named Keg, lame and starving, hiding in some bushes. He said his band had taken his ponies and blankets, leaving him to die beside the river. Some soldiers who knew him—he had lived for years near Sioux City—vouched for him as a "good Indian." Sully had someone treat the inflamed sores on the old man's feet.

Keg said after Sibley's forces killed sixty-eight Indians during fighting about fifty miles to the northeast, Sioux scouts followed the army east until it crossed the James River. Then the main body of Sioux broke up, with some heading north but most returning to hunt buffalo near Long Lake. Other Sioux, Keg said, might be near the Missouri. Only a few days after Sibley left, Hunkpapas and Sihasapas from Black Moon's and Fire Heart's bands attacked a mackinaw of returning miners, killing everyone—twenty-one men, three women, and several children—and burned the boat. Keg said thirty Sioux died from fire, whereas Standing Buffalo counted ninety-one burned to death.[21]

Realizing his scouts might be in danger, Sully sent one Sixth Iowa and four other Nebraska companies to find them, only to have the original two units return the next day. La Boo's men, while marching 187 miles, lived off buffalo and other game as they scoured the country west to the Missouri. They saw no one but destroyed a small Indian camp. On its ninety-mile scout, the other party found nothing but treeless country with plenty of grass and stagnant lakes. A third scouting detail sent to Apple Creek located Sibley's fortified campsite but discovered no evidence of any mackinaw boat attack.

La Framboise was Sully's official translator and guide, but the "real guide," according to Sixth Iowa cavalryman Frank Myers, was Melvina Ingalls' rescuer, Fool Dog. Myers recalled how, on one scouting foray, he "caused considerable comment by sticking a couple of arrows in the

---

[20] Sully report, OR, vol. 22, pt. 1, pp. 555–56; Pope to Kelton, 1 June 1863, 304, and Pope to Halleck, 14 Aug. 1863, 451, both in OR, vol. 22, pt. 2; King to Libby, 14 Oct. 1914, 8, folder 9, box 32, Libby Papers, SHSND Archives; and Gray, "Story of Mrs. Picotte-Galpin," 11. See also Drips, *Three Years*, 41.

[21] Collins, "Larned," 50–52; and Belden, *White Chief*, 357. Black Moon and Sitting Bull were cousins (see Utley, *Lance*, 22). See copy of Fire Heart's map (H. H. Larned had the original), in Collins.

ground and refusing to inform the soldiers why he did it." Returning after dark, the troopers worried he had led them astray, but about midnight Fool Dog pulled those same arrows out of the ground.[22]

On September 3 Sully halted his army beside a lake near where Indians had recently killed a large number of buffalo. With La Framboise as guide, he sent Major Alfred E. House's 300-man battalion of Sixth Iowa Cavalry to find and attack Indians if they were few but otherwise to send for support. While riding ahead of House's men, La Framboise spotted up to 600 Sioux tipis in a ravine near a small lake southeast of Sully's location. Perhaps 1,200 warriors could muster from these families, who were putting up stores for the winter. Before he could report his discovery to House, upwards of 200 Indians surrounded him. From his years as a trader, La Framboise must have known, and might have had kinship ties to, many of these Sioux. Their message to Sully was boilerplate bluster. They "could not see why the whites wanted to come to fight them, unless they were tired of living and wanted to die." La Framboise rode back to brief Major House and, moving quietly between hills, guided the battalion to the Indian camp. As soon as House saw it, he sent La Framboise and two soldiers to alert Sully, some ten miles away with the rest of the force. When La Framboise reached Sully's camp at about four o'clock, he told him these were the same Sioux who fought Sibley—Minnesota Santees, Cutheads from the coteau, Yanktonais, and Sihasapas from west of the Missouri. (Sully later learned some Hunkpapas and perhaps some Brulés were also there.)[23]

The horses were grazing, but when the bugle sounded, Sully was pleased to hear his men cheer. In minutes they were saddled up and ready. Leaving four companies in camp, Sully took a position in the middle with the artillery battery and the Seventh Iowa and set off at full gallop, with the Second Nebraska on the left and the Sixth Iowa on the right. Nebraska private Joseph S. Phebus recalled men shouting encouragements to one another: "Remember New Ulm," "Don't shoot until you can see the whites of their eyes," and "Don't take any prisoners." Phebus claimed Sully had told them they would fight "under the black flag," a reference to the black flag Quantrill's Partisan Rangers flew to indicate they would

---

[22]Myers, *Soldiering*, 7; Z. T. Mullin speech at 3 Sept. 1909 Whitestone Hill battlefield monument dedication. See "Soldier Writes: Battle Was of 'Pathetic Scenes'" in Whitestone booklet, 14–15.

[23]Richards, in Drips, *Three Years*, 53–57; Luce, "Battle of White Stone Hill," 417–19; Sully's Whitestone report, 557–58. (Richards's account, though eyewitness, was reminiscent.)

give "no quarter" to prisoners. In reality, Phebus noticed, the expedition "had no flag at all."[24]

While waiting for Sully's reinforcements, House deployed his four companies, armed with carbines and pistols, "in four different directions." When the Indians became aware of the soldiers, Sergeant Elkanah A. Richards, Sixth Iowa, saw young warriors rush to a small lake near the camp and, "with a wild yell that still lingers in my ears," scrape up clay to daub on their bodies, "marking themselves hideously."[25]

House ordered Captain Lucien A. Ainsworth's Company C to reconnoiter from atop Whitestone Hill. When Indians came down the hill to meet him with a white flag, Ainsworth sent for House. The ensuing confab between a few officers and several chiefs was brief. Corporal Julius C. Luce remembered a hundred or so well-mounted Indians. "Every warrior . . . had a long pole on the end of which was fastened a white woman's scalp," or several in "all different colors of hair, yellow and brown and black." The Indians, some speaking English, said they wanted to smoke peace pipes with the soldiers and even offered to surrender some of their chiefs. House, however, demanded unconditional surrender. This may have been when, as Luce remembered, the chiefs "all suddenly stood up with their hatchets raised ready to kill the officers."[26]

Both parties backed off, but during the talk other troops kept advancing. When they all reached higher ground, House ordered his men to dismount and stand armed but not fire "under any circumstances."[27] Soldiers watched women and old men take down tipis while others continued to work on buffalo hides in various stages of drying and curing. Still others packaged meat in two- by three- by five-foot-long bundles weighing, Luce estimated, 300 or 400 pounds. It was a tense time. Sergeant Richards, who knew a little Sioux, heard young warriors yell, "Kill them, kill them! money plenty." Older men answered, "No, no these are all the soldiers there are. We will kill them at sundown." Richards had learned that sundown was the Sioux's favorite time to fight. As the soldiers continued to shift position and otherwise delay, "the hideous howl of the wolf-dog" and the "savage faces of the reds" were, Richards

---

[24]Phebus to Libby, 6 Dec. 1915, 4, folder 9, box 32, Libby Papers, SHSND Archives. For Quantrill, see Goodrich and Goodrich, *Black Flag*.

[25]Quotes by Richards are from Drips, *Three Years*, 53–57.

[26]Quotes by Luce are from Luce, "Battle of White Stone Hill," 417–19. Details of Whitestone battle are primarily from House report.

[27]House report, 564–65.

recalled, "enough to make the strongest heart nearly fail." The Sioux added war songs to the cacophony until, with a sunset as backdrop, the Second Nebraska arrived in advance of Sully's forces. Richards heard Indians cry out that "soldiers are coming out of the ground." Women hastened to take down the remaining lodges and pack the dog and pony travois. Families ran off in all directions with what they could carry, leaving some lodges standing.

Sully sent his Nebraskans to the right to help House and ordered his four fresh Sixth Iowa companies to surround the fleeing Sioux and drive them back. Thousands of people, horses, and dogs were trapped in a deep ravine. Although Colonel David S. Wilson, Sixth Iowa, and House thought the Indians opened the battle, Colonel Robert Furnas, Second Nebraska, reported that he had. When he realized how little daylight remained, he did not wait for a directive from Sully before ordering his men to dismount, form a battle line, and send out a volley from their Enfield rifles. This they did "with precision and effect, creating quite a confusion in the enemy's ranks."[28]

While fighting raged in the ravine, Sully led his Seventh Iowa body-guard, two Sixth Iowa companies, and the battery of four twelve-pounder mountain howitzers into the center of the Indians' camp, where he found the Lower Yanktonai chief Little Soldier and a few of his people. "This Indian," Sully reported later, "has always had the reputation of being a 'good Indian' and friendly." He left them under guard and, farther on, met the Upper Yanktonai chief Big Head and about thirty of his war-riors. Although dressed for battle, they had women, children, dogs, and ponies nearby. When the soldiers cut them off, Big Head surrendered himself and about 120 people.[29]

Leaving the Indians' camp, the general formed a battle line on hills overlooking the ravine and centered his battery on the highest rise—prob-ably Whitestone Hill—with his Little Soldier and Big Head prisoners under guard below it. The fight continued with soldiers dismounted in order to better their aim at enemies sometimes no more than forty to sixty paces away. Although one soldier thought he heard cannons roaring during the battle, he was mistaken. According to Sully, "The Indians had formed line of battle with good judgment, from which they could be dislodged only by a charge. I could not use my artillery without greatly

---

[28]Wilson report, 563–64; Myers, *Soldiering*, 8; House report, 564–65; and Furnas report, 565–68. Compare Sully report, 555–61.

[29]Sully report, 555–61.

endangering the lives of my own men; if I could, I could have slaughtered them." With gunsmoke deepening the darkness, Sully had such difficulty distinguishing his men from the enemy he feared friendly fire casualties. Finally, after one last "desperate resistance," the Indians gave up and scattered. Sully claimed he had the Nebraska riflemen—some of whom he considered among the best shots in the world—mount their horses and, with others, pursue them until his buglers called them in. However, Furnas was out of communication with Sully and, on his own, judged it too dark to do so.[30]

Sully believed that if there had been an hour or two more of daylight, he could have "annihilated the enemy." While army doctors ministered to wounded soldiers by firelight produced by burning the Indians' pine tipi poles, picket guards killed two more Sioux. Expecting to re-engage in the morning, Sully ordered buglers to sound rally call to collect his men on the Indians' deserted campground, where they remained under arms all night, arranged in a square with their mounts and the injured protected inside.[31]

By morning, only dead or dying warriors remained on the battlefield; those who were able slipped away during the night. Dead Indians were "found in so many different places" Sully and his officers estimated Sioux dead at 150 to 200. Knowing they always tried to remove their killed and wounded, Wilson doubled that estimate.[32]

According to Nebraska trooper George P. Belden's account in a book he later wrote, Indians, including women, overnight attacked "our helpless wounded with long-handled tomahawks, [and] beat their brains out, after which they took a butcher-knife and cut out their tongues." Second Lieutenant Thomas J. Leavitt, Company B, Sixth Iowa, with a serious leg wound, lay near his dead horse, unnoticed until one woman approached to ransack his saddlebags. She realized Leavitt was alive and struck him with her tomahawk, whereupon he "thrust at her with his saber, but could not reach her." She tried to kill him, and then called for

[30]Ibid., 558–60; Drips, *Three Years*, 44; Libby to Phebus, 30 Nov. 1915 and Phebus to Libby, 6 Dec. 1915, folder 9, box 32, Libby Papers, SHSND Archives; and Furnas report, 567.

[31]Pierce diary entry in Rowan, "Second Nebraska's Campaign," 48; and Sully report, 559. According to U.S. Naval Observatory web site, on 3 Sept. 1863, sunset was at 7:11 p.m. (Central time) and end of civil twilight was 7:42 p.m.

[32]Wilson report, 563–64. For Iowa and Nebraska casualties, see Wilson to Pell, 5 and 9 Sept. 1863, and Furnas to Pell, 9 Sept. 1863, in Secretary of War, "Expedition of Sully against the Northwest Indians," 38th Cong., 1st sess. 1 (1863), 503–504 (listed under "Misc. MP" in the bibliography). See also Andreas, *Andreas' History*, pt. 18, 2nd Neb. Cav.

help. With a half-dozen women attacking him, Leavitt slashed about
with his saber, severely wounding one. As her friends took her away, the
lieutenant fainted. "We found the poor fellow in terrible condition, and
brought him to camp," Belden wrote, where he died "after a day of great
suffering." Another Nebraskan, Private Francis E. Caldwell, saw thirty
dead Indians "piled and covered with stones and rubbish" among some
tipi wreckage. Along with "dead soldiers, dead Indians, dead horses,
[and] hundreds of dogs howling for their masters," he saw dead and
wounded women and about sixty children, still alive, of every age.[33]

While looking among debris for dried buffalo meat for the prisoners to
eat, Phebus found eight children huddling together. "This was a critical
time; our men had blood in the eye. If any one had said, 'nits make lice,'
they would have been destroyed." He cautioned the men, "We were sent
out after meat, these babies are meat, we will take them in. So on to the
wagons they went, and they were turned over to the prisoners." Belden
marveled how "the little babies, that the dogs were dragging about on
their travaises, never cried, but lay perfectly still, though the dogs galloped over ditches and gullies, shaking and jolting them at a terrible
rate." Because the soldiers could not always catch the dogs, they "shot
them, and it sometimes happened the dog would move, or the aim not
be good, when the baby, instead of the dog, would receive the ball." He
justified this: "If left out on the prairie it [the baby] would have starved
to death; if brought in, we had no way to keep it or take care of it, but if
dead it was at rest. Poor little creatures, however much we pitied them
we could not help them." Sully turned the surviving children over to
the prisoners.[34]

For some, fighting did not end on September 3. At daylight, Sully sent
out scouting parties to overtake Indians and search for some missing men.
About fifteen miles from the battlefield, First Lieutenant Charles W.
Hall, Company F, Second Nebraska, and his detail of twenty-seven men
from the Sixth Iowa and Second Nebraska skirmished with some 300
Indians. Perhaps Belden was describing this encounter when he related
how First Lieutenant John J. Bayne, Company L, Second Nebraska, and

---

[33]Belden, *White Chief*, 360–62; Wilson report, 563–64; and Caldwell's 1901 letter to 6th Iowa
Cav. veteran Jeptha M. Van Meter, quoted in Whitestone booklet, 12–14. Caldwell offered this
caveat: "This is the history of the battle of Whitestone Hill, as near as I can recollect, after the
lapse of nearly 38 years as seen from my point of view."

[34]Belden, *White Chief*, 366–67; Caldwell's 1901 letter in Whitestone booklet, 12–14. The phrase
"nits make lice" and its application to enemy noncombatants may be centuries old.

his searchers came across two Indians walking toward some bluffs. A guide warned the lieutenant they might be decoys, but Bayne ignored him. When he approached the two men, they disappeared into the rough terrain as, simultaneously, hundreds of warriors appeared and trapped the soldiers in a ravine. Sergeant Hugh S. Blair, Company K, directed Bayne's attention to the top of the bluffs where two lines of Indians were advancing toward them. Because Bayne seemed paralyzed, Blair took command. Responding to his orders, the soldiers wielded their sabers so effectively and with such zeal that they freed themselves.[35]

Officially, Hall reported little more than the outcome of this adventure to Sully. He admitted to a "retreat, without orders," in the face of so many enemies, but added that, even while retreating, his men killed six Indians, four ponies, and wounded an unknown number. These casualties matched his own losses—six men and four horses killed. Not long after Hall's party returned, the missing men they had gone to find turned up in camp. All told, on that day, eight Iowans died, and, of twenty-two wounded, three later died. Furnas reported two dead and thirteen wounded Nebraskans. In his own diary, Furnas wrote on September 5: "I found 4 stragling Indians who I killed[,] and brought in one small Indian prisoner."[36]

Over two days, the army burned many tons of dried buffalo meat, 300 tipis, and other Indian property. Wagon master Captain R. B. Mason estimated they destroyed a thousand pounds of buffalo meat alone. Estimates differed. Sully's, for example, went as high as 500,000 pounds. According to Private Caldwell, "After all the Indian property . . . was gathered in wagons, piled in a hollow and burned, melted tallow ran down that valley in a stream." They threw "hatchets, camp kettles and

---

[35]Sully report, 558–59; Hall's "Skirmish" report, 5 Sept. 1863, OR, vol. 22, pt. 1, p. 611; Phebus to Libby, 6 Dec. 1915, folder 9, box 32, Libby Papers, SHSND Archives; and Belden, *White Chief*, vii, 367–70, 370n. Belden's editor, Gen. James S. Brisbin, misidentifies Sgt. Blair, who died 5 Sept. 1863, as "Bain."

[36]Hall's "Skirmish" report, 5 Sept. 1863, 611; Sully report, 558–59; and Wilson report, 563–64, all in OR, vol. 22, pt. 1. For Iowa and Nebraska casualties, see Wilson to Pell, 5 and 9 Sept. 1863, and Furnas to Pell, 9 Sept. 1863, in Secretary of War "Expedition of Sully against the Northwest Indians," 503–504; Felthauser (Feltheizer) to Libby, 30 Nov. 1915, folder 9, box 32, Libby Papers, SHSND Archives; and Furnas and Pierce diaries, 5 Sept. 1863, both in Rowan, "Second Nebraska's Campaign," 24, 48. See also Andreas, *Andreas' History*, pt. 18: 2nd Neb. Cav. Felthauser claimed Furnas educated the boy. However, he may have mistaken this boy for an Oglala boy Furnas wrote about in response to the boy's obituary. See "John Sioux," *Nebraska Advertiser*, 19 Aug. 1869. I thank John Ludwickson and James E. Potter, Sr. Research Historian, Nebraska State Historical Society, for bringing the article to my attention.

all things that would sink" into a lake. What they did not destroy, they looted. Among Indian possessions left strewn about were rifles, cartridges, and boxes of army revolvers. On one Indian body, Colonel Wilson found letters enclosing gold dollars and gold dust, implicating him in the attack on the miners' mackinaw.[37]

Years after the encounter, William V. Wade, Dakota Territory rancher, legislator, deputy marshal, and author, overheard one of Two Bear's sisters tell of hiding in some bushes by Elm Creek after the fighting. While a soldier dismounted and lay on his belly to drink from the stream, she stole up and stabbed him, then hid again until a second soldier came by. When his horse mired itself in mud, then fell on its rider, she stabbed this man, too. She claimed both died, but perhaps they were the two men a Nebraska detachment found wounded on September 5 while "hunting an Indian in some tall grass."[38]

Sully was proud of his troops, most of whom had no battle experience, but he regretted the casualties. Among the 600 or 700 men actually engaged, he counted twenty killed and thirty-eight injured. Hundreds of horses and mules died in battle in addition to those Sully ordered killed because they were in bad condition. Possibly some casualties could have been avoided. According to Private Spencer, supported by Sergeant Drips, Colonel Wilson ordered men to mount up, "then, without giving the order to load their pieces, he marched them up to within thirty feet of the enemy, one company with their rifles unloaded."[39]

On September 6, Sully started his army and his 156 prisoners—32 men and 124 women and children—south. According to Drips, the Indians marched behind the mountain howitzers. One company rode guard, "keeping chiefs, bucks, squaws, pappooses, ponies and dogs, all hemmed in with men, horses, rifles, revolvers and sabres." Corporal Henry A. Pierce, Second Nebraska, called the prisoners "the most ridiculous looking outfit of human beings I ever saw." Private Caldwell recalled that the

[37]Furnas report, 567; Sully report, 559; Caldwell letter; Pierce 4 Sept. 1863 diary entry in Rowan, "Second Nebraska's Campaign," 47–48; and Wilson report, 564.

[38]Dickey County (N.Dak.) Historical Society, *History of Dickey County*, 25–30. See also Wade, "Wades Stories," in Paha sapa tawoyak'e/William V. Wade Collection, MSS 20038, SHSND Archives; Crawford, *Exploits*, 302; and Furnas 5 Sept. 1863 diary entry in Rowan, "Second Nebraska's Campaign," 24. Elm Creek is a tributary of Crow Creek.

[39]Spencer to Father and Sister, 18 Sept. 1863, in Goodwin, "Letters of Spencer," 251. See also Drips, *Three Years*, 45. For the Nebraska and Iowa dead, respectively, see Furnas's and Wilson's 9 Sept. 1863 reports in Secretary of War "Expedition of Sully against the Northwest Indians." See Andreas, *Andreas*, pt. 18, 2nd Neb. Cav. Other casualties are from Sully's Whitestone report and its appended list, 561.

children rode in two government wagons. One soldier watched another feed the children crowded into a wagon box by dumping an opened box of hard tack on them. The march was cruel, exhausting livestock and people alike. Rations were low. After seven days, the soldiers and captives reached the confluence of the Cheyenne and Missouri Rivers, where the steamboat *Alone*, carrying supplies and grain, waited.[40]

When the returning army neared the new military post's construction site, Sergeant Nelson N. Fuller and a Thirtieth Wisconsin detail brought dispatches for Sully. The wounded boarded the *Alone*, but Sully's army and captives resumed their brutal march south. The captured men called themselves "good Indians" who were forced into fighting when the others joined them uninvited. On the way, Sully learned from captive women that the same Hunkpapas who fought Sibley were among those who had attacked the mackinaw boat.[41]

Keg was among others who claimed Inkpaduta's band had been part of the Sioux force, and some said Inkpaduta had acted as the Indians' general at Whitestone. Inkpaduta may not even have been there, however. Late in life, Phebus, claiming he never heard of Inkpaduta, said "Two Bear was supposed to be a leader with them if they had any leader." He added that the ordinary soldier "generally knows but very little about what is going on at headquarters and often cares much less." Descendants of Sioux who were at Whitestone agree that Two Bear, despite being about sixty-six, figured prominently there.[42]

With his 156 Indian prisoners, Sully stopped only briefly on October 5 at the Crow Creek reservation's agency, Fort Thompson, where Company L, Sixth Iowa, replaced the Nebraskans, whose enlistments were up. Sully left what Whitestone Hill prisoners he had not freed or stashed at Crow Creek at Fort Randall, where Captain William Tripp's Dakota Cavalry Company A and the five Sixth Iowa companies who had been with Sully would remain the winter. Major Thomas Shephard, Sixth Iowa, commanded while Pollock remained under arrest until November 2. On

[40]Drips, *Three Years*, 48, 44–57; Pierce 10 Sept. 1863 diary entry in Rowan, "Second Nebraska's Campaign," 49; "Soldier At Whitestone Gives Eyewitness Account," Whitestone booklet, 12–14; and Unnamed veteran, in Dickey County (N.Dak.) Historical Society, *A History of Dickey County, North Dakota*, 25–30. See also Sully's, Wilson's, Furnas's, and House's Whitestone reports, 555–68; Scott and Kempcke, "Journey," 7; and Myers, *Soldiering*, 5.

[41]Nelson N. Fuller, Reminiscence, folder 32, box 20, Libby Papers, SHSND Archives; Pierce diary in Rowan, "Second Nebraska's Campaign," 49; and Sully's Whitestone report.

[42]Phebus to Libby, 6 Dec. 1915, folder 9, box 32, Libby Papers, SHSND Archives; and Beck, *Inkpaduta*, 123–25. Two Bear's age from birth/death dates (1797–1877) in Whitestone booklet, 4.

October 25, Shephard reported on Sully's Indian prisoners' condition: "The Children amoung them are destitute of clothing and suffering from the inclemency of the weather. Two of them have died the past week."[43] Even Pope wrote to Washington asking what to do with them, to no avail.

Shephard had other concerns as well. He ordered a detail of Dakota Cavalry to bring back some Winnebagos camped below Fort Randall opposite the Yankton Agency. When, meantime, ten additional canoe loads of Winnebagos fled the reservation, Shephard figured all he could do was warn Dakota Cavalry officers dispersed at Yankton and Vermillion to watch the river and try to stop further exodus. After taking back command at Fort Randall from Shephard in November, Lieutenant Colonel Pollock wrote headquarters for instructions concerning the 300 Winnebagos camped on an island seven miles above the post as well as the 140 Captain Nelson Miner, Dakota Cavalry, retrieved. Pollock believed rumors that "the balance of the Indians from the Crow Creek agency are now on their way and will be here in a few days." Although he considered his supplies too low to "warrant issues to them," Pollock had a large store of condemned pork and rice on hand. "I believe these Indians to be in destitute Condition[.] . . . Are they to be subsisted [the words 'or not' were crossed out]," he asked headquarters, "and if so, how?"[44]

In mid November, Pollock turned the Whitestone Hill prisoners over to the Yankton chief Little White Swan. "He has gone on a Hunt to the part of the County near where they were taken and can return these children and old Squaws to their tribes." Pollock sent a copy of the "invoice" for the prisoners to Sully's adjutant. The document, headed "Census of Indian Prisoners," includes thirty-one Sioux names, spelled out and translated. The nine males were all under age seven. The rest were girls, except for five women between the ages of thirty-three and eighty. All were either from the Sweat on the Upper Lip Lower Yanktonai sub band, from Two Bear's Lower Yanktonais (also called Hunkpatinas), or from Big Head's Upper Yanktonai Wazikute group. None was a Minnesota Santee.[45]

[43]Shephard to Pell, 25 Oct. 1863, in Ft. Randall LS, 1856–67, RG 393, NA.

[44]Thomas, diary, 13, 14 Sept. and 5 Oct. 1863, River Falls Area Research Center, University of Wisconsin (hereafter cited as Thomas diary). Thomas estimated 250 prisoners, but Sully's 11 Sept. report was "by actual count." Fort Randall PR, Oct. and Nov. 1863, reel 938, M617, NA; Shephard to Pell, 25 Oct. 1863, and Shephard to COS at "New Fort opposite Farm Island," Yankton, Vermillion, and Tackett's Station, 26 Oct. 1863, and Pollock to Pell, 6 Nov. 1863, all in Fort Randall LS, 1856–67, RG 393, NA; Pope to Kelton, 12 Oct. 1863, OR, vol. 22, pt. 2, p. 642.

[45]"Census of Indian Prisoners Taken at the Battle of White Stone Hill D.T. 3 Sept. 1863 (now confined here [Fort Randall])," in Pollock to Pell, 18 Nov. 1863, Fort Randall LS ledger, vol. 3; and "Wičíyela or Middle Dakota," 8. Little White Swan was also known as Little Swan or White Swan.

BECAUSE SO MANY INDIAN WOMEN AND CHILDREN DIED AT
Whitestone Hill, the Sioux regarded it a massacre. The loss of so much
property and food was catastrophic. In a 1915 stage play he wrote, an
Episcopal missionary presented the Sioux point of view as he heard it
from participants and descendants. Its premise was that Sully considered
the battle "all a mistake." Whether Sully had regrets or not, some of his
soldiers did. Decades later, Private Phebus's mixed feelings were apparent
when he wrote to an inquirer: "There was no glory in this whole campaign
not even a little bit for the general. . . . I don't care whether you call it
a battle or a massacre. I am a friend of the Indian, but I am glad that I
helped to drive them out of the Dakotas." Some soldiers questioned if
the Indians they fought were the guilty Santees they had been sent to
chastise. Sergeant Martin heard from returning soldiers that "only a part
of the Santees were engaged," and the Indians in the fight were those
living near Fort Pierre last winter and spring. Martin predicted "a big
Indian war in Dakota."[46]

Acting governor Hutchinson, as ex officio Indian agent, believed Sully's and Sibley's battles had only begun a wider war and recommended
another expedition. "These hostile tribes *must* be conquered, and *must*
be compelled to make new treaties" to ensure whites' safety in his super-
intendency. He commended Sully for overcoming obstacles to fight "a
glorious battle," and for "his persevering efforts and good generalship,
manifested throughout the campaign."[47]

Others thought differently. Mixed-blood interpreter Samuel J. Brown
wrote his father, Joseph, the former Santee agent: "I don't think he
[Sully] ought to brag of it at all because it was, what no decent man
would have done, he pitched into their camp and just slaughtered them,
worse a great deal than what the Indians did in 1862, he killed *very few*
men and took *no* hostile ones prisoners . . . It is lamentable to hear how
those women and children were slaughtered." Calling Whitestone "a
perfect massacre," Brown, whose mother was Sisseton, scorned Sully
for "saying that we need fear no more, for he has 'wiped out all hostile
Indians from Dakota.' If he had killed men instead of women & children, then it would have been a success, and the worse of it, they had no
hostile intention whatever." Nebraska veteran Phebus, late in his long life

---

[46]Beede, *Heart in the Lodge*, preface, SHSND Archives; Phebus to Libby, 6 Dec. 1915, folder 9,
box 32, Libby Papers, SHSND Archives; and Martin to brother Bill, 12 Sept. 1863, Martin Papers,
Yale Beinecke Library. For an analysis of the battle's ramification and for the historical value of
Beede's play, see Jacobson, "Battle of Whitestone Hill," 4–14.

[47]Hutchinson to Dole, 23 September 1863, no. 67, in CIA report, 270–71 (italics in original).

remarked of Whitestone: "It isn't every body that would acknowledge to being there."[48]

Henry Boller summarized the campaign in his book, *Among the Indians*, published around 1867: "The army took the field—the bugles were blown, the antelopes, badly frightened, sped over the hills, while from the distant bluffs 'the d——d redskins' defiantly waved their breech-clouts. Some few squaws were captured, and the army went into winter-quarters, the Indians having gone out of sight and the safety of the frontiers thus being assured." Pope wanted another campaign, but Halleck hesitated, saying Sully should continue to solicit treaty signatures. "If we want war in the spring a few traders can get one up on the shortest notice."[49]

Sibley and Sully, with nearly 5,000 troops between them, did not destroy or even discourage the Sioux. Sibley pushed his foe temporarily west and south of the Missouri. His modest victories left Sully's forces the ignominy of attacking and destroying a hunting camp where women and children were among the dead and comprised most of the captives. This first attempt to punish fugitive Minnesota Santees failed dismally and made enemies of former friends. However, Sioux warriors did learn what they were up against in fighting the U.S. army. That knowledge frightened some chiefs into signing Sully's peace treaty and others into desperately defending their territory and way of life.

---

[48]Samuel Brown to Joseph Brown, 13 Nov. 1863, quoted in Carley, *Dakota War*, 91 (Brown's italics); and Phebus to Libby, 6 Dec. 1915, folder 9, box 32, Libby Papers, SHSND Archives.

[49]Boller, *Among the Indians*, 358; and Halleck to Pope, 10 Oct. 1863, OR, vol. 22, pt. 2, p. 633.

Chapter 10

"A Reservation of Desolation"

WHILE SULLY AND SIBLEY WERE BATTLING SIOUX ON THE UPPER Missouri in 1863, the Santee Sioux men who had been judged guilty of 1862 violence but were not sentenced to die remained under military guard in Davenport, Iowa. In 1863, thirty prisoners died there of old age, disease, or cramped and unhygienic conditions. Newspaper reports blamed the prisoners for their own misery, contending that, rather than clothing and feeding the "murderous devils," the government should hang them. Other Sioux men who were innocent or helpful to whites during the outbreak worked as guides and scouts for Sibley in Minnesota, but he sent their families to the new reservation on the Missouri's east bank. Those families—1,306 Dakotas, most of whom were women, children, and old men—arrived by steamboat at Crow Creek Reservation on May 30, 1863, wretched, anxious, and sick. Thirteen died during the 800-mile river trip from Minnesota by way of St. Louis. Three groups of Winnebagos, 1,945 in all, arrived between June 8 and June 24. Before the trip, Winnebagos had killed and scalped three Sioux, perhaps in a misguided attempt to please Minnesota whites enough to let them remain in the state. Instead, the murders exacerbated fear and hatred between the new Upper Missouri neighbors.[1]

The Winnebagos, Sergeant Martin wrote his parents, "talk very good English and are near white as can be and not be white." As soon as they arrived, they began building a fleet of dugout canoes in which some hoped to return by the Missouri and Mississippi to Minnesota or, more realistically, to join their kinsmen, the Omahas, on their reservation downstream. Martin blamed food rationing, which began the month they arrived, for their dying at such a rate that "they will soon be out

---

[1]*Campbell*'s log, 2 and 24 June 1863, 271, 274; Lass, "Removal," 362–63; Thompson to Dole, 1 June 1863, no. 153, 424–25, 28 May 1863, no. 157, and 1 July 1863, no. 158, 437–41, all in CIA annual report; Mix to Dole, 21 and 29 May 1863, nos. 154 and 155, CIA annual report, 426–27; Pope to Halleck, 9 May 1863, OR, vol. 34, pt. 3, p. 532; Carley, *Dakota War*, 80–81; and "Indian Guard," *Davenport (Iowa) Democrat*, 3 Dec. 1863. The *Campbell*'s log mistakes the Winnebagos for Sioux.

of the way and some speculator will lament it and he only . . . for profit sake." He thought it "too bad to treat civilized Indians as these are now being treated," but said nothing of Sioux in the same situation.[2]

Observing the Crow Creek Indians' deplorable living conditions in July 1863, Sully petitioned Pope and the new secretary of the interior, John P. Usher, to allow a Winnebago transfer to the Omaha Reservation. Calling Sully's report to Halleck's attention, Pope said he had "little expectation that the Indian Department will be able to maintain the Indians [at Crow Creek] through the winter."[3]

Sergeant Spencer of the Sixth wrote his family that the reservation Indians' "morals and general behavior is much better than that of many of the soldiers. The white men they have to deal with would corrupt any community, and I wonder that the redskins are half as decent as they are." On the other hand, Sergeant Abner M. English, Dakota Cavalry, recalled how Te Maza, or Iron Door, in a fit of jealousy brutally beat his "handsome young squaw" and disfigured her face with his knife. When her friends petitioned Captain Miner to punish Te Maza, Miner thought it best to allow a panel of Indians to handle it. They decreed he should die but that the military should administer the sentence. When Miner refused, Te Maza's tribesmen decided the injured woman's fifteen-year-old brother should shoot him. With a military guard and a crowd witnessing, the frightened, trembling boy fired his rifle but missed. Instantly, "Te Maza sprang forward, brandishing a large knife which he had managed to conceal about his person, and slashing right and left, wounded several in a serious manner." The boy dropped his rifle and ran for cover as the crowd scattered. Miner, "the coolest man on the field" according to English, "drew his revolver and brought down" Te Maza.[4]

As the 1864 Sioux expedition came together, Sully did not need to whip up his soldiers' fighting spirit. While Private Henson Wiseman, Second Nebraska, was on duty at Crow Creek that summer, Indians had murdered his seven children at the family's northern Nebraska home. Only Wiseman's wife, on an errand at Yankton, survived. Without witnesses, many blamed White Lodge's and Inkpaduta's bands. Captain Wolfe sent out two First Dakota detachments, but neither could track

    [2]Martin to parents, 2 Aug. 1863, Martin Papers, Yale Beinecke Library; and Lass, "Moscow Expedition," 232–37.
    [3]Sulley [sic] to Secretary of the Interior, 16 July 1863, no. 159, 442–43, and Sulley [sic] to Meline, 15 July 1863, no. 161, 443, both in CIA annual report; Pope to Kelton, 18 Feb. and 30 March 1863, OR, vol. 22, pt. 2, pp. 117–18, 186; and Lass, "Moscow Expedition," 228.
    [4]Goodwin, "Letters of Spencer," 253; and English, "Dakota's First Soldiers," 303–304.

the perpetrators. Also, nearly simultaneously to the Whitestone battle, some Sioux attacked a stagecoach about forty miles above Fort Randall and killed passenger Sergeant Eugene F. Trask, Seventh Iowa. According to his friend Sergeant Martin, Trask was the "pet" of Company L. His killing "has raised a spirit of 'Indian hatred' to such a pitch that we would not feel fully avenged could we exterminate" all Indian people. Wolfe believed the Indians fled with the stolen stage horses to a group of mound houses on the James River known as the Dirt Lodges, where the Drifting Goose and Sweating Lips bands of Lower Yanktonais farmed and fished. However, only fifty-five men at Randall were fit for duty, and Wolfe had no cavalry to send after the attackers.[5]

On September 23, acting governor Hutchinson told Commissioner Dole such incidents had given militants an opportunity to vent their feelings. Now whites could distinguish friend from foe. Even so, he admitted that no one could tell if the Santees or Yanktonais were guilty, but it was "possible and probable" both were. He also considered Miniconjous, Hunkpapas, and some other bands "hostile."[6]

WHEN COMPANY F, THIRTIETH WISCONSIN, ARRIVED AT CROW Creek late in October 1863, Captain Edgar A. Meacham also assumed command of the Sixth Iowa Company already there. Because the Indian Department counted on the Sioux and Winnebagos instantly becoming farmers, it had only sent them subsistence provisions.[7] They arrived

---

[5]Wolfe to Pattee and Wolfe to Pell, 2 Sept., 1863, Wolfe to Pell, 4 Sept. 1863, Wolfe to Pattee, 5 Sept. 1863, and Wolfe to Trask, 20 Sept. 1863, all in Fort Randall LS, 1856–67, RG 393, NA; Martin to brother, 12 Sept. 1863, Martin Papers, Yale Beinecke Library; "Drifting Goose's Village," 2, and "Wičíyela or Middle Dakota," 2–3; Drips, *Three Years*, 23; English, "Dakota's First Soldiers," 267–69; Doane Robinson, "History of the Dakota," 329; Van Nuys, *Inkpaduta*, 263–66; and Beck, *Inkpaduta*, 123. James River earth lodges' inhabitants deduced, in part, from Pollock to Pell, 18 Nov. 1863, with attachment titled "Census of Indian Prisoners Taken at the Battle of White Stone Hill," both in Ft. Randall LS, 1856–67, RG 393, NA. Unless Wolfe dated his letter incorrectly, the attack was on or before 2 Sept.

[6]Hutchinson to Dole, 23 September 1863, no. 67, CIA annual report, 270–71.

[7]Meacham to Pell and to Shephard, 8 Jan. 1864, and Meacham to King, 1 March 1864 and 11 April 1864, all in Meacham order book, 30th Wis. Vol. Inf., Co. F., in Misc. records of Civil War regiments, Wisconsin Historical Society Archives (hereafter cited as Meachum order book); Lass, "Removal," 353–64; and Lass, "Moscow Expedition," 227–40. Co. D, 30th Wisc. stayed the winter at Fort Sully. Companies I and K, transport guards, left for Milwaukee in Aug. 1863. Other regimental changes in Thomas diary, 4, 5, and 15 May 1863; 11 July 1863; 2, 6, 10, and 12 Aug. 1863; 28 Sept. 1863; and 27, 28, and 29 Oct. 1863.

too late to plant, but the severe 1863 drought probably precluded a crop anyway. It became obvious that neither Indians nor soldiers would have enough to eat. According to missionary John P. Williamson, the agency daily fed its 3,000 wards about a quarter-pound of flour, pork, and corn each and had no extra food or medicine for the many ill Indians. After only a month at Crow Creek, 70 of the 1,300 Sioux had died.

Agent Saint Andre D. Balcombe was away from the reservation during August and September establishing his family at Sioux City and caring for his own sick child. Because the Indian Department wanted one agent to serve both tribes at Crow Creek, Chester Adams, whom Balcombe originally hired to supervise civilian employees, was in charge. Superintendent Thompson, the agency's namesake, was in Washington, D.C., but Adams kept him informed. It is possible Thompson did not act to assuage conditions at Crow Creek until he could be sure his friend James B. Hubbell and Hubbell's partner, Alpheus F. Hawley, would secure the contract for hauling emergency supplies overland from Minnesota to the reservation. When Minnesota newspapers questioned why it would not be easier and faster to procure goods from points lower on the Missouri, Thompson cited low water and the late season.

The relief expedition Hubbell began organizing at Mankato in October was so huge one editor called it the "Moscow Expedition" after Napoleon's disastrous wintertime Russian invasion. From concept to implementation, the Minnesota mission reeked of shady deals and greedy maneuvering to control Missouri River access to Rocky Mountain gold districts. With most able-bodied men at war in the South, attempts to recruit civilian teamsters failed. Pope allowed three Sixth Minnesota Cavalry companies—men just back from campaigning with Sibley—to fill in as teamsters. The reluctant soldiers sabotaged wagons and employed work stoppages to demand outrageous wages, forcing abandonment of ten to twelve wagonloads of food and supplies. The expedition's chief scout, William Duley, husband of White Lodge's former captive and executioner at the mass hanging, likely did not sympathize with the relief mission's purpose.[8]

Sully sent a Sioux City beef contractor to Crow Creek with army provisions, and Pollock acknowledged that Lieutenant Wallace Pattee (John's brother) delivered a hundred pounds of flour to the agency in mid

---

[8]Lass, "Moscow Expedition," 232–37.

October. After resuming command at Randall on November 2, Pollock seemed proud that he gave Indians no more than a hundred pounds of hard tack plus damaged and spoiled provisions considered unfit for soldiers. As conditions worsened at Crow Creek, Captain Meacham tightened security, ordering that no Indians, male or female, enter the stockade without a pass, even if they were on agency business. Soldiers would need passes to leave after retreat.[9]

The mile-and-a-half-long string of wagons—the Moscow Expedition—started west from Minnesota on November 5 and arrived at the reservation on December 2 with approximately 100 tons of provisions—mostly poor-quality flour and salt pork—and 500 or so tired, starving cattle. By then, not only had some 600 Winnebagos fled Crow Creek, now the Dakotas wanted to move to the Yankton reservation. When Pollock learned of the relief train's arrival, he saw a way to rid himself of the runaway Winnebagos General Cook had ordered him to detain and subsist at Fort Randall. He suggested Agent Balcombe send down a wagon train to transport them and their belongings back to Crow Creek. In mid-December, Pollock reminded headquarters he still had provisions "unfit for issue to troops" at Fort Randall. Perhaps he was creating a delay when, instead of just giving even this awful stuff to the Indians, he wondered in a letter if Sully thought he should give it out to them.[10]

The Moscow Expedition hardly helped relieve hunger at Crow Creek. As an emergency measure, Superintendent Thompson, who came with the train, ordered a huge, thirty-barrel-capacity box filled with soup for the masses. In January 1864, Williamson wrote his colleague, Reverend Stephen R. Riggs, that "they put into [this box] 600 lbs beef 100 lbs pork & 1 brl flour—filled up with water & turned the steam from the sawmill into it all night & give it out." An appalled army surgeon called this gruel—which included hearts, entrails, heads, and lungs of cattle—offensive, and said what settled to the bottom smelled like carrion. In February and March, Williamson led several hundred Sioux and Winnebagos on a buffalo hunt. While they were gone, someone got rid of the trough and returned to a ration system.[11]

---

[9]Pollock to Pell, 24 Nov. 1863, Fort Randall LS, 1856–67, RG 393, NA; and Meacham order book, SO 6, 24 Nov. 1863.

[10]Sibley to Pope, 6 Feb. 1864, OR, vol. 34, pt. 2, 265–66; Meacham to Pell, 12 Dec. 1863, Meacham order book; Lass, "Moscow Expedition," 238–39; Pollock to Balcomb [sic] 7 Dec. 1863, and Pollock to Pell, 17 Dec. 1863, both in Fort Randall LS, 1856–67, RG 393, NA.

[11]Goodwin, "Letters," 254; and Lass, "Moscow Expedition," 239–40.

The soldiers at Crow Creek suffered even while consuming supplies meant for Indians. On January 8, Captain Meacham wrote in a receipt book: "We have had no flour for thirty one days, except what we have borrowed of Maj. [Balcombe] of the Indian Dept., which takes us up to the 10th of the present month. The whole amt of flour at this Agency including that in hands of traders and Indian Dept. will . . . last only to the 15th of February." In January and February, Meacham purchased beef for his soldiers from Galpin, now sutler at Fort Sully, the new military fort four miles east of present Pierre, South Dakota.[12]

WHILE SANTEE WOMEN, CHILDREN, AND OLD MEN LED A concentration camp existence at Crow Creek, their few white neighbors feared them, loathed them, and worried their presence in Dakota would impede further immigration. Reverend Riggs, who during his lifetime published a book of Dakota grammar and a Dakota translation of the Bible, taught Sioux children and adults to read and write in their own language and, at the same time, worked to Christianize them. In his opinion, many Santees converted because they were convinced their predicament proved the failure of their animistic religion. Disease followed starvation at Crow Creek, driving some women, Riggs wrote, to do "whatever they could to earn a living—supplying wood to steamboats, cleaning white peoples' houses, even digging cellars and trenches for farmers. Some turned to prostitution." He observed that Santee men incarcerated at Davenport became "students, soon able to write letters in the Dakota language to their families at Crow Creek, urging their wives, and especially, their children, to learn all they could of the white men's ways." Ironically, Santee and mixed-blood men employed as army guides and scouts in Minnesota missed this opportunity to become literate in their own language. In August, President Lincoln pardoned twenty-seven Sioux prisoners, and Davenport residents lost enough fear that some Sioux could labor in farmers' fields.[13]

In February, Private George Thomas recorded in his diary that forty-six lodges of Yankton buffalo hunters passed by Fort Sully. A week

---

[12]Meacham to Pell, 8 Jan. 1864, Meacham order book. It was initially called Fort Antietam, then Fort Bartlett.

[13]Kingsbury, *History of Dakota Territory*, vol. 1, 755; Riggs, *Tah-koo Wah-kan*, 342–69; and "Put Them Where They Belong," *Davenport (Iowa) Daily Gazette*, 2 June 1865. Gideon H. Pond and Thomas S. Williamson contributed to a Sioux Bible translation.

later, Captain Meacham, at Crow Creek, issued fifteen pounds of coffee to Yankton chiefs Feather-in-the-Ear and Little Swan, who was likely returning the Whitestone prisoners home on this trip. In March, still worried about his troops, Meacham exchanged salt pork and ham with Agent Balcombe for the Indians' beef. By April, some soldiers had scurvy, but without fruits and vegetables, the post surgeon could do nothing.[14]

ALTHOUGH MOST FUGITIVE SIOUX REMAINED NORTH OF THE international border over the winter, some stayed on the James River, and two small camps of Sissetons were at or near Devil's Lake. Sibley argued for an offensive movement; it would cost less than defensive measures, which might be "calamitous" to Minnesota, Iowa, and Dakota Territory prosperity. Lakotas, he heard, had invited such traditional enemies as the Assiniboines, Blackfeet, and Crows to form a coalition of perhaps 8,000 or 9,000 warriors.[15] Joseph Brown, now Sibley's special military agent, informed the general in March that Yanktonais had invited disaffected Sioux to join them in attacking "any boats or parties found within the limits of their country." Even as a public notice warned of this (although also saying that by mid-summer, Sully's new expedition should make the overland route "as safe as travel usually is in the Indian country"), citizens clamored for access to northern Rocky Mountain mining areas.[16]

Major Edwin A. C. Hatch commanded an independent cavalry battalion headquartered at Fort Pembina whose job was to monitor Dakotas who fled north of the line. In December 1863, a governor of the British possessions sent Hatch a letter granting permission to American forces to pursue Sioux into his part of British territory. Sibley warned Pope no good would come of that. For one thing, Hatch had no horses for pursuit. Besides, those bands were reportedly on their way south to join the war.[17] In mid-December, Hatch sent a squadron to "fall upon and destroy" a camp of three lodges located five miles west of the Red River settlement, St. Joseph, in present Kittson County, Minnesota. When

---

[14]Thomas diary, 9 Feb. 1864; 16 Feb. 1864, Meacham order book; Meacham to Pell and Shephard, 8 Jan. 1864, and Meacham to King, 1 March and 11 April 1864, Meacham order book.

[15]Sibley to Pope, 25 Jan. 1864, OR, vol. 34, pt. 2, pp. 152–56.

[16]Sibley to Pope, 23 March 1864, OR, vol. 34, pt. 2, 712; Carter reminiscence, 2; and "Important to Gold Seekers," St. Cloud (Minn.) Democrat, 14 March 1864.

[17]Sibley to Sully, 28 March 1864, OR, vol. 34, pt. 2, p. 768; and Sibley to Pope, 2 Apr. 1864, OR, vol. 34, pt. 3, pp. 23–24.

Sibley learned the six people they killed included women and children, he rebuked Hatch and advised him to avoid "confounding" peace-seeking leaders like Standing Buffalo.[18]

At Christmastime 1863, Hatch's men conspired to kidnap Little Six (Shakopee)—who, with Cut Nose, had captured Melvina Ingalls—and Medicine Bottle, another Sisseton leader during the 1862 fighting. When Hatch offered a reward for the two, now living north of the border, two British subjects accepted the challenge. First, one of Hatch's lieutenants crossed the border to visit the chiefs and plant the idea that the British were about to cut off their rations. After he urged them to go to Fort Garry (present Winnipeg, Manitoba) to discuss this situation with the governor, Hatch's lieutenant set out with the two locals. The two locals drugged Little Six and Medicine Bottle with opium-laced alcohol, then administered chloroform for good measure.[19] Tying the two captives on dogsleds, the British men handed them across the border to Hatch's waiting troops. Although Little Six and Medicine Bottle were sentenced to death after their Fort Snelling trial, they were imprisoned with other convicted Santees at Davenport for a year and a half before both were hanged in November 1865.

Taoyateduta's four wives and two half brothers were among some ninety Sioux men, women, and children surrendering to Hatch over the 1863–64 winter. He transferred them to Fort Snelling, where Sibley proposed to Pope that a military commission try the men for 1862 crimes and that the families be sent to Crow Creek.[20]

HUNDREDS OF MILES AWAY, ON THE NORTHEAST BANK OF THE Missouri, Lieutenant Colonel Edward M. Bartlett, Thirtieth Wisconsin, was building a new palisaded fort. At first it was called Fort Bartlett, but ultimately it was named Fort Sully. Bartlett was in charge of three Seventh Iowa cavalry companies as well as his own two infantry companies. He passed along to Sioux City headquarters whatever he learned about

[18]Sibley to Pope, 3 Jan. 1864, OR, vol. 22, pt. 2, 768; and Richard Ellis, *General Pope*, 26.

[19]Boutin, *Cut Nose*, 54, describes a similar attack but names no one.

[20]Sibley to Pope, 9 June 1864, 288–89, and 30 May 1864, 135, OR, vol. 34, pt. 4; Sibley to Pope, 5 Feb. 1864, 249, and 23 March 1864, 712, OR, vol. 34, pt. 2; Schultz, *Over the Earth*, 274–75; and Carley, *Dakota War*, 75. See also Anonymous, "Lo! the Poor Indian," *Brooklyn (N.Y.) Eagle*, 7 Oct. 1854, republished from a Minnesota paper.

militant Sioux from the mixed band camped near his fort and the two trading posts. He heard that Hunkpapa headmen had failed to persuade the Cheyennes to join a war against whites because peace had brought them prosperity in the form of more and better horses. Miniconjous also refused Hunkpapa overtures. In early November 1863, Lone Horn said they had no access to ammunition, and besides, if they did go to war with whites, they would not tell the Hunkpapas about it. However, some Miniconjous were apparently part of a delegation of Hunkpapas and Santees who approached Oglalas with a war pipe, hoping to form an alliance. Grass Rope, a peace-faction Miniconjou, revealed that Hunkpapas, Sans Arcs, Sihasapas, and a few Yanktonais were threatening a winter attack on Fort Sully. In his report, Bartlett said he feared this less than attacks on parties away from the post. Even those Sioux who had suffered through Whitestone seemed of two minds. Eighty lodges of Yanktonais separated from those at Devil's Lake in order to join Two Bear, who had decided to sue for peace at Fort Sully.[21]

On November 10, the Yanktonai chief Mad Bear came in from Two Bear's camp inquiring about what peace would entail. He signed the treaty "without the least hesitancy." Although Two Bear was influencing Indians "in the soldiers' favor," small bands of Yanktonais were robbing and murdering any whites they encountered. When Mad Bear remonstrated with them about this, they threatened his life and stole his horse. Big Head and several other Whitestone veterans called on Bartlett with similar information about the roaming bands but added that some were tiring of war. A majority, according to Big Head, planned to use winter to recuperate and consolidate their forces. He also said many destitute Indians were camped at Berdache Creek far to the north. Bartlett knew these groups constantly visited one another, but as winter set in his attention turned to keeping his men warm. Their barracks were under construction, they needed clothing, and their stoves, discards from Fort Randall, were inadequate.[22]

By December, Sans Arcs formerly at Devil's Lake moved south to the Painted Woods. Although buffalo was scarce up north, the Sans Arcs obtained a large supply of ammunition from the Red River mixed-bloods.

---

[21]Bartlett to Pell, 8 Nov. 1863, and letter no. 2, undated in the ledger but positioned between 31 Oct. and 8 Nov. documents, "Fort Sully, S.D. Selected Telegrams Sent, 1863–66, v. 19," pt. V 9W2 39/20/1, reel 2, microfilmed as job no. 1276439 on microfilm reel 1, RG 393, NA (hereafter cited as FS Selected LS, RG 393, NA), 31–33; and Kingsley Bray, Crazy Horse, 76, 414n10.

[22]Bartlett to Pell, 16 and 24 Nov. 1863, FS Selected LS, RG 393, NA.

The Yanktonai chief White Crane, who came to sign the treaty, confirmed that northern traders were supplying Sioux with powder and
lead. He offered to accompany the next expedition, if there was one.[23]

Big Head renounced the treaty he had signed apparently only to secure
his own and the other Whitestone prisoners' freedom. Nevertheless,
evidently he had visited the militant camp only to bring his relatives
to Fort Sully. While approaching the post on the ice, he suffered a fit
or stroke and died. Several winter count calendars depicted Big Head's
death as the premier event of the year.

By February 1864, Lakota bands camped in small parties between the
Grand and Little Missouri Rivers as far west as the Black Hills. Santees
were living along the Missouri's east bank between Painted Wood and
Berdache Creeks.

A Miniconjou chief Bartlett called Medicine Bones came to Fort Sully
representing himself as favoring peace. In reality, he tried to convince
resident Indians that the government, whom he accused of fighting solely
to take possession of Sioux country and open the Black Hills to gold
seekers, would not uphold Sully's treaty. Medicine Bones admitted killing "a few" white men himself, but he considered this nothing compared
with how many Indians died from "sickness caused by the White Man."[24]

Late in February the Yanktonai headmen Bone Necklace, White
Bear, and Buck stopped by Fort Sully with about 280 people to sign
the treaty and express "strong friendship" for whites. However, they
complained about their agent's mismanagement and censured traders
for selling goods at inflated prices. Militants were continually stealing
horses peaceful Indians needed for hunting. Consequently, they did not
have enough clothing or robes to meet their own needs, let alone did
they have any robes to trade. Fearing others would impede their summer hunts, the peace bands wanted their annuities. They predicted they
all would die unless whites chastised the militants and concluded "an
honorable peace." To show good faith, Bone Necklace, White Bear, and
Buck offered their young men as guides "or in any other capacity" for
the summer's campaign.[25]

By the third week of February, Bartlett counted 125 lodges of peace-

---

[23]Bartlett to Pell, 2 Dec. 1863, in ibid.

[24]Blue Thunder and No Two Horns 1863–64 winter counts in Howard, "Dakota Winter
Counts," 388; Bartlett to "Capt.," 22 Feb. 1864, FS Selected LS, RG 393, NA; Mallery, *Picture-
Writing*, 285; and Candace Greene and Thornton, *Year the Stars Fell*, 252–53. Bartlett's mention
predates by a decade Custer's confirmation of Black Hills gold.

[25]Bartlett to "Capt.," 22 Feb. 1864, and FS Selected LS, RG 393, NA.

seeking Yanktonais, Hunkpapas, Miniconjous, Brulés, Two Kettles, and Sans Arcs camped near the fort. Even so, he requested more cavalry or at least more horses—he had only ten—in order to fight off attacks on the post from small bands; in addition, he requested a strong guard to ensure safe mail delivery. The three Yanktonai chiefs had told Bartlett, who was having trouble with drunken mail carriers losing dispatches in transit to Randall, of two places between Fort Sully and Crow Creek where Indians could buy whiskey.[26]

The peace faction was eager to learn Sully's intentions, yet Bartlett did not trust them and advised commanding officers of the various posts to "keep faith with both friends and foes." Because everyone understood the fight would be to the "bitter end," Bartlett believed disaffection among the bands would cause more people to join the peace faction. However, as a precaution against compliant Sioux supplying their dissatisfied kinsmen with ammunition, he wrote the Chouteau firm about "professed friendly Indians" purchasing ammunition for resale and ordered restrictions on sales of "other articles of warfare." He would allow small sales to certain "known friendly Indians" who applied to a commanding officer.[27]

By late March nearly all the Santees, Sissetons, Cutheads, and some sixty lodges of Yanktonais were hunting buffalo east of the Missouri in the James River country. An Indian who lived with them all winter said they had ammunition that, despite Sully's admonitions, Berthold trader Fred Gerard had sold them, telling them he was "no soldier" and his reason for bringing guns into Indian country was to trade them. Furthermore, he added six kegs of free powder to their purchase.

When the influential Miniconjou chief Lame Deer could not trade buffalo robes for ammunition at Fort Sully, he supposedly told others he met on the trail who intended to sue for peace at the post "they would be disarmed and sent off to some distant Military Post and confined" like the Minnesota Indians. Bartlett was convinced Lame Deer was "doing his utmost to concentrate" Sioux forces in the spring.[28]

Perhaps to allay suspicions that the AFC's Chouteau family had Southern sympathies and to keep its steamboat line competitive for lucrative government transportation contracts, AFC management in March reported belligerent Sioux gathering in the angle formed by the Yellowstone and

---

[26]Bartlett to "Capt.," 6 Feb. and 14 March 1864, and Bartlett to Pollock, 14 and 17 March 1864, all in FS Selected LS, RG 393, NA.

[27]Bartlett to P. Chouteau and Co., 5 Feb. 1864, and Bartlett to "Capt," 22 Feb. 1864, in ibid.

[28]Bartlett to "Capt.," 14 and 25 March 1864, and Bartlett to Pollock, 14 and 17 March 1864, in ibid.

Missouri Rivers across from Fort Union and threatening to "clear out
all the whites."[29]

At the end of March, Sioux killed a soldier three miles from Fort Randall, possibly to avenge an earlier incident involving a Yankton Indian
returning from hunting. Curious about a wagon train stopped at Bon
Homme, the Indian had approached a driver described by Private Spencer as "a green kind of fellow, who knew nothing about [I]ndians and
supposed every one to be after his scalp." When the Yankton offered his
hand in greeting, the teamster grabbed his gun and shot him dead.[30]

EARLY IN 1864, SIBLEY EMPLOYED A CATHOLIC PRIEST, FATHER
Alexis André, and special agent Joseph Brown, who through his wife was
kin to several prominent chiefs, to negotiate surrender with the Sissetons.
The two were making progress, but in the end, Sibley's adjutant, R. C.
Olin, condemned Father André's peace overtures as being "of a compro-
mising nature with regard to the Indians." Then, in March 1864, Hatch's
men killed two Sisseton peace emissaries "in the most odious manner,
and notwithstanding all the information which clearly proclaimed their
quality and the object of their journey." Soon thereafter, Hatch's battalion
left Pembina for Fort Abercrombie, where they would free companies of
the Eighth Minnesota Volunteer Infantry to join Sully's 1864 expedition.[31]

AFTER ICE BROKE UP ON THE MISSOURI RIVER IN APRIL, GERARD,
the Fort Berthold trader so willing to trade ammunition to the Sioux,
arrived at Fort Sully with five other men and a hair-raising story. Some
1,500 Sihasapas, Hunkpapas, and other "mixed Indians" trading at Berthold had turned belligerent. According to Gerard, in parties of 300 and
400 warriors, they tried but failed to break into the fort. They turned

---

[29]P. Chouteau and Co. to Halleck, 26 March 1864, OR, series 1, vol. 34, pt. 2, p. 744.

[30]Spencer to Sister, 2 March 1864, in Goodwin, "Letters of Spencer," 257; and Sully to Sibley,
28 March 1864, OR, vol. 34, pt. 2, p. 767.

[31]Gary Anderson, Kinsmen, 266; Sibley to Hatch, 5 Jan. 1864, 29, Sibley to Pope, 25 Jan. 1864,
152–56, Olin to Hatch, 18 March 1864, 653, and Sibley to Pope, 21 March 1864, 687, all in OR, vol.
34, pt. 2; Olin to Hatch, 15 April 1864, OR, vol. 34, pt. 3, p. 168; Standing Buffalo's letter in Gary
Anderson and Woolworth, Through Dakota Eyes, 294; Diedrich, Odyssey, 58; and Pfaller, "Peace
Mission," 307, 310–12.

their wrath on Gerard, but after their third attempt to kill him, he got away. He credited Hunkpapa shirt-wearers Red Horn, Four Horns, and Running Antelope with saving his life.[32] Gerard knew these Sioux had a white woman living with them, but they would not sell her for any price. Meanwhile, two of Big Head's brothers and an uncle wanted Gerard to communicate their wish to surrender. Apparently, some sixty lodges tried repeatedly to do so, but militants always thwarted them. On the other hand, according to Gerard, the Yanktonai chiefs Little Soldier and Two Bear were now "very hostile."

In mid-May, Indians attacked two soldiers posted at Spirit Lake in Iowa. The soldiers fought them off, killing three. The following day, a white boy died after an attack near Minnesota's Lake Changuska, and soon after a soldier fishing near a small post at Lake Hanska died from bullet and arrow wounds. Sibley anticipated more such raids by White Lodge's and Sleepy Eye's bands and other refugees.[33]

In addition, that month a war party of Hunkpapas and Yanktonais threatened some Indian boys looking after Fort Sully horses. One boy caught a pony from the horse herd and sped to the fort, yelling that a large party of warriors intended to attack the post. The peace band and some mixed-bloods, starting ahead of the soldiers, chased them to about a mile above Peoria Bottoms, where the thieves swam the Missouri. When the cavalry caught up, the pursued Indians left behind all the horses. The fort's Indian protectors claimed as booty robes and blankets dropped during the chase.[34]

More than 140 lodges of friendly Indians lived around the post by then, and 200 more camped nearby. What Two Bear's and Little Soldier's Lower Yanktonai bands would do was still a mystery, but sixty or seventy lodges of Medicine Bear's Upper Yanktonais joined the war faction. Bartlett estimated the large hostile camp waiting to fight Sully comprised some 900 lodges of Hunkpapas, Sihasapas, Yanktonais, Two Kettles, Sans Arcs, Miniconjous, and Brulés. Bartlett's frayed nerves were apparent when he confined three very young and supposedly hostile Indians in the post's guardhouse. Fool Dog and others petitioned him to free the youngsters, and after lecturing them, he did so.[35]

[32]Bartlett to Pell, 13 April 1864, 41–43, FS Selected LS, RG 393, NA; De Trobriand, *Army Life*, 273; and De Trobriand journal, 11 April 1868.

[33]Sibley to Pope, 20 May 1864, OR, vol. 34, pt. 1, p. 937.

[34]Bartlett to Pell, 14 May 1864, FS Selected LS, RG 393, NA.

[35]Bartlett to Pell, 24 May 1864, FS Selected LS, RG 393, NA; and Candace Greene and Thornton, *Year the Stars Fell*, 252–55.

THE SECRETARY OF THE INTERIOR AND THE INDIAN COMMISSIONER, at cross-purposes as usual with the war department, persuaded the well-known Catholic priest Pierre-Jean De Smet to talk peace with the Lakotas and Yanktonais. The Belgian, sixty-three and ailing, was a longtime friend of Upper Missouri tribes, including the Sioux. This year De Smet took advantage of the *Yellowstone*'s wooding stops to talk with and baptize Winnebagos hiding from soldiers trying to force them back to Crow Creek. After visiting there himself, De Smet called it a "reservation of desolation."[36]

When the *Yellowstone* stopped at Fort Sully, bands of Two Kettles and Yanktonais greeted De Smet, their beloved "blackrobe." On the chiefs' invitation, he baptized some children and instructed his audience (with Zephyr Rencontre translating) in religion. He also told his Indian friends that army officers would protect peaceable bands, but "a terrible retribution, nothing short of utter extermination, must overtake the hostile bands, if they persist in their present reckless course of hostility against the whites." He asked his listeners to take that message—and his invitation to meet him at Fort Berthold—to Sioux bent on fighting Sully.[37]

On June 3, the Yanktonais chief Man-Who-Runs-the-Bear of Two Bear's band and Death-of-the-Bull beckoned the boat ashore to invite De Smet to talk with them. Only part of the Sans Arcs, Oglalas, Brulés, and other Yanktonais had attended a recent war council, they said. Two Bear and The-Man-Who-Runs-the-Bear did but left determined not to join the war faction. The Miniconjous also leaned toward peace.

On June 4, the passengers buried a man who had died of smallpox. For Indians on shore, the disease aboard the boat posed deadly danger, which—had they known about it—would have frightened them more than the prospect of war.[38] On April 24, twenty-eight soldiers—part of Company I, Thirtieth Wisconsin, bound for Fort Union and ill with smallpox—had been put off the boat at Nebraska City.

---

[36]Chittenden and Richardson, *Life, Letters*, vol. 3, 816, 820–30 ("reservation of desolation" quote on p. 821); Iowa Adj. General's Office, *Roster and Record of Iowa Soldiers*, vol. 4, 1124n5; Dole to De Smet, 21 March 1864, no. 122, and Dole to Sully, 22 March 1864, no. 124, 275–76, both in CIA annual report; Hoffman to Edmunds, 20 Aug. 1864, no. 118, and Stanton to Usher, 15 June 1864, no. 130, 265–69, 286, both in CIA annual report; and Buchanan, "Trip to the Gold Fields." See also Pfaller, "Sully Expedition"; Pfaller, *Father De Smet in Dakota*, 49–50; and Antrei, "Father DeSmet [*sic*]," 26.

[37]Chittenden and Richards, *Life, Letters*, 820–30; and De Smet report, 24 June 1864, no. 125, CIA annual report, 276–77. See Doane Robinson, ed., "Fort Tecumseh and Fort Pierre Journals," 235.

[38]Buchanan, "Trip to the Gold Fields"; and De Smet report, 24 June 1864, no. 125, CIA annual report, 276–78.

On June 10, the *Yellowstone* dropped De Smet off at Fort Berthold, then continued to Fort Union, which the army had recently commandeered from the AFC to store supplies for Sully's summer campaign. It was shabby now, with a fur industry declining partly because of disruption caused by Indian wars. The soldiers disembarked there on June 13 to learn that Sioux recently had killed an AFC employee and stolen $4,000 in goods from a pack train.[39]

While De Smet waited at Fort Berthold for his messenger—Big Head's Brother, who lived with the Arikaras—to return from the militants' camp, he and Upper Missouri agent Mahlon Wilkinson heard the three affiliated tribes' concerns. The Rees were grateful to the Hidatsas and Mandans for taking them in after the Sioux drove them from their country south of the Missouri River, but they wanted that country back or else "pay for it." On June 13, Sioux proved the tribes' accusations when they attacked, killed a Hidatsa, wounded a Ree, and stole horses. On June 29, the Yanktonai chief Medicine Bear came to Berthold to assure De Smet his delegation wanted peace, and he agreed to take De Smet's invitation to bands on a Heart River tributary.[40]

With the horrible conditions at the Crow Creek Reservation as an example of what they believed could happen to their bands, many Sioux leaders were agitated and indecisive as they awaited Sully's second campaign. Whites and their Indian friends pried information from one another, but no one knew whom to trust. Nervousness and suspicion had permeated the Upper Missouri for so long that Sully's imminent approach could only relieve it.

---

[39]Sunder, *Fur Trade*, 220; P. Chouteau and Co. to Halleck, 26 March 1864, OR, vol. 34, pt. 2, pp. 743–44; Buchanan, "Trip to the Gold Fields"; and Dill to Greer, 11 Apr. 1864, in U.S. Army, *General Orders, 1st.*, Fort Union Trading Post National Historic Site (NHS) Library. Sunder, 215–65, discusses Civil and Indian war effects on the fur trade.

[40]Wilkinson to Edmunds, 31 Aug. 1864, no. 117, CIA annual report, 264; Chittenden and Richards, *Life, Letters*, 820–30; and De Smet to Dole, 15 July 1864, no. 126, CIA annual report, 279–80. Buchanan says the boat reached Berthold 10 June; De Smet says 9 June.

Chapter 11

Tahkahokuty

BANISHING DAKOTAS AND WINNEBAGOS TO CROW CREEK Reservation resulted in starvation and disease exacerbated by ill-conceived and insincerely executed rescue missions that were motivated by greed. Over the 1863–64 winter, General Pope, who regarded the nation's policy toward Indians a woeful failure, presented his solution. Government should cease annuity payments and appropriations for land claims and remove all Indians "to some point far in rear of frontier settlements." Money should instead "be devoted to building villages for them and supplying them with food and clothing." Government could then civilize, educate, and Christianize Indians while simultaneously eliminating barriers to American emigration and travel. Why should the nation retain "in wildness and unproductiveness, for the scanty subsistence of a few thousand savages, regions which would support many millions of civilized men[?]" History, he claimed, demonstrated the inevitability of "the dispossession of the savage and the occupation of his lands by civilized man." Government need only decide how to do it "with the greatest humanity, the least injustice, and the largest benefit to the Indian morally and physically." Pope saw the 1864 Sioux campaign as an opportunity for government to apply his suggestions: "These operations will bring us into contact with tribes of wild Indians with whom treaties have never been made, and with powerful bands of annuity Indians . . . who have violated their treaties." Furthermore, he asked that the "military be left to deal with these Indians without the interposition of Indian agents."[1]

Pope had berated Sully for his failure to meet Sibley, but Sully's subsequent Whitestone Hill victory earned him Pope's praise and his own military district encompassing Iowa and Dakota. Wearing a dilapidated hat and civilian clothes, Sully often walked anonymously through Davenport, his winter headquarters. Although he was only forty-three in 1864, his long graying beard aged him. One observer remarked, "The

---

[1]Pope to Stanton, 6 Feb. 1864, OR, vol. 34, pt. 2, pp. 259–64. See also Richard Ellis, *General Pope*.

General, when in full uniform, was a fine looking officer, and of a very commanding appearance, but when not in uniform, his appearance was that of an ordinary and common person." Once, when a drunken man, unaware of who he was, insulted him on the street, Sully knocked him down with one punch, then went on his way.[2]

Though he was tough like Harney, Sully's background was genteel. Son of the famous portrait painter Thomas Sully, he grew up privileged. He inherited some artistic ability, but his bent was more toward engineering, steering him to West Point. He drew and painted often while on the Upper Missouri.[3]

After graduating in 1841, Sully fought Seminoles in Florida and then went to war in Mexico. Promoted to first lieutenant, he served next in California, first at Benicia, then Monterey. There he befriended the local don and married his beautiful daughter. Their son was a newborn in 1851 when his wife Manuela ate an orange a former suitor sent her and died soon after. Sully suspected murder by poison. Almost immediately, his beloved black servant, apparently as despondent over Manuela's death as Sully, committed suicide. The tragedy tripled when his mother-in-law, who was wet-nursing the baby, accidentally smothered the one-month-old boy in her bed. Sully remained on the west coast until 1854, when his company (F, Second Infantry) transferred to Fort Ridgely.[4]

Now, in summer 1864, Sully would personally command the Second Northwest Sioux Expedition. Pope could not persuade Sibley to take the field. Instead, Colonel Minor T. Thomas would command the Minnesota brigade. To avoid problems with Indian agents, Sully asked Pope to assure that Sioux annuity goods be shipped no farther than Fort Pierre and that none be distributed until any fighting was over. Accordingly, Commissioner Dole instructed Agent Latta to consult Sully before delivering goods to tribes in his jurisdiction.[5]

The campaign shaped up earlier and better than in 1863. Sully's Missouri River brigade—1,800 men and all their equipment—comprised eleven Sixth Iowa companies under Pollock; three Seventh Iowa companies under Pattee; both Dakota Cavalry companies under Captain Miner; Brackett's Minnesota Battalion under Alfred B. Brackett; an

    [2]Pope to Sully, 25 and 31 Aug. 1863, 496–97, 502–503, and 5 Oct. 1863, 608, OR, vol. 22, pt. 2; Levering, "Recollections"; and Moe, *Last Full Measure*, 117.
    [3]Sully, *No Tears*, 122, 243n13.
    [4]Sully, *No Tears*, 22–27, 55–71, 104–115. See Diedrich, *Odyssey*, 8, 11, 24, 43.
    [5]GO 45, Dept. NW, 4 Dec. 1863, OR, vol. 22, pt. 2, 730–31; Sully to Asst. Adj. Gen., 21 March 1864, OR, vol. 34, pt. 2, 688; and Dole to Latta, 22 March 1864, CIA annual report, no. 123, p. 276.

independent company of scouts, mostly white, but including some Winnebagos, Omahas, a few Sioux, and some mixed-bloods, all under Captain Christian Stufft; and the Prairie Battery, commanded by General Pope's nephew Nathaniel Pope.[6]

Agent Burleigh proposed that Sully formally induct into service fifty-one Yankton Indians Burleigh already had protecting his agency and nearby settlements. Sully liked the idea and enrolled them all as scouts for nine months. He issued arms, clothing, and subsistence and promised them $300 each when they mustered out. On June 9, Sully wrote Colonel Thomas, explaining he had "given the Yanktons the privilege of hunting up the James River. With them are a party of Indians . . . [who] are to burn down the dirt lodges situated on the James River . . . and draw out the small bands of Santee Sioux in that locality." The Minnesota Brigade could identify these Yanktons by their manner of waving a white flag. Because this detachment often would be away from their families, Sully instructed Fort Randall's commanding officer to issue these scouts and their families rations during field assignments. Continuing upriver, Sully took the Nebraska scouting unit but left the Yanktons to guard settlements along the river.[7]

Captain John Fielner, the expedition's Bavarian-born topographical engineer, immediately began collecting plant, animal, and fossil samples for the Smithsonian Institution. Two days out from Fort Sully, in today's Potter County, South Dakota, Fielner and two others were exploring near the Little Cheyenne River when three Indians hiding in the grass rose up and shot and killed him.[8]

Captain Miner and his Dakota Cavalry caught and killed all three. Scouts recovered horses the attackers stampeded and learned they were Cuthead Yanktonais camped along Apple Creek near present Bismarck. When the Dakotans reported to Sully, he directed Lieutenant Bacon to bring back the Indians' heads. Sergeant Benjamin S. Estes and Corporal

[6]Stufft's 2 Aug. 1864 report, no. 7, OR, vol. 41, pt. 1, pp. 163–64; Abstract, OR, vol. 34, pt. 4, p. 628; and Pattee, "Reminiscences," 301–302, 305. In one report, Sully called this unit, commonly known as "Nebraska scouts," his "Independent Company of Indian Scouts." Records show 65 Nebraska and Dakota frontiersmen, 8 Omaha Indians, 8 Winnebagos, 4 Indians (probably Sioux), and 3 mixed-bloods—a total of 3 officers and 85 enlisted men. I thank John Ludwickson and Patrick A. Bowmaster for sharing their Nebraska Scouts research (Ludwickson, e-mail message to author, 20 June 2005).

[7]General Sully's Company of Yankton Scouts, 3–9 (listed under "Misc. MP" in bibliography); Edmunds to Dole, 20 Sept. 1864, and Edmunds to Burleigh, 21 Oct. 1864, both in CIA annual report, no. 115, pp. 261, 284–85.

[8]English, "Dakota's First Soldiers," 277–80; and Myers, Soldiering, 10–11.

Joseph Ellis severed them with a butcher knife and brought the grisly trophies to camp in a gunnysack. Bacon, who was, according to Sergeant English, "highly elevated over the success of [the] chase," liberally rewarded the victors from two kegs—one of water, the other containing "commissaries." Next morning, Sully directed Sergeant English "to hang the heads on poles on the highest hill . . . as a warning to Indians who might travel that way." Although many soldiers mentioned the three bloody heads in their diaries, few offered any comment. "It was curious to note the effect of this melanchoy [sic] incident on the men of the command," John Pattee wrote later. "On every face appeared a sort of grim earnestness." Reflecting later, Sergeant English concluded, "General Sully's brutal and reprehensible conduct, instead of acting as a warning and as a restraint on the Indians, worked quite to the contrary and made them furious and determined upon reprisals."[9]

GEORGE WASHINGTON NORTHRUP, A YOUNG SERGEANT IN Brackett's Battalion, did double duty as a *St. Paul Daily Press* correspondent, writing as "Icimini." He also wrote personal letters, but while with Sully's brigade, he seemed disheartened. From camp on June 10, he complained to his brother-in-law of apathy. He philosophized that it would not be long until, "'three score and ten' rolls around if [I] am *un*fortunate enough to live that length of time."[10]

Northrup was locally famous for his frontier exploits long before becoming a soldier. In one adventure, he set out with his dog, pushing a handcart west from Minnesota determined to reach the Pacific coast. Though he aborted the trip, it earned him his Sioux appellation, "Man-that-Draws-the-Hand-Cart." While living in a cabin near Fort Abercrombie, he trapped and traded furs, carried mail between posts, and guided wealthy hunters on woodland and prairie excursions. He made enemies and friends among Sioux he encountered. Once, when

---

[9]Drips, *Three Years*, 69; English, "Dakota's First Soldiers," 277–80; Pattee, "Reminiscences," 304; and Wieneke narrative in Shambaugh, "Iowa Troops," 369. For diary mentions, see English, diary, 29 June 1864, Abner M. English Collection, H85.78, SDSHS Archives (hereafter cited as English diary); Ole W. Orland (Co. A. Dak. Cav.), diary, 28 June 1864, Orland Papers, MSS 20442, SHSND Archives. Many soldiers' diaries, letters, and reminiscences about Sully's 1864 expedition are in the Dakota Conflict of 1862 MSS at MNHS Archives.

[10]Northrup to Miss Alice Humphrey, 26 May 1864, Northrup Letters, 1852–65, MNHS Archives.

some Lakotas captured his party of English hunters, his friend Standing Buffalo came to his aid. The two were *kodas*—a relationship Sioux considered as close as blood ties.

While serving in Brackett's Battalion in the South, Northrup, unmarried, began corresponding with a woman who had knitted him some socks. He never met Alice Humphreys, but he wrote her from Sioux City that he did not think "Genl" Two Bear would "exhibit the necessary skill . . . to hurl back" Sully's column. He enclosed a picture of Standing Buffalo, who, he expected, would be among those waiting in force for Sully's army. (However—possibly to protect his koda's reputation—as Icimini he wrote the opposite about Standing Buffalo.) Mato Nopa or Two Bear, "is the most influential among the Western Sioux, and his word will go far to inflame the hostile party," he told *Daily Press* readers. He wrote his brother-in-law that peaceable Indians at Fort Sully were "few and we hav[e] the whole [S]ioux nation nearly to fight." In a later letter to him, he enclosed a bloody lock of one of Fielner's murderers' hair. "If you wish to preserve it you can wash it out," he advised. In closing a letter to Alice, he remarked: "Perhaps this may be the last [letter] you will ever receive from me."[11]

Two to three hundred lodges of Yanktonais, Two Kettles, Sihasapas, Miniconjous, Sans Arcs, Brulés, and "warlike" Hunkpapas had signed Sully's peace treaty since the Whitestone Hill fight, but Sully suspected they would "take either side according to the success of my expedition." He told Pope, "They are perfectly aware . . . this is their last hope; that if we succeed they will not have one foothold that they can claim their own, and that the whites, who are now coming into their country, will overrun it." Bands ready to fight might muster 6,000 warriors; he expected a desperate fight.[12]

ON JUNE 6, COLONEL MINOR THOMAS'S MINNESOTA BRIGADE started west from near Fort Ridgely, an area still scarred with 1862 reminders. Many of the brigade's approximately 1,600 members had

---

[11]Diedrich, *Odyssey*, 13; Bergemann, *Brackett's Battalion*, 74; Pfaller, "Sully Expedition," 46, 46n57; Northrup, "Icimini" reports, *St. Paul (Minn.) Daily Press*, 11 and 29 May, 2 and 7 June, 17 July, and 6 Aug. 1864; Northrup letters dated 26 May, 10 and 18 June, and 1 and 11 July 1864 in Northrup Letters, 1852–65, MNHS Archives; "Icimini" 26 June 1864 letter in Libby Papers, box 32, MS 10085, SHSND Archives; and Eggleston, "George W. Northrup," 4–21.

[12]Sully to Asst. Adj. Gen., 21 June 1864, OR, vol. 34, pt. 4, p. 497.

served with Sibley in 1863. On the first day out, some Eighth Minnesota men dug up bodies of an Indian man and woman and, as one witness put it, "kicked them around just as they pleased."[13]

Sully had orders to escort approximately 200 men, women, and children in 123 oxen-pulled wagons partway to the Montana mining districts. The train's leader, Thomas A. Holmes, led a group to the mines in 1862 without incident, but this year he took the opportunity of an escort Pope offered through public notices in newspapers during March. The Holmes train added more than 100 teams and nearly 300 people to Thomas's procession. Pope must have bemoaned this impediment to the expedition as much as Sully, but both knew the Union needed Montana's gold to help pay Civil War debt.[14]

Several of Thomas's scouts reported in their diaries that they met Sully's detachment of Yankton scouts near present Mobridge, South Dakota, and, on June 30, the brigades converged at Swan Lake Creek, seven miles from the Missouri. The Minnesotans added considerable strength to Sully's fighting force. Along with ten companies of his own Eighth Minnesota Infantry, mounted for the expedition, Thomas had six companies of Second Minnesota Cavalry under Colonel Robert N. McLaren. The Third Minnesota Battery Light Artillery trundled two sections—one with two brass six-pounder smooth-bore guns and the other with two brass twelve-pounder mountain howitzers. Captain Jones, defender of Fort Ridgely in 1862 and an 1863 campaign veteran, commanded one section.[15]

The Fourth of July was a day for orations in the combined Sully and Thomas camp. Thomas C. Hodgson, Eighth Minnesota, recalled an Adventist preacher named Harris from his regiment who began with

---

[13]George W. Doud, diary, 6, 7, and 9 June 1864, MNHS Archives (cited hereafter as Doud diary). See also Doud, "Doud Diary," 471–74.

[14]Helen White, *Ho!* 108 (quoting Weydert's "Biography"), and appendix; Josephy, *Civil War in the American West*, 148. After Montana Territory was created in 1864, the gold region was in Montana, not Idaho. The number of wagons varies with every diary. Gilbert Benedict's diary, 13 July 1864, tells of cutting 117 cords of wood—one for each emigrant wagon—to pay for crossing the Missouri by steamboat (Benedict Papers, 1865–67, SC410, Montana State Historical Society Archives Collections—hereafter cited as Benedict diary).

[15]James Benton Atkinson, diary, 21–25 June 1864, 2nd Minn. Vol. Cav. Reel 1, Dakota Conflict of 1862 MSS (hereafter cited as Atkinson diary). Doud diary, 30 June 1864. Doud counted 18 "Sully scouts." Andrew J. Fisk, diary, 30 June 1864, 2nd Minn. Vol. Cav., Fisk Family Papers, P622 M538, MNHS Archives (hereafter cited as Andrew Fisk diary). See SO 176 Dist. of Minn., Dept. NW, 9 Aug. 1864, OR, vol. 41, pt. 2, 629; "Summary of the Principal Events," 131, and Thomas's Killdeer report, no. 9, 9 Oct. 1864, 168–69, both in OR, vol. 41, pt. 1. Williams, "Narrative of the Second," in *Minnesota in the Civil and Indian Wars*, vol. 1, 544.

the expected tributes, then gave the Sioux "such a roasting as only a silver tongued Irishman can. The boys fairly howled with delight. The more barbarous the speech became the more the boys applauded. There were to be no prisoners taken—even children and women were to be butchered if we ever got at them." When another clergyman "severely rebuked Harris for his un-Christian speech, [he] . . . boldly declared that the Christian method was not adapted to warfare with savages; that the old testament method was the only practical method when we deal with barbarous people." He cited the Bible story of God sending Saul to destroy Amelek, "utterly, root and branch," as an example. The preacher then related a version of "nits make lice" using ganders and goslings. "This was a clincher, and the humane preacher was vanquished utterly." Hodgson mentioned this, he said, to "show the spirit of the boys toward the savages in their front. It is plain the boys were to favor the Old Testament method of dealing with enemies."[16]

On July 5, some Yanktonais who knew Sully from Whitestone Hill signaled the *Island City* from a bluff. They wanted a parley. Afterward, these seven lodges surrendered, saying forty more would do the same but some 1,600 lodges high up the Heart River or on the Little Missouri were eager to fight.[17]

Four companies of the Thirtieth Wisconsin Volunteer Infantry were already eight miles north of the Cannonball River at a spot where they would build Fort Rice, named for Brigadier General James Clay Rice of Wilderness Campaign fame. Meanwhile, the regiment's Company I guarded Sully's supplies at Fort Union. After Sully's steamboats ferried his army and the Holmes train across the Missouri to the Fort Rice site on the west bank, Sully spoke to the emigrants: "Gentlemen, I am damn sorry you are here, but so long as you are, I will do the best I can to protect you." After warning them he might stop longer or march harder than they would like, he concluded, "I expect to jump an Indian camp and give them hell. . . . Keep together for in union there is strength."[18]

While his men helped the Thirtieth Wisconsin prepare lumber and bake clay for the new fort, Sully kept scouts busy reconnoitering to the west. Three Second Minnesota men deserted, but death also diminished his expedition. A citizen from Minneapolis who had come west to

[16]Hodgson, *Personal Recollections*, 28–29.
[17]Price, "Colonel D.J. Dill," 33, River Falls Area Research Center, University of Wisconsin; and Sully to Asst. Adj. Gen., 7 July 1864, OR, vol. 51, pt. 2, pp. 80–81.
[18]Chaky, "Wisconsin Volunteers"; and Pfaller, "Sully Expedition," 36.

benefit his health died July 8 of consumption, and an Eighth Minnesota soldier, Andrew Doud, died July 16. Mortality was on soldiers' minds. In his diary that day Major Ebenezer Rice, Second Minnesota, wrote, "Saw a Meteor fall last evening afterwards had a Dream all foreign to my previous thoughts[.] I have therefore noted the circumstance and wait for events." Private John W. Wright, Sixth Iowa, wrote, "We go to battle feeling that right and justice are on our side and we are resolved to conquer or die. Knowing that some must fall, we all feel that our lives will not be lost in vain."[19]

Meanwhile, Father De Smet talked at Fort Berthold with 200 to 300 militant Sioux who appeared July 8 on the opposite bank. The *Yellowstone*'s timely return from above made it the venue for the conference. The boat's captain, Charles Chouteau, spoke first, urging the Sioux to seek and keep peace with whites. After De Smet addressed them, spokesmen Black Eyes and Red Dog "expressed their great desire of keeping peace with the whites, and of preventing their young men from breaking it." De Smet believed his meeting had concluded favorably after "the great chiefs . . . heard with pleasure and satisfaction the words I addressed to them on the part of the Government." He also thought the Santees were ready to consider peace terms. De Smet rode the *Yellowstone* down to Fort Rice to tell Sully, who listened but told the priest he had come to punish the Sioux, not negotiate with them. Labeling his peace mission "bootless," De Smet returned, dejected, to St. Louis. What he told Sully was useful; now Sully knew the location of about 470 Yanktonai lodges.[20]

Joseph Brown, the former Indian agent commanding the Minnesota brigade's scouts, according to Sully, left "at his own request" on July 15 with twelve of his men and new orders for duty where Wisconsin infantrymen were building another military post, Fort Wadsworth (later Fort Sisseton), eighty-five miles southwest of Fort Abercrombie in the Kettle Lakes region. Brown carried a message from Sully to General Sibley:

---

[19]David N. Jenkins, diary, 10, 11, and 12 July 1864, Jenkins Papers, MNHS Archives (hereafter cited as Jenkins diary); Atkinson diary, 14 July 1864; Doud diary, 10 July 1864; Ebenezer A. Rice, diary, 9, 10, and 16 July 1864, Rice Diaries, 1864, M646, MNHS Archives (hereafter cited as Rice diary); William L. Silvius, diary, 9 and 21 July 1864, 8th Minn. Vol. Inf., Reel 3, Dakota Conflict of 1862 MSS (hereafter cited as Silvius diary); Washburn, diary, 16 July 1864, Washburn Diaries 1863–65, MNHS Archives (hereafter cited as Washburn diary); Wright's diary, 25 July 1864, quoted in Scott and Kempcke, "Journey," 9; and Welsh, *Medical Histories*, 327–28. See also Helen White, *Ho!* 125, 125n31. George Doud did not say if Andrew Doud was a relative.

[20]Chittenden and Richardson, *Life, Letters*, 833–35; Pfaller, "Peace Mission," 312–13; and Pfaller, *Father De Smet in Dakota*, 42–52.

"We see Indians now and then, and some have sent word they want to give themselves up, but I have not time to attend to them."[21]

ON JULY 19, THE EXPEDITION, NUMBERING ABOUT 3,000 PEOPLE, began following the Cannonball River's northern branch westward. Less than a week out, messengers from Fort Rice alerted Sully that Indians had attacked government boats, but further word came a few hours later that the steamers suffered no real damage. The few hours' delay gave his men time to explore the "fantastical shaped" buttes—some layered with coal and scattered on the sparse buffalo-grass plain—so different from the hilly country east of the Missouri.

When scouts found an Indian trail trending northwest toward Heart River, the long, hot march resumed. The temperature soared to 110 degrees. Dogs and oxen died. Men suffered heat stroke.[22] In camp at Heart River, Sully unpacked what he would need during battle. First, he looked for saddle blankets but found none and made do with gunnysacks. Next, he searched for the wide webbed duck *cincuas* that went over packs and under mules' bellies, but he found only narrow, hard leather bands. "These instruments of torture," he told Pope, provoked his mules to kick and jump until they had either rid themselves of their packs or broken them open. Sully gave up on the mules and impressed the Holmes train's light wagons to haul more than a thousand pounds each. Finally, on July 26, Sully left the emigrant train corralled at the camp with Captain William Tripp, Dakota Cavalry, commanding the Second Minnesota's band and a guard force of soldiers who were too sick or incapacitated for an active fight.

That afternoon the army of some 2,200 men, burdened with thirty-five wagons and carrying seven days' rations, began a forced march to meet the enemy. An officer— probably John Pattee—acting as correspondent for the *Sioux City Journal* described wagons moving in two parallel lines about 300 paces apart, with Sully and his staff between, followed by

---

[21]Sully to Sibley, 15 July 1864, 617; Clowney to Olin, 29 July 1864, 514–15; Brown to Clowney, 1 Aug. 1864, and Sibley to Pope, 8 Aug. 1864, 616–17; and SO 176 Dist. of Minn., Dept. NW, 9 Aug. 1864, 629, all in OR, vol. 41, pt. 2; Schuler, *Fort Sisseton*, 9.

[22]Jenkins diary, 10, 11, and 12 July 1864; Atkinson diary, 14 and 22 July 1864; Doud diary, 10 July 1864; Rice diary, 9, 10, and 16 July 1864; Silvius diary, 9 and 21 July 1864; Washburn diary, 16 July 1864; Wright's diary, 25 July 1864, quoted in Scott and Kempcke, "Journey," 9; Welsh, *Medical Histories*, 327–28; Pfaller, "Sully Expedition," 36; Myers, *Soldiering*, 13–14; McLaren diary, 23 and 24 July 1864, McLaren Papers, MNHS Archives; and Bluemle, *Face of North Dakota*, 3–5. See also Helen White, *Ho!* 125, 125n31.

the provost guard, some scouts, the battery, headquarters wagons, and ambulances. The Seventh Iowa marched on the left flank with Brackett's Battalion and the two Dakota cavalry companies. Eight Sixth Iowa companies marched on the right flank. Two other Sixth Iowa companies and some scouts formed an advance guard, and the other Sixth Iowa company guarded the rear. Loose livestock walked between the two lines of wagons. Thomas's Minnesota brigade marched in a single line, which the correspondent found "objectionable in a country like this, which is favorable for marching after the manner proposed by General Sully."[23]

The army trudged on for about half an hour when the Nebraska scouts' commander, Captain Christian Stufft, dashed in at a gallop to report that a large force of Indians had attacked his company and "cut [it] to pieces." Stufft was drunk. Sully arrested him and ordered him to march behind the ambulances as punishment, but according to Amos Cherry, Stufft's offense went beyond drunkenness. Stufft apparently ordered a retreat at the same time a lieutenant ordered the men forward, then drew his revolver against the lieutenant. Twenty-five or thirty scouts followed Stufft in retreat. Sending Brackett's Battalion ahead to aid the fifteen or so who had not retreated, Sully hurried his army forward to find the scouts "all in good healthy condition waiting for us." Sully worried, however, that their skirmish gave the Sioux notice of his army's approach.[24]

About nine the next morning, soldiers glimpsed the Indians the scouts had fought and followed their trail. By mid-afternoon on what Major Atkinson called a "day hot as thunder," they had covered more than twenty-eight miles. On July 28, they started at 3:00 A.M. and covered thirty-five miles before stopping at about 9:00 A.M. to rest and drink coffee. They were on the move again by 10:00 A.M., and at about 11:00 A.M., chief guide Frank La Framboise rode in to report the Sioux camp's location. Lieutenant Colonel Pollock, standing with Sully, called out to one of his Sixth Iowa officers: "Well, Captain, we have found the sons of bitches at last."[25]

[23]Myers, *Soldiering*, 13–14. Unidentified 6th or 7th Iowa Cav. officer (possibly John Pattee) acting as correspondent, "From the Indian Expedition," *Sioux City (Iowa) Journal*, vol. 1, no. 1, 20 Aug. 1864.

[24]Atkinson diary, 26 July 1864; Cherry diary, in Shambaugh, "Iowa Troops," 26 July 1864, 422; Drips, *Three Years*, 76; Pattee, "Reminiscences," 306–307; Dugas to parents, 3 June, 1 July, and 10 Sept. 1864, in Charles Dugas, Letters, Reel 1, Dakota Conflict of 1862 MSS; and Sully to Pope, 31 July 1864, OR, vol. 41, pt. 1, p. 142. For Minnesota brigade scouts, see Sibley to Pope, 10 Oct. 1864, OR, vol. 41, pt. 1, p. 40.

[25]Rice and Atkinson diaries, 26 and 27 July 1864; Drips, *Three Years*, 77; Scott and Kempcke, "Journey," 10; Williams, "Narrative of the Second," in *Minnesota in the Civil and Indian Wars*, vol. 1, 545; and Sully, Abstract of Sully to Asst. Adj. Gen., Dept. NW, 30 June 1864, NA (under "Misc. MP" in bibliography).

Based on what the scouts and guides told him, Sully estimated that up to 1,600 lodges stood protected against hills the Sioux called *Tahkahokuty*, or The Hunting Ground Where They Killed the Deer. The soldiers called it Killdeer Mountain. Estimates of the camp's size ranged from four to five miles long in one direction to much larger. Using eight people per lodge, including two fighting-age men, Sully estimated the camp might muster 5,000 or 6,000 warriors.[26]

Those scouts who were dressed in Indian fashion changed to uniforms to guard against accidents. Sully had soldiers count off by fours, assigning every fourth man as horse holders, thereby cutting his fighting force by 25 percent. His army advanced, cavalry dismounted, in battle formation—a mile-long, mile-wide hollow square enclosing horses and horse holders, artillery, supply wagons, and ambulances. As Pattee and his three Seventh Iowa companies led the slow-moving square over the rugged country, Henry Wieneke saw what they were facing. "Indians appeared covering plains 6 miles or more front and back to the Hills." Even above the racket the army created behind him, he could hear warriors whooping.[27]

Against the backdrop of the huge Indian camp, one warrior charged toward the front of the marching square, then turned and raced across their ranks. Pattee described how this warrior "very gayly dressed, carrying a large war club gorgeously ornamented appeared in front of the 6th Iowa cavalry and called loudly to us and gesticulated wildly . . . Major Wood, chief of cavalry, approached my position and said, 'The general

[26]Sully to Pope, no 2, 31 July 1864, OR, vol. 41, pt. 1, p. 142; and Larson, *Gall*, 113, 255–56n3. Larson believed the Killdeer village was larger than the 1876 Greasy Grass village.

[27]Myers, *Soldiering*, 13–14. (Myers, with Sully's battalion, possibly meant Sully's mostly white "Nebraska scouts" when he wrote "Dakota scouts," rather than the Dakota Sioux and mixed-blood scouts with the Minnesota brigade.) Pattee, "Reminiscences," 307–308; Shambaugh, "Iowa Troops," 370–71; and Sully's Killdeer report, 31 July 1864, vol. 41, pt. 1, p. 142 (see below in this footnote for documents included in Killdeer report). See Doane Robinson, "Rescue," 111. See also Utley, *Lance*, 55–64, and Vestal (Campbell), *Sitting Bull*, 50–57. Sully's and his officers' 1864 expedition reports are in OR, vol. 41, pt. 1 as follows: (a) Sully, Report no. 2, Sully to Asst. Adj. Gen., Dept. NW, 31 July 1864, 141–44; 13 Aug. 1864, 144–49; 29 Aug. 1864, 150–51; 9 Sept. 1864, 151–52; 11 Sept. 1864, 152–55; and 10 Oct. 1864, 155–56; (b) Pollock, Report no. 3, Pollock to Pell, 29 July 1864, 156–58, and 9 Aug. 1864, 158–59; (c) Pattee, Report no. 4, Pattee to Pell, 2 Aug. 1864, 160; (d) Brackett, Report no. 5, Brackett to Pell, 1 Aug. 1864, 161, and 13 Aug. 1864, 161–62; (e) Miner, Report no. 6, Miner to Sully, 2 Aug. 1864, 162–63; (f) Stufft, Report no. 7, Stufft to expedition Asst. Adj. Gen., 2 Aug. 1864, 163–64; (g) Nathaniel Pope, Report no. 8, N. Pope to Pell, 1 and 13 Aug 1864, 164–65; (h) Thomas, Report no. 9, Thomas to Pell, 1 Aug. 1864, 165–66, 13 Aug. 1864, 167–68, and 9 Oct. 1864; (i) Rogers, Report no. 10, Rogers to Butterfield, Acting Asst. Adj. Gen., 1 Aug. 1864, 170–77; (j) Camp, Report no. 11, 1 Aug. 1864, 172; and (k) McLaren, Report no. 12, McLaren to Pell, 29 July 1864, 172–73. (Hereafter cited collectively as Killdeer reports; specific reports are cited to author, e.g., "Sully's Killdeer report.")

sends his compliments and wishes you to kill that Indian for God's sake.'"
The Seventh Iowa's rifles and revolvers did not have enough range, but
three men still carried old infantry Springfield rifle muskets that did.
When they shot at the warrior, the Indian "immediately stretched himself
out flat along the horse's back and plied his left heel vigorously against
the flank of his pony and disappeared from my sight over the hill." Sully,
on higher ground, watched him fall off his horse, then saw his friends
put him on another and lead him to the hills. This man may have been
Sitting Bull's uncle, the shirt-wearer Four Horns, who suffered a bullet
wound to his back at Tahkahokuty. If so, Sitting Bull and his fourteen-
year-old nephew White Bull were his rescuers.[28]

The battle began then in earnest. The soldiers fought their way to the
Indians' camp, which Colonel Thomas described as "on a plateau . . . with
great rugged buttes overhanging it. The position for defense and safety
could not have been better, being protected in front by almost impassable wooded ravines, and in rear . . . [by] hills [that could be] ascended
[only] through narrow chasms." During the approach, Sully's brigade
fought on the right of the square formation, opposing Yanktonais and
Inkpaduta's Dakotas, while Thomas's brigade faced Lakotas on the left.
Although the formation marched dismounted, Brackett's Battalion, in
Sully's brigade, made one successful mounted thrust against attackers. Near the camp, however, all dismounted, each man carrying about
twenty-five pounds of gear and arms.[29]

The Killdeer battle was a stage for heroic and bizarre dramatics on
both sides. Soldiers and Sioux both recalled how, as the soldiers neared
the hostile camp, a cream-colored horse pulling a man riding in a travois
basket galloped toward them. He guided the horse with long reins as
bullets struck the horse and finally upset his travois. This warrior without
weapons sat still on the ground, facing the soldiers, singing his death
song. It did not last long. When the soldiers investigated later, they
found the body of a man of about forty with twisted, paralyzed limbs.

St. Paul Pioneer Press correspondent "M" (Sergeant Eugene Marshall

---

[28]Diessner, *No Indians Left*, 44; Pattee, "Reminiscences," 308; Larson, *Gall*, 47; and Wright
diary, 27 July 1864, quoted in Scott and Kempcke, "Journey," 10. Sioux oral history tells a similar
story of Long Dog, a warrior who believed he was "with a ghost" and therefore invincible. Cf.
Utley, *Lance*, 55–56.

[29]Diessner, *No Indians Left*, 43–46; Utley, *Lance*, 55–56; Vestal (Campbell), *Sitting Bull*, 50–57;
Kelly, *My Captivity*, 92–111; Sully's Killdeer report, 31 July 1864, 142–43; Thomas Killdeer report,
9 Oct. 1864, 168–70; and A. Brackett, "Gen. Sully's Expedition, The Fight With the Indians,"
St. Paul (Minn.) Pioneer Press, 6 Sept. 1864.

of Brackett's Battalion) described, with admiration, the way the Sioux fought. Yelling their war whoops and striking without hesitation, they "fought over every foot as they retired and yielded up no vantage ground until its capacities for defense had been tested to the utmost." He told how Brackett's mounted charge against the Yanktonais and Inkpaduta's Dakotas became "a succession of desperate hand-to-hand encounters, which ended only in the death of one or the other parties."[30]

Many of these encounters were personal—one-on-one fights motivated by vengeance—as for Corporal James Edwards of Brackett's Battalion. Sioux murdered his father near Mankato in 1862. At Tahkahokuty he drew his saber and galloped toward a lone Indian on foot, shouting, "Now is the time for revenge." Years later, a fellow soldier described how it was: "When Jim had almost overtaken him, the Indian suddenly turned, and waiting until the last moment, with his gun pointed directly at Jim's head, he took deliberate aim and fired. . . . With one jerk on his bridle, [Jim] threw his horse back on his haunches, which elevated his head just enough to receive the fatal bullet designed for Jim's brain. The horse dropped dead." Other Sioux came to the warrior's rescue at about the same time Company B's Captain Reed ordered men to Edwards's assistance. Edwards and the warrior remained focused on one another. The Sioux tried to club him with his empty gun, but Edwards parried with his saber and thrust it into his opponent's chest. Edwards then coolly grabbed the dead man's gun, moccasins, and the dead horse's bridle and saddle and returned to his battalion the "hero of the hour."[31]

Armed only with bows and arrows, lances, clubs, and some old muskets, the Indians held their own against the army's Sharps carbines, Colt navy revolvers, cavalry sabers, and formal military tactics until the artillery surprised them with the power and range of its cannon. Private Spencer described their reaction: "At first the reds appeared to be astonished. And after three or four rounds of shell [they] plainly showed sig[n]s of fear, began to complain that we were not fighting fair. Said iff we would leave the wagons that 'shot' twice at home they would come out and fight us."[32] (The artillery guns shot first when shells were

---

[30]Diessner, *No Indians Left*, 44; and Vestal, *Sitting Bull*, 52–55. Sioux tradition says his tribesmen honored The-Man-Who-Never-Walked in death with a new name, Bear's Heart; "M" (Sgt. Eugene Marshall) to "Editor of Press," 1 Aug. 1864 letter, Alfred B. Brackett Papers, Pl568, MNHS Archives.

[31]Bergemann, *Brackett's Battalion*, quoting Isaac Botsford, 113.

[32]Spencer to Father and Sister, 10 Sept. 1864, in Goodwin, "Letters of Spencer," 261. For armaments, see Sibley to Pope, 26 March 1864, 744, and Sibley to Sully, 28 March 1864, 767–68, both in OR, vol. 34, pt. 2.

fired, then again when they exploded.) Indeed, as the army marched, fighting, anywhere between four and ten miles toward the Indian camp, the Sioux learned to respect the battery. One shell lobbed at a crowd of noncombatants watching from a hill missed, but the second killed many and sent survivors scrambling. When several hundred warriors attacked the supply train, the Dakota Cavalry held the Sioux back mainly with revolvers until Sully sent Lieutenant Jones with a gun from his Minnesota battery to help. Sergeant English recalled how the "steady fire of the musketry and the shells of Jones' guns made sad havoc in their ranks and they went scurrying off, to seek and strike some other weak spot in our ranks, but not once did they succeed in piercing that line of blue."[33]

Warriors made a final grand assault to give their families time to escape, but the warriors could not ward off the horseless men with rifles trampling through their camp, especially with artillery shells bursting in their vanguard. "Sharpshooters cleaned the sides [of the hill] with their carbines," wrote "M," "and foot by foot the men won their way to the top and sweeping down the opposite side drove the last of the savages to the hills beyond." At sunset, the Indians vanished up steep gullies, and the battle was over.[34]

If Sully doubted the Nebraska scouts' loyalty after the incident involving their inebriated captain, he was reassured early in the fighting. According to Private Spencer, they "fought like tigers" with their carbines. Those who spoke Sioux interpreted conversations between antagonists and "abused [enemy Sioux] terribly in their way of blackguard."[35]

The Sioux exploited their superior numbers and hit-and-run way of fighting from about ten in the morning until dark all that hot, dry day, paying dearly in killed and wounded. "The slaughter of the reds was terrible," Private Myers recalled, but it was uncountable because when one warrior fell another would slip his lariat over him "as quick as a flash and drag him off."[36]

Though victorious, the soldiers did not rest easy the night of July 29. Indians killed two Second Minnesota Cavalry pickets, thirty-three-year-old

---

[33]Myers, *Soldiering*, 16; English, "Dakota's First Soldiers," 282–83; and English diary, 28 July 1864.

[34]"M" to "Editor of the Press," 1 Aug. 1864, in Brackett Papers, MNHS Archives. See also Brackett, Pollock, Sully and Thomas Killdeer reports, 156–58, 161, 143, 168–70.

[35]Spencer to Father and Sister, 10 Sept. 1864, in Goodwin, "Letters of Spencer," 261.

[36]Myers, *Soldiering*, 15; "M" to "Editor of the Press," 1 Aug. 1864, and Brackett's 1 Aug. 1864 handwritten report to Sully, both in Brackett Papers, MNHS Archives. Cf. Brackett's Killdeer report, 1 Aug. 1864, 161.

David LaPlante and eighteen-year-old Anton Holzgen, leaving nine arrows in one's naked, mutilated body, fifteen in the other's, and a butcher knife stuck in each. According to most accounts, the Indians did not take time to scalp them. In addition, that night another picket shot and killed Isaac Winget, a Sixth Iowa sergeant he had mistaken for an Indian. All told, Sully lost two killed and eight wounded in Brackett's Battalion on July 28; two Second Minnesota men killed by Indians; and one Sixth Iowa cavalryman killed accidently on July 29. A Sixth Iowa man and a Dakota Cavalry man also suffered injuries. The Brackett's Battalion wounded included Major Brackett, who shot his own hand while pulling his pistol from its holster yet remained in command throughout. Arrows twice pierced Sergeant Marshall but only injured him.[37] His fellow newspaper correspondent, Sergeant George Washington Northrup, was not so lucky. Only a few days earlier, Northrup had asked Marshall to "write his obituary in case he died." After the battle, Marshall informed Northrup's editor that "your Special Correspondent, G. W. Northrup . . . died in the front of the battle as a soldier should and we burried him by a small lake near the head of Knife River. He rests in the prairies of the great North West which he loved so well." In his official report, Major Brackett revealed that Northrup "fell after receiving eight or ten wounds one of which pierced his heart." Northrup's biographer, Edward Eggleston, wondered if the frontiersman had chosen that day at Killdeer Mountain as his "good day to die."[38]

Returning to the Indians' former camp the day after the battle, Colonel McLaren, Second Minnesota, reported that "after the work of destruction commenced[,] the Indians carried a white flag on the bluff close to the camp." He explained to Sully—possibly tongue-in-cheek—that, "as I could not interpret the meaning at this particular time, I did not feel called upon to report the fact to you until I had accomplished the object" and destroyed the camp. Sully spared the surviving Sioux nothing. As at Whitestone, fleeing Sioux left behind hundreds of dogs and a few ponies. Tipis, food, and equipment of all kinds fed bonfires that spread destruction even to trees on the hills.[39]

[37]Sully's Killdeer report, 31 July 1864, 144; Edward Bondiette, Co. H. 2nd Minn. Cav., reminiscence, fldr. 3, Fort Rice ND Collection, 1864–1921, SHSND Archives (hereafter cited as Bondiette reminiscence); and Bergemann, *Brackett's Battalion*, 108. Winget was in Co. G. Bondiette mentions scalping. Horatio N. Austin, Co. D, also died, along with 22 horses.

[38]Eggleston, "George W. Northrup," 20; and Patton diary, p. 31, Patton Papers, 1861, MS 20028, SHSND Archives.

[39]Sully's 31 July 1864 and McLaren's 29 July 1864 Killdeer reports, 144, 173; and Diessner, *No Indians Left*, 44.

Unlike at Whitestone, however, Sully had no prisoners to protect and feed. Private Myers recalled that only one Indian "fell into our hands, and that was a wounded one who had been found in a small clump of bushes by the Indian soldiers among Sully's scouts. They set him up on one side of the brush, mounted their ponies and rode around the brush in single file, each one shooting the poor wretch every time they came around."[40] As at Whitestone, soldiers discovered children alive amidst the camp chaos. Lieutenant Benjamin W. Brunson, Eighth Minnesota, remembered how soldiers set two baby boys on a buffalo robe and gave them hardtack. However, some Indian scouts "coming up struck their tomahawks into their brains, saying as they did so, and for the excuse of the cold blooded murder that 'Nits Make lice.'" Lieutenant G. Merrill Dwelle, Minnesota Light Artillery, found two babies dead, along with a fifteen- or sixteen-year-old girl. "Is it not sad," Dwelle asked his sister in a letter, "to think that the inocent should suffer with the guilty[?] Such children never did us any harm—Such is war."[41]

BACK AT THE HEART RIVER CAMP, SIXTH IOWA SERGEANT Nicholas Overholt, left behind because of illness, had trouble sleeping the night of July 28 because of a disturbance at the absent general's campsite. "One of Sully's squaws had a young brigadiere last night and judging from the fuss she made having it, it was a pretty good sized one." Sully was not in his tent to welcome the baby born the night following the Killdeer battle, but he was on his way back. According to Private Spencer, after attempting to follow the retreating Sioux into the rugged hills that morning, the general "gave up in disgust, saying it was the damdest country he ever saw." On July 31, Sully's fighting force united with the others.[42]

[40]Myers, *Soldiering*, 16–17; English, "Dakota's First Soldiers," 282; and Benedict diary, 28 July 1864 memorandum following 23 Sept. 1864 entry. See also Scott and Kempcke, "Journey," 11–12.

[41]Brunson, "Reminiscences of Service," 372–73, Reel 1, Dakota Conflict of 1862 MSS (hereafter cited as Brunson reminiscence); Pfaller, "Sully Expedition," 52; and Merrill Dwelle to "Sister Carrie," 25 Sept. 1864, Dwelle Papers, AD989, MNHS Archives.

[42]Overholt diary, 29 and 31 July 1864, Nicholas Overholt diaries, MNHS Archives. See also Athearn, *Forts of the Upper Missouri*, 136; Spencer to Father and Sister, 10 Sept. 1864, in Goodwin, "Letters of Spencer," 261; and Atkinson diary, 31 July to 4 Aug. 1864. This baby was apparently a boy, but Mary Sully Bordeaux, mother of famous siblings Vine Deloria, Sr., and Ella Deloria, was born of a relationship between Sully and a Yankton Sioux woman. See Sprague, *Images of America*, 101, 111, 118; and Hoxie, *Encyclopedia*, "Vine Deloria Sr.," 161–62, and "Ella Deloria," 159–61. Sully's Killdeer report, 29 Aug. 1864, 150; Thomas's Killdeer report, 168; and Williams in "Narrative of the Second," in *Minnesota in the Civil and Indian Wars*, vol. 1, 548–49.

At Tahkahokuty, Sully engaged not just a small hunting camp as at Whitestone, but warriors from the entire Sioux Nation who knew he was coming and were as prepared for a fight as they could be. Many died and many lost nearly all their possessions, but most Sioux winter counts again ignored the obvious.[43] Underlying its importance to the Sioux and American nations, the battle was personal—to Sully because of Fielner's murder, to soldiers still seeking vengeance for 1862 violence against their families, and to the Sioux whose very existence and livelihood was at stake. An expanding American nation, never mind the soldiers, considered Sioux demands—essentially that whites leave them alone to live as they pleased—unrealistic. As Sully posited beforehand, if his 1864 campaign succeeded, whites would surely overrun Sioux country.

---

[43]Cf. "Big Missouri" winter count in Cheney, *Sioux Winter Count*, 32; Howard, "Dakota Winter Counts," 389–90; Mallery, "Picture Writing," vol. 1, 285; and Candace Greene and Thornton, *Year the Stars Fell*, 253–55.

Chapter 12

"Abomination of Desolation"

AFTER THE KILLDEER BATTLE, THE YANKTONAIS AND INKPADUTA'S band departed for Dogden Butte, which lies about halfway between Fort Rice and the international border. Sitting Bull and his Hunkpapas headed south to hunt buffalo. The Sans Arcs and Miniconjous rested at a new camp near the Little Missouri River. Although Sully was running dangerously low on rations, he let his army rest two days before setting out for the Yellowstone River, where he had a fort to build. Its valley was unpopulated but for temporary Indian villages along its 600 or more miles, and the swift-flowing shallow stream was considered unnavigable by steamboats, yet Sully was counting on meeting three supply steamers more than fifty miles from its mouth.

The march began anew on August 3. Sioux scouts watching from a distance may have been surprised when Sully turned his expedition west. At first grass and water were plentiful, but after two days, they reached the badlands. From their camp on high ground near present Medora, North Dakota, they looked down on an eroded landscape. "M" told his readers: "It was a perfect labarynth to which there seemed no outlet and where no eye could trace out a path for a man to walk much less for the passage of loaded wagons."[1] Sully held a council to determine if he could cut through this country he called "hell with the fires burned out" before his six days of full rations ran out. A young man Brackett called a "Blackfoot Indian" thought he could take the expedition to the Yellowstone in eight days. He was a child when he last crossed the badlands with his father's band; nevertheless, Sully took the chance he offered.[2]

---

[1]Sully's Killdeer report, 29 Aug. 1864, 150; Thomas's Killdeer report, 168; Williams, "Narrative of the Second," in *Minnesota in the Civil and Indian Wars*, vol. 1, 548–49; Utley, *Lance*, 55–56; "M"'s (Marshall) handwritten 15 Aug. 1864 letter to "Editor of [Pioneer] Press," in Brackett Papers, MNHS Archives; Pfaller, "Sully Expedition," 56; and Lingk, "Northwestern Indian Expedition," 182.

[2]"Biography of Old Settlers," 342; Bondiette reminiscence; Helen White, *Ho!* 128n49; Sully report, 13 Aug. 1864, 144; Seelye reminiscence, fro241r, reel 3, M582, Dakota Conflict of 1862 MSS; and Lingk, "Northwestern Indian Expedition," 183n2, 188–90.

Fool Dog, Sully's oldest scout, predicted Sully would "smell the blood of his enemies within two days." Indeed, when the Sans Arcs and Miniconjous realized soldiers were coming, they sent runners to alert other scattering bands. For the first time, Cheyenne tribesmen and Brulé Sioux joined the others ready to fight Sully.[3]

"M" told readers how "slowly and surely under the guidance of our faithful Blackfoot we wound our way amongst the hills[,] now climbing a sharp ridge twenty or thirty feet high[,] ever skirting the base of a perpendicular clay wall two or three hundred feet high[,] or driving along the bottom of a dry water course." As the army inched forward, Sioux drove off horses and rolled boulders down on men struggling to cut a road. However, soldiers guarding the workmen managed to fend off a larger attack and retrieve some horses.[4]

Sully's column crossed the Little Missouri on August 7 accompanied by band music. At one point, some Sioux on high ground shouted across the river in English that, since the fight at Tahkahokuty, 500 more lodges joined them, and that 10,000 warriors had the expedition surrounded. According to Lieutenant Ben W. Brunson, Eighth Minnesota, they "proposed to take us all prisoners, and make the officers eat the soldiers." They bragged they had a white woman captive and dared the soldiers to rescue her. They may have exaggerated their numbers, but they did have a captive. The soldiers, intent on making it through this hellish landscape, paid little heed to this information.[5]

Some Eighth Minnesota men, though out of range of Sioux shooting from the bluffs, grew exasperated enough with their taunts to set their small brass howitzer almost on end to use like a mortar. Sergeant Fisk described how this was done: "They had to dig holes in the ground in order to get an angle sufficient to throw shells up on top of [the] mountain." According to Private George Cambell, they fired twice to determine the range. Emboldened by these two apparent failures, the hecklers approached a third shell, which exploded with deadly effect.[6]

The Sioux, at home in the badlands, used the terrain to advantage.

---

[3]Sully report, 13 Aug. 1864, 147. See also Utley, *Lance*, 55–64. Williams names Fool Dog in "Narrative of the Second," in *Minnesota in the Civil and Indian Wars*, vol. 1, 547.

[4]"M" to *Pioneer Press*, 15 Aug. 1864, Brackett Papers, MNHS Archives; and Brunson reminiscence, 372–73.

[5]Rice diary, 7 Aug. 1864; and Brunson reminiscence, 372–73.

[6]Andrew Fisk diary, 7 Aug. 1864; Cambell, reminiscence, 23, Cambell Papers, MNHS Archives; and Hodgson, "Personal Recollections," 34.

Cambell marveled at how they scaled the near vertical topography, jump-ing "off their horses, catching them by the tails." Thus, men and horses were "back over the bluff like a flash." That night, according to Sergeant Fisk, Indians high on the hills "fired flaming arrows down into our cor-ral, hoping to stampede the mules and horses." The attempt failed, and artillery shells sent the archers away.[7]

Sully, ill in his tent the evening of the seventh, turned over command for the next day's fighting to Colonel Thomas. In fact, Sully spent most of the campaign riding in an ambulance suffering from rheumatism and dysentery. Rheumatism also kept him from field duty during the Civil War, but he seemed to rally during battle and had war wounds to prove it. At Fair Oaks, a bullet grazed his ear; at Fredericksburg, one brushed his leg. Sully's illness may have been partly due to alcoholism; early in the march, 8th Minnesota soldier William L. Silvius made a blunt diary entry: "Sully drunk."[8] That evening, Thomas recalled, about a thousand mounted warriors sat on every elevation "quietly . . . observing our move-ments." Sully commented that Thomas would "have the biggest Indian fight that ever will happen on this continent." In the morning, Sully lay in his ambulance watching the troops. He advised Thomas to "push for the Indians' camp . . . They will fight for their families; protect your flanks and I will protect the rear." Later, as Thomas prepared to attack, Sully pointed to some hills a few miles distant and said: "You will find the camp beyond those buttes."[9]

The Battle of the Badlands took place in the six-mile space between what the Indians called "Two-Buttes-that-Stand-Facing-Each-Other." Sometime during the day, scouts had a shouted conversation with Sitting Bull, who identified the warriors as Hunkpapas, Sans Arcs, Yanktonais, and others, then asked who they were. "Some Indians with the soldiers," a scout told him, volunteering that "an Indian named Stuck-in-the-Mud" had been shot in the arm. Possibly, he meant Sully's indispensable guide

[7]Cambell reminiscence, 26, Cambell Papers, MNHS Archives; and Andrew Fisk diary, 8 Aug. 1864.

[8]Jenkins diary, 10, 11, and 12 July 1864; Atkinson diary, 14 July 1864; Doud's diary, 10 July 1864; Rice diary, 9, 10, and 16 July 1864; Silvius diary, 9 and 21 July 1864; Washburn diary, 16 July 1864; Wright diary, 25 July 1864, quoted in Scott and Kempcke, "Journey," 9; and Welsh, *Medical Histories*, 327–28. See also Helen White, *Ho!* 125, 125n31.

[9]Thomas quoted by Houlton, "Narrative of the Eighth," in *Minnesota in the Civil and Indian Wars*, vol. 1, 392, and in Hilger, "General Alfred Sully's Expedition," 325–26; and Pfaller, "Sully Expedition," 61. Some think Thomas exaggerated his role.

who, shot through the shoulder that day, had become delirious. Sitting Bull scolded the Sioux-speaking scouts for being with the soldiers.[10]

"M" wrote that the Indians "completely surrounded our Command and could be seen in great numbers on every hill top. Their line could not have been less than ten miles long." Nevertheless, they lost heavily during the long battle that ensued. One Eighth Minnesota soldier succinctly summed up his day: "Broke camp and march[e]d 12 miles and fought the enemy all day[.] Killed 6 Indians[;] captured one Horse and one Scalp. Bivouacked."[11]

On August 9, Nathaniel Pope's Prairie Battery marched in front of Brackett's Battalion blasting with shrapnel any Sioux who dared attack. "The Indians came on stronger than ever and attacked us on all sides," emigrant Nicholas Hilger wrote in his diary. He and others climbed a butte where they could "overlook the whole field of battle. Indian chiefs and commanders could be seen in all directions, signalling and directing the movements of their forces. . . . About two miles west of us our front seemed to have been checked by the hostiles, while the reports of firearms and artillery indicated a desperate struggle. About this time the rear of the train got in motion, and shortly thereafter the firing ceased."[12]

Losing the advantage the badlands terrain afforded, the Indians gave up. Colonel McLaren described their exit: "A great cloud of dust was seen rising about two miles to the south-west of our advance, which upon close inspection proved to be a living mass of warriors, with their families and herds, stampeding in a south-easterly direction into the badlands." The Sioux now knew that archery and old guns were ineffective against the army's Springfield rifles, artillery, and long-range carbines, which, in the hands of excellent marksmen, could hit targets at 300 yards.[13]

[10]Sully to Pope, 13 Aug. 1864, OR, vol. 41, pt. 1, pp. 145–74; Lingk, "Northwestern Indian Expedition," 182–85; Williams quotes Mrs. McLaren from her husband's diary in "Narrative of the Second," in *Minnesota in the Civil and Indian Wars*, vol. 1, 547; Vestal, *Sitting Bull*, 60; and Pfaller, "Sully Expedition," 64. I disagree with those who identify Sully's guide as William or Robert Jackson, mixed-blood white and Blackfeet—Siksika, not Sioux—brothers. The arm/shoulder injury fits Stuck-in-the-Mud. Furthermore, diaries, reminiscences, and letters call the guide "Little Blackfoot" or "the Little Blackfoot," not a mixed-blood.

[11]"M" to "Editor of [Pioneer] Press," 15 Aug. 1864, Brackett Papers, MNHS; Silvius diary, 8 Aug. 1864; and Dugas to parents, 10 Sept. 1864, Charles Dugas, Letters, Reel 1, Dakota Conflict of 1862 MSS.

[12]Nathaniel Pope's Killdeer report, 13 Aug. 1864, 164–65; and Hilger, "General Alfred Sully's Expedition," 319.

[13]McLaren to "My dear wife," 15 Aug. 1864, McLaren Papers, 1862–77, MNHS Archives; and Utley, *Lance*, 58–59.

Even without threat of attack, the expedition's troubles were not over. "M" wrote, "The men were already on one third rations[.] Grass had been growing scarce as we advanced and . . . our Blackfoot guide . . . was unable to sit up in an ambulance and no one else knew the country. But in difficult places and when a good view could be obtained[,] supported by two men he looked around and pointed out the General direction but was too week to do more."[14] Rattlesnakes and swarms of grasshoppers also plagued them. The latter destroyed grass that could have sustained livestock.[15]

Those in advance at the western edge of the badlands soon saw a Sioux camp stretching some three miles alongside a creek. "Their fires were yet burning," Hilger recalled, "and many of their effects, including the corpses of warriors, were left in the camp to tell of the hasty and unexpected flight." Although the Indians' livestock had used up most of the grass, water was abundant. The expedition camped nearby that night.[16]

From there to the Yellowstone, they encountered further difficulties. "M" told *Pioneer Press* readers: "We have passed through a country which can be none other than the 'Abomination of Desolation' written of by Daniel the Prophet . . . One day we marched thirty five miles over a country incapable of supporting any living thing. The grass there was absolutely none. Horses and mules fell dead by the way[. M]en parched with thirst and sick from alkali water staggered along leading the horses which could no longer carry them." John Henry Strong, Eighth Minnesota, wrote in his diary that the animals "would [fall] down and lay there[.] If they could not get up, "our orders were to shoot them." People of the Holmes train, with no choice but to struggle on with the soldiers, tried various methods of keeping animals alive. Strong watched women harvest grass for livestock too weak to graze. Some families tapped their own kegs of drinking water for their animals. Major Rice blamed Sully for this terrible trip. "I hear some bitter complaints" about his management. "Were I to say anything it certainly would be *strong language*."[17]

---

[14]"M" to "Editor of [Pioneer] Press," 10 Aug. 1864, Brackett Papers, MNHS Archives.

[15]Benedict diary, 6 Aug. 1864, in Helen White, *Ho!* 110, 126; and "From the Indian Expedition," *Sioux City Register*, 30 July 1864.

[16]Hilger, "General Alfred Sully's Expedition," 319.

[17]"M," to *Pioneer Press*, 15 Aug. 1864, Brackett Papers, MNHS Archives; Williams, "Narrative of the Second," in *Minnesota in the Civil and Indian Wars*, vol. 1, 544–48; John Henry Strong, diary, 11 Aug. 1864, 8th Minn. Vol. Inf., Reel 3, Dakota Conflict of 1862 MSS (hereafter cited as Strong diary); Rice diary, 9 and 11 Aug. 1864 (Rice's underlining).

John E. Robinson, Second Minnesota, wrote of passing near a dead five- or six-year-old Indian boy. Studying the body with its bullet wound to the temple, Robinson meditated "upon the unhappy condition of the race and their superstitious ideas of religion. I could but feel sorry for and pity them, to think that they could not have been civilized and enlightened and taught the true religion of Christ, that they might not have commited such heathenish and unheard of crimes as they did in the outbreak of 1862." This boy might have been a Lakota who had never been near Minnesota, yet Robinson further concluded that "none but the most heathen and savage minds could have thought up such heart rending and soul sickening crimes as they [meaning the Minnesota Sioux] perpetuated upon poor defenseless females. When I would get to thinking of these things my blood would boil and I would almost ache to send a bullet through their hearts."[18]

The expedition reached the Yellowstone's bottomland on August 12. Soldiers, animals, and emigrants gratefully refreshed themselves with cool water in this veritable oasis. Deer, elk, and all manner of game in the riparian woods provided feasts for the half-starved soldiers, who, since leaving the badlands, marched on only two hardtack crackers, a little bacon, and black coffee per day. Although he was downstream from his intended rendezvous, Sully was in luck. Two of his steamboats, stopped by rapids, waited nearby with food and supplies. The small sternwheelers *Chippewa Falls* and *Alone* displaced only twelve inches of water unloaded, but each carried fifty tons of freight. Not all supplies made it to the famished army, however. Corn for livestock and barrels of pork sank with the *Island City*, which also carried materials for the Yellowstone fort. This loss, low water, and the lateness of the season induced Sully to go home. He crossed his expedition to the Yellowstone's west bank. Boats hauled baggage, while men and livestock conquered the swift current any way they could. Two emigrants and many animals drowned.[19]

Once across, Sully sent Captain Moreland with Company G, Sixth Iowa, to scout upstream while the expedition followed the Yellowstone downstream to the Missouri and Fort Union. The steamboats could not carry freight in the low water, but the trip by land with overburdened wagons was leisurely and relatively pleasant. Moreland's party caught

---

[18]John E. Robinson, reminiscence, 2nd Minn. Vol. Cav., Reel 3, Dakota Conflict of 1862 MSS; and Kelly, *My Captivity*, 98–99. Kelly mentions her captors burying a dead boy after the Killdeer battle.

[19]Seelye reminiscence, fr02242r, reel 3, M582, Dakota Conflict of 1862 MSS; Helen White, *Ho!* 111; and Benedict diary, 13 and 14 Aug. 1864, in Helen White, *Ho!* 127. Xavier Kopp and John Brounworth, both of Shakopee, drowned. Estimates of today's Yellowstone River width average 100–50 feet.

up to Sully after reconnoitering 150 miles, seeing only a "few scattering bands" of Indians but, according to Private William M. Cuppett,
wildlife in astounding abundance. Another arduous river crossing (of
the Missouri) necessary to reach Fort Union took the lives of a Seventh
Iowa soldier and three animals.[20]

Sully saw that Assiniboines had waited there a long time for annuity
goods consisting only of "a spoonful of sugar, or a few beads, and part
of a blanket per head." He took the opportunity to criticize the Indian
Bureau's annuity system in a letter to headquarters. He thought Indians
should not have to "leave their hunting grounds and bring their families
to some fort, where there is no game, to starve" while waiting for such
a paltry reward.[21]

The prospect of traveling without a military escort frightened a few of
the Holmes people into returning east with Sully, but stalwarts hired a
guide to take them west to the mining regions. Sully worried that "twenty
Indians" could have captured them, although some had thought to trade
whiskey for, or buy, arms and animals from soldiers. A number of his men
deserted in the same direction. Sully sent a detail after them to no avail.

After moving his army several miles downriver of Fort Union to camp
near better grass, Sully, not liking Fort Union's location, had Fielner's
replacement as the expedition's topographical engineer choose a site for a
new military post. Captain Henning von Minden, Brackett's Battalion,
marked off a four-square-mile reserve "at and below the mouth of the
Yellowstone River, taking in all the heaviest bodies of timber."

Many expedition soldiers visited Fort Union and mingled with the
Wisconsin men of Company I who had been there since mid-June. In
the newspaper their officers published—the *Frontier Scout*—they read
news of an attack on the steamboat *Benton* upriver from the post on July
14, four days before the expedition left Fort Rice.

Three days before the Killdeer battle, Sioux attacked the *General Grant*,
a Sully boat, from a ridge on the south bank of the Missouri near Fort
Union. A crewman suffered a slight injury before a charge of canister
fired from the *Grant*'s big iron deck gun frightened the Indians away.[22]

---

[20]W.M. Cuppett to Libby, 31 Aug. 1914, folder 1, box 33, Libby Papers, SHSND Archives;
"Arrival of Gen. Sully," (*Fort Union*) *Frontier Scout*, 17 Aug. 1864; and Larpenteur, journal, 17
Aug. 1864, Fort Union NHS Library (hereafter cited as Larpenteur journal).

[21]Quotes in this and the following two paragraphs are from Sully to Asst. Adj. Gen., Dept.
NW, 18(?) Aug. 1864, OR, vol. 41, pt 1, p. 149 (OR editor questioned the date).

[22]Ibid., 148–49; Love, *Wisconsin in the War*, 833–39; "Two Interesting Stories," 28 June 1927,
Fort Union NHS Library; Larpenteur journal, 14 July 1864; "Attack on the Benton," and "The Battle of Glass Hills," (*Fort Union*) *Frontier Scout*, 27 July 1864; and Larpenteur journal, 27 July 1864.

Another item reported Sioux killing three men and wounding another while stealing cattle from a trade house named for Charles Galpin fifteen miles above the Milk River's mouth. However, the greatest excitement occurred July 27 when a Sioux raiding party stole some Fort Union horses. The infantrymen shot at them with their rifles, perhaps wounding one. First Lieutenant Charles Buckman led his foot soldiers out after them, but without horses, the attempt was futile. About a mile and a half from the fort they found a disabled horse shot dead and "a scalp-pole already prepared." According to Fort Union trader Charles Larpenteur, "had the Indians been so disposed, they could have destroyed [Buckman's] men with all ease."[23]

While Sully's men were obliterating the Killdeer Sioux camp, Sioux warriors—possibly fresh from the battle—stole two horses owned by Fort Union Assiniboines. The *Frontier Scout*'s "Extra" edition reported, "After a few minutes skirmishing . . . the big gun was brought to bear and a shrapnel shot [was] fired at them which killed one as it burst." The soldiers, Assiniboines, and a few visiting Mandans and Hidatsas who still had horses chased them for more than two miles when the Sioux "turned and gave battle." A Mandan killed a Sioux, whom the Assiniboines scalped, "bringing both head and scalp to the Fort as their trophies." They celebrated by "brandishing their bloody trophies aloft, singing, dancing, drumming, etc., in honor of the great victory." The *Frontier Scout*'s account emphasized, "Had we been mounted this morning we might have captured the whole of them. Give us some horses by all means!" The first news Fort Union residents had of Sully's victories and his successful rendezvous with the boats came August 13 when the *General Grant* returned to Fort Union from upriver on the Missouri.[24]

While soldiers were in the vicinity, the *Frontier Scout* published an anonymous soldier's account of the trip that closely followed the expedition officers' official reports. A final paragraph ticked off Sully's accomplishments. Between July 19 and August 16, the expedition traveled 457 miles, "fought three days, forded rivers and dug the way through a country so broken as to seem utterly impassable, often suffering for days together for want of grass and good water, [and] taught the combined

---

[23]Larpenteur journal, 19 July 1864; Larpenteur, *Forty Years*, 306; "Extra," (*Fort Union*) *Frontier Scout* 29 July 1864; "Surprise Party," (*Fort Union*) *Frontier Scout*, 27 July 1864; and Regimental Muster and Descriptive Rolls 1861–65, Wisc. Historical Society Archives.

[24]"Desperate Attack by Sioux!" (*Fort Union*) *Frontier Scout* (extra ed.), 29 July 1864. The *Eau Claire Free Press* reprinted the *Frontier Scout*'s account 8 Sept. 1864. Larpenteur journal, 28 July, 2 Aug., and 13 Aug. 1864; and Sully to Asst. Adj. Gen., 13 Aug. 1864, OR, vol. 41, pt. 1, p. 147.

forces of the Indians a lesson they will never forget. For the first time [Sully] demonstrated the practicability of steamboat navigation of the Yellow-stone." He also "surveyed an unexplored country and found its immense resources" of exposed coal beds.[25]

Because Captain Napoleon B. Greer's original orders were to protect Sully's boats and prevent government stores and annuity goods for tribes who traded at Fort Union from "falling into the hands of hostile Indians," he and his Company I expected to leave with the others. However, Sully ordered them to remain the winter and erect temporary sheds inside the fort's walls to store materials for the Yellowstone post.

On August 22 Sully hurried his expedition downriver. About eighty miles from Fort Union, they noticed thousands of pony tracks trending northeast. Sully guessed they were Yanktonais he had fought at Killdeer Mountain.[26] At Fort Berthold, the affiliated tribes were busy harvesting corn. While his men enjoyed themselves with all that the trading post and Indians had to offer, Sully met with Arikara, Hidatsa, and Mandan leaders, who told him "they now felt as if they were relieved from [the] slavery" of Sioux intimidation. To protect them and to keep communication open on the river, Sully left Captain Moreland's company, G, Sixth Iowa, to garrison the trading fort.

The Rees believed the Sioux who made the trail Sully crossed were on their way to Dogden Butte. However, Father De Smet's courier, Big Head's Brother, heard from Yanktonais that the northern mixed-bloods supplied them with seven powder kegs and some balls and invited them across the border. Big Head's Brother also attested that Yanktonai chiefs Black Catfish, Medicine Bull, Two Bear, and other headmen wanted to make peace. They claimed they never would have fought Sully if the Hunkpapas and other Lakotas did not talk them into it. At Tahkaho-kuty, these Yanktonais realized the Hunkpapas were "better at talking than fighting."

Sully reached Dogden Butte on September 2, where its height provided a forty-mile view of the country that verified Big Head's Brother's intelligence. He saw no Indians, only signs of the northern mixed-bloods'

---

[25]"Arrival," (*Fort Union*) *Frontier Scout*, 17 Aug. 1864. According to the Lignite Energy Council, in 2008, North Dakota produced 29.7 million tons of coal.

[26]Dill to Greer and GO 6, both 11 Apr. 1864, and SO 70, 19 Aug. 1864, NW Indian Expedition, all in U.S. Army, *General Orders, 1st.*, Fort Union NHS Library; Napoleon B. Greer, pension records, file 679179, CAN 14-400, bundle 62, RG 94, NA; Atkinson diary, 22 Aug. 1864; Sully to Pope, 29 Aug. 1864, 150, and Thomas to Asst. Adj. Gen., Dist. of Minn., 13 Aug. 1864, 167–68, both in OR, vol. 41, pt. 1; English, "Dakota's First Soldiers," 292–93; and English diary, 27 Aug. 1864.

recent passage. "We can never expect to have quiet on this frontier till this unlawful traffic on the part of people from the English possessions is put down. An expedition into their country," Sully reported, "would have a very beneficial effect."[27]

He turned his army toward Fort Rice, one day marching it through a buffalo herd so large he "had to send out men dismounted as skirmishers to drive them off." Major Atkinson scoffed, "Talk of starving the Indians, it is damed nonsense." Sully's horses and other livestock, competing for grass, continued to suffer. Cold weather and rain magnified the misery for man and beast, leading one Second Minnesota diarist to call this "the hardest days march I have ever seen in the army." Another wrote more livestock gave out and were shot that day than at any other time on the campaign. In camp near Apple Creek, amid remnants of Sibley's 1863 camp, fifty horses died in one day. Here, Sully had Lieutenant Beaver's body exhumed and prepared for shipment to his family in Cardiff, Wales.[28]

As the expedition approached Fort Rice September 8, Sully was pleased to hear the Thirtieth Wisconsin had made good progress building the post. However, he was furious when he learned that another bothersome emigrant train from Minnesota was in trouble out on the prairie.[29]

JAMES LIBERTY FISK'S FASCINATION WITH THE IDEA OF A NORTHERN wagon road began when he worked for Nobles's 1857 road-building expedition. Fisk was only a private early in the Civil War, yet Minnesota promoters, including Nobles, facilitated his commission as captain in the quartermaster department and his congressional appointment as superintendent of emigration to establish such a route. In 1862, Fisk's expedition rendezvoused at Fort Abercrombie well before the August mayhem erupted in southwestern Minnesota. Their trip across the plains

[27]Sully to Asst. Adj. Gen., 29 Aug. 1864, 150–51 ("better at talking" quote on p. 150), and 11 Sept. 1864, p. 153, both in OR, vol. 41, pt. 1; GO 78, 30 Aug. 1864, Brackett Papers, MNHS Archives; Atkinson diary, 31 Aug. 1864; Gary Anderson, *Kinsmen*, 217; Strong diary, 2 Sept. 1864; and Pfaller, *Father De Smet in Dakota*, 45–46, 46n85.

[28]Sully to Asst. Adj. Gen., Dept. NW, 11 Sept. 1864, OR, vol. 41, pt. 1, p. 153; Atkinson diary, 5 Sept. 1864; Rice diary, 6 Sept 1864, 29; Jenkins diary, 6 Sept. 1864; Pfaller, "Sully Expedition," 75; and Pattee, "Reminiscences," 316–17.

[29]Sully to Pope, 11 Sept. 1864, OR, vol. 41, pt. 1, pp. 152–53.

to the diggings in what was then Idaho was uneventful. In 1863, Fisk led his train through parts of Minnesota barely scabbed over from the previous year's depredations. Fisk and his train caught up to Sibley's forces but, feeling secure enough with Fisk's fifty-man private guard force, did not stay with them and safely reached their destination. In 1864, Fisk's would-be miners and merchants met at Fort Ridgely too late to avail themselves of Colonel Thomas's Minnesota Brigade as escort. General Pope knew how determined the captain was to cross Dakota, notwithstanding that the territory might become a battleground. However, since Fisk was on detached service for the secretary of war, Pope could not stop him.[30]

Although instructed to follow his same Fort Abercrombie to Fort Benton route, Fisk burned to open a new one, shorter by some 500 miles, that would pass between the Black Hills and the badlands Sully negotiated, roughly today's Highway I-94. This was Sully's planned route before his pursuit of the Sioux diverted him farther north. When his train reached the Kettle Lakes region where Major John Clowney was building Fort Wadsworth, Fisk asked for an escort. From his command comprising Company I of the Second Minnesota Cavalry and four Thirtieth Wisconsin companies, Clowney assigned the Second's Lieutenant Henry F. Phillips, with fifty men, to take Fisk to the Missouri.[31]

At Fort Rice, Fisk was miffed at Sully for three weeks earlier taking the Holmes train with him. "I was not aware until I reached Fort Rice that this distinguished military leader was authorized or disposed to supercede me in the special duties of pioneering routes and protecting emigrants. However, I suppose I can square accounts with the General by offsetting my battles with his Indians against his pains with my emigrants." Fisk's sniping remark would prove prescient.

Citing Clowney's orders to return to Fort Wadsworth, Lieutenant Phillips refused to obey Fisk's order to continue as escort to the Yellowstone River. At Fort Rice, Colonel Dill reluctantly allowed Fisk fifty men from among his recuperating cavalrymen and enough serviceable horses to carry them. Second Lieutenant Dewitt C. Smith, Company

---

[30]Pope to Halleck, 6 Oct. 1864, OR, vol. 41, pt. 1, p. 132; and Helen White, *Ho!* 28, 136. White (132–57) copied and annotated James Fisk's 13 Jan. 1865 official report.

[31]Clowney to Olin, 29 July 1864, 463, and Pope to Halleck, 12 Aug. 1864, 675, both in OR, vol. 41, pt. 2; and Helen White, *Ho!* 137–38. The fort was established 1 Aug. 1864 to honor Brig. Gen. James F. Wadsworth.

A, Dakota Cavalry, had orders to accompany the train only to the Yellowstone River.[32]

Fisk followed Sully's tracks to where the army headed north. With
nary a Sioux in sight, he left Sully's path to head west through uncharted
territory. Then, 180 miles from Fort Rice, Indians suddenly "swarming
in the bluffs on all side[s]" attacked. Badly injured, Corporal Thomas C.
Williamson, Sixth Iowa, who had been in advance with the military
guard, alerted Fisk to his predicament. According to Fisk, Lieutenant
Smith, without waiting for orders, sped to the fight joined by soldiers and
emigrants responding to bugle calls and signal guns.[33] Meanwhile, civilians and teamsters pulled the wagons together to corral livestock inside
and partition off a safe place for women, children, and the wounded.
Along with the twelve-pounder mountain howitzer and additional men
Smith requested once he knew the situation, Fisk sent an ambulance to
bring in the injured and dead.

It would have meant little to Captain Fisk had he realized his attackers
were Sitting Bull's Hunkpapa band. Neither Sitting Bull nor Pizi (Gall),
also present, were yet famous. They had tracked Fisk's train for days, then
attacked when emigrants and soldiers were trying to right an overturned
wagon. The Hunkpapas took two wagons, one of which had a man tied
to it as punishment for thievery. Later, Porcupine, one of the attackers,
told a Fisk expedition member, "We Indians have different customs from
you whites. The last thing this white man saw was a bright light at his
feet." The two-hour fight, during which Smith's outnumbered men meted
out what Fisk called "considerable punishment," ended at sunset. Sitting
Bull suffered a gunshot wound to his hip. Fisk's cost was six soldiers and
two teamsters dead, two men missing, and several seriously injured.[34]

That night the emigrants dared not light fires or pitch tents. They
cared for the wounded and buried their dead. Camped between two

---

[32]Helen White, *Ho!* 140 ("I was not aware" quote); Sully to Pope, 9 Sept. 1864, OR, vol. 41, pt.
1, p. 151; correspondence concerning Phillips's refusal in OR, vol. 41, pt. 2, pp. 947–49; Daniel J.
Dill, "Fort Rice," fldr. 10, box 33, Fort Rice ND Collection, 1864–1921, SHSND Archives (hereafter
cited as Dill, "Fort Rice"); "From the Frontier," *Saint Paul (Minn.) Pioneer*, 19 Sept. 1864; English,
"Dakota's First Soldiers," 308–309; and English diary, 12 July 1864.

[33]Sully to Pope, 9 Sept. 1864, OR, vol. 41, pt. 1, 151–52; and Helen White, *Ho!* 142–43, 143n23.

[34]Helen White, *Ho!* 144–45; Utley, *Lance*, 59–60; Larson, *Gall*, 50–51, 235; and Collins, "Larned,"
9, 9n6, 17n17. Killed were Theodore Rasch, Co. K, and Joseph Delaney, Co. I, 8th Minn.; John
Quinn, Co. I, 6th Iowa Cav.; William H. Chase and Ernest Hoffmaster, Brackett's Battalion;
H. Higgins, cavalry; Walter Fewer and Walter Greaves, teamsters; and Louis Nudick (or Neudick),
emigrant. Wounded were Corp. Marmaduke Betts, Co. F, 6th Iowa Cav., mortally; Thomas C.
Williamson, Co. A, 6th Iowa Cav.; Jefferson Dilts, signal scout; and L. Dostaler, teamster, slightly.

ridges, they were out of range of the Indians' own guns but not of the Sharps carbines the attackers had unwittingly acquired with the captured wagons. The Sioux's aim with these new weapons was poor, however. That night, as a "grand and terrific" thunderstorm raged, Fisk wrote that "hundreds of Wolves, attracted by the scent of blood and of corpses set up a most unearthly howling and yelping." By morning, cattle enclosed in a natural basin were "standing . . . in two feet of water."[35]

Come Hunkpapas or high water, Fisk insisted on continuing west. For two days, the train moved ahead in five columns, all the while under attack. More Sioux arrived to harass the travelers, but the emigrants' superior firepower kept them at bay. Fisk inched his party westward until September 4, when he decided to appeal to Colonel Dill for help. Lieutenant Smith volunteered as messenger, and Fisk wrote a letter to Dill describing what had happened but insisting that "to turn back would be certain destruction to my little party."[36]

On a hill on the east side of the Little Missouri River, Fisk ordered his people to dig in. The Sioux departed temporarily, uncharacteristically leaving behind their dead. The Fisk party found drinking water, dug rifle pits, and began surrounding their camp with sod walls. They named this makeshift fortification near present Rhame, North Dakota, Fort Dilts to honor scout Jefferson Dilts, who lived on for days tortured by injuries incurred in hand-to-hand combat during the initial attack.[37]

Carrying Fisk's letter, Lieutenant Smith arrived at Fort Rice after traveling thirty-eight hours. Colonel Dill recalled later that Smith "had to be taken off his horse, his feet and legs were so swollen that he could not use them for a time." Another messenger, whose horse had given out the previous day, staggered in the next day on foot. The two, Dill said, were lucky they avoided Indians arriving at the fort to sue for peace.[38] When Sully read Fisk's letter, which Dill forwarded to him, Sully ordered Dill "with all the troops of his garrison" to "proceed without delay to [Fisk's] assistance." He also ordered 600 of his own tired troops to go along dismounted and told Captain Nathaniel Pope to take two guns and one caisson. With rations for eighteen days and sixty rounds of

[35]Helen White, *Ho!* 143–44, 149; expedition surgeon William D. Dibbs, quoted in Pearson, *Fort Dilts*, 56–57; and Utley, *Lance*, 59–60.

[36]James Fisk to Dill, 4 Sept. 1864, OR, vol. 41, pt. 3, p. 466; and Helen White, *Ho!* 145–46, 150, 269. Teamster Charles L. Libby was wounded.

[37]Collins, "Larned," 10; and Helen White, *Ho!* 20, 116, 152, 168.

[38]Helen White, *Ho!* 146, 152; Fisk to Dill, 4 Sept. 1864, OR, vol. 41, pt. 3, p. 466; Collins, "Larned," 16; and Dill, "Fort Rice."

ammunition per man, the force would march in light order, carrying no supplies or baggage. Sergeant Andrew Jackson Fisk, a Second Minnesota infantryman with Sully's expedition, eagerly joined the rescuers going to the aid of his brother James and the others. In addition to James and his wife and daughter, another Fisk brother, Van, was with the emigrants.[39]

THE NIGHT SMITH HAD DEPARTED FOR FORT RICE CARRYING THE message, Sitting Bull's warriors fired arrows and bullets into the emigrant camp. In the morning, Fisk wrote, Sioux "appeared in force gathering and closing around us." One man wearing a long robe seemed to make a speech to the emigrants as a diversion while others worked their way around to the other side of the camp. Because the Indians had 2,000 rounds of ammunition in the wagons they captured, Fisk knew he could not withstand a lengthy siege. Complicating matters, these Hunkpapas had the white woman they had bragged about to Sully's scouts during the badlands fight. A band of Oglalas had attacked her party on the Oregon Trail in July and kidnapped nineteen-year-old Frances Kelly, but she now belonged to the Hunkpapa Brings Plenty. When they forced her to write the "soldier chief" (Fisk), she recognized opportunity. Although none of her captors could read English, some could understand it and they counted her words. The result was a confused communication integrating what they demanded she say with what she wanted to tell her potential rescuers.[40]

From a crowd of Indians on a hill about a mile from Fort Dilts, three warriors came forward to fasten a paper to a stick in the ground. Written with a pointed bullet, the note's gist was that the Sioux were tired of fighting and would turn Kelly over in exchange for forty head of cattle. Her phrase "many killed by the goods they brought into camp" referred to bread Fisk's 1864 emigrants poisoned with strychnine and purposely left lying about. The paragraphs in Fisk's official report concerning the poisoning were censored for a hundred years. Kelly wrote, "They have killed many whites. Help me if you can." Fisk replied, offering "three good American horses" for her. In her garbled notes, Fanny identified several of her captors by name.[41] In her memoir, Kelly explained that one

[39]James Fisk to Dill, 4 Sept. 1864, and Sully to Dill, GO 80, 9 Sept. 1864, both in OR, vol. 41, pt. 3, pp. 466–67; Fisk diary, 9 Sept. and 20 Sept. 1864; and Helen White, Ho! 168.

[40]Helen White, Ho! 149; Utley, Lance, 60; and Kelly, My Captivity, 147–52, 274–78.

[41]Helen White, Ho! 133, 147–51, 269; Kelly, My Captivity, 129, 276; and Collins, "Larned," 26. White reproduced the censored paragraphs.

named Porcupine arrived at the Sioux camp "well dressed, and mounted on a fine horse, and brought with him presents and valuables that insured him a cordial reception." He told her he was sent from Fort Laramie to negotiate her release. After a few days, he gave her a letter from Captain Levi G. Marshall, Eleventh Ohio Volunteer Cavalry, telling of previous unsuccessful attempts to rescue her and vouching for Porcupine as a "friendly Indian [who] had undertaken to bring me back, for which he would be rewarded." Kelly was overjoyed at the prospect of rescue, but Porcupine dashed her hopes by preparing to return to Fort Laramie without her. According to Kelly, "Porcupine said he should report me as dead, or impossible to find." When Kelly reminded him Marshall's letter said the soldiers had his three wives in custody and would kill them if he did not return with Kelly, Porcupine scoffed. "White soldiers are cowards; they never kill women; and I will deceive them as I have done before."[42]

One note Porcupine carried to Fisk demanded four wagons and "40 cattle to eat" in return for stopping the fighting. They wanted Fisk to come to them, but Kelly, warning Fisk not to read aloud or to come, added: "They say this is thier ground. They say go home and come back no more . . . and they say they want knives and axes and arrow Iron [guns] to shoot Buffalo. . . . They are very anxious for you to move now." Ultimately, negotiations broke down. Fisk justified his stubbornness in bargaining for Kelly: "Although we were bound to do all that lay in our power to ransom Mrs Kelly, we could not, with safety to ourselves, show our weakness, and lay it at the mercy of that fiendish treachery, against which Mrs Kelley had herself warned me."[43]

Fighting was finished at Fort Dilts; dying was not. Two Sixth Iowa soldiers, Manfred D. Betts and Thomas Williamson, died of their wounds on September 8. Williamson had been delirious for days. Jefferson Dilts, the brave scout for whom Fisk named their makeshift fort, also died after eleven long days of suffering. Altogether, the expedition lost six soldiers and two teamsters. Porcupine later said at least twenty-five Sioux died from strychnine-laced bread and the party's bullets.[44]

As the nearly 900-man rescue party marched west at the pace of its oxen, Sergeant Andrew Fisk, eager to see his brothers, complained about the slow-moving beasts, a number of which gave out after two days' work. After passing where the emigrants' and Sully's trails diverged, the soldiers sighted Indians nearly every day. Captain Peter B. Davy, Second

---

[42]Kelly, *My Captivity*, 129–30. Marshall identified in Ware, *Indian War*, 197, 479.
[43]Helen White, *Ho!* 148–50.
[44]James Fisk quoted in Helen White, *Ho!* 149–52; Collins, "Larned," 10n7, 12–13, 12n9.

Minnesota, commanding the small cavalry contingent, ordered the men to "close picket" their horses overnight and have them in hand before dawn. It was good advice. As the men saddled up early on September 16, Thomas Hodgson recorded in his diary that "a band of Indians dashed across a corner of the camp, firing guns, shaking buffalo robes and yelling like [mad]." They stampeded all the grazing horses, but mounted soldiers chased them and recovered all but fifteen.[45]

The rescue party reached Fort Dilts on September 20. The brothers Fisk celebrated their reunion, and according to Andrew, the emigrants were "delighted to once more be assured of safety." James, too, was happy. "The first thing Fisk did," Hodgson recalled, "was to present Col. Dill with a barrel of whiskey." Fisk's warm welcome cooled, however, when Dill insisted he take his train back to Fort Rice. Because the Sioux had not bothered them since Smith left, James Fisk requested an escort farther west, arguing that in three or four days they would be in Crow country and out of danger. Dill refused, calling such a move "folly and madness." Fisk continued cajoling his emigrants to go forward and, in Dill's words, "insulting them for what he called backing out." Meanwhile, one of the emigrants, who had planned to start a saloon in the mining districts, offered his stock for sale to the soldiers. Dill, who had been a liquor dealer, did not stop his men from enjoying what Hodgson called "one vast whiskey camp."[46]

In the morning, James Fisk relented: the entire party would return. In his report, Dill commented, "I think Captain Fisk deserves censure for trying to urge the emigrants forward under the circumstance, and knowing as much as he should of the Indian character." On September 30, Fisk's party and its rescuers safely reached Fort Rice, with Colonel Dill counting as casualties fifteen horses, fifteen or sixteen oxen, and one missing man— Augustine Carpenter of the Eighth Minnesota. "We think he was captured by Indians," Andrew Fisk wrote in his diary, "and will never be seen alive again." According to Dill, he "became intoxicated the morning we left the corral and [is] supposed to have laid down and [been] left behind."[47]

<hr>

[45]Andrew Fisk diary, 9–15; and Hodgson, *Personal Recollections*, 36.

[46]Andrew Fisk diary, 20 Sept. 1864; Hodgson, *Personal Recollections*, 37; Dill to Asst. Adj. Gen. Pell, 4 Oct. 1864, OR, vol. 41, pt. 1, p. 795; and Dill, "Fort Rice."

[47]Dill to Asst. Adj. Gen. Pell, 4 Oct. 1864, OR, vol. 41, pt. 1, pp. 795–96; Dill, "Fort Rice"; Mattison, ed., "Fisk Expedition: Diary of Larned," (hereafter cited as Larned diary), 23, 26, and 30 Sept. 1864, 237; Collins, "Larned," 9n6, 18n19; Helen White, *Ho!* 151; Houlton, "Narrative of the Eighth," in *Minnesota in the Civil and Indian Wars*, vol. 1, 410; Andrew Fisk diary, 21 and 22 Sept. 1864; and Dill, "Fort Rice."

While the rescuers were away, Sioux on a horse raid at Sully's camp east of the Missouri killed and scalped Sergeant Alfred Murphy, Sixth Iowa, after a furious fight. The four men with him escaped, but barely. A few days later, Sioux killed Sixth Iowa wagoner Sanford Murphy during an attack on a herding party.[48]

SULLY FEARED THE SIOUX WOULD ASSUME FISK'S TRAIN WAS PART of his command and, if they captured it, might "boast of it and urge the rest to continue the war." Despite this concern, his stay at Fort Rice was fruitful. Three to four hundred lodges of Sioux met him there, suing for peace.[49] Although Sully remained in camp across from Fort Rice during the rescue of Fisk's train, he led his main expedition away from Fort Rice the day before Colonel Dill's return. Neither did the colonel waste time sending off his soldiers. Most of Fisk's people joined those returning to Minnesota or Sioux City. Julia and William Larned and their son Horatio were among a few who remained at Fort Rice. James Fisk's assistant, Sam Johnston, and his brother Van Haden Fisk stayed on to look after property and livestock until James could get up a new expedition.[50]

Because Sully did not have enough rations to keep his army together for long, he had sent off all but enough men to garrison Fort Rice. Lieutenant Colonel Pattee, who estimated the distance to Sioux City by water at about 1,000 miles, had his men build boats for the infantry bound for Kentucky and for cavalrymen whose horses died during the campaign. On October 1, a fleet of eight fifty-five-foot-long boats left Fort Rice.[51] The Nebraska Scouts, five companies of Sixth and three Seventh Iowa companies; the two Dakota Cavalry companies, Nathaniel Pope's Prairie Battery, and Brackett's Battalion marched south with Sully.

Communication between Fort Rice and Sioux City—450 miles apart by land—required some twenty-four days. Furthermore, delivering

[48]Sergeant Alfred Murphy, Co. L, 6th Iowa Cav., Iowa's Adj. General's Office, *Roster and Record of Iowa Soldiers*, 1125; Drips, *Three Years*, 93–94; English, "Dakota's First Soldiers," 298–99; and English diary, 21, 22, and 27 Sept. 1864.

[49]Sully to Pope, 9 Sept. 1864, 152, and Sully to Asst. Adj. Gen., 11 Sept. 1864, 154, both in OR, vol. 41, pt. 1.

[50]Dill to Asst. Adj. Gen. Pell, 4 Oct. 1864, OR, vol. 41, pt. 1, p. 796; Dill, "Fort Rice"; Col. C.A.R. Dimon to Asst. Adj. Gen. Pell, 17 Oct. 1864, OR, vol. 41, pt. 4, p. 65; Larned diary, 15 and 17 Oct. 1865, 241–43; Collins, "Larned," 20–21; and Helen White, *Ho!* 133, 153.

[51]Sully to Asst. Adj. Gen., 11 Sept. 1864, 154, and Dill to Asst. Adj. Gen. Pell, 4 Oct. 1864, 796, both in OR, vol. 41, pt. 1; and Pattee, "Reminiscences," 317–18.

dispatches, especially between Forts Sully and Rice, took courage. Soon after leaving Rice, Sully's brigade met a mail courier, George Pleets, whom Indians had captured on his way to Fort Sully, releasing him only because his Indian wife's relatives pleaded his case. Sully ordered Captain Miner, with a detachment of Dakota Cavalry, to find the band who detained Pleets—according to Amos Cherry, it was Two Bear's band—and invite them to Fort Sully to make peace. After passing Swan Lake, the Dakotans found an Indian camp with meat from several freshly killed buffalo still on the ground. Another group of Sioux admitted they "had broken up into small parties the better to subsist" and were "discouraged and disheartened." Their supplies were destroyed during the summer's fighting; they were ready to come in for talks. Meanwhile, scouts reported seeing a white woman (not Kelly) near a lake on the east side of the Missouri but took no action to rescue her. (Pizi [Gall] later confirmed they had taken Kelly to the Grand River area, but that was west of the Missouri.)[52]

When Sully's column reached Fort Sully on October 6, he learned the Yanktonai chiefs Two Bear and Little Soldier as well as another chief he fought over the summer had come in earlier to ask the terms of peace. Captain David C. Fuller gave them two conditions: that they behave themselves and that they stop attacking whites. The three chiefs promised to bring in their headmen to talk it over. But when Fuller did not help them, they explained, they had to choose between letting their families starve or living in the hostile camp. They, and many others, did not want war with whites but akicita (Indian soldiers) guarding them would have "cut up their lodges, seized all their property, horses, everything" if they had tried to leave. They had already lost many lodges as a result of the two summers' defeats. The chiefs gave Sully a clearer idea of whom he had fought this season—"nearly all the Indians out west"—and a better enemy casualty count. Two Bear and Little Soldier did not know how many Sioux had died but could account for some 400 to 500 wounded. The two did not relish living around a garrison begging for their food, although they did want to join the band of friendly Indians at Fort Rice. Sully liked that idea, too. "I gave them a letter to the commanding officer, with orders to treat them well, for Two Bears can be made of great use. He is a very influential man in his nation; a very brave and

[52]Pattee, "Reminiscences," 317–18; land mileage from Pope to Halleck, 12 Aug. 1864, OR, vol. 41, pt. 2, p. 675; Cherry diary, 1 Oct. 1864, in Shambaugh, "Iowa Troops," 435; Drips, *Three Years*, 96; English, "Dakota's First Soldiers," 299–300; Larson, *Gall*, 247n22; and Larson, "Chief Gall," 20–21.

very shrewd Indian." Perhaps because he regretted Whitestone, in his report Sully reported that Two Bear and Little Soldier had "always been strong friends to the whites."[53]

Sully left his adjutant-general, Captain Pell, to meet the large congregation of Sioux expected to arrive for further talks, but Whitestone Hill veteran Major House would command the three Sixth Iowa companies— B, H, and K—who would winter at Fort Sully.[54] On October 10 Sully arrived at Crow Creek Reservation, where he saw little if any improvement. Agent Balcombe permitted the starving Sioux to hunt east of the Missouri, but some twenty-four lodges crossed the James River and did not return. According to the *Sioux City Register*, another train from Mankato was supposed to supply Crow Creek that summer. "As was the case last fall . . . this train is probably loaded with suttlers goods with which to absorb the Indian annuities. The people of Minnesota, who'd not rest until the Winnebago Indians were removed from their State, yet they seem to have no compunctions about receiving their money for supplies." The summer supply mission never materialized. While criticizing Minnesotans, the Iowa paper also wanted the Winnebagos out of their neighborhood, fearing "there will be more trouble if they are allowed to roam over the country annoying the people."[55] The Mandans, Hidatsas, and Arikaras proposed that the Winnebagos, distant kin to the Mandans, have a reservation near them. Ultimately, their new agent, Whitestone Hill veteran Colonel Robert Furnas, helped them find a permanent home with the Omahas in Nebraska. On March 8, 1865, the tribe signed a treaty with Commissioner Dole and agents Thompson and Balcombe ceding their interest in Crow Creek to the government and accepting as their new reservation the Omaha tribe's cession of some land along the Missouri River in Nebraska.[56]

Proceeding down the river, Sully found the Yanktons also near starvation. Because they had received no annuities, they were forced to hunt north of their reservation. Sully feared they might hamper peace efforts

[53]Sully to Asst. Adj. Gen., Dept. NW, 7 Oct. 1864, OR, vol. 41, pt. 3, pp. 698–99. Fulton, 30th Wis. Vol. Inf., commanded Fort Sully when Bartlett moved to Rice with the expedition.

[54]Sully to Asst. Adj. Gen., Dept. NW, 7 Oct. 1864, OR, vol. 41, pt. 3, pp. 698–99; and Drips, *Three Years*, 96–97, 99.

[55]Brown to Rose, 26 Oct. 1864, OR, vol. 41, pt. 4, p. 293; "Indian Supply Train," *Sioux City (Iowa) Register*, 23 July 1864 (item copied and embellished from *The Mankato (Minn.) Record*).

[56]Kappler, *Indian Affairs*, vol. 2, *Treaties*, 8 March 1865 (Winnebagos), 874–75, ratified 13 Feb. 1866, proclaimed 28 March 1866. See also Farb, "Military Career" and "Omaha Agent." *Sioux City (Iowa) Register*, 23 July 1864; Pope to Sibley, 10 Oct. 1864, OR, vol. 41, pt. 3, 772; and De Smet to Dole, 23 Sept. 1864, no. 128, CIA annual report, 282.

through propinquity to the militant bands, or they might spread word about whites' "continued abuses to friendly Sioux." With only about 1,500 men in his own vast jurisdiction, he suggested to Pope that the army use other Upper Missouri tribes to help control the Sioux. He argued it would be economical "for the Government to expend a few thousand dollars and get these Indians into a war with the hostile portion of the Sioux, and to assist them also with troops, till all the posts are permanently established." At his district headquarters (now at Dubuque), Sully awaited word from Captain Pell about unfinished 1864 business—Fanny Kelly.[57]

ON OCTOBER 23, PELL HOSTED A PRELIMINARY COUNCIL AT FORT Sully with Bear Rib's delegation of 200 Hunkpapa and Sihasapa headmen. His opening speech almost certainly insulted his audience: "News was brought to General Sully that you wished to come in and talk with him. He had more important business to care for elsewhere . . . Whatever you say to me I will tell him. He could not stay and left me in his place." Pell grumbled to Sully about the post's interpreter being unskilled but gave Sully a detailed synopsis of speakers' "thoughts, sentiments, and comparisons."

Bear Rib, only twenty-four, spoke first, blaming traders, agents, and other whites for getting them into war. His camp was glad the president "would make peace with those who were sick of fighting and wished to be friends to the whites." The Sihasapas and Hunkpapas now knew that "whites go wherever they want to, that nothing can stop them; that where they want to stay we can no more drive them away than we can a wall of solid rock. We used to think we could fight like men, but now we know we can only fight like boys when we fight with the whites."[58]

To speakers who complained the summer's campaign and new forts drove away their game, Pell responded that until they turned over Fanny Kelly, the government would continue to send expeditions and build posts. At this they "looked very much cast down; in fact," Pell said, "they

[57]Sully to Asst. Adj. Gen., Dept. NW, 11 Sept. 1864, OR, vol. 41, pt. 1, p. 155; Pell to Sully, 26 Oct. and 1 Nov. 1864, OR, vol. 53, p. 602; Sully to Asst. Adj. Gen., 22 Nov. 1864, OR, vol. 41, pt. 4, pp. 651–52; and Moe, *Last Full Measure*, 97.

[58]Bear Rib's age inferred from U.S. Bureau of the Census, Indian Census Rolls, 1885–90, Standing Rock Reservation. Speeches in Pell to Sully, 26 Oct. and 1 Nov. 1864, OR, vol. 53, pp. 599–602. See also Pope to Halleck, 17 Nov. 1864, OR, vol. 41, pt. 4, pp. 599–600.

seemed much cast down during the entire council." As incentive, he promised a feast when they brought Kelly in. In addition to the "nearly 200 pounds condemned meat" he told Sully he could use for this purpose, Pell promised them "papers from the general showing we are at peace." These papers would serve until Sully could come to make an official treaty.

Six chiefs left Fort Sully ahead of the others to find Kelly. The rest of the delegation promised to contact the Miniconjous and Sans Arcs, who, they were sure, would also sign the treaty. In an October 26, 1864, letter to Sully, Pell wrote, "As far as I could judge by their actions, speeches, and what they said to outsiders after the council, all I said met their Indian ideas of justice perfectly."

A runner from the large Sioux camp brought word on October 31 that the delegation of chiefs bought Kelly for three horses. She was presently a guest at their camp, but they had to hunt buffalo before bringing her to Fort Sully. Pell assured Sully he "made no bargain to pay for the woman," thinking it better to reimburse the individual Indians involved. He wished for "a few well-expended presents" to cement "the friendly feeling that they now express." He was optimistic about a general peace. "The hostile bands now suing for peace are numerous, influential, and have long been the greatest trouble makers among all the Indians of this country." The Miniconjous and Sans Arcs wanted peace, but were "afraid of the way they will be treated if they come in." Pell reasoned that once the Sihasapas and Hunkpapas signed a treaty, the others would, too, because "they will no longer fear that these other tribes will charge them with cowardice because they make peace" and "if they continue the war they will stand the brunt of it alone without the assistance of the others."

Pell regarded Medicine Bear's Upper Yanktonais "more uncertain than any other [bands], as they have been tampered with by the traders of the north and offered munitions of war and a city of refuge in the British Possessions." Although Two Bear assured Pell he could make peace for all the Yanktonais, Pell was "afraid he is somewhat of an Indian braggart." He pointed out Two Bear had "only about forty lodges, while Bone Necklace has about the same number in the friendly camp, and Medicine Bear has over 100." These Sioux bore witness to how severely Sully's expedition had punished them: "They say they have lost but few men in the fight, but the large proportion of those whose hair is cut as mourning and the wailing and lamentation about their camp prove this to be entirely false." However, Pell thought severe treatment could be the basis for a lasting peace "if they could . . . be treated with justice

and humanity instead of being preyed upon by a horde of Indian traders and speculators." It would be good if they could "remember that the
same hand which confers benefits inflicts punishment when occasion
demands."[59]

Sully authorized Pell to give "$200, or three unserviceable horses and
a lot of rations, &c." for Kelly's release. Sully would see the president
in a few days, and Pell should assure them that although the "Government is determined to fight till they either exterminate all the Indians
or have no more war," the president would be "glad to hear he had no
more trouble with his red children." Pell should tell them Sully would
come in winter to tell them what the president said.[60]

Sully forwarded Pell's report to Pope and asked authorization for making a treaty that would "save the Government hundreds of thousands."
He regretted he could not go immediately to the Indian camp. "But,
general, you know Indians well enough to know if an officer visits them
as a peacemaker, and has no money to make them presents, they look
on him as a small individual. . . . If a permanent peace can now be made
with the Sioux, I look upon it as one of the greatest achievements in our
Indian troubles."[61]

Pope agreed with nearly everything Sully wanted Pell to tell the Sioux,
"except in regard to presents to the Indians and a renewal of their annuities. The latter they have forfeited by the act of war, and the former I have
always been opposed to in Indian treaties." The treaty must hang "on the
sole understanding that they do not commit acts of hostility against the
whites" and the knowledge that it would be nullified by "the first hostile
act." It should offer "no consideration" to either side, except that Indians
keep the peace and the United States "protect them against wrong" from
whites. Because Indians blamed agents for the war, until he heard what
the War Department or Congress intended to do, he would permit no
intercourse between the Sioux and their agents. "Fair treatment and fair
dealing are now alone necessary to keep peace."[62]

Meanwhile, Fanny Kelly's rescue was progressing. Chief Crawler later
recounted how he and three other Sihasapas—Magpie Eagle, White
Thunder, and Bear Fur—set out from Fort Sully with their wives to secure

---

[59]Pell to Sully, 26 Oct. and 1 Nov. 1864, OR, vol. 53, pp. 599–602; and Pope to Halleck, 17 Nov.
1864, OR, vol. 41, pt. 4, pp. 599–600.
[60]Sully to Pell, 10 Nov. 1864, OR, vol. 41, pt. 4, pp. 514–15.
[61]Sully to [Pope], in OR, vol. 41, pt. 4, p. 514.
[62]Pope to Halleck, 17 Nov. 1864, OR, vol. 41, pt. 4, pp. 599–600.

her release from the Hunkpapas. The other wives waited at the Sihasapa camp at the mouth of the Moreau River, but Crawler's wife, Sunflower Face, accompanied the men to the Hunkpapa village Laughing Wood, near today's Bull Head on Standing Rock Reservation. The Hunkpapas who greeted them were receptive to trading Kelly for horses, but Brings Plenty preferred to exchange her for food at a trader's store. As Crawler told it, he followed Brings Plenty to his tipi, where Kelly was sitting beside him in front of a fire. Negotiations between the two men stalemated until Brings Plenty unsheathed a knife and laid it down. Crawler drew his revolver, grabbed Kelly, and forced her behind him, backing with her out of the lodge. His friends grabbed Kelly and helped her mount a pony. The camp, divided between those who supported Brings Plenty and those who wanted to trade Kelly for horses, was in turmoil but let her go. At the Sihasapa camp, Hollow Horn's wife gave Kelly some clothing. When they arrived at Long Soldier's lodge, the entire Sihasapa band joined the procession to Fort Sully, which convinced Kelly they meant to use her as a pawn to attack the post. She warned in a note she sent to the fort with Charger: "Be guarded, as they are making all kinds of threats and preparations for an attack." Charger denied this, saying they came only for the feast Pell promised.[63]

First Lieutenant G. A. Hesselberger recalled how, on December 9, some 1,000 to 1,500 "war-painted" Indians appeared on the hill behind the fort. Major House, in response to Kelly's warning, allowed only chiefs to enter with her. When she and ten or twelve chiefs were inside, soldiers slammed shut the gates. Hesselberger and others attested that her warning had been "very valuable to us . . . and enabled us to ward off the threatened attack of the Indians. In my opinion, had the Indians attacked the fort, they could have captured it." It was cold, Hesselberger recalled, "and she was very poorly clad, having scarcely any thing to protect her person. Her limbs, hands, and face were terribly frozen." Kelly remained hospitalized at Fort Sully nearly two months.[64]

On December 16, Sully forwarded news of Kelly's release to Pope along with word from Pell that "the Indians talked humbly" at the council

---

[63]Doane Robinson, "Rescue," 111–17. Hollow Horn's camp was high up Little Oak Creek, a Grand River tributary. Robinson interviewed Crawler when Crawler was 77 and "in full possession of his mental faculties," 8 July 1908. Carlisle Institute graduate Joseph Fly, a Sisseton, translated. Robinson also drew on Crawler's account to missionary Mary C. Collins.

[64]Kelly, *My Captivity*, 280–83. Hesselberger and six other Sixth Iowa men attested to the same story in affidavits Kelly solicited for her book.

after her transfer and "seemed delighted to be at peace." However, they expected Sully "here with presents to ratify a peace." Sully telegraphed that he could not come then but would send the Sioux a written report of what he told President Lincoln on their behalf.[65]

In 1871, the Senate passed a bill stipulating Kelly be paid "five thousand dollars in full for property taken and destroyed by the Sioux Indians" in 1864. The money would "be taken from any money in the Treasury which is due or which may become due" the Brulé, Oglala, Sans Arc, and Miniconjou bands.[66]

From August 22—when he left Fort Union—into December, Sully was officially on sick leave, but only those in direct contact with him probably realized it. Despite that and other problems—boat wrecks, annoying emigrants, failure to build the Yellowstone fort—Sully was satisfied. The 1864 expedition "met the combined forces of the Sioux Nation at points they chose to give us battle, and in these engagements completely routed them, destroyed a large portion of their camps and baggage, and scattered them in all directions, completely breaking up their combination, and proved to them that in spite of their boasts and threats they were no match for the whites." Because he was convinced the Sioux "never will again organize for resistance against a large body of troops," Sully thought this would be his last Upper Missouri campaign.[67]

What the consensus was among the Indians about the summer's campaign cannot be gleaned from winter-count calendars. For 1864, the Big Missouri Winter Count depicts a circle with four appendages and a dot inside that Kills Two translated as, "This year nearly all the Sioux bands camped together," which might refer to the gathering at Killdeer or the earlier one near Bear Butte. Some Sioux, reflecting on 1864 events years later, regarded their siege of Fisk's wagon train and harassment of Sully's forces in the badlands as partial victories.[68]

---

[65]Sully to Asst. Adj. Gen. [Pope's], 16 Dec. 1864, OR, vol. 41, pt. 4, p. 874.

[66]Kelly, *My Captivity*, 114–19, 138–41; and Sen. Bill 1315, *A Bill for the Relief of Mrs. Fanny Kelly*, 41st Cong., 3rd sess., in Library of Congress, *Century of Lawmaking*, http://memory.loc .gov/ammem/amlaw/.

[67]Welsh, *Medical Histories*, 327–28; and Sully to Asst. Adj. Gen., 11 Sept. 1864, OR, vol. 41, pt. 1, p. 155.

[68]Larson, *Gall*, 247n22; Larson, "Chief Gall," 20–21; Cf. "Big Missouri" winter count in Cheney, *Sioux Winter Count*, 32; Howard, "Dakota Winter Counts," 341, 348, 359, 388–90; Mallery, "Picture Writing," vol. 1, 285; and Candace Greene and Thornton, *Year the Stars Fell*, 252–55.

Chapter 13

"King of the Uncultured Waste"

DESPITE HIS CIVIL WAR INVOLVEMENT, PRESIDENT LINCOLN IN 1864 signed into law a bill chartering the Northern Pacific Railway, which, in Dakota, would follow Fisk's approximate 1864 route. The law also gave the company forty-acre sections of land north and south of its tracks. Railroad construction required peaceful conditions, which Sully thought would follow only if Indians were treated "in future with justice." When Pope solicited his input, Sully advised, "Let them understand that the Government intends to see that they will no longer be the prey of dishonest agents and traders." Sully suggested a three-man military commission to oversee annuity payments and make sure traders offered Indians credit only at the traders' own risk.[1]

Sully believed it a good idea to aid surrendering Sioux by subsidizing their families for a short time, giving them blankets, and lending men horses for hunting. He considered all-out war unwise and made his point bluntly in a letter dated October 7, 1864: "If a war of extermination is called for, it will be necessary to shoot everything that wears a blanket; but it would be very expensive . . . The cheapest and easiest way to exterminate the wild Indian is to bring him into a civilized country in contact with the whites (the women would soon become prostitutes and the men drunkards)."[2]

In the same letter, Sully went on to say that once enough Indians came to live near a military post, the work of "civilizing, and, finally, Christianizing them" could begin. Let missionaries not preach the Gospel— "they can't understand that yet"—but teach the boys trades and the girls homemaking. He expected more benefits from educating girls because "Indian women are probably the most industrious, hard-working beings

---

[1]Larson, "Chief Gall," 18, 21–26; and Sully to Asst. Adj. Gen., 22 Nov. 1864, OR, vol. 41, pt. 4, pp. 651–52.

[2]Brown to Clowney, 18 Sept. 1864, and Sully to Asst. Adj. Gen., Dept. NW, 7 Oct. 1864, OR, vol. 41, pt. 3, pp. 626–29 (Sully's parentheses).

in the world. Elevate the female portion of this race and you civilize the male." Sully believed this transformation would take more than one generation, however, because "an Indian, in some respects, is like a child, a few kind words of praise, a small reward for a brave or worthy act, has a great effect on them, and when he is your friend he is a staunch one."

Sully hired two interpreters to live with and spy on Sioux living around Fort Rice. He also issued some damaged clothing to the fifty new Yanktonai soldiers he organized into a company. They set up their family lodges in a stockade outside Fort Rice and reported to the commanding officer for duty as pickets and scouts. As pay, each received two rations and adequate ammunition. Besides serving as spies when militant bands were nearby, they would form a nucleus for those wishing to desert from those bands. Until they became used to white ways, Sully thought it inappropriate to discipline them the same as white soldiers. They were proud of their jobs, and Sully predicted they would be the best troops for the frontier. Furthermore, he had no trouble with his Indian soldiers obeying orders.[3]

General Pope's opinion incorporated Sibley's and Sully's ideas and had weight. Although prejudice and motivation to accommodate white expansionism rather than to ensure Indians' basic survival colored their opinions, these three military leaders knew Sioux ways in some measure; knew, liked, and respected individual Indians; and together could influence government policy.

Governor Edmunds, as ex officio Indian agent, recommended that all peace-minded Indians, including Sioux, settle on reservations as a "matter of justice" to them and to reduce government expenses. He wanted Indian trade reformed in order to convince Indians "of the fidelity and good faith of the government towards them." He praised the Yankton Sioux soldiers based at Fort Randall: they "faithfully executed the trusts committed to them" and were "more effective than twice the number of white soldiers for the kind of service they have been called on to perform." So far, they "killed several hostile Indians and the result is that our settlers . . . have met with no losses from roving bands of hostile Indians."[4]

Agent Burleigh detailed the Yankton scouts' accomplishments. Those sent to destroy the Dirt Lodges some 200 miles up the James River had done so, driving the occupants a hundred miles away. Those patrolling the Missouri to Sioux Falls "overtook a war party on their way down the

---

[3]Sully to Asst. Adj. Gen., Dept. NW, 7 Oct. 1864, OR, vol. 41, pt. 3, pp. 699–700.

[4]Edmunds to Dole, 31 Aug. and 20 Sept. 1864, nos. 115 & 117, 261–64, and Dole to Edmunds, 8 Sept. 1864, no. 136, 292–93, all in CIA annual report.

Vermillion, arrested the ringleaders, and shot them on the spot." Among them were two who "confessed to having killed 10 white persons in the Minnesota massacre" and to having killed Private Wiseman's seven children in northern Nebraska. Burleigh believed justice demanded that the Yanktons be paid the same as other soldiers, and he wanted more Indians to be recruited to patrol the frontier. Sioux soldiers "have the will, a knowledge of the country and of Indian warfare . . . without which our frontiers can not be efficiently protected."[5]

The full pay Burleigh advocated for the original fifty Yankton scouts was not forthcoming. Years later, in an effort to obtain compensation as government employees, some surviving scouts and their descendants testified to their accomplishments since June 1864. They said they "went wherever the commander of Fort Randall and Agent Burleigh told us to." They made "two scouts up the Niobrara River toward the Black Hills," once to as far as the Loup Fork in Nebraska. They caught and killed an escaped Fort Randall prisoner and a "hostile crawling up on one of our scouts to shoot him." Another scout carrying dispatches to Sully in the field "met a hostile and shot him dead." When at their home bases at Fort Randall and Yankton Agency, they "scouted the country daily to give notice of the approach of hostiles." Sometimes during long marches, they "had to live on what they could pick up, sometimes on nothing but pieces of buffalo skins." These long trips "used up their horses, and sometimes they were raided by the hostiles."[6]

FEEDING UPPER MISSOURI SIOUX DURING THE 1864–65 WINTER posed a problem. Calling prices for food and other goods from Iowa, the nearest supply point, exorbitant, Edmunds encouraged the Yanktons and Poncas under his supervision to hunt and stay out where they could sustain themselves for as long as possible. With no extra congressional help forthcoming for the two reservation tribes, Dole advised Edmunds to borrow money from their education and building funds in order to feed them until spring.[7]

[5] *General Sully's Company of Yankton Scouts*, 3–4; and Burleigh to Dole, 21 Oct. 1864, CIA annual report, no. 129, 283–86.

[6] "Statement of the Services Performed by the Yankton Indian Scouts," by Rev. Williamson (on their behalf), in *General Sully's Company of Yankton Scouts* 4–5.

[7] Burleigh to Dole, 21 Oct. 1864, no. 129, 283–86; Edmunds to Dole, 5 Aug. 1864, no. 134, 290–91; and Dole to Edmunds, 8 Sept. 1864, no. 136, 292–93, all in CIA annual report.

Burleigh asked Dole if, because of the Yanktons' faithfulness and their "reduced condition in consequence of the failure of their crops for two successive years," a small congressional appropriation might be "both an act of justice and of charity." Burleigh held racist beliefs common to nineteenth-century Americans: "The North American Indian, like the rest of the dark-skinned races, cannot cope with the Caucasian single-handed and alone. He is not the equal of the white man, and never can be; he is an inferior being, physically and mentally." Therefore, "the Indian is either to be protected, as indicated by every principal of humanity, and allowed to slide gently down that declivity, which seems to be his inevitable fate, or, abandoned by the protecting arm of government, and rushed ruthlessly out of existence, with the stain of his extermination upon our hands." Convinced "the race is passing away," Burleigh thought the only question was how this destiny could be "fulfilled with the greatest good to [the Indian], and the least evil to ourselves."[8]

AWAY FROM THE MISSOURI OVER THE 1864–65 WINTER, BANDS UNDER White Lodge, Sleepy Eye, and others intimidated Sioux who wanted to join the 170 or so lodges of Sissetons living near Fort Wadsworth. Introducing special military agent Joseph R. Brown's peace ambassador, Wausukige (or Wauskiye), at the Cuthead camp, Sisseton chief Burning Earth's son urged cooperation. "This man has traveled on foot a great distance to carry good news to the Sioux who desire peace." Because Americans struck the Cutheads while they were with the Lakotas, are these Cutheads to remain their enemies and "be hunted over the prairie like buffaloes? What are you waiting for? . . . Our Great Father holds out his hand to us. Will we permit him to draw it back without taking hold of it? If not, arise. . . . Go and take a strong hold of the friendly hand that is extended toward you." Some Cuthead Sioux did surrender.[9]

This was a season of surrender on the Upper Missouri and of widespread condemnation of the atrocities committed against Indians at Sand Creek. On November 29, 1864, Colonel J. M. Chivington attacked Chief Black Kettle's camp of about one hundred Cheyenne and thirty Arapaho lodges at Big Sandy Creek. These Cheyennes and Arapahos

---

[8]Burleigh to Dole, 21 Oct. 1864, CIA annual report, no. 129, 283–86.
[9]Brown to Clowney, 18 Sept. 1864, OR, vol. 41, pt. 3, 626–28; and Diedrich, *Odyssey*, 67.

had negotiated a peace with whites at nearby Fort Lyon and were flying a U.S. flag in their camp to indicate such. With the promise of peace, the Indians had sent most of their warriors to hunt; hence, the camp was filled primarily with women, children, and old men. After the bloodshed that took place at Sand Creek and the condemnation that followed, the U.S. government perceived the need for new Indian policy throughout the country. Indeed, even some soldiers who participated in it called what happened at Sand Creek a massacre.[10]

EARLY IN NOVEMBER 1864, WHEN FANNY KELLY'S RESCUE WAS imminent, Lieutenant Colonel John Pattee set off from his Sioux City headquarters to look for Indians accused of raiding in the Big Sioux River country and to leave behind troops to establish a military presence at Firesteel Creek and Sioux Falls. The trip was also a personal quest. On April 9, 1864, Indians had killed his brother Frederick and a companion, William Tennis, as they traveled down the Big Sioux River. At the place where some Sioux City men had found Tennis's wooden leg with his revolver strapped to it, John Pattee and his men, including his other brother, Lieutenant Wallace Pattee, made a gruesome discovery—Frederick's boot and "in it the bones of his foot." Wallace and some men scouted west of the river, finding no one, while John stayed two nights in camp because he was "too sick to ride [his] horse." Approaching Sioux Falls, the grieving brothers "discovered a little twist of smoke arising from behind a small patch of timber on the river [and,] . . . with the batteries, made a headlong dash . . . into a little camp of Yankton Indians." Fortunately for the Yanktons, someone John knew was with them. "They were fearfully frightened at the impetuosity of our charge," he recalled.[11] The brothers never did avenge Frederick.

Hunger was widespread during fall and winter. At Fort Randall, Private Spencer, now Colonel Pollock's orderly, wrote his sister in November that his job was "to carry orders and keep the Indians, of which there is a plenty in the office every day, from stealing anything. They plague the Col nearly to death for something to eat." At that moment, eleven

---

[10]Bartlett to Pell, letter no. 2, undated, but between 31 Oct. and 8 Nov. 1863, FS Selected LS, RG 393, NA; and Jerome Greene and Scott, *Finding Sand Creek*, 4–25. See official reports, "Engagements with Indians on Sand Creek, Colo. Terr.," OR, vol. 41, pt. 4, pp. 948–72.

[11]Pattee, "Reminiscences," 318–19.

"painted and streaked warriors" were there to visit Pollock, who "shakes hands with them, and says, damn the Indians. That they cannot understand, of course."[12]

At the Crow Creek Agency, Superintendent Thompson wanted a military escort for yet another Minnesota-based winter expedition to supply the Sioux and the few Winnebagos still on the reservation. Pope let Sibley decide if he could spare troops for what might be a second "Moscow" disaster. Sibley ordered Lieutenant Frank McGrade, Second Minnesota, stationed at Fort Ridgely, to escort the train and round up and return to Crow Creek any Sioux who had wandered away. Although McGrade's orders did not specify that he go to the Missouri with the train, teamsters threatened to vandalize the wagons if he did not. He relented and on November 5 dropped off twenty-two Sioux, including only three men, at the reservation before accompanying the supply train back to Minnesota without incident.[13]

Spurred partly by hunger, Sioux in Sibley's districts sporadically surrendered over the winter. Four Second Minnesota Cavalry companies now garrisoned Fort Wadsworth, where Major Robert H. Rose commanded. Early in November, the Sisseton chief Scarlet Plume, never involved in the 1862 violence, came to the post and began employment with other Indian men as a scout.[14]

On Christmas Day 1864, Pell reported to Sully from Fort Sully. Because the summer's fighting drove away buffalo from west of the Missouri, the Miniconjous and Sans Arcs were destitute and almost starving. Given that these bands were eager to make peace but could not travel far, Pell suggested Fort Rice as a better venue for future treaty talks. Sully advised Fort Sully's commander, Major House, to be friendly to, yet wary of, Indians seeking peace. Have "plenty of canisters ready for your howitzers," and keep the garrison well supplied with water and fuel in case of seige.[15]

---

[12]Spencer to sister, 25 Nov. 1864 and 5 Feb. 1865, in Goodwin, "Letters of Spencer," 263–65.

[13]Pope to Sibley, 10 Oct. 1864, OR, vol. 41, pt. 3, p. 772; and McGrade to Olin, 20 Nov. 1864, OR, vol. 41, pt. 4, pp. 632–34.

[14]Sully to Pope, 10 Oct. 1864, OR, vol. 41, pt. 3, p. 773; Sibley to Meline, 17 Oct. 1864, OR, vol. 41, pt. 4, p. 64; Brown to Rose, 26 Oct. 1864, 292–93, and Rose to Olin, 2 Nov. 1865, 408–10, both in OR, vol. 41, pt. 4; Brown to Rose, 9 Jan. 1865, OR, vol. 48, pt. 1, pp. 647–48; and Diedrich, *Odyssey*, 62, 67, 69.

[15]Sully to Asst. Adj. Gen., Dept. of NW, 6 Jan. 1865, OR, vol. 48, pt. 1, pp. 438–39; Schuler, *Fort Sully*, 6; and Sully to House, 16 Dec. 1864, FS Selected LS, RG 393, NA.

EARLIER THAT FALL, WHEN SULLY LEFT HIS NAMESAKE FORT ON October 8 with his army, he met Colonel Charles A. R. Dimon, who was on his way with six companies of First United States Volunteer (USV) Infantry to garrison Fort Rice. Because the First's steamboat could not make it past the mouth of White River—about halfway between Forts Randall and Sully—they had been marching for days. Their meeting with Sully was a lucky break. Noticing their inadequate equipment, Sully gave them shelter-tents and hired a few wagons to facilitate their further travel. Although Sully was impressed with their military appearance, others thought they were a sorry-looking lot. Many, too sick to go on, remained in Fort Sully's hospital.[16]

By the time Dimon and his men reached Fort Rice on October 17, his cattle had given out and three men were dead from chronic diarrhea, a fourth from heart disease. As he led his paroled Rebels, nicknamed "Galvanized Yankees," to the Upper Missouri, twenty-three-year-old Dimon owed much to his mentor, General Benjamin F. Butler, who had rewarded the New Englander's heroism in saving the USS Constitution from falling into Rebel hands by making him a lieutenant in the Thirtieth Massachusetts Volunteer Infantry. By exhibiting valor and leadership in combat at Vicksburg and elsewhere, Dimon had earned rapid advancement. In Louisiana, he commanded a unit of paroled Rebel soldiers—the Second Louisiana Volunteers—in action at Forts Jackson and St. Philip. His success there influenced Butler to put him in charge of this regiment of Rebels paroled from the Union prison at Point Lookout, Maryland.[17]

The First USV soldiers chose to enlist as Union soldiers as one of four options offered them: the others being "to be exchanged, paroled, [or] to go north and work on Government fortifications." In the Fort Rice version of the *Frontier Scout*, their officers explained, "They made the choice at a time when the Southern Confederacy was as likely to succeed as at any time in its history. But they cast their mite in with the United States, when she needed every man she could muster. No bounty was

---

[16]Olin to Pfaender, 4 Oct. 1864, OR, vol. 41, pt. 3, p. 629; Sully to Asst. Adj. Gen., Dept. NW, 10 Oct. 1864, OR, vol. 41, pt. 1, pp. 155–56; C. Dimon to "My dear Sis," 24 Sept. addition to 22 Sept. 1865 letter, Dimon Papers, Yale Beinecke Library; Fulton to Pell, 17, 20, and 26 Sept. 1864, FS Selected LS, RG 393, NA; and Schuler, *Fort Sully*, 145. Companies A, F, G, and I, First USV, served in Sibley's Minn. district.

[17]Townsend to Dix, Dept. of the East, 16 and 17 Aug. 1864, and so 118 in U.S. Army, *General Orders, 1st.*, Fort Union NHS Library; Olin to Pfaender, 4 Oct. 1864, OR, vol. 41, pt. 3, 629; and Tucker-Butts, *Galvanized Yankees: Face of Loyalty*, 12, 165.

offered them, no glaring inducements were held out, no chicanery or flattery was employed."[18]

Nevertheless, by the end of August Dimon's regiment lost seventy-three men by desertion, and on the steamboat trip up the Missouri, forty-four more vanished. Therefore, when Private William C. Dowdy indicated he might try to leave the boat, Dimon made him an example. At a general court martial, officers condemned the twenty-two-year-old to death. After passing Omaha, a detail dug a grave on the Iowa side of the Missouri, four men positioned the coffin to accept the body, and the officer of the day, to the beat of drums and in the presence of all six companies, shot the manacled Private Dowdy dead. After reading the proceedings, Sully accepted Dimon's circumstances as mitigating and said so to General Pope. Halleck and Secretary of War Stanton also tacitly approved the "irregular" proceedings.[19]

Many Iowans, Minnesotans, Nebraskans, and Dakotans who soldiered in Dakota with Sully nursed personal antagonism toward Indians stemming from the 1862 uprising and other encounters. Dimon and his fellow New England officers and southern soldiers brought different sensibilities and prejudices to the Upper Missouri. After witnessing the bloody tearing of flesh at a sun dance on the Yankton reservation, Dimon was appalled. He called the Yanktons barely civilized and proclaimed Dakota itself an "uncivilized out of the world" place. Chief Eagle Face compounded Dimon's culture shock by pointing out the "hair from ten scalps suspended from his girdle." Because one scalp was blond, Dimon assumed it belonged to "a white woman but as these are friendly Indians they wont acknowledge it."[20]

Three days before arriving at Fort Rice on October 17, Dimon had a portentous meeting with Two Bear. An officer later recalled his first impression of the Yanktonai leader: "In simple majesty, he stood, this king of the uncultured waste. Gay as an eastern king in his fancy trappings, a combination of simplicity and style which no being exhibits so

---

[18]"A Misrepresentation Corrected," (*Fort Rice*) *Frontier Scout*, 15 June 1865. Rules for former prisoners' enlisting changed over the course of the war. See Tucker-Butts, *Galvanized Yankees: Face of Loyalty*, 3–5.

[19]so 64, 30 Aug. 1864, Dimon on board *Effie Deans*, in U.S. Army, *General Orders, 1st.*, Fort Union NHS Library; Tucker-Butts, *Galvanized Yankees: Face of Loyalty*, 67, 69–73; and Dee Brown, *Galvanized Yankees*, 74–78.

[20]Tucker-Butts, *Galvanized Yankees: Face of Loyalty*, 77, 101; Lamar, *Dakota Territory*, 96; Jerome Greene, *Fort Randall*, 95; and C. Dimon to "My dear Sis," 22 Sept. 1864, Dimon Papers, Yale Beinecke Library.

much in the wide world as an Indian."[21] The Sioux and soldiers were wary of one another, both lining up to fight if necessary, but in the end, Two Bear and Dimon sat down to a council. The chief impressed him favorably and promised to send runners to invite other chiefs to meet him at Fort Rice. In his report, Dimon assured Sully he would only greet the Indians "with such overtures as I felt you gave me authority to make."[22]

Many of Dimon's command, in poor physical condition anyway, sickened during the trip, and five died during the regiment's first two weeks at Rice. In October, fifteen Fort Rice men, some left behind from other regiments, died, all but one of disease.[23] Soon after arriving at the post, Dimon wrote a woman named Sis that he was "neither pleased or disappointed" with Fort Rice, although he had never seen "such a forsaken place as it is here for Five Hundred miles round."[24] With ordnance and one unmounted cannon, and "two years supply of provisions, clothing, emigrant wagons, mules, 40 milch cows and the like," he set his men to work at construction. To make lumber at the post's sawmill, they harvested a stand of timber some two hundred yards to the north.

Dimon considered his most "delicate and important" task to be building relations with the Indians. "I am authorized," he wrote Sis in the same letter dated October 21, 1864, "to enter into a treaty with all the hostile Indians which number about 50,000. All the treaties thus far have not been lasting. I hope by proper management to do something better." He gave rations to some "Unkapas"—probably Bear Rib's band—who were so near starvation they had eaten "about sixty" ponies. Even in their dire condition, they impressed Dimon. The "chiefs are very eloquent," he told Sis. "Its not senseless talk . . . but good, sensible, eloquent language, the

---

[21]Quoted in "March of the 1st U.S. Vol. Infantry to Fort Rice, D.T.," (*Fort Rice*) *Frontier Scout*, 29 June 1865, possibly inspired by a poem, "To Walter Scott," by Mary Leadbeater (1758–1826): "Where candour reigns, and native taste/Fair beams o'er an uncultured waste—/Where freedom, candour, taste agree/To pay the tribute due to thee."

[22]"March of the 1st U.S. Vol. Infantry to Fort Rice, D.T.," (*Fort Rice*) *Frontier Scout*, 29 June 1865; Dimon to Pell, 17 Oct. 1864, OR, vol. 41, pt. 4, p. 65; and Dee Brown, *Galvanized Yankees*, 74–78.

[23]Bodies from regional fort cemeteries were transferred to the nearest national cemetery in the 1890s. Fort Rice burial records (including names, rank, and unit) are at Montana's Little Bighorn Battlefield National Monument. Other deaths gleaned from Drips, 25, 26, and 27 Sept. 1864 diary entries in *Three Years*, p. 95; Leonard Aldrich, 8th Minn., Co. F., to brother, 16 Sept. 1864, Aldrich Letters, MNHS Archives; Doud diary, 11 and 15 Sept. 1864; Washburn diary, 11 Sept. 1864; Rice diary, 9 Sept 1864; and *Medical History of Fort Rice*, 5. Names from "Record of Interments at Post Cemetery at Fort Rice, D.T.," 218–21, Custer National Cemetery, Little Bighorn Battlefield. See also Billings, *Report on Barracks and Hospitals*, 390–94.

[24]All quotes in this and the following four paragraphs are from C. Dimon to "my darling in America Sis," 21 Oct. 1864, Dimon Papers, Yale Beinecke Library.

evident result of thought and reflection. Their minds are not polished but are keen and their expressions to the point." Their arguments require "much skill and thought to answer." She would "laugh to be present at some of our councils. They come in making friendly signs and express a desire to see the 'great Captain' as they call me." They would shake his hand, squat silently in a circle, light and pass a pipe. "This you must take or the council ends abruptly, puff two or three times in silence, and that silence except while talking is always maintained." Their speeches, Dimon told Sis, "would charm you."

With Frank La Framboise interpreting, Dimon learned that, in general, old men wanted peace; young men, war. He expected peacekeeping to be difficult because the Indians were "too proud to beg for anything and the chiefs have more in view the future good of their band than its present necessities." Despite regarding them as superstitious, Dimon perceived "some noble traits of character."

He considered Two Bear and Fool Dog "good Indians," but he refused to make peace with the Upper Yanktonai chief Little Soldier until he freed a white girl his band held captive. To monitor nearby bands, Dimon utilized the fifty Indian soldiers Sully employed at Fort Rice, paying them "a ration a day for themselves and one for their squaws." Cold weather made finishing construction work urgent; Dimon hurried to make Fort Rice defensible. One-story, mud-chinked, dirt-roofed barracks would house the men.

Although game was plentiful, Dimon wrote Sis, the resident Indians could kill only enough with bows and arrows to feed themselves. Fur-bearing animals such as mink and beaver were also abundant, but Dimon believed trade "at this post will depend on the result of my conference with the Indians." Possibly mistaking the Red River of the North for the Red River of the South, Dimon was convinced that "the South are trying to get this trade down to the Red River for their benefit."

Late in October, when an Indian returned two stolen horses to Major House at Fort Sully, House gave the man "some little pay for his Honesty" and sent him to Dimon at Rice. The horses and their accoutrements seemed in good condition. In fact, a revolver remained fastened to one of the saddles. "Please pay the Honest Indian something for his generosity and integrity," House wrote, adding that, "this Indian is one of a friendly Band which has always been friendly toward the whites."[25]

---

[25]House to "Col. Diamond," 24 Oct. 1864, Dimon Papers, Yale Beinecke Library; and McDermott, *Frontier Scout*: View of Fort Rice," 29.

On November 21, some decidedly unfriendly Indians attacked Fort Rice soldiers, wounding a private. A week later, they attacked three men lagging behind a detail returning from the Cannonball River, slightly injuring Second Lieutenant Samuel B. Noyes, the post's quartermaster, and the quartermaster Sergeant Charles E. Thompson. Two Bear and his Lower Yanktonais chased them but returned without Private G. W. Townsend. Dimon, who personally joined the search party, did not know which band of Indians to blame. However, believing this incident was due partly to soldiers being too trusting of Indians, he issued an absurdly impractical order intended to prevent such mistakes. It decreed that "all armed Indians except those dressed in soldier uniforms and on the west side of the Missouri River will be regarded as enemies and be immediately fired upon and if possible killed."[26]

Helpful as Two Bear's band and the other Sioux who lived near Fort Rice were, they did present Dimon disciplinary problems. Fool Dog early on set up what could only be termed a brothel in his camp across the Missouri. When married Captain Enoch G. Adams, who was a Yale graduate and distant relative of President John Adams, attempted more than once to force favors from Indian women in Fool Dog's camp, Dimon strongly reprimanded him. Adams's criticism (as the *Frontier Scout*'s editor and otherwise) of Dimon, as well as his frequent drunkenness, created tension between these two, who were first and second in command at Rice.[27]

During winter, disease and weather became the soldiers' worst enemies. In December, seven men perished from chronic diarrhea, one died from the respiratory disease phthisis, and another from typhoid fever.[28] With December temperatures as low as thirty-four below zero, Dimon relieved his guards every fifteen minutes. Frozen feet, faces, and fingers

---

[26]SO 67, Fort Rice, 28 Nov. 1864, in U.S. Army, *General Orders, 1st.*, Fort Union NHS Library; Sully to Asst. Adj. Gen., Dept. NW, 6 and 22 Jan. 1865, OR, vol. 48, pt. 1, pp. 438–39, 614; McDermott, *"Frontier Scout*: View of Fort Rice," 27; Tucker-Butts, *Face of Loyalty*, 121; Helen White, *Ho!* 154–55; Adams, "The Resurrected Soldier," (*Fort Rice*) *Frontier Scout*, 14 Sept. 1865; and Brown, *Galvanized Yankees: Face of Loyalty*, 83. Sully reported Townsend's body found, but Fort Rice burial records do not list him.

[27]"Letter from the Hub of the Universe," (*Fort Rice*) *Frontier Scout*, 7 Sept. 1865; Tucker-Butts, *Galvanized Yankees: Face of Loyalty*, 97–98, 178, 216; McDermott, *"Frontier Scout*: View of Fort Rice," 28; and Athearn, *Forts of the Upper Missouri*, 196–97.

[28]*Medical History of Fort Rice*, 4; and "Record of Interments at Post Cemetery at Fort Rice, D.T.," 218–21, Custer National Cemetery, Little Bighorn Battlefield. First USV dead listed in "List of Deaths in Six Companies of 1st U.S. Vols in Dacotah Territory," (*Fort Rice*) *Frontier Scout*, 15 June 1865.

were common. One man lost a foot; another, a hand. A party of miners arrived at the fort having left a companion "with his collar bone broken and freezing to death 40 miles from the Fort." Rescuers found him barely alive, but he recovered. After an Indian arrived with the mail, Dimon marveled at what seemed Indians' superior ability to withstand cold. He found it astonishing that "they go when the therm is 40° below with bare breast and arms."[29]

Despite December cold, Dimon visited all the Indians within a forty-mile radius of Fort Rice. Among the many gifts they gave him were "three fine horses," six buffalo robes, a beaver pelt, and "a large Pipe decorated with scalps, Porcupine quills and paint." Perhaps mistaking characteristic Sioux generosity for something more, the young colonel marveled to Sis how they "look up to me with great superstition as the agent of their Great Father at Washington and pay me the most reverential homage," even asking him to "pray to the Great Spirit to give them success in their hunts."

Dimon told Sis that during his tour of Indian camps, he had found a young white woman (whom he does not name), in Mad Bear's Yanktonai band. Her owner had purchased her for two horses from Santees who captured her after murdering her father during the 1862 conflict. Dimon had written about her to Sis in an October letter, saying then that Little Soldier's band had her and that he would only make peace with the band if they brought her in to Fort Rice. Dimon described the nineteen-year-old girl as "perfectly beautiful" and added that the "Poor girl she dont know what to do with her children[.] [S]he has three little Indians." Dimon seems to have left her with the Indians—perhaps she was reluctant to leave her children—telling Sis only that he would "send her to her friends as soon as I can." Although the facts in Dimon's letters to Sis conflict considerably with those given by Fanny Kelly in her book, she thanks "Diamond" for visiting her at Fort Sully once the Indians brought her there on December 12, 1864.[30]

By late November, Sully estimated that about eighty-five lodges, housing some 300 warriors, lived near Fort Rice. At Christmas, Dimon hosted a celebration and invited the chiefs of these bands, including Black Catfish,

[29]Quotes in this paragraph and the following one are from C. Dimon to "My dear Sis," 16 Dec. 1864, Dimon Papers, Yale Beinecke Library.

[30]C. Dimon to "My darling in America Sis," 21 Oct. 1864, and to "Dear Sis," 16 Dec. 1864, Dimon Papers, Yale Beinecke Library. Kelly, *My Captivity*, 215–16.

whom Two Bear had convinced to come to the fort, to join the feast. Black Catfish brought three warriors with him and pledged, in turn, to try to bring in Medicine Bear's people. Other Indians danced and sang as entertainment. Half a year later, Adams could still describe the scene for the *Frontier Scout*: "Variegated as Joseph's coat of many colors was the garb of these Beaux Brummels of the Wilderness. Bears' claws, bears' teeth, feathers, fringes, beads and porcupine quills, and an abundant supply of red and yellow paints, helped to complete their costume."[31]

Company G, Sixth Iowa, separated from their regiment at Fort Berthold since August 29, 1864, built wooden winter quarters inside the 250-foot-square hewn cottonwood stockade that stood on a point jutting out on the Missouri's eastern bank. Like-a-Fishhook's earthen houses were east and northeast of the fort on bench land extending back to a line of bluffs. However, when severe weather hit, villagers moved to skin lodges or log houses in the woods. The 1864–65 winter produced three feet of accumulated snowfall and thermometer readings as low as fifty-two below zero. Fortunately, buffalo were plentiful near the post. Even so, many Sioux living nearby in tipis at the mouth of Douglass Creek died of cold and starvation.[32]

In November, the Miniconjou chief Red Moccasin came to Fort Berthold with forty warriors from their camp near the Cannonball's headwaters. Red Moccasin was "anxious to make peace," and the Yanktonai chief Medicine Bear—whom Sully considered "one of the biggest scoundrels in the Sioux Nation"—came there with one hundred warriors from his camp near Dogden Butte, telling Moreland it was "no use of Indians trying to fight the whites."[33] Northern mixed-blood people were constantly traveling near the post, trading with Sioux bands and supplying them with arms and ammunition while inciting them to "drive the whites from the country or exterminate them." Captain Moreland, who commanded the unit of soldiers at Fort Berthold, believed these mixed-blood people were mercenaries and feared serious trouble from their interference. Sully sent a copy of Moreland's letter to department

[31]Capt. Enoch Adams, "Fort Rice, D.T.," (*Fort Rice*) *Frontier Scout*, 22 June 1865. Sully's estimate from Sully to Asst. Adj. Gen., Jan 1865, OR, series 1, vol. 48, pt. 1.

[32]Frazer, *Forts of the West*, 110; Goodwin, "Letters of Spencer," 267; Cuppett to Libby, 21 Aug. 1914, Libby Papers, SHSND Archives; and Doane Robinson, *History of South Dakota*, 1:689–90. Cuppett identified this band as Two Bear's, but they lived at Fort Rice then. Douglass Creek today flows into Lake Sakakawea west of Garrison, N.Dak.

[33]Sully to Asst. Adj. Gen., Dept. NW, 6 Jan. 1865, OR, vol. 48, pt. 1, pp. 438–39; and Jacobson, "History of the Yanktonai and Hunkpatina Sioux," 17.

headquarters, adding a comment that these mixed-bloods would "always be a great obstacle to any permanent settlement of difficulties in this section of country." To manage them, U.S. troops would have to "follow them into the British possessions."[34]

At the end of January 1865, Man-that-Strikes-the-Ree's determinedly militant Upper Yanktonai band moved to the Painted Woods area. Some 600 Santees also camped along the Missouri between Forts Berthold and Rice. Hunkpapas, Sihasapas, and Miniconjous remained across the Missouri southwest of Berthold. Moreland also heard that some Cheyennes had set up 200 lodges near Medicine Bear's band.[35]

Since the Sand Creek bloodshed, Cheyennes had their own quarrel with the U.S. military. The Upper Missouri Sioux learned about the atrocities that Chivington and his troops committed at Sand Creek when survivors of victims sent runners north and west to recruit others to fight the whites with them. Meanwhile, the Cheyennes took refuge south of the Arkansas River. Word was that previously peaceable Indians were so outraged that even many so-called "Laramie Loafers" joined the Sioux, Arapahos, and Northern Cheyennes planning revenge. Meanwhile, small groups of Indians sabotaged telegraph poles and lines and raided traffic on the Oregon Trail and its offshoots.[36]

Early in 1865, mixed-blood traders brought Sioux camped near Fort Berthold sleigh loads of goods, including, according to Moreland, "five kegs of powder and a quantity of balls." Two Bear's two sons, spying for Dimon, reported that Upper Yanktonai chiefs Medicine Bear and Strikes-the-Ree were emboldened now to blatant hostility toward whites. Moreland feared they would attack Fort Berthold.[37]

On January 19, thirty warriors stole sixty horses from Two Bear's camp near Fort Rice, but Two Bear's warriors caught them and recovered some horses. During the raid, Fort Rice Indians learned the mixed-blood traders, while doing business with Medicine Bear's and Strikes-the-Ree's

[34]Moreland to Sully, 16 Nov. 1864, and Sully to Asst. Adj. Gen., Dept. NW, 6 Jan. 1865, both in OR, vol. 48, pt. 1, pp. 438–39.

[35]According to Miller et al., *History of the Assiniboine and Sioux*," 51, this Strikes-the-Ree (a.k.a. Struck-by-the-Ree) was the famed Yankton chief's son.

[36]Moreland to Sully, 31 Jan. 1865, OR, vol. 48, pt. 1, pp. 700–701; Bartlett to Pell, letter no. 2, undated, but between 31 Oct. and 8 Nov. 1863, FS Selected LS, RG 393, NA; Jerome Greene and Scott, *Finding Sand Creek*, 4–25; official reports in "Engagements with Indians on Sand Creek, Colo. Terr.," OR, vol. 41, pt. 4. pp. 948–72; Livingston to Charlot, 2 Jan. 1865, OR, vol. 48, pt. 1, pp. 948–72.

[37]Dimon to Ten Broeck, 24 Jan. 1865, 636–38, and Moreland to Sully, 31 Jan. 1865, 700–701, both in OR, vol. 48, pt. 1.

people, flew the English flag and boasted, "This flag will not be put down for anybody, only for God Almighty. Those who join us will not get hurt. Those who join the Americans will get hurt." The informants said Strikes-the-Ree pledged to the traders he would never "shake hands with the whites," and Medicine Bear concurred, "I am the man to make war with the Americans; kill all you can, I shall say nothing against you." The mixed-bloods promised more guns and ammunition and said they would bring with them 1,500 or more lodges of Santees wintering at Devil's Lake and on the Mouse River. Together they would "take Fort Berthold and then Fort Rice." The coalition fizzled, however. Seventy lodges defected in order to sue Dimon for peace.[38]

In a January 31 letter to Sully, Moreland described how his garrison of only forty-nine men were holed up in "a frail, inflammable, ill-constructed stockade, easily fired, hard to defend, cut off from water (in case of an attack), isolated . . . and in the heart of the hostile Sioux country." With Indians "gathering like birds of ill-omen around us and their threats reaching us daily, our situation is one of extreme peril." Moreland told Sully "the Sioux are determined to allow no communication between this place and points below." He assumed papers he sent to Rice in January were lost.[39]

Dimon tried to calm Moreland: Medicine Bear "makes assurances of good will and says the majority of the camp below you is for peace, and all to be feared from them is small war parties of young men, which he cannot control." Based on this and other intelligence, Dimon cautioned Moreland to await overt aggression before taking injudicious action Indians might see as a war overture. Dimon assured him he was "in communication (by Indian scouts) almost daily with the camp below you. The fact of your mail having passed through that camp unmolested is proof of some change in their feeling. It may be treachery, but as the men I employed were in the camp several days, and only heard expressions of peace and weariness of the late war, I think you have not much to fear, if you are careful." Dimon ended his communication with a veiled reprimand: "Medicine Bear complains that his young men go out in the night to the Ree village and trade with your traders for all

---

[38]Dimon to Ten Broeck, 24 Jan. 1865, OR, vol. 48, pt. 1, pp. 636–38. The spies also communicated the puzzling information that "Five hundred lodges of half-breeds have started for Fort Abercrombie to join the whites."

[39]Moreland to Sully, 16 Nov. 1864, 439, and 31 Jan. 1865, 700–701; Dimon to Moreland, 5 Feb. 1865, 785–86, and Dimon to Ten Broeck, Dist. Iowa, 8 Feb. 1865, 784–85, all in OR, vol. 48, pt. 1. Tucker-Butts, *Galvanized Yankees: Face of Loyalty*, 118.

they want to make war with, and he cannot control them and wishes it could be stopped."[40]

Big Head's Brother, who lived with the Rees, continued his chivalry toward whites, but when he escorted a party of miners to Fort Rice in late January, he could not protect them from Santees near the Painted Woods, who stole their rations and a gun. However, as Sully pointed out to Pope, the Santees "did not kill them, which is a remarkable instance of forbearance on their part." Sully thought these Indians were ripe for accepting a lasting peace with the government, although he realized "there will always be some little trouble in that country so long as there is an Indian and a white man in it and the line of the British Possessions is so near to it." He believed "a few military posts judiciously situated will put an end to that."[41]

Over the winter, Dimon wrote several orders to keep his men from entering the local Indians' lodges, to keep Indians from entering cookhouses, and to forbid issuing Indians papers vouching for them as "good Indians." By January's end, Dimon believed the Indians' "war spirit" was broken and the peace party predominated. He asked Sully's permission to "break up these trading parties from the British possessions and execute summary justice on the principals engaged this winter." He added, without substantiation, that he did not doubt "there is a Confederate element at work" among these interlopers. Dimon also took it upon himself to regulate trading at posts where soldiers he supervised were stationed. At Rice, he seized ammunition from Berthold's Frederick T. Pease, whom he accused of trading guns to Indians. Then, as Pease traveled on to Fort Berthold, warriors stopped the unarmed man, stole his horses, some of his oxen, and about $4,000 worth of goods. As with Pleets, Pease's Sioux kinsmen's intercession saved him from a possibly worse experience.[42]

In March 1865, the Chouteau family sold Forts Berthold and Union as well as most of their Upper Missouri business interests to Pease's employers, the Northwest Fur Company, a firm that Hubbell and Hawley of "Moscow Expedition" fame formed with another partner, lawyer James A. Smith. Consequently, in April, Company D moved out of Fort

[40]Dimon to Ten Broeck, 8 Feb. 1865, and Dimon to Moreland, 5 Feb. 1865, 784–86, both in OR, vol. 48, pt. I.

[41]Sully to Asst. Adj. Gen., Dept. NW, 22 Jan. 1865, OR, vol. 48, pt. I, p. 614.

[42]GO 2 et al. Dimon during Jan. 1865, in U.S. Army, *General Orders, 1st.*, Fort Union NHS Library; Dimon to Ten Broeck, 24 Jan. 1865, OR, vol. 48, pt. I, pp. 636–38; and Athearn, *Forts of the Upper Missouri*, 171–72.

Berthold and into log buildings they erected outside the stockade. After investigating Pease and Moreland, accused of illicit trading, Dimon in May sent his brother, Captain Benjamin Dimon, with Company K, First USV, to replace Moreland's Iowans. A military commission later found insufficient evidence to charge Pease, and although investigators found evidence at Fort Berthold of blatant illicit trading, Moreland vehemently denied any transgressions in testimony at Davenport in October 1865.[43]

Soon after arriving at Fort Berthold, Ben Dimon infuriated Upper Missouri Indian agent Mahlon Wilkinson when he barred him from an important council. "I was not permitted to talk with the Indians except in his presence." After Colonel Dimon learned that some Assiniboines had made peace with the Sioux, he decided that tribe "should have no goods this year." Both Dimons' refusal to acknowledge Indian Bureau-licensed traders was only one of many complaints Wilkinson made to his superiors.[44]

For the Wisconsin soldiers who had remained at Fort Union during the winter of 1864–65, mail was a rarity. It was December 15 before anyone at Fort Union knew of Abraham Lincoln's reelection. With Sioux threatening dispatchers with death, one carrier from Fort Berthold refused to turn over his missives unless each addressee paid him an extra fifty cents for his trouble. They paid but stole his rifle. In February, only local mail between forts reached Union. Isolation also affected the soldiers' nutrition. By the end of April, four men succumbed to scurvy. Captain Napoleon Greer, also afflicted, departed for better hospital facilities first at Fort Rice, then at Sioux City. He did not rejoin his company until after they had left Fort Union.[45]

On April 27, Sioux attacked three soldiers hunting below Fort Union, leaving First Sergeant Orrin C. Hall dead, stripped, and stuck with

[43]For the Northwest Fur Company, see Lass, "Northwest Fur Company," 21–40; Hubbell Papers and Smith Papers, MNHS Archives; Frazer, Forts of the West, 110; and Athearn, Forts of the Upper Missouri, 171–72. Moreland's situation is discussed in Goodwin, "Letters of Spencer," 265–67; Cuppett to Libby, 21 Aug. 1914, Libby Papers, SHSND Archives; Medical History of Fort Rice, 5; "Arrival," (Fort Rice) Frontier Scout, 15 June 1865; and in Abraham Moreland service records, 30 Oct. 1865 affidavit, box 8263, RG 94, NA. Capt. S. G. Sewall, Fourth USV Inf., notified Sully about lack of evidence against Pease.

[44]Wilkinson to Edmunds, 5 Sept. 1865, CIA annual report.

[45]Larpenteur journal, 22 Sept. and 25 Nov. 1864; 1 Feb., 14, 17, and 18 March, and 2–6, 14, 16, and 24 April 1865; SO 21, 27 Apr. 1865, Northwest Sioux Expedition, U.S. Army, General Orders, 1st, Fort Union NHS Library; Regimental Muster and Descriptive Rolls 1861–65, Wisconsin Historical Society Archives; and Napoleon B. Greer, pension records, file 679179, CAN 14-400, bundle 62, RG 94, NA.

eleven arrows. They wounded Private George P. Vaux severely, but nine-teen-year-old Private Erastus Livermore managed to kill a warrior and escape unhurt. After burying Hall, the soldiers suspended the Indian's body from an elm tree. That night, people in the fort could hear his kinsmen mourning. Finally, Captain William Upton's Company B, First usv, arrived on May 18 from Fort Rice, freeing Greer's Wisconsin men to join their regiment in Kentucky.[46] Upton was of the same mindset as the Dimon brothers. He enraged Fort Union's traders by evicting them from their quarters inside the fort. Also, when he heard that Blackfeet were in the area, he may have cost the Blackfeet tribe of western Montana their annuities when, possibly mistaking them for the Sihasapas or Blackfeet Sioux, he ordered the tribe's annuities offloaded at Fort Union.[47]

---

[46]GO 16, 22 March 1865, Dist. Iowa, and SO 26, Fort Rice, 11 May 1865, both in U.S. Army, *General Orders, 1st*, Fort Union NHS Library. D. W. Babcock told Livermore's story in the December 1919 issue of *Outers Book* (a magazine published in Milwaukee), according to "Two Interesting Stories" (Fort Union NHS Library), which also mentions an account by company I private Charles E. Brown that was published "about 15 years earlier" in the *Eau Claire (Wisc.) Tribune*. Brown identity from Regimental Muster and Descriptive Rolls 1861–65, Wisconsin Historical Society Archives; Larpenteur journal, 27 April 1865, 18 May to 4 June 1865 entries; and Chaky, "Wisconsin Volunteers," 175–78. The Wisconsin men left June 4.

[47]SO 21, 27 Apr. 1865, and Upton's military records in U.S. Army, *General Orders, 1st*, Fort Union NHS Library; and Athearn, *Forts of the Upper Missouri*, 170. Recall Pope's intent to interfere with Indian agents in Pope to Halleck, 17 Nov. 1864, OR, vol. 41, pt. 4, pp. 599–600.

Chapter 14

Indecision

WHEN THE CIVIL WAR ENDED IN THE SPRING OF 1865, THE U.S. military entered a period of unprecedented transition. However, Upper Missouri Sioux chiefs would have to react to change that began immediately after the carnage at Sand Creek. On November 30, 1864, Lieutenant General Grant made Major General Pope head of a new Division of the Missouri to include the former Departments of the Northwest, the Missouri, and Kansas. Grant explained to President Lincoln that Pope would be subordinate and was an intelligent administrator.[1] His jurisdiction included Platte River Sioux, the Cheyennes, and several other Plains Indian tribes and reached to the Rocky Mountains. It also included his old Department of the Northwest, now headquartered in Milwaukee, where Major General Samuel R. Curtis—who was in overall command of the Department of Kansas at Leavenworth when the atrocities at Sand Creek happened—would command. Curtis, a sixty-year-old West Point graduate, Mexican War veteran, and former Iowa congressman, had proven his administrative skills in Missouri early in the Civil War and his battle command prowess at Pea Ridge and Helena, Arkansas.[2]

Curtis turned to Sully for information about the settlements and Indians in Dakota Territory. Sully reviewed where he thought the Sioux bands were and warned Curtis about the northern traders. Again, he singled out Two Bear: "Near [Fort Rice] on the east bank of the Missouri, near Beaver Creek, is a large camp of Yanktonnais, of which Two Bear is the chief. These Indians were at war with me last year, but made peace and have since shown every disposition to keep it." Sully told Curtis how the Winnebagos and some Minnesota Sioux had been "starved out" of Crow Creek. He described the Yankton Sioux as a "fine body of Indians, who have always been peaceable and deserve the care and protection of the

---

[1]Utley, *Frontiersmen*, 304. Townsend to Pope, 28 Nov. 1864, 709; Grant to Halleck, 30 Nov. 1864, 716–17; and Grant to Lincoln, 7 Dec. 1865, 784–85, all in OR, vol. 41, pt. 4; Halaas and Masich, *Halfbreed*, 198; and Larson, *Gall*, 253n5.

[2]Perret, *Lincoln's War*, 140–41, 266; and Hyde, *Spotted Tail's Folk*, 101.

Government." He advised Curtis that the "part of Dakota south of a line running from Vermillion due east to the Big Sioux is pretty thickly settled, being about the only really good land I have seen in the Territory."[3]

In February 1865, Pope sent orders to Sully and Sibley that, because surrendering people were to be considered U.S. prisoners, "no white man whatever will be allowed to visit them except by special permit . . . from the district commander." In addition, the government suspended all Sioux treaties and decreed that "payment of annuities or distribution of goods under any former treaties will not be permitted by the military commanders of districts or posts on the frontier, unless contrary orders are received from the War Department." Assimilation was not a goal: Indians would have to remain behind "a line from Fort Abercrombie through Fort Wadsworth to Fort Pierre, and from Fort Abercrombie along the line of the Cheyenne [*sic* Sheyenne] River; east and south of this line all Indians are prohibited from coming on any pretext, under the penalty of immediate hostilities with the tribes to which they belong." Should surrendering Indians have to defend themselves against other Indians, "such service for their own protection will furnish no ground for any claim for services against the United States," although post commanders could assist and direct surrendered Indians in such military actions. Furthermore, Indians were expected to "subsist themselves by hunting and trading at the military posts." Traders must not live in Indian camps. Rather, post commanders would assign them a store location at or near posts. Soldiers caught trading with Indians would face court-martial. As inducements to live near posts, military commanders must offer surrendering Indians kindness as well as protection from other Indians and from traders.[4]

ON FEBRUARY 20 AT FORT RICE, THREE SANTEES KILLED PRIVATE Francis Connor, who, Colonel Dimon reported to Sully, had violated orders by leaving camp alone. Dimon also reported that Two Bear was sure the Heart River and Little Missouri camps, among others, would come to Fort Rice to discuss peace terms. Dimon suggested mid-May as a deadline, after which they would be regarded as enemies.[5]

³Sully to Curtis, 25 Feb. 1865, OR, vol. 48, pt. 1, pp. 979–81.
⁴Pope to Sully, 1 Feb. 1865, OR, vol. 48, pt. 1, pp. 719–20.
⁵Dimon to Cram, Fort Rice, 3 March 1865, OR, vol. 48, pt. 1, p. 1080.

In Sibley's Minnesota District, military agent Joseph Brown reported some Hunkpapas and other Lakotas had joined Yanktonais under Mdoka (the Buck) at Oak Grove, east of the James River. Reservation Yankton hunters, too, were in the area, along with the mixed-blood traders who supplied them all with liquor and other goods. Despite this volatile mix of Sioux, traders, and soldiers, calm prevailed at Forts Wadsworth and Abercrombie and their environs. With everyone complaining about the northern traders, President Lincoln proclaimed that "all persons engaged in that nefarious traffic shall be arrested and tried by court-martial at the nearest military post, and if convicted shall receive punishment due to their [just] deserts."[6]

Despite talk of peace, Sully planned to lead a third Northwest Sioux Expedition near, if not into, the Black Hills where Pope wanted to build one of several new military posts. Therefore, Sully ordered Lieutenant Carter Berkeley, Sixth Iowa, to report on the area's geography. Instead of going there, Berkeley relied on local long-time residents as sources.[7]

When a war party passed Fort Rice on March 30, Dimon sent out mounted men to disperse them. That night, Eagle Woman Galpin, hearing something, looked out her window to see two men lighting matches. When she heard them whispering to each other in the Santee dialect, she asked them what they wanted. "We are hungry," they said, but fled toward the river. The next night they returned. When Eagle Woman threatened them with exposure again, they fled to Two Bear's camp, claiming they had come to the fort to hear the news. Two Bear turned them over to the soldiers. Because one of the men had an English gun, Dimon arrested them both.

On April 3, Santees and perhaps others attacked and badly injured two mail carriers near Fort Rice. Sioux from the fort recovered stolen horses and the dispatches, but later in April, Strikes-the-Ree, with about 200 Yanktonais and Santees, rode down from the hills behind the fort to attack a herding party composed of soldiers, sutlers' employees, and some of James Fisk's men. Dimon reported to Sully that the storekeepers' men, who ran away, together with the Fisk men, lost sixty-eight animals in the attack. The soldiers successfully defended their stock but at a cost of two men killed. Next, the Indians attacked soldiers who were cutting timber but were repulsed and suffered some losses. Having no cavalry to send

---

[6]Brown to Everest, 28 Feb. 1864, OR, vol. 48, pt. 1, pp. 1144–45; and Lincoln, "A Proclamation," 18 March 1865, OR, vol. 48, pt. 1.

[7]Berkeley to Sully, 20 Feb. 1865, in Sully to Pope, 15 March 1865, OR, vol. 48, pt. 1, pp. 1188–90.

after them, Dimon retaliated by ordering his Santee prisoners executed. When Frank La Framboise told them their fate, Eagle Woman recalled one replying, "We can't help it. We had no business to come here to steal."[8]

Over the winter, militant Oglala and Brulé Sioux, Arapahos, and Cheyennes had rendezvoused at Bear Butte to discuss operations. Sacred to the Sioux, who used it for vision quests, Bear Butte was also where the Cheyenne's prophet, Sweet Root, received tribal laws. Spotted Tail and the aging Little Thunder attended the meeting but left in April 1865 to integrate their sixty lodges into the Fort Laramie Loafer band; however, Spotted Tail's fellow former Leavenworth prisoner, Red Leaf, joined those determined to fight.[9]

In May, Sully knew Cheyennes from the Platte were with Sioux war parties harassing Fort Rice pickets, but he was also aware of, and told Pope about, the "great amount of sickness and death at Fort Rice . . . There are now 207 on the sick list and 11 per cent of [Dimon's] command have died this winter." Despite that, Sully commended Dimon for his and his men's conduct. He was also pleased with the peaceful Sioux and recommended their chiefs be rewarded because "with very little induce-ment they could be made to turn against these hostile bands, and either rid the country of them or force them to become peaceable." If Sully had his way, he would pit friendly Indians against the others, "assisting them with all my troops," and give them provisions, blankets, ammunition, and exclusive hunting rights in "lands they now live in."[10]

Sully's May 13 update reached Pope when he was participating in an effort to capture Jefferson Davis and persuade General E. Kirby Smith to accept the same surrender terms General Lee had at Appomattox Courthouse.[11] Minnesota events also vied for Pope's attention. On the heels of a February scandal involving illegal traders and scouts in Sib-ley's district, a mixed-blood named Jack Campbell led a Santee raid May 2 at the Andrew J. Jewett farm, where they killed all five family

---

[8]Holley, Once Their Home, 303.

[9]Utley, Frontiersmen, 303–304. Townsend to Pope, 28 Nov. 1864, 709; Grant to Halleck, 30 Nov. 1864, 716–17; and Grant to Lincoln, 7 Dec. 1865, 784–85, all in OR, vol. 41, pt. 4; Halaas and Masich, Halfbreed, 198; Larson, Gall, 253n5; Hyde, Spotted Tail's Folk, 106–110; and H. E. Car-rington, "The Indian Question," in Cozzens, ed., Eyewitness, vol. 5, 108.

[10]Sully to Asst. Adj. Gen., Div. of the Missouri, 13 May 1865, OR, vol. 48, pt. 2, pp. 434–35.

[11]"Naval Forces on Western Waters"; S. P. Lee to Pope, 14 and 26 May 1865, 196–98; Pope to Lee, 9 May 1865, 162; and Lee to Wells, 28 Apr. 1865, 219, all in Official Records of the Union and Confederate Navies (hereafter cited as ORN) vol. 27; and Pope to Pleasonton, 22 May 1865, OR, vol. 48, pt. 2, p. 556.

members. Campbell, a sometimes member of Brackett's Battalion, may have been avenging his brother, who was among the thirty-eight executed at Mankato. All but Campbell, whom a white mob caught and summarily lynched, initially escaped, triggering panic among settlers. When Mrs. Jewett's brother wrote General Curtis suggesting he use bloodhounds to chase down the remaining perpetrators, Curtis reassured the distraught man. Santees would be caught, but bloodhounds would be unnecessary. "Our Indian scouts are far better followers and hunters of vagrant Indians," he wrote. "Besides, Indians are not afraid of dogs; they like and eat them."[12]

By the end of May, most Jewett murderers were dead, but a few blundered into a camp of those very Dakota scouts Curtis touted to Mrs. Jewett's brother. Solomon Two Stars, the scouts' leader, recognized one as his nephew. Nevertheless, because his orders were to take no prisoners, he personally shot him dead. The scouts chased the lone survivor to Fort Wadsworth, where soldiers captured him. Major Rose praised them for their efficiency and fidelity and bragged to Sibley that his hundred Indian scouts were "more valuable for the particular service in which they are engaged than would be a regiment of cavalry."[13]

Settlers remained nervous, and when the Fort Abercrombie commander reported a "threatened assault from Devil's Lake," Pope and Curtis abruptly pointed Sully's expedition north toward Devil's Lake instead of west to the Black Hills. Sully sent Berkeley's Black Hills report to Pope anyway for its valuable updates and corrections to Warren's and Raynolds's explorations.[14] Sibley, with eighteen companies of cavalry and four of infantry, called for more troops, although only sixteen Sioux were involved in the Jewett murders. Nevertheless, Pope told Sully, "If this nest of hostile Indians at Devil's Lake can be broken up this summer it will be best for you to do so." However, his main job was to make a treaty.[15]

As usual, supply problems plagued Sully: four steamboats sank. Furthermore, his latest intelligence was that the real threat, instead of coming

[12]Bergemann, *Brackett's Battalion*, 143–51; and Curtis to Finch, 6 June 1865, OR, vol. 48, pt. 2, p. 801.

[13]Sibley to Charlot, Asst. Adj. Gen., Dept. NW, 26 May 1865, 616.

[14]Curtis to Pope, 31 May 1865, 710; and Pope to Pleasonton, 22 May 1865, 556, all in OR, vol. 48, pt. 2. Sibley to Charlot, 28 May 1865, OR, vol. 48, pt. 1, p. 275; Pope to Sully, Sully to Pope, and Curtis to Sibley, all 26 May 1865, OR, vol. 48, pt. 2, pp. 616–20; and Berkeley to Sully, 20 Feb. 1865, in Sully to Pope, 15 March 1865, OR, vol. 48, pt. 1, pp. 1188–90.

[15]Pope to Sully, 22 May 1865, 557–58, and Sully to Pope, 3 June 1865, 766, both in OR, vol. 48, pt. 2.

from Indians near Devil's Lake, came from 10,000 Cheyennes, Arapahos, Brulés, and Sihasapas who were waiting for him north of the Black
Hills at Bear Butte. Conceding that his Miniconjou sources might have
exaggerated the number, Sully assured Pope he still planned a northern campaign. Curtis, to whom Sully would report officially during his
campaign, sent supplies to Fort Rice to replace those lost on the sunken
boats. "Your troops may have to winter at Fort Rice," Curtis warned,
"and you may have starving Indians also to feed."[16]

Sully complained to Pope. "Of course I will go where the general
orders me, but I fear I will meet no Indians whatever." Wintering his
troops at Fort Rice would be expensive. Besides, a large force there
would discourage Indians from coming anywhere near it. "A sufficient
number of men left at these very remote points to protect themselves
and the friendly Indians against the aggressions of the hostile Indians
is all that is required." Furthermore, his troops' terms of service were
expiring. Unless he left Brackett's Battalion to garrison Fort Rice, he
would have only the First and Fourth USV battalions to leave there, but
the new crop of "galvanized Yankees" assigned to his department was
"fast mustering itself out by desertion." However, the Fourth had enough
men to garrison Fort Sully with three companies, allowing three of the
Sixth Iowa cavalry companies stationed there to join the expedition.[17]

In May, Colonel Dimon sent First Lieutenant Horace Cyrus Hutchins
and ten soldiers of Company H, First USV, to arrest unauthorized traders
doing business with Indians upriver of Fort Union. On June 4, Sioux fired
on their patrol steamboat, but charges of grape canister and passengers'
gunfire dispersed them.[18]

To RETALIATE FOR SAND CREEK, A LARGE COALITION OF SOME 2,000
Oglala and Brulé Lakotas, Cheyennes, and Arapahos began in January
1865 to attack military camps, stage stations, and private ranches in Colorado Territory, killing whomever they could and destroying telegraph

---

[16]Sully to Pope, 26 May 1865, 617–18, and 3 June 1865, 766; and Curtis to Sully, 26 May 1865,
618–20, all in OR, vol. 48, pt. 2.

[17]Sully to Pope, 28 May 1865, 647, and 3 June 1865, 766, both in OR, vol. 48, pt. 2; and Dee
Brown, *Galvanized Yankees*, 112–14.

[18]Tucker-Butts, *Galvanized Yankees: Face of Loyalty*, 151; Dee Brown, *Galvanized Yankees*, 91;
and Overholser, *Fort Benton*, 339.

lines and poles. They were well mounted and equipped with plenty of ammunition and some rifled muskets. In February, Lieutenant Colonel William O. Collins, Eleventh Ohio, advised his superiors that the Black Hills, Big Horn Mountains, and Yellowstone country were "all rich in minerals, but this wealth cannot be made available while hostile bands of Indians are roaming over the country." In order to open promising mining and agricultural areas, he suggested moving Indians north toward the Missouri, where they "would be in a fine buffalo country, and out of the way of collisions with the whites, which are always liable to occur if they are near together." Separating them from southern Indians would prevent them from "plotting and combining" with one another. He recommended building posts on the Little Missouri and Powder Rivers.[19]

The mixed-blood half-brothers Charles and George Bent, sons of former fur trader and former Upper Arkansas Indian agent William Bent, though usually dressed as warriors, sometimes were taken for whites. The officer reporting an attack on Deer Creek Station in May 1865 said a white man (probably George) "seemed to have command of the Indians." They were paroled Rebel soldiers freed, in their case, on their promise to remain in the West. They joined their mother's people, the Cheyennes and, along with their married sister and their stepmother, were at Black Kettle's camp when Chivington attacked it. Furthermore, Chivington compelled the Bents' other brother, Robert, to guide him to the camp. George, injured, and Charles, captured and held for nearly a week, afterward rode with the Cheyenne Dog Soldier fraternal society, avenging Sand Creek at every opportunity.[20]

In May, two Oglala chiefs, Two Face and Blackfoot, brought to Fort Laramie a white woman, Lucinda Eubanks, whom they had purchased from her Cheyenne captors. She was nearly naked and attributed to the two Oglalas enough bad treatment to raise the commanding officer's suspicions. When both boasted of killing whites, Colonel Thomas Moonlight, who in January replaced Chivington, hanged them. Indians were incensed about the hangings and became further angered when, at the Miniconjou's Cottonwood Creek camp, soldiers killed a sleeping

[19]For "Operations against Indians on the North Platte River," see Livingston report, no. 1, 18 Feb. 1865, 88–92, and Collins report, no. 2, 15 Feb. 1865, 92–98. For "Operations on the Overland Stage Route," see Livingston report, no. 1, 5 Feb. 1865; Kennedy report no. 2, dated 16, 17, and 29 Jan. 1865, 41–42; and Walter report no. 3, 1 Feb. 1865, 43–44, all in OR, vol. 48, pt. 1.

[20]Hyde, *Life of George Bent*, 137–63, 204–205, 209–22; and Halaas and Masich, *Halfbreed*, 1, 93, 149–53, 164–69, 180–86.

youth and the sergeant later flaunted the boy's scalp as a decoration on his horse's bridle.[21] By June, Moonlight counted about 4,000 warriors among the Sioux and their allies.

The secretary of war, Stanton, thought it wise to move the Fort Laramie Indians away from transcontinental travelers. On June 11, Captain William D. Fouts, with 135 Seventh Iowa cavalrymen and some uniformed Indian police, began leading some 1,500 Sioux to Fort Kearny in the heart of Pawnee country, notwithstanding Pawnees and Sioux were decades-long enemies. Vowing secretly to one another to die rather than go to Kearny, the headmen and chiefs, including Spotted Tail, led a revolt on June 15 during which the Brulé chief White Thunder shot and killed Fouts. The Indians—including the Indian police guards—rode north to join camps on Powder River. The Iowans under Lieutenant John Wilcox killed twenty to thirty warriors guarding their families crossing the Platte River, but in addition to Fouts, they lost four killed and four wounded. Afterward, the soldiers took the women and children prisoners to Indian agent Vital Jarrot for safekeeping. Jarrot took them first to Fort Kearny, then sent them up the Missouri to the Yankton reservation. In assessing the incident when Fouts was killed, Major General Grenville Dodge blamed Colonel Moonlight for allowing Indian soldiers to set out from Fort Laramie with worn-out animals. George Bent attributed the rebellion partly to the soldiers' forcing sexual favors from Sioux women.[22]

AFTER LEAVING FORT UNION, COMPANY I, THIRTIETH WISCONSIN, dropped off their printing press in time for the Fort Rice version of the *Frontier Scout* to report the May 26 ambush of construction superintendent First Lieutenant Benjamin S. Wilson as he rode north to check on his loggers. As his horse reared, the injured Wilson hit the ground, dislocating his hip. Even so, he fired back but hit no one. Eagle Woman

---

[21]"Operations against Indians," Moonlight report, no. 1, 27 May 1865, 276–77; "Expedition," Moonlight to Price, 6 June 1865, 255–56; Curtis to Halleck, 12 Jan. 1865, 502–503, all in OR, vol. 48, pt. 1; Jones, *Guarding the Overland Trails*, 239–41; Utley, *Frontiersmen*, 317; and Bettleyoun and Waggoner, *With My Own Eyes*, 66.

[22]Connor to Dodge, 15 June 1865, 895, and 16 July 1865, 1086, both in OR, vol. 48, pt. 2; "Action with Indians," Wilcox and Moonlight reports, 21 June 1865, OR, vol. 48, pt. 1, pp. 322–24, 325–28; Utley, *Frontiersmen*, 319–20; Hyde, *Life of George Bent*, 209–10; *Spotted Tail's Folk*, 120–21, 121n3; and Jones, *Guarding the Overland Trails*, 249–52. These 7th Iowa units served separately from Pattee's companies.

Galpin rushed to Wilson's aid and later recalled shouting at the approaching attackers, "This man belongs to me now! You can not mutilate him
nor touch him! Begone, every one of you!" Circling Bear, the Sans Arc
chief who mortally wounded Wilson, and the others backed off but seized
the lieutenant's horse. Eagle Woman swung her shawl in the air to attract
the garrison's help, and soldiers soon chased the attackers away. Later,
Circling Bear (perhaps known in 1865 as Son-of-The-Man-That-Howls)
told Eagle Woman he would have killed her had he realized who she
was. Wilson lived on in agony from three arrow wounds until, on June
2, he called for Eagle Woman and died holding her hand. Later that
day, warriors appeared in force near the fort. "Every ravine and knoll for
two miles contained squads" of them, Dimon reported. The mounted
infantry and some sixty warriors from Two Bear's and Bear Rib's bands
withstood the attackers' initial fire until a few artillery shells chased
the enemy Indians off. Shouted conversations with the fort's Indians
established that the assailants were based at Young Man's Butte near
present Richardson, North Dakota, and that a new attack on the fort
would come in a few days.[23]

WITH SULLY SET TO GO NORTH, POPE ORDERED DODGE TO HAVE
General Patrick E. Connor's Powder River Expedition deal with the
Sioux, Cheyennes, and Arapahos purportedly still at Bear Butte. The
expedition was meant also to punish Indians who had destroyed telegraph
lines and targeted travelers going to Montana and would be in the field
simultaneously with Sully's.[24]

On June 5, Curtis updated Sully that some Santees from the Devil's
Lake and Turtle Mountain areas had been marauding near the settlements
and their old Minnesota reservation. Twenty-five hundred Yanktonais
were also supposedly camped in scattered groups south of the Mouse

---

[23]Larpenteur journal, 14 Nov. 1864; Chaky, "Wisconsin Volunteers," 174; "Tribute to Lieut.
B. S. Wilson," (*Fort Rice*) *Frontier Scout*, 15 June 1865; Dimon to Sully, 2 June 1865, OR, vol. 48,
pt. 1, pp. 304–305; Holley, *Once Their Home*, 301–302; and Gray, "Story of Mrs. Picotte-Galpin,"
14. Note that in the (*Fort Rice*) *Frontier Scout* for 12 Oct. 1865, Ft. Rice's attackers are identified
by Hunkpapas as Son-of-the-Man-That-Howls and Sitting Bull. If this is not another name for
Circling Bear, this more contemporary account is probably correct. A photo of Circling Bear
follows p. 196 in Holley.

[24]For a summary, see Hampton, "Powder River Expedition, 1865," 2–15; for source material,
see Hafen and Hafen, *Far West and the Rockies*, vol. 12, *Powder River Campaign*.

River. "Strike these hostile bands," Curtis ordered, "so as to destroy or drive them still farther from our settlements." Sully was also to locate a fort at Devil's Lake. A few weeks later, Lieutenant Colonel C. Powell Adams, commanding at Fort Abercrombie, suggested that "an expedition composed of 200 or 300 cavalry and a section of mountain howitzers fitted out at this post [Abercrombie], . . . could, in my opinion, inflict a terrible blow" on the Indians. Adams could organize such an expedition in five days if only he had "one more company of cavalry at [his] command." Accordingly, Sibley ordered Colonel R. H. Carnahan, at Fort Snelling, to combine his Third Illinois Cavalry with two battery sections under Killdeer veteran Captain John Jones to "scour the country" for Sioux camps from Devil's Lake to the international border. Carnahan was to respect any Indians friendly to the government and was to treat any others with fairness and humanity. He should avoid injuring women and children "as far as practicable" and teach the "savages" that the president's troops "are as merciful to the helpless and unresisting as they are formidable to an armed foe." Special military agent Joe Brown from Fort Wadsworth and veteran guide Pierre Bottineau would show the way. Carnahan was not to cross into British territory "under any circumstances," but he should arrest any illicit traders he might encounter south of the border.[25]

Sully informed Pope and Curtis on June 6 that some Sioux had joined the Platte Indians, who were now aware of Connor's troops. Sully also learned from Fort Rice sources that the Platte Indians intended to abandon territory south of the Big Cheyenne River in favor of the game-rich country farther north. To do this, they would "clean out all posts, commencing with Rice." Even so, Pope immediately telegraphed with instructions for Sully to keep his expedition focused northward.[26]

The last of Sully's troops left Sioux City June 9, but the general delayed his own departure a few days to write more letters. One to Pope concerned Colonel Dimon, whom Sully admired for his pluck and determination to obey orders. However, Dimon was "too young—too rash—for his position . . . He is making a good deal of trouble for me, and eventually for you, in his overzealous desire to do his duty." Sully did not want to

---

[25]Curtis to Sully, 5 June 1865, 789; Adams to Olin, 27 June 1865, 1013–14; and Olin to Carnahan, 28 June 1865, 1022–24, all in OR, vol. 48, pt. 2.

[26]Pope to Dodge, 29 May 1865, 665; Pope to Sully, 2 June 1865, 742; Sully to Pope, 2 June 1865, 743; Sully to Asst. Adj. Gen., Dept. NW, 6 June 1865, 800–801; and Pope to Sully, 7 June 1865, 812, all in OR, vol. 48, pt. 2.

"hurt his feelings, but I think the interests of the Government would be advanced by having an older and cooler head at Fort Rice." That older, cooler head belonged to Lieutenant Colonel John Pattee, whose moccasin- and buckskin-wearing frontier style differed considerably from Dimon's.[27]

Not knowing if the muster out order for his troops would be extended past October, Sully worried that instead of securing a lasting peace, too small a force left on the Upper Missouri after his expedition would make garrisons vulnerable to attacks they could not punish. If the militants prevailed, he warned Pope, his previous two expeditions would have been in vain. Connor's Powder River Expedition, he predicted, "will have a long march of it" to catch up to any southern Indians who joined the Sioux from the Heart River camp. What if some of those Cheyenne and other Platte Indians wanted peace in exchange for a promise to "occupy the country north of the Big Cheyenne River and behave themselves[?]" What would he tell friendly Indians about that? If he had "500 more good cavalry," Sully was confident his own expedition could intercept the Indians Connor was after. "Although I may not be able to make a big fight and accomplish all, as I have heretofore, yet I can hold my own against any number of Indians."[28]

Many of Sully's 800–900 soldiers and 100 or so teamsters and other men were veterans of his past two campaigns. He had four Sixth Iowa Cavalry companies under Lieutenant Colonel Ten Broeck; Major Brackett's Battalion; three Seventh Iowa Cavalry companies under Pattee; and Captain Nathaniel Pope's battery, with its four twelve-pounder howitzers. Part of Company B, Dakota Cavalry, again served the general as bodyguard. The Fourth USV "galvanized Yankees" were the only Upper Missouri neophytes.[29] Sully again pestered Pope to authorize using Indians as soldiers and suggested "paying them the same as [white] soldiers and giving them rewards for every scalp they bring in—say, $50." They would be trustworthy, he argued, because he had "so compromised them with their nation that it is to their interest to serve me."[30]

---

[27]Sully to Pope, 10 June 1865, OR, vol. 48, pt. 2, pp. 851–52; and Pattee, "Reminiscences," 326. Pattee took command of Fort Rice 24 July 1865.

[28]Sully to Pope, 10 June 1865, OR, vol. 48, pt. 2, pp. 851–52.

[29]Pope to Sully, 8 Feb. 1865, OR, vol. 48, pt. 1, p. 784; Sully to Pope, 14 June 1865, OR, vol. 48, pt. 2, pp. 887–88; and Hill to Dutton, 22 Oct. 1865, in Shambaugh, "Iowa Troops," 440–43.

[30]Sully to Pope, 10 June 1865, OR, vol. 48, pt. 2, pp. 851–52.

SULLY WAS ABOUT A WEEK INTO HIS MARCH WHEN, LATE ON JUNE 17, 800 Sioux signaled from the river bank opposite Fort Berthold that they wished to come across and trade. Captain Ben Dimon would not allow it and told them to leave. When they did not do so immediately, Dimon opened fire on them with his artillery, killing some. That was what passenger Hiram Upham heard the next morning when the *Twilight* arrived just as 600 Fort Berthold Indians were crossing the river to go after the Sioux. A Fort Berthold Indian arriving at Rice a few days later said that Yanktons and Two Kettles had killed two Rees and stolen many horses. In reporting this to Curtis, Sully commented, "I suppose as these Indians are not allowed to fight the whites, it is necessary for them to fight somebody in order to keep up their habits and customs."[31]

Sully arrived at Fort Sully on June 27. "I made the trip in a light wagon with three persons in all," he reported. "When I first came into this country I would not have run the risk. Now two or three white men think nothing of traveling all the way to Fort Rice. . . . I mention this to show the great improvement in Indian affairs." However, the Indians Sully expected to meet at Fort Sully were hunting buffalo east of the Missouri. They asked to be notified when Sully arrived, but his emissaries could not find them.[32]

Sully wired Pope from Fort Sully on June 28—but because the nearest telegraph was in Sioux City, Pope did not receive the message until July 8—that 3,000 Cheyennes, Arapahos, and militant Sioux were still camped at the head of Knife River where Sully had fought them in 1864.[33]

Perhaps a more accurate sense of what Indians, friends and foe, were thinking about this 1865 campaign came from ordinary soldiers, not commanders. Private Myers, stationed at Fort Sully over the winter, befriended "the Little Blackfoot," Sully's badlands guide. The young man was bitter toward those who injured him. "He frequently came to me, and, placing his hand over the wound, would say, 'seachy'—it hurts me." As spring approached, the same guide accompanied a party of soldiers to a Sioux camp to retrieve three men who wished to surrender. On the way back, Myers and his fellow soldiers "had to watch both the

---

[31]Upham letters, 18 June 1865, in Hakola, *Frontier Omnibus*, 280–84; and Dimon to Norton, 23 June 1865, and Sully's 1 July 1865 endorsement, 984, both in OR, vol. 48, pt. 2. Dimon erroneously called the Yanktons "Yanktonais"; see Sully to Asst. Adj. Gen., Dept. of the Missouri, 15 Aug. 1865, OR, vol. 48, pt. 2, p. 1186.

[32]Sully to Asst. Adj. Gen., Dept. NW, 17 [27] June 1865, OR, vol. 48, pt. 2, p. 916.

[33]Sully to Pope, 28 June 1865, OR, vol. 48, pt. 2, p. 1024; and Drips, *Three Years*, 104–106, 137.

hostiles and the Blackfoot guide, who seemed determined to kill the three Indians, if he got an opportunity."[34]

While traveling north with messages for Fort Rice that spring, Myers and his companions came across a Sioux camp located where Captain Fielner died a year earlier. Although wary, they affected a friendly demeanor and approached the 400–500 Sioux. Not all in the camp were cordial; some pointedly refused to respond to greetings in the Sioux language. Myers and his friends were relieved to recognize some people who had wintered at Fort Sully, especially two women to whom Myers had once given some leftover beans. Now they repaid him and his party with enthusiastic hospitality. Myers talked with one young man who showed where the soldiers' bullets pierced his arm during the previous summer's fighting but seemed not to "hold any resentment toward us for it." Later, another Fort Sully mail party had to turn back in the face of these same Indians' threats.

On their own return from Fort Rice, Myers and his friends, accompanied now by twenty-two soldiers, met two Indian men afoot. One turned away, but the officer in command took the other—a young man who had escaped Fort Sully's guardhouse—into custody. Later, when the detainee complained he could walk no farther, the soldiers allowed him to lag behind with only one private guarding him. Taking an opportunity, the captive bolted and the private reacted by shooting him dead.[35]

With Sully's expedition nearing Fort Rice, the post celebrated a Fourth of July enhanced by the soldiers' full appreciation that, with the War Between the States ended, unity prevailed. The Indians donated a buffalo and calf killed near the fort, and for the first time since the post learned of President Lincoln's death, the U.S. flag flapped at full mast. Decorations paid tribute to Presidents Washington and Lincoln and featured a multitude of flags. Colonel Dimon reviewed the troops. Then, after he and Captain Adams made speeches, games began west of the fort. Eagle Woman, her three daughters, and William Larned's wife joined officers and other civilians to watch foot races, wheelbarrow races, and other sports from the parapet. Among onlookers were "soldiers and frontier's men with slouched hat, moccasins and Canadian sashes." Also, "lounging and leaning against the Fort's sides were the Indians in their grotesque costume, young boys with nothing but a breech-clout on,

---

[34]FS Selected LS, 1865, RG 393, NA; and Myers, *Soldiering*, 40–41.

[35]Myers, *Soldiering*, 42–48.

and squaws bearing their offspring—a la pig-back—their faces painted with vermillion and a streak of red showing the parting place of their hair.—Fringes, beads, feathers, paints, buffalo robes, tassels and a conglomeration of everything that hangs, shines and flutters, they exhibited like a Punchinello."[36]

Target practice, sack races, and other contests offered participants opportunities to win modest money prizes. The final race featured Sioux riders and Indian ponies in a half-mile heat. Two Bear's nephew raced on Bear Rib's pony against Mad Bear's son, The-One-that-Runs-In, on Mad Bear's pony. Mad Bear's son Whirlwind raced another of Mad Bear's horses, and Mad Bear's nephew, The-One-that-Looks-to-the-Ground-as-He-Walks, rode another. Two Bear, on Bear Rib's pony, won by two lengths. A sack of flour was his first prize. The-One that-Runs-In took second place and a sack of meal. A mock dress parade, with outlandishly costumed soldiers poking fun at their officers, each other, and the local Indians introduced more hilarity until, as the *Scout* reported, "the sun set on the happiest Fourth of all time, past, present, or to come."

It was fitting that Indians shared in this small but momentous celebration. July 4, 1865, was as much a marker for them, had they known it, as it was for the American nation. With Sully on the march against them here, and Connor's troops marching against them elsewhere, Sioux could choose peace at the price of surrender and all the life changes that would entail or they could choose a mere chance of freedom bought with the hardships of war. What it came down to was either accepting or fighting the inevitable encroachment of whites. With the Civil War over, the government's attention was turning toward Indian policy reform at the same time the U.S. military was transforming itself into a frontier army ready to do battle in the spirit of, if not the name of, manifest destiny. For both soldiers and Sioux chiefs, a new era was beginning on the Upper Missouri.

---

[36]All quotations in this paragraph and the following one are from "July 4th, 1865, at Fort Rice, D.T.," *Frontier Scout*, 6 July 1865.

Chapter 15

The Battle of Fort Rice

DAYS BEFORE SULLY'S ARMY'S EXPECTED ARRIVAL AT FORT RICE, Fire Heart's Sihasapa band brought news that, at the Heart River camp, "two thousand lodges of Indians, [were] fighting among themselves, some being for peace and some for war." At present, the *Frontier Scout* reported, the elders, advocating peace, prevailed, but the Sihasapas said the Hunkpapas were especially "bitter in their hostility."

Sully's expedition was two days from Fort Rice when Curtis wrote the general that Carnahan's Third Illinois cavalrymen were coming to join him. By now, Curtis realized the Sioux probably would not confront Sully and only hoped the expedition would "scare them still farther from the settlements." Of premier importance now was selecting a fort site "at or near Devil's Lake."[1]

On July 14, Sully arrived at Fort Rice gratified to find about 250 lodges housing perhaps 8,000 people dotting the hills behind the post. Two Bear, Black Catfish, Little Soldier, and Medicine Bear, all Yanktonais, were there as were the Hunkpapa chief Bear Rib and the Sihasapa chief Fire Heart, each with his peace faction. Basil Clément, witness to Mato-cu-wi-hu's assassination, arrived with a multi-band group. With even Lame Deer's, Lone Horn's, and White Swan's Miniconjou bands and Four Horn's and Black Moon's Hunkpapa bands expected (although they apparently did not come), the *Frontier Scout* was optimistic about the talks. The "Indians, like the Rebels, seem anxious to take the amnesty oath. Gen. Sully . . . will accomplish more than a hundred thousand dollars expended in annuities to the hostile tribes."[2]

The newspaper named participants in the July 16 council: Fool Dog, Two Bear's Son, Black Catfish, Lousy Man's Son or Four Legs, Yellow

---

[1]"Local Items," (*Fort Rice*) *Frontier Scout*, 13 July 1865; and Curtis to Sully, 12 July 1865, OR, vol. 48, pt. 2, p. 1074.

[2]"Local Items," (*Fort Rice*) *Frontier Scout*, 15 June 1865; "Local Items," (*Fort Rice*) *Frontier Scout*, 13 July 1865; and "Local Items," (*Fort Rice*) *Frontier Scout*, 20 July 1865.

Robe, Big Head's Brother, Bear Rib's Son, Little Blackfoot, Long Soldier, Stinking Foot, Yellow Legs, and Grass or Shield. Fool Dog presented his credentials, shook hands with everyone, and made the opening
speech, saying everyone was happy the general had come. Young Bear
Rib, still known to some as Mato-cu-wi-hu's or Bear Rib's Son, spoke
next, admitting Sully scared him the previous summer. He did not want
Sully here again and blamed him for his people not being able to obtain
such things as gunpowder. He wanted friendly relations with traders
lower on the river.

White Shield recalled 1863. "My friend, you came down here two years
ago, and fought the Brulés, and killed some, and took prisoners down
below." Perhaps pointing out certain ones, he informed Sully that "All
these men here are relations of Bear Rib's," whose papers were buried
with him at Fort Sully [*sic* Pierre]. He spoke of one Indian agent who,
claiming to be a big chief, told them "to catch white men, and . . . we
did it. My friend, I say now hang all the Agents!" The statement elicited
a chorus of approving "haus." To Sully, he said, "This is the third time
you come, and you kill some every time." Those gathered here had "their
bellies full of fighting," but when Sully invites Indians for talks and soldiers "stick out the guns," meaning cannons, he wonders if they are in
earnest. Even starving Indians are frightened away when they hear guns.

The Hunkpapa Long Soldier said he wanted to go to Fort Sully [*sic*]
"and die there. Bear Rib lies there, and all these men wanted to go there
last fall, but you know who kept them from it." Grass remarked that
when he and others brought Sarah Morris to the fort, "I thought it would
make you feel proud." He and her other rescuers "want to sleep well,
and hunt buffalo." Grass's final remark—that "Bear Rib went under the
ground, and I think I want to be there too"—echoed Long Soldier's. It
is unclear if they were expressing despair.[3]

Sully reported to Pope that although all these Indians professed to
want peace, many war-minded Sioux remained at the Knife River camp.
Because the Fort Rice group told Sully some others would meet him
anywhere but Fort Rice, Sully said he would host them at Fort Berthold.
At the time, Sully did not understand the Indians' depth of fear of Fort
Rice beyond hearing that some mixed-blood trader had convinced them

---

[3]"Notes of the Council with the Sioux . . ." (*Fort Rice*) *Frontier Scout*, 20 July 1865. Regarding
White Shield's recollection of Brulés being at Whitestone, perhaps he was referring to a Yanktonai subgroup of that name. In the same account in the *Scout*, Long Soldier also says, "You came
up here, and killed Brulés."

that a boat was bringing Sully and his army across to the fort in order to kill them all. Actually, the big guns saluting Sully's arrival frightened away even the fort regulars until they learned the truth. Sitting Bull, approaching, turned his party away and supposedly "went through the different villages cutting himself with a knife and crying out . . . and calling on the nation to avenge the murder." A Sitting Bull relative later confirmed his distress, but denied he cut himself.[4]

ALTHOUGH HE DID NOT BELIEVE ANY FOES WERE NEAR THERE, SULLY would go to Devil's Lake as ordered. He reminded Pope there are "plenty of Indians between the Missouri and the James, probably over 3,000 warriors, but they are all Indians who have made peace with me, and I feel sure they will molest no one." He defended his decision to let them hunt there; because he had no rations to give them, they would otherwise starve.[5]

The bountiful and "most splendid dinner" the expedition officers hosted for departing First USV officers at Fort Rice was in stark contrast to the Indians' condition. The *Scout* exclaimed, "Green peas raised at Fort Berthold in Dacotah! Every luxury of the season was furnished in great abundance."[6] It also contrasted with regular fare. Sully wrote Curtis: "Last winter [the soldiers] suffered terribly by death and sickness, and all the medical officers agree that they fear they will suffer more next winter." Given that two potato plantings at Fort Rice had failed, Sully suggested the garrison purchase potatoes as soon as boats could bring them up. "It may be the means of saving the lives of a good many men" because the fort's garden only fed grasshoppers. Sully followed his medical officers' "urgent recommendation" to relieve the Union and Berthold garrisons even though Sixth Iowa soldiers stationed at Fort Berthold, where William Cuppett recalled no one dying and very little sickness, remained relatively healthy. On July 30 Captain Adam Bassett left Fort Rice with Company C, Fourth USV, to replace Company B, First USV, at Fort Union.

[4]"Local Items," (*Fort Rice*) *Frontier Scout*, 13 July 1865; Sully to Asst. Adj. Gen., Dept. of NW, 20 July 1865, 1109–10, and 8 Aug. 1865, 1172–74, both in OR, vol. 48, pt. 2; Sully to Sawyer, 20 July 1865, CIA annual report, no. 60, 204–205; Utley, *Lance*, 67–68; and Vestal (Campbell), *Sitting Bull*, 73–74.

[5]Sully to Asst. Adj. Gen., Dept. NW, 20 July 1865, OR, vol. 48, pt. 2, pp. 1109–10.

[6]"Local Items," (*Fort Rice*) *Frontier Scout*, 27 July 1865.

On July 22, Sully sent Colonel Dimon away by steamboat on trumped up "important business" and a furlough. With more than eighty deaths over the winter and twenty-two men then in the hospital, one of Lieutenant Colonel Pattee's tasks as the new Fort Rice commander would be improving the garrison's health.[7]

Sully left Fort Rice on July 25 with about 800 soldiers and enough officers, teamsters, herders, and other camp followers to total 1,000. When messengers forwarded mail to Sully, including an order to muster out the First and Fourth USV, Sully immediately complained: without replacements for garrisons at Forts Union, Berthold, and Rice, he would have to abandon them. He wanted further orders on the subject to intercept him at Fort Berthold. The mail also included papers Pope described as "relating to claims of Yankton Indians, or rather of Indian Agent Burleigh, for damages done them by soldiers." Sully should make necessary statements and pass these papers along to a congressional committee that was on its way to the Upper Missouri to look into Indian affairs. Replying, Sully told Pope he knew Burleigh had taken to Washington "a large pile of documents against me, sworn to by Colonel Pollock, half-breeds, and others." (Sully had arrested Pollock, perhaps partly for a comment about Sully chasing Indians with ox teams, but his case was never tried.)[8]

These papers could disastrously affect Sully's career. Lieutenant General Ulysses S. Grant telegraphed Pope for an explanation. Pope, who had tried to keep Sully out of his department, now defended him: "Sully's case . . . I think should be dealt with, not so much with reference to his special qualifications for his command as the fact that he is complained of by persons whose personal views and objects he will not promote at the expense of the public interests."[9]

---

[7]Sully to Asst. Adj. Gen., Dept. NW, 20 July 1865, OR, vol. 48, pt. 2, pp. 1109–10; Pattee, "Reminiscences," 339, 342; Dee Brown, *Galvanized Yankees*, 112–14; Cuppett to Libby, 21 Aug. 1914, Libby Papers, SHSND Archives; Dimon to Acting Asst. Adj. Gen. Ten Broeck, Dist. Iowa, 24 Jan. 1865, OR, vol. 48, pt. 1, pp. 636–38; and SO 21, 27 Apr. 1865, in U.S. Army, *General Orders, 1st*, Fort Union NHS Library. According to the (*Fort Rice*) *Frontier Scout*, 27 July 1865, Pattee officially assumed command by SO 12, HQ NW Indian Expedition, 21 July 1865.

[8]Herrick ("MEDICUS"), "March of the North-West Indian Expedition," (*Fort Rice*) *Frontier Scout*, 17 Aug. 1865; "Local Items," (*Fort Rice*) *Frontier Scout*, 27 July 1865; Sully to Asst. Adj. Gen., Dept. of NW, 23 July 1865, 1116–17, and 31 July 1865, 1145–47, both in OR, vol. 48, pt. 2; and Pope to Sully, 22 May 1865, and Sully to Pope, 3 June 1865, both in OR, vol. 48, pt. 2, pp. 557–58, 766.

[9]Pope to Sully, 22 May 1865, and Sully to Pope, 3 June 1865, both in OR, vol. 48, pt. 2, pp. 557–58, 766; Drips, *Three Years*, 132; Pattee, "Reminiscences," 339. Sully to Pope, 14 July 1865, 1080; Grant to Sherman, 20 July 1865, 1108; Pope to Grant and Grant to Pope, 21 July 1865, 1111; Pope to Grant, 27 July 1865, 1125–26; and Curtis to Sully, 12 July 1865, 1074, all in OR, vol. 48, pt. 2. Cuppett to Libby, 21 Aug. 1914. See "Organization of troops," 28 Feb. 1865, OR, vol. 48, pt. 1, p. 1031.

Out of touch while on the expedition, Sully did not know that, when he was nearly to Devil's Lake, some 500 warriors in the Knife River camp had responded to Sitting Bull's call to avenge the imaginary massacre the salute to Sully had conjured. Pattee was at the cattle yard some distance from Fort Rice when, early on July 28, a sutler's store employee saw a "friendly Indian flying with the greatest celerity towards him pursued by seven savages on horseback." Leading the chase was a warrior "nearly naked, and painted with ochre," wearing "a head dress of feathers and plumes that fell halfway over his back." Trader Hubbell's horses drew their attention from the man, but Captain Adams, writing as *Frontier Scout* editor, reported that "south of the post near the sawmill, a warrior chasing Private Hufstudler, Fourth USV, shot him with an arrow. Private Andrew F. Burch got a good look at Hufstudler's assailant: "His pony was hung with red tassels; he, himself had a red blanket around his waist, his shoulders were naked and painted red, his hair was hanging loose, two feathers fluttering in it. He had a rifle or shot-gun in a fringed covering hanging on his back and in one hand his bow and arrows. His horse was streaked off with red paint over his haunches."[10]

Pattee, returning from the cattle yard, hurried to find his company commanders, whose names he did not yet know. Near the fort, Captain Moreland and a number of Sixth Iowa men were engaged in a fierce fight with the attackers. Three Indians fell; survivors dragged their injured away. First Sergeant Charles F. Hobbs and three other dismounted cavalrymen joined infantry companies holding the hills behind the stockade. The Indians charged, and when the infantrymen ran away, Hobbs and his friends had to follow or die. Halfway down the hill, a hundred or so warriors began "whirling down the slope" toward them, shooting at Private James C. Hoffman with guns and bows. Hoffman ran toward Hobbs and the other Iowans until an Indian hit him with a lance. Hobbs fired at the warrior from about ten or twelve feet away. "[The warrior] dropped down, catching his horse by the mane, whirled him round and started off up the hill." Someone saw two men tie him on his horse and take him away. Post surgeon George Herrick extracted an arrow buried six inches in Hoffman's side.[11]

---

[10]Many sources mention the battle. Sully to Asst. Adj. Gen., Dept. NW, 8 Aug. 1865, OR, vol. 48, pt. 2, pp. 1172–74; Utley, *Lance*, 67–68; Vestal (Campbell), *Sitting Bull*, 73–74; Adams, "Battle at Fort Rice," (*Fort Rice*) *Frontier Scout*, 3 Aug. 1865; Pattee, "Reminiscences," 340–41; Tucker-Butts, *Galvanized Yankees: Face of Loyalty*, 193–96; and Dee Brown, *Galvanized Yankees*, 105–107.

[11]"Battle at Fort Rice," (*Fort Rice*) *Frontier Scout*, 3 Aug. 1865; Pattee, "Reminiscences," 340–41; McDermott, *Frontier Scout: View of Fort Rice*, 33–34, quoting Herrick ("MEDICUS"), *Sioux City Register*, 12 Aug. 1865; and "Local Items," (*Fort Rice*) *Frontier Scout*, 10 Aug. 1865.

Pattee, unable to rescue Hoffman, led two infantry companies to the hill, where Captain Bassett's Fourth USV got off a few shots with the howitzer. These, Adams wrote, "scattered terror among the natives, they believing shells . . . living, shrieking demons." At a distance from the post, Captain Samuel G. Sewell and thirty Fourth USV infantrymen made three dismounted charges at a hundred or so warriors, killing two. When more infantry under Sergeant S. P. Morgan, First USV, appeared on the scene, those Indians retreated. The Battle of Fort Rice ended by noontime. Hoffman lived, but Hufstudler died a week later. A third soldier survived an arrow wound in his thigh.[12]

In the *Frontier Scout*, Adams predicted "many a squaw will bewail" their dead warriors. "Poor dear creatures! As though Indians possessed . . . attributes of humanity, or the affectionate instincts of the higher order of brutes. As though their fiendish hearts were susceptible of one spark of the anguish they so gloatingly inflict upon others! They are devoid of every ennobling emotion of the human heart—intuitively brutal—preternaturally degraded—essentially heartless, vindictive and remorseless. Their stately pride and nobility of character exists only in the ideal fancies of imaginative flash novel writers." Hobbs, one of the soldiers involved in murdering the seven Sioux in 1863, marveled at how the Indians charged, "rushing from all points" against the Iowans' fire, to fight hand to hand. "Indians [had] never fought so gallantly before," he said. Adams told *Scout* readers Fort Rice could add "a day of glory to its calendar that will give it a name and fame in the annals of Indian warfare."[13]

During another attack on July 30, artillery killed one Indian; in addition, a company of First USV soldiers prevented the Indians from stampeding the livestock. On August 1, the *Scout*'s local items column reported Indians watching and waiting, perhaps for a chance to shoot a sentinel.[14]

AS THE JULY 28 BATTLE RAGED AT FORT RICE, SULLY'S SOLDIERS surprised a large group of mixed-blood people drying meat some twenty-six miles from Devil's Lake. Besides "a French nobleman lately from

---

[12]"Battle at Fort Rice," (*Fort Rice*) *Frontier Scout*, 3 Aug. 1865; and Pattee, "Reminiscences," 340–41.

[13]"Battle at Fort Rice," (*Fort Rice*) *Frontier Scout*, 3 Aug. 1865; C. F. Hobbs, letter to editor, (*Fort Rice*) *Frontier Scout*, 10 Aug. 1865; and McDermott, "*Frontier Scout*: View of Fort Rice," 34.

[14]"Local Items," (*Fort Rice*) *Frontier Scout*, 3 Aug. 1865.

Paris," Sully reported, "they had with them their women and children and even their priest," on what they said was a two-month-long hunting trip. Nevertheless, they knew about the American president's order concerning trading. After searching their camp, Sully concluded they were indeed hunters; they had killed 600 buffalo in one day. When he told them that "their coming into our country to hunt in large parties would have to be stopped," they acknowledged that "perhaps . . . they had no right to hunt in our country without permission, but if they could not do so [they] would starve." Besides, they argued, American mixed-blood people trapped furs north of the border. When Sully underscored how much "trouble their people gave us in furnishing ammunition to the Indians," they admitted some of their people did do this and professed eagerness to stop them. They showed Sully a written copy of their colony's laws, which included a law fining anyone £5 for selling ammunition to Indians. Sully explained in his report that these mixed-blood people, whether north or south of the line, shared a culture, spoke French in common, and were intermarried to the extent they considered themselves one family. They paid no taxes and recognized no laws but those each colony devised for itself.[15]

As he guessed, no militant Sioux remained east of Devil's Lake. The mixed-bloods "felt sure if any large body of Indians had left for Minnesota they would know it," and these would probably "be glad to come in and make peace, for they were very poor." A couple of Santee bands had crossed the border. Others found shelter in the Turtle Mountains, which straddled the international line, and about 500 lodges of Santees, Cutheads, and Upper Yanktonnais might be on the Mouse River south of the border. That night, Sully camped near the hunters, some of whom volunteered to take him to the Sioux camp; however, Sully, afraid they would plunder while his men fought, declined the offer.

Sully's command found no Indians near Devil's Lake, but they did come across some American mixed-bloods who confirmed that some Santees were along the Mouse River. Searching their camp turned up nothing, but Sully left a detail to guard them "for fear that they might give the Indians information of my coming." He selected a camp on the south shore of Devil's Lake and waited for Major von Minden to prepare maps and find the best location for a new post. He forwarded von

---

[15]All quotes in this paragraph and the following one are from Sully to Asst. Adj. Gen., Dept. of NW, 31 July 1865, OR, vol. 48, pt. 2, pp. 1145–47. See also Hill to brother, 22 Oct. 1865, in Shambaugh, "Iowa Troops," 441.

Minden's reports to headquarters with his own assessment of the area as an "oasis in the desert, dreary prairies of Dakota" that would likely remain remote from civilization for a long time. With its rich soil and abundant timber, game, and fish, Sully believed the Devil's Lake area would be "a convenient point to assemble together such Indians who are disposed to be friendly and to adopt somewhat the civilized modes of living." He suggested that whoever served so remote a location be selected because they "would prefer this service." The post's commander should be a strict disciplinarian who "would teach the Indian to respect him by his daily habits, firmness, and the interest he would take in their welfare." This man should study Indian character and learn the language. That way, he would not need to "[take] into his confidence one he can not depend on." In Sully's experience, a post interpreter "is, in fact, the commanding officer, as far as the Indians are concerned, for . . . he will interpret the Indian speech just as it suits him, or is to his interests."[16]

Nevertheless, Frank La Framboise, who interpreted for him in 1864, left Fort Rice on the *Big Horn* on August 7, presumably at Sully's request, to interpret for the general's expected meeting with Sioux at Fort Berthold. La Framboise's trip was potentially more dangerous than was Sully's. On August 8, another boat arrived at Fort Rice with its "'Texas,' cabin, and stacks full of bullet-holes."[17]

The expedition found no Indians along Mouse River, although scouts encountered additional mixed-blood families during an exploration north to the border. Sully suspected they would not dare enter this country unless they were on "very good terms with the Indians." Arriving at Berthold August 8, Sully sent runners to the Sioux camp on Knife River to invite those who wanted peace to "come in and see me, and those who did not I would make war on." Returning runners reported many leaning toward peace. If they fought Sully, they expected to fail. Nevertheless, they feared Sully's invitation was a trap "to capture and slay them."[18]

Sully knew from experience that the camp's location provided warriors excellent defense and easy escape into the badlands. This year, his 800–900 men would be no match for a large Indian force holding such

---

[16]Sully to Asst. Adj. Gen., Dept. of NW, 30 July 1865, 1136–37, and 31 July 1865, 1145–47, and Von Minden to Norton, 4 Aug. 1865, 1137–39, all in OR, vol. 48, pt. 2.

[17]"Local Items," (*Fort Rice*) *Frontier Scout*, 10 Aug. 1865; and "Log of the Steamer Benton," 285–313. According to Hunter, *Steamboats*, 90–91, a "texas" was "a short and boxlike extension aft of the lower part of a . . . pilothouse."

[18]Sully to Asst. Adj. Gen., Dept. NW, 8 Aug. 1865, OR, vol. 48, pt. 2, pp. 1172–74; Utley, *Lance*, 67–68; and Vestal (Campbell), *Sitting Bull*, 73–74.

good ground. However, if Connor's Powder River expedition was on its way to find the "very large numbers" of Miniconjous, Sans Arcs, Oglalas, and Brulé Sioux (along with some Cheyennes, Arapahos, and other tribes) that Sully believed were in that camp only sixty miles from Fort Berthold, he told Curtis he was "in an excellent position to co-operate" with it. He sent his report from Berthold to the nearest telegraph office "by an Indian who has to run the gauntlet to get through the hostile country."[19]

However, Connor's expedition was already in motion with different objectives. Connor instructed Colonel Nelson Cole, Second Missouri Light Artillery, to proceed with his column from Omaha "to the east base of the Black Hills, . . . move thence along the east base of the Black Hills to Bear's Peak [*sic*, Bear Butte], . . . where a large force of hostile Indians are supposed to be camped." From there, Cole was to scout the creeks in the Black Hills and attempt to surprise these Indians, then head northwest to meet Connor's command. To his individualized orders to Cole and his other commanders, Connor added: "You will not receive overtures of peace or submission from Indians, but will attack and kill every male Indian over twelve years of age." Lieutenant Colonel Samuel Walker, with the same orders, left Fort Laramie with about 600 men on August 6. When Pope received copies, he demanded General Dodge countermand these "atrocious" instructions, which were "in direct violation of my repeated orders. . . . If any such orders as General Connor's are carried out it will be disgraceful to the Government, and will cost him his commission, if not worse." Connor received the telegram too late—on August 11—to rescind orders to the expedition's eastern prong commanders. On August 13, Cole's column reached Bear Butte. Six days later, Walker's column, traveling rapidly with pack mules instead of wagons, found Cole.[20]

Because Sully received no new orders from Curtis, he sent word to the usv company's officers at Fort Union to sell at cost what government property they could not move and bring the rest down to Fort Rice.[21] Still at Fort Berthold in mid-August, Sully learned about Sitting Bull's skirmish at Fort Rice from Indians who said the approximately 300

---

[19]Sully to Asst. Adj. Gen., Dept. NW, 8 Aug., 1172–74, and Sully to Asst. Adj. Gen., Dept. of the Missouri, 13 Aug. 1865, 1180–81, both in OR, vol. 48, pt. 2.

[20]Connor to Cole, 4 July 1865, in OR, vol. 4, pt. 2, p. 1049; and Pope to Dodge, 11 Aug. 1865, in OR, vol. 48, pt. 1, p. 356.

[21]Utley, *Frontiersmen*, 306n13; Hampton, "Powder River," 7; Sully to Asst. Adj. Gen., Dept. NW, 8 Aug. 1865, OR, vol. 48, pt. 2, pp. 1172–74; Sully to Asst. Adj. Gen., Dept. of the Missouri, 13 Aug. 1865, OR series 1, vol. 48, pt. 2, pp. 1180–81; SO 72, Fort Rice, 31 Aug. 1865, in U.S. Army, *General Orders, 1st*, Fort Union NHS Library.

warriors had paid for the dozen or so horses they stole during the raid with nine badly wounded warriors. Months later, Hunkpapas arriving at Rice for peace talks confirmed that Sitting Bull and The-Man-That-Has-His-Head-Shaved led the attack. Adams reported their version of what happened afterward in the *Scout*. For "cowardice in leaving the fight . . . Sitting Bull was whipped[.] . . . To use their own words enforced by appropriate gestures, he only lived by the little end of his little finger." The participants would not let the disgraced leaders keep two horses they stole that day. Instead, "in the dispute the poor animals were killed, thus satisfactorily arranging the division of plunder."[22]

When the war party returned to the Knife River camp and learned that Sully was a few days from Fort Berthold, the entire camp fled south because peace party Indians had said the general would not make peace with them after their attack on Rice. Sully sent Bloody Knife—whose Arikara mother had left his Hunkpapa father to return to her people when Bloody Knife was ten—to track them.[23] After following them to Beaver Creek's confluence with the Little Missouri, Bloody Knife concluded they were heading toward Powder River. Sully knew it would take too long to build rafts to cross his army over the Missouri to pursue them.

However, Sully learned that 300 to 500 lodges of Cuthead Sioux and Medicine Bear's Upper Yanktonais were hunting buffalo north of Fort Union near the international border. Knowing he could not overtake them before they reached safety, Sully sent for Medicine Bear. Some who knew him considered Medicine Bear the most intelligent of Sioux chiefs; in addition, he held the Sioux record for coups counted now that Big Head was dead. His people feared Sully would hang Medicine Bear, a bitter enemy to whites and a leader in all the fights against Sully. Nevertheless, he came to see the general. When Sully informed him he would "take his advice and not go after his people," Medicine Bear said most Sioux wanted peace but "their heart[s] felt bad" against Sully because the prairies "were not yet dried from the blood" he had spilled. Hundreds of Yanktonai men, women, and children had died from wounds or deprivation. Of the hundred men Medicine Bear personally commanded during the 1864 fighting, thirty died in battle or later from their wounds. He would not reveal his band's location, but he said he would bring them in after Sully left the vicinity.[24]

[22]Larson, *Gall*, 35; and "Local Items," (*Fort Rice*) *Frontier Scout*, 23 Oct. 1865.

[23]Innis, *Bloody Knife*, 45; Gray, "Bloody Knife," 89; and Larson, *Gall*, 35.

[24]Sully to Asst. Adj. Gen., Dept. of the Missouri, 13 Aug. 1865, OR, vol. 48, pt. 2, pp. 1180–82; and Pattee "Reminiscences," 335–36.

Sully's stay at Berthold prompted him to urge government to act to help the Arikaras, Mandans, and Hidatsas, "all speaking different languages, but banded together for protection against their powerful neighbors, the Sioux." Because of their small and decreasing population, "they dare not go far from their village to hunt, and are quite poor." To replace the First USV company there, "partly for [the Indians'] protection, as well as to stop illegal trading with hostile Sioux," he set up forty Indian soldiers, issued them arms, and recommended the government supply them with distinctive uniforms. Because the Yanktons' and Two Kettles' attack on the Berthold Indians that spring violated the Yanktons' treaty promise not to leave their reservation without a permit, Sully recommended the Yanktons pay restitution to the three tribes for the two dead Rees and the stolen horses.[25]

The expedition left Fort Berthold August 20. Despite the commotion the guns caused at his previous arrival, a week later Sully crossed the river to Fort Rice to "customary salutes fired." The celebration was marred when Indians killed Corporal Horace Jameson of Brackett's Battalion. Moccasins and a painted medicine-stone left at the scene along with the lariats identified the assailants as Cuthead Yanktonais. Even soldiers due to muster out vowed not to leave Fort Rice until they had "revenge on some Indian" for Jameson. When Two Bear's band and other fort regulars returned from a hunt, skittish soldiers waylaid their advance party and, "in the excitement would have killed them had it not been for the officers." Emotions ran so high Sully sent runners to warn Indians to keep away until the expedition left. By then, soldiers captured three men in Bear Rib's band on suspicion of killing Jameson, but Adams defended them in the *Scout*. He knew one—Left Hand Bull—personally. "During all the spring Bear Rib's and Two Bear's men proved their loyalty and good faith. While they were here we lost no men—no cattle—not even a shoe-latchet. Honor to whom honor is due even if an Indian. Let not our prejudices 'hang all the Johnsons.'"[26]

When the expedition reached Fort Sully on September 11, the Seventh Iowa garrison expected to muster out right away, but instead, they would relieve the Sixth Iowans. On his way home, Sergeant Drips of the Sixth visited Camp McLelland in Davenport, where he found the Minnesota Sioux prisoners "fat and hearty, well fed and clothed in government

[25]Sully to Asst. Adj. Gen., Dept. of the Missouri, 15 Aug. 1865, OR, vol. 48, pt. 2, p. 1186.

[26]"Local Items" and "Another Soldier Killed by Indians," (*Fort Rice*) *Frontier Scout*, 31 Aug. 1865; Sully to Pope, 2 Sept. 1865, OR, vol. 48, pt. 2, pp. 1222–23; Bergemann, *Brackett's Battalion*, 160–61, 193; and "Local Items," (*Fort Rice*) *Frontier Scout*, 7 Sept. 1865.

clothing and guarded by U.S. soldiers. It would not have been very healthy for these red gents if the soldiers just from Dakota had been placed on guard over them." Drips would not have been happy to know that Reverend Williamson, who also ministered to their families at Crow Creek, had petitioned President Lincoln a year earlier to pardon the Davenport detainees.[27]

ARMY REORGANIZATIONS AND PERSONNEL SHIFTS LEFT NEWLY brevetted Major General Sully commanding the new District of Dakota, which included fourteen Iowa counties and Dakota Territory, excepting parts under Minnesota and Nebraska military districts. Sully would retain command of the First and Fourth USV and take on other Galvanized Yankee units. He was grateful the Fiftieth Wisconsin Volunteer Infantry Regiment would relieve the First USV at Fort Rice. He lamented to Pope that the post's cemetery "tells a fearful tale of sickness and death, and already scurvy is again beginning to show itself. The men are so disheartened and have such a perfect fear of staying . . . I verily believe many of them would die of fear alone should sickness break out among them again as it did last winter." Although he regarded Fort Berthold as important for regulating Sioux trade, Sully acceded to abandoning it. Unsure if the new order removed Fort Rice, located west of the Missouri, and Fort Union, on the Montana and Dakota border, from his command, he reported he would "not so consider the order, till I get further orders."[28]

Also because of post-war reorganization, Major General Pope now headed the Department, not Division, of the Missouri. He wrote Division Commander Sherman's adjutant on August 1, 1865, expressing his views and requesting clarification of his duties. It was a crucial time, he wrote: "Today we are at one grasp seizing the whole region of country occupied by the Indians and plunging them without warning into suffering and starvation." That meant "either a large force must for a time

[27]Drips, *Three Years*, 125. See also Hill to Dutton, in Shambaugh, "Iowa Troops," 442–43; and Williamson to Lincoln, 27 April 1864, Abraham Lincoln Papers at the Library of Congress, series 1, http://memory.loc.gov/ammem/alhtml/malhome.html..

[28]Dodge to Tichnenor, 12 Aug. 1865, 1179; Sully to Asst. Adj. Gen., Dept. of the Missouri, 14 Sept. 1865, 1228–29; GO 20, Dept. of the Missouri, 22 Aug. 1865, 1201; Sprague to Sully, 20 Aug., 1193–94; Sully to Asst. Adj. Gen., Dept. of the Missouri, 13 Aug. 1865, 1180–81, all in OR, vol. 48, pt. 2. "Local Items," *The (Fort Sully) Independent*, 16 Sept. 1855 [sic 1865]; and SO 37 and GO 38, Fort Rice, 6 Oct. 1865, in U.S. Army, *General Orders, 1st*, Fort Union NHS Library.

be kept there, or we must furnish insufficient protection to our citizens in that region." He hoped "the expeditions now marching against the Indians will be able to inflict such damage upon them that they will prefer to undergo much wrong and suffering rather than again break out in hostilities. This is a cruel process, but the only one which under the present system seems to be in my power." There were logistical problems: "The remote stations of these troops and the necessity of hauling in wagons from the Missouri River all supplies needed for them, renders the protection required and demanded by the mail service, the emigration and the remote settlements an expensive undertaking." He had questions for his new boss. "Is it designed that such military pressure be kept upon the Indians that small parties of adventurers prospecting the plains and mountains in every direction, and in the most remote and uninhabited regions of the country, will be unmolested by Indians, whatever such parties may do or wherever they may go?" Pope also asked if, as department commander, he was "responsible for hostile acts of Indians against such parties." Is the army "to be made responsible for every murder or outrage committed in the great plains by Indians or white men, who are officially at peace according to the records in the office of the Commissioner of Indian Affairs?" He suggested that "when there is divided action, as in the case now in the management of Indian affairs, there should be divided responsibility."[29]

Once the Sully and Connor expeditions were over, five infantry and two cavalry regiments would be the only military serving in Kansas, Nebraska, Colorado, Utah, Montana, and the part of Dakota Territory later included in Wyoming Territory. In the old Department of the Northwest, Brevet Major General J. M. Corse would command the District of Minnesota. General Sibley would serve on an investigative Indian commission.[30]

Public outrage over abuses against Cheyennes and Arapahos at Sand Creek had spurred Wisconsin senator James R. Doolittle, Indian Affairs Committee chairman and President Lincoln's friend, to introduce a joint resolution to investigate Indian affairs on a broad scope. To finance peace talks with the Upper Missouri Sioux, Dakota governor Edmunds had gone to Washington to appeal for an extra $20,000 appropriation to the Indian Appropriations Act passed in February. When Edmunds approached President Lincoln with his plan to end the war by negotiation,

---

[29]Pope to Sawyer, 1 Aug. 1865, OR, vol. 48, pt. 2, pp. 1149–53; and GO 44, OR, vol. 48, pt. 1, p. 1225.
[30]Townsend to Sherman, OR, vol. 48, pt. 2, p. 1056; and Gilman, *Henry Hastings Sibley*, 208.

Lincoln gave Edmunds a personal card on which he instructed the U.S. House Ways and Means Committee chairman Thaddeus Stevens to "give Governor Edmunds what he wants." Stevens and Edmunds enlisted Commissioner Dole's support, and the three approached Senator Doolittle. Despite opposition from Ohio senator John Sherman, General Sherman's brother, the amendment passed on March 1.

The prospect of this congressional committee's trip to Sioux country further complicated post–Civil War military reorganization, but not even Lee's surrender to Grant or Lincoln's assassination during April interrupted the controversy over Indian affairs on the Upper Missouri. Edmunds had his money plus Commissioner Dole's and Dakota Territory representative Burleigh's support; now he wanted the military's cooperation. He wrote Sully to that effect, but General Pope replied, informing Edmunds "there are no Sioux Indians in Dakota Territory with whom it is judicious to make such treaties of peace as you propose. . . . I do not feel authorized to assist, or permit any arrangements for a treaty with them." Furthermore, Pope regarded Indians who came to the forts prisoners of war. "With such prisoners I do not understand that the Indian Department has anything to do."[31]

In response, Edmunds wrote the Andrew Johnson administration's interior secretary James Harlan in May, enclosing Pope's letter to him and a copy of another letter Pope sent to Major General Halleck. Halleck weighed in, saying "military commanders were long since instructed to permit no treaties . . . and that no presents or ammunition [should] be given or provided" until set aside by superior military authority. Edmunds hoped Secretary Harlan would agree that the "military commander of this department has his face firmly set against making peace with these Indians, notwithstanding the evident desire of [C]ongress."[32]

Harlan took up the fight, asking of Secretary of War Stanton that civil and military authorities "alike conform to the policy adopted in relation to the Indian tribes." When the public, critical of both entities, became aware of the conflict, Pope warned Sully to keep official communications out of newspapers and Harlan instructed acting Indian commissioner Dennis Nelson Cooley to do the same. (President Andrew Johnson had accused Dole of inefficiency and corruption in connection with Sand Creek, forcing his July resignation.) Cooley put out a circular to his superintendents

---

[31]Pope to Edmunds, 8 May 1865, OR, vol. 48, pt. 2, 357–58.
[32]Edmunds quotes Halleck in Edmunds to Dole, 9 May 1865, OR, vol. 48, pt. 2, p. 663; Edmunds to Harlan, 10 May 1865, OR, vol. 48, pt. 2, 661–62.

and agents informing them the "department will subordinate its actions and intercourse with the tribes and bands in hostility to the United States to the policy and operations of the War Department." That meant not delivering "goods, money, or other property" to any tribe or band "in hostility to the government." Agents and superintendents should also revoke licenses from traders who had dealings with such Indians.[33]

AFTER SOME MONTHS LIVING AMONG INDIANS AND AGAINST THE backdrop of a Civil War fought partly because of racial differences, the Galvanized Yankee units' eastern officers and southern soldiers seemed to have been of two minds about the Sioux, alternately admiring and disparaging them. The tendency of some Fort Rice soldiers to consider Indians less than human showed itself in their disregard for the dead. *Frontier Scout* editor Adams wrote that he "obtained an Indian's skull to add to my cabinet of curiosities. It is securely perched on the summit of my hat-tree, like Poe's raven on the bust of Pallas, just above his chamber door."[34]

In one of a series of essays about the Sioux published and copied in area newspapers, John Pattee revealed his own prejudices. He did not doubt the Sioux are the "most degraded set of savages on this continent. There is but little among them that can be found to interest anyone." This man the Indians called "Big Heart" concluded that Sioux were "almost entirely without tradition and with but little skill in fabricating those things that they use most." He contrasted his own experience with the sentiments in William Wadsworth Longfellow's famous poem, "Hiawatha." "Why wonder at Mr. Longfellow's ideas, and not at the many erroneous ideas entertained by almost all eastern people, who cry out against every attempt to chastise these vagrants as their past conduct merits. I think if some of them could visit this country . . . they would cease their senseless sympathy."[35]

---

[33]Follow the controversy in Sully to Pope, 14 June 1865, 887–88, Pope to Harlan, 19 June 1865, 933, Harlan to Pope, 6 July 1865, 1056, Pope to Corse and Pope to Sully, 25 Aug. 1865, 1213, all in OR, vol. 48, pt. 2; "Report," CIA annual report, 28 Oct. 1865, 537; and Kvasnicka and Viola, *Commissioners*, 94–95, 104–105. See also U.S. Senate, *Condition of the Indian Tribes* (hereafter cited as Doolittle report), no. 156.

[34]"Local Items," (*Fort Rice*) *Frontier Scout*, 3 and 10 Aug. 1865.

[35]Pattee, "Reminiscences," 338. The same wording is in an unsigned editorial in the (*Fort Rice*) *Frontier Scout*, 17 Aug. 1865.

By contrast, while at Fort Rice, Sully sent Charles Galpin and his universally respected wife, Eagle Woman, on a secret mission to the militant camp. While they were away, the *Scout* profiled Eagle Woman as "one of the finest women in the world" who "makes us believe that Pocahontas is no myth or fabrication of the poet. . . . She is the friend of her own race, and also of the whites. Her friendship is not proved by words but by deeds." The article detailed her heroism in rushing to Lieutenant Wilson's aid during the attack on the fort and her bravery when Santees stopped the Galpins' mackinaw in 1862. "She has been placed in scenes of great danger, but she has always stood the test, and proved a golden link in the chain between the savage and the civilized."[36]

On September 23, the Galpins returned to Fort Rice after, according to William Larned, extracting promises from many chiefs to meet the commissioners at Fort Rice. Sully told Pope that because Eagle Woman "got thrown from her horse and hurt a little," the Galpins remained longer at Fort Berthold than planned. They reported that Carnahan's Illinois cavalrymen had camped on the Sheyenne River while a major brought a contingent to Berthold. Along the way, Carnahan's men chased, but fortunately did not catch, a small party of Indians who were local Berthold residents. Had they killed them, Sully told Pope, "Indian affairs would have been in a bad state and [have] no prospects of peace."[37]

Sully predicted the Sioux would "never try a combination again to resist our troops, for they frankly admit it is useless for them to fight us, for we are better mounted and armed." There would not be "perfect peace immediately," however. He told Pope he expected "small war parties of young bucks, who have nothing to lose by war, [to] . . . continue to rob when they get a good chance." Even this guerilla warfare would stop "if peace is made with the major portion of the Indians, and particularly if the posts in the Indian country are commanded by officers of sound judgment and some little knowledge of the Indian character."[38]

EVERYONE KNEW SULLY'S 1865 CAMPAIGN HAD FAILED. THE expedition's surgeon, Dr. Herrick, ended his journal account, published

---

[36]Larned diary, 28 Aug. 1865 and 23 Sept. 1865, 264–65; Pattee, "Reminiscences," 342–49; "An Heroic Woman," *Frontier Scout*, 31 Aug. 1865; and Gray, "Story of Mrs. Picotte-Galpin," pt. 1, 14.

[37]Larned diary, 28 Aug. 1865 and 23 Sept. 1865, 264–65; "Local Items," (*Fort Rice*) *Frontier Scout*, 7 Sept. 1865; Sully to Pope, 2 Sept. 1865, 1222–23, OR, vol. 48, pt. 2, pp. 1222–23; and Gray, "Story of Mrs. Picotte-Galpin," pt. 1, 14.

[38]Sully to Asst. Adj. Gen., Dept of the Missouri, 26 Aug. 1865, OR, vol. 48, pt. 2, pp. 1215–16.

in the *Scout* under the pseudonym Medicus, this way: "Let the blame fall where it should, upon those who sit at home and order, but not on those who take the field and obey orders . . . Just so long as these Indian Expeditions are controlled altogether by Generals at home, they can accomplish comparatively nothing."[39]

Would Indians fare better under the aegis of the U.S. War Department than under the corrupt Indian Bureau? Dr. Stephen P. Yoemans, Seventh Iowa surgeon, thought so. The expedition's failure, he wrote under the pen name SPY in the *Scout*, meant that "in the future Indians will be sought where they are to be found." Had Sully been permitted to go after the Knife River group, "he would have been between the two columns, and it is scarcely possible that [the Indians] could have escaped a decisive engagement with one or the other." Considering "all the difficulties surrounding this Indian question," Yoemans argued, the military would accept its responsibilities if "protected from the intermeddling of that class of frontier vultures whose only aim is to dispossess Indians of the scanty means which God and our Government have given them for sustenance."[40]

SINCE JULY 1, WHEN COLONEL COLE BEGAN MOVING HIS EASTERN column of Connor's 1865 Powder River Expedition west from Omaha, mutinous troops, unbroken mules, and Pawnee guides who did not know the country were only a few of the difficulties that plagued him. After Colonel Walker and his Kansas cavalrymen found Cole's Missourians near Bear Butte on August 20, Walker's greater mobility allowed him to move ahead faster, but the columns kept in contact. So far, neither Cole's nor Walker's men had fought any battles, but they would continue to operate under orders that allowed no immunity to peace-minded Indians.

When an Indian presence became apparent, Cole regretted that his orders "confined [him] to moving to Powder River and Panther Mountain," where Connor expected to arrive first and leave supplies. As they traveled beside Box Elder Creek, many men were sick with scurvy. Wild onions proved a valuable discovery.[41]

---

[39]Herrick ("MEDICUS"), "March of the North-West Indian Expedition," (*Fort Rice*) *Frontier Scout*, 17 Aug. 1865.

[40]Yoemans ("SPY"), editorial, (*Fort Rice*) *Frontier Scout*, 24 Aug. 1865.

[41]Pope to Dodge, 11 Aug. 1865, OR, vol. 48, pt. 1, p. 356; and Hampton, "Powder River," 2–15. Walker's 25 Sept. 1865 report to Price in Hafen and Hafen, *Far West and the Rockies*, vol. 12, *Powder River Campaign*, 92–100. (See also Cole's report in Hafen & Hafen, 60–91.)

Scouts returning from Panther Mountain on September 1 reported no indication Connor had been there. On the heels of this disappointment, the several hundred Hunkpapas, Sihasapas, Miniconjous, and Sans Arcs returning to the Powder River country from the Knife River camp attacked Cole's herders and stole some animals. The advance recaptured the stock, but six Missouri artillerymen died in the attempt. When the main force moved up in support, the Sioux fell back. Cole estimated twenty-five enemy killed and many wounded.[42]

Cole continued toward the Yellowstone with his animals foraging on nothing but cottonwood bark. On September 3, a new obstacle arose—quicksand, "in which our horses could not for an instant maintain control of themselves." That night, a terrible storm finished off the already famished and weak. In all, 225 horses and mules died of "excessive heat, exhaustion, starvation, and extreme cold." The men destroyed some wagons and quartermaster's stores because they lacked enough animals to haul it all.

While Cole waited for his surviving animals to recuperate, some seventy-five Indians attacked a Twelfth Missouri Cavalry detachment, which chased them away. Cheyenne Dog Soldiers, Oglalas, and Arapahos joined the Knife River Sioux coalition, and early on September 5, Sitting Bull and others attempted to block teamsters rounding up stray mules.[43] A volley from men with the pack train turned them away, but more Indians appeared on the hills. As he advanced, Cole discovered hundreds more in the gulches and large numbers also moving south up the valley. Another warrior force occupied the riverbank.

After about three hours of fighting, the thousand or so Indians attacked an isolated Twelfth Missouri detachment, killing two soldiers and wounding two others. Among the Sioux heroes on September 5 were the Hunkpapas Bull Head, Stand-Looking-Back, and Bull Eagle. Jumping Bull, Sitting Bull, his nephew White Bull, and cousin Black Moon also participated.

On September 8, Walker, about three or four miles ahead, sent word to Cole that some 3,000 to 4,000 Indians were trying to drive him back. Cole corralled his train and went to the rescue. The foes now were Oglala Sioux and Cheyennes under Red Cloud and Little Wolf, respectively, whom the Knife River group had alerted about the soldiers before continuing to their destination.[44]

---

[42]Utley, *Lance*, 69.

[43]Halaas and Masich, *Halfbreed*, 196–98; and Utley, *Lance*, 69.

[44]"Local Items," (*Fort Rice*) *Frontier Scout*, 29 Sept. 1865; Cole to U. S. Grant, 10 Feb. 1867, OR, vol. 48, pt. 1, pp. 366–74; and Utley, *Lance*, 22, 69–70.

Cole found these Indians less eager for battle than the others, but that night a terrible storm killed 414 more of Cole's animals, forcing him to destroy additional wagons and equipment. On September 10, as Cole's train began to move, warriors harassed the column's rear until artillery pushed them beyond range. Moving upriver, the soldiers passed a deserted Sioux, Cheyenne, and Arapaho camp that might have included 1,500 to 2,000 households. Cole regretted his starving and exhausted command could not have "overtaken and destroyed" this group. The Indians attacked once more, losing several killed and wounded before leaving entirely.[45]

Men marching on quarter rations began eating their horses and mules. As soon as a horse or mule died, Colonel Walker wrote, "twenty men would pounce on . . . [it;] in less time than I can tell it his bones would be stripped and devoured raw."[46] On September 18, Cole's column met soldiers bringing food and supplies from Fort Connor (later Fort Reno), the new post on the Powder River near present Kaycee, Wyoming. Connor's western columns, with better luck, had sustained themselves and, on August 29, wiped out thirty-five Arapahos at a cost of five killed and two wounded.

When all Connor Expedition components returned to Fort Laramie in late September, two-thirds of the men were barefoot. Cole later complained to Major General Grant, "Starving soldiers might well wonder . . . why old Indian fighters had not, with their knowledge, planned a more consistent campaign; created depots here and hunted Indians there; not had a command starving here, unfit to cope with the Indians everywhere around them, and the supplies they needed . . . no one knew where."[47]

While Connor's campaign was in motion, James A. Sawyers of Sioux City was roughing out a road meant to put Iowa in the running for the lucrative traffic to the mines in southwestern Montana. It was an ambitious project. Part would traverse the Missouri River valley from Sioux City north to the Sheyenne River near the Dakota and Minnesota border. From there a branch would lead to the main road west of the Black Hills. Sully refused to provide an escort for a crew heading west from Fort Pierre, but they went anyway, making it to within forty miles of their planned endpoint west of the Black Hills before their guide, Charles Picotte, sensed danger and persuaded them to turn back.

[45]Cole to U. S. Grant, 10 Feb. 1867, OR, vol. 48, pt. 1, pp. 366–74.

[46]Walker to Price, 25 Sept. 1865, in Hafen and Hafen, *Far West and the Rockies*, vol. 12, *Powder River Campaigns*, 98.

[47]Ibid.; Dodge to Pope, 1 Oct. 1865, OR, vol. 48, pt. 2, p. 1237; Hampton, "Powder River," 11, 11n32, 13–14; and Cole to Grant, 25 Dec. 1865, OR, vol. 48, pt. 1, p. 382.

In August, Sawyers's wagon train and escort of twenty-five Dakota Cavalry and two companies of "galvanized" Fifth USV under Captain George W. Williford were west of the Tongue River when several hundred Indians tried to run off the livestock. After an initial attack that failed, these Cheyennes and Lakotas, among whom were Charles and George Bent, asked for a parley." George represented the Indians, interpreting for the Dog Soldier chief Bull Bear, Northern Cheyenne chief Dull Knife, and the Oglala chief Red Cloud. At one point in the negotiations, George grew angry and, without consulting the chiefs, demanded from Sawyers a promise that the government hang Chivington. Ultimately, the Indians accepted a wagonload of peace offerings. Nevertheless, during the transfer of goods, the Lakotas attacked. Afterward, others joined this group to dog the road party for days. After reaching Fort Connor on August 23, Sawyers continued west, but Connor kept Williford there. With a smaller party, Sawyers improved parts of his road the following year, but it never caught on as a route to Montana's mining districts.[48]

Another road to Montana that emigrants called the Bozeman Trail became the focus of Sioux wrath and inspired a new war in which a few Upper Missouri Sioux warriors would participate, but that primarily would pit Platte River Sioux and their Cheyenne and Arapaho allies against regular army soldiers. The Sioux war that had spread to the Upper Missouri from Minnesota and that was influenced by the one that Harney had declared against the Sioux after the fight at Blue Water was essentially over.

---

[48]Armstrong, *History and Resources*, 40–41; Holley, *Once Their Home*, 67–69; Johnson, *Bloody Bozeman*, 169–70; Andrist, *Long Death*, 89; Halaas and Masich, *Halfbreed*, 149–53, 164–69, 180–85, 187–89; Sawyers' 15–26 Aug. 1865 diary entries, in Hampton, "Powder River," 255–58, 256n27; and Dee Brown, *Galvanized Yankees*, 132–33.

(*left*) Little Crow, Taoyateduta. *Courtesy State Historical Society of North Dakota.*

(*below*) Henry Hastings Sibley. *Courtesy State Historical Society of North Dakota, 0036-0050.*

General Sibley's Indian Expedition pursuing the Sioux.
Courtesy State Historical Society of North Dakota, Harper's Weekly.

(*above*) The execution of Sioux Indians at Mankato, Minnesota, 1862.
Courtesy State Historical Society of North Dakota.

(*below*) Fort Rice garrison during the 1860s.
Courtesy State Historical Society of North Dakota, C-1628.

(*left*) Alfred Sully.
Courtesy State Historical Society of North Dakota, A-4447.

(*below*) Two Bear, Yanktonai Nakota. *Courtesy State Historical Society of North Dakota, 0004-024.*

(*left*) Mato-cu-wi-hu's son
Bear Rib. *Courtesy
State Historical Society of
North Dakota, B-298.*

(*below*) One of Sully's 1864
camps. *Courtesy
State Historical Society of
North Dakota, 0004-009.*

(*left*) James Liberty Fisk. *Courtesy Minnesota Historical Society.*

(*below*) Officers' Row at Fort Sully II in 1867. *Courtesy of the State Archives of the South Dakota State Historical Society.*

(*above*) Charles A. R. Dimon (*fourth from left*) with local Sioux chiefs at Fort Rice, ca. 1864–65. This image includes unidentified people who are nevertheless recognizable by comparing faces with other known portraits. For example, the short man second from right may be Two Bear; the man on the far right may be post interpreter Frank La Framboise. © *Corbis.*

(*left*) John Pattee. *Courtesy of the State Historical Society of Iowa, Des Moines.*

PART III
Resolutions with Reservations
1865–1868

Chapter 16

Like a Snow Bank in Summer Sun

AFTER CONNOR'S EXPEDITION TOOK THE FIELD, VANDALISM TO telegraph lines and pillaging of mail deliveries along the Platte River emigrant route in retaliation for Sand Creek abated as Indians moved north to the game-rich Powder River country. Meanwhile, Congress had joined the Cheyennes and their Lakota and Arapaho allies in their outrage over Sand Creek and had launched a major investigation into Indian affairs.

In addition to Connor's and Sully's 1865 campaigns, Pope had ordered Brigadier General John B. Sanborn, commanding the District of Upper Arkansas, to send three columns against Indians south of the Platte River. Sanborn, a Minnesota lawyer before the Civil War, started July 25, but by August 8, Pope, at Secretary James Harlan's behest, ordered him instead to represent the army on one of the congressional delegations charged with investigating "the condition of the Indian tribes and their treatment by the civil and military authorities of the United States."[1]

The commissioners sent questionnaires to Indian agents, army officers, missionaries, and others. Twenty-seven military men, thirteen Indian agents or superintendents, a teacher, a missionary, and a physician answered the questionnaires.[2] Sully seemed eager to express his opinions.

The first question required the respondent's credentials. Sully had been "constantly in the Indian Country" since entering the army in 1841. Asked for a population prediction, he answered that tribes "in close contact with the Whites and civilization are fast decreasing" because of lifestyle changes and their adoption of "all the vices and few of the virtues of the whites." Indian Affairs system reform, Sully thought, could remedy the "decay" in Indian population that another question assumed. With

---

[1]Inventory of Sanborn's papers at MNHS Archives.

[2]Dodge's report, OR, vol. 48, pt. 1, p. 335–66; Sanborn to Dodge, 25 July 1865, 1122, Sanborn to Pope, 8 Aug. 1865, 1172, Dodge to Pope, 24 Aug. 1865, 1208, and 15 Sept. 1865, 1229, all in OR, vol. 48, pt. 2; Doolittle report, 424–92; Chaput, "Generals, Indian Agents, Politicians," 264, 269–82; and Utley, *Indian Frontier*," 96–97, 102–103, 105–106.

reform, "Indians who are now a curse and a nuisance to the country can be made a peaceful part of our community if not a beneficial part."[3]

Asked to assess Indians' health, Sully replied that venereal diseases and alcoholism were the most common maladies among Indians near white settlements. Smallpox was often fatal. A question about intoxication prompted him to argue that, although it was prevalent among Indians near settlements and among the elderly, he would not conclude that Indians in general were addicted to intoxicating drink. He knew non-treaty bands to shun spirits altogether. However, "the Indian, like the White man, if he lives where whiskey is plenty, will acquire a taste for it, and when he does will become as debased as the lowest white drunkard." He thought current liquor laws, if enforced, were adequate.

As to morality among Indians, Sully saw a "wide and remarkable difference in different tribes." Women in the "wild bands of Sioux . . . set an example of virtue worthy of being copied by any white civilized nation." He blamed "contact with depraved specimens" of the white race, as well as a yen for luxuries, for Indian women taking up prostitution. "When they do, they become very much depraved and disease naturally follows."

Sully thought concentrating Indians from all over the country into one area would only transfer trouble from one place to another. However, he did not completely disapprove of reservations. He thought Indians should own land in severalty, but he would not "confer the power of alienation of real estate upon Indians for this generation." Instead, give the privilege to their "civilized and educated" children. Answering another question about Indian land ownership, Sully advised they own their land but in separate places in such a way as to destroy each tribe's conception of, and pride in, its nationhood. Eventually, Indians would "consider themselves citizens of the United States and be proud of that."

How suited to agriculture were Indians? "Among these nomadic tribes who live in a country abounding with game, with wild fruits and roots . . . it is hard to bring them down to cultivate the soil. Their instinct teaches them to wander out on the prairie to hunt." Although he acknowledged that the tribes near Fort Berthold successfully raised crops, he considered Indian country generally unsuitable for agriculture. Sully would "inculcate a taste to raise stock" among Indian children like Jesuits did in their California missions.

Because money Congress appropriated for education seldom was used for it, Sully recommended boys learn trades and girls learn domestic skills.

---

[3]Sully's questionnaire answers from Sully, *No Tears*, chap. 11, 200–209.

"Above all teach them the habits of cleanliness." Do these things, "and you do all required to reclaim the savage, and make him a useful human being."

Another question asked how Indians should be subsisted. Sully, calling money annuities the "principal source of all our trouble at Indian Agencies," wanted them *entirely* discontinued."[4] Instead, he advised issuing clothing and supplies on an as-needed basis; the present system of ordering and distribution was "very bad." Without naming specific tribes, he lamented the long wait for annuities Indians experienced. He did not think significant Indian money was "squandered for intoxicating drink for the simple reason that the trader . . . pockets most of the money." He also castigated agents, giving a no-names-mentioned example of one persuading Indians to go hunting and then distributing the goods only to those left behind.

His opinion about who should administer Indian affairs was unequivocal: the War Department. "It is to the troops the friendly Indian looks for protection against hostile bands, and from the troops the Agent or Trader looks for protection when his Indians, exasperated at repeated impositions, threaten to take his life." At present, Sully wrote, "it is a common saying among the Indians that when they are in want of more annuities, all they have to do is kill a few white men and steal a few horses."

What should be done with mixed-blood people? They were "a very bad mixture," because in general, "they retain too many of the bad qualities of the Indians and too few of the good qualities of the Whites." The War Department should set apart reservations for them, perhaps by treaty. On the subject of what should be done with Indian orphans, he was succinct: "I approve very much of the placing of orphan children in the families of Christians for education and civilization."

Sully's idea for improving conditions for Indians was specific: He would locate agencies, each with a missionary school, at military posts with commanding officers as supervisors. Ideally, three senior officers would examine shipments of goods and their invoices and then report, under oath, to the commanding officer, who would distribute goods in the presence of other officers. Sully surmised fewer men would seek work as Indian agents when they had no chance of "making a fortune on a salary of $1500 a year."

He advocated recruiting Indians for a frontier military force. As examples of "what good can be done in the way of improving the Indian race and making them useful," he would have them work as builders, farmers, mill workers, cattle herders, and similar occupations as at the New Mexico

---

[4]Sully's underlining.

and California missions. Although he was not Catholic, he noticed that the mystery and solemnity of the service "strikes the ignorant Indian with awe, or as they term it 'Big Medicine.'" He would "capture the women and children. Make the women work at the mission, and the children, by force." He acknowledged how "unchristianlike" this might seem, "but with the savages a woman is treated as bad as any negro slave formerly was in our country, and it would be a mercy to her to be under the control of a Christian Mission." An Indian war might result from this policy, but when it ended, Sully would allow husbands and fathers to visit their women and children. Then, after being "in charge of the mission as prisoners," the women could "rejoin their husbands, or the husbands . . . [could] come and live at the missions." After a few years of army protection, Sully envisioned "flourishing settlements, strong enough to protect themselves, and as soon as they became sufficiently strong and civilized," he would allow them "all the benefits of the laws of the country, like any white man."

After advocating slavery in answer to one question, he nevertheless conceded in answering another that Indians "certainly have an equal right to the land we occupy, and as soon as they are fitted for it they have the right to be citizens of the United States." Instead of treating them as foreign nations, Sully suggested not moving Indians away from white settlements but purchasing for them tracts in densely populated areas, where, within a few years, they would either adopt "civilized life, or . . . become extinct." He gave the Minnesota Sioux as an example. "It would have been far better to say to them: We must have your land. Each family will select his locality or farm. Settlers would then be allowed to settle around each separate band." In return for land taken, the Government would help them with agriculture and establish schools for Indian children. They would be "protected in law in all their rights, the same as the white man."

Sully saw only two options regarding reservations already established. "Drive [the Indians] off further, starve them and drive them to desperation, till we have to adopt some other mode of ridding ourselves of an encumbrance [or] . . . reclaim them from their savage life, and by kindness and education make them peaceable." He warned, "But don't send Indian Agents and traders among them to rob them of what the Government appropriates for their improvement."[5]

Although some of Sully's responses were shocking, contradictory, and often at odds with other respondents' opinions, he was certainly the most knowledgeable about Upper Missouri Sioux, who, by now, realized their

---

[5]Sully, *No Tears*, 200–209. Cf. Chaput, "Generals, Indian Agents, Politicians."

age-old Lakota, Nakota, and Dakota social mores and customs did not work in a whites-dominated world. During the decade since General Harney invaded the Upper Missouri, Sioux society endured tremendous upheaval. At this crossroads, some Sioux would take the warrior's way; others—some under the duress of circumstances, others out of conviction—were eager to tell their troubles to Doolittle's commissioners and acquiesce to trying to live like whites.

AFTER DOOLITTLE'S JOINT CONGRESSIONAL COMMISSION DIGESTED the questionnaires, three delegations set out to visit Indians and examine conditions firsthand. Harney, now a retired brevet major general, General Sanborn, and Brevet Major General E. M. McCook would represent the military with the group assigned to Indians of the southwest. Doolittle so valued Harney's experience that he recommended secretary of war Stanton study Harney's 1856 Fort Pierre Sioux peace talks.

Chairman Doolittle personally visited the Sand Creek site and spoke to people in Denver in July, but full delegations did not travel to their destinations until Pope's military campaigns were completed.[6] Pope instructed Sully specifically to make sure the Upper Missouri Doolittle delegation heard about the Winnebago removal and "everything connected with the Crow Creek Agency." Sully acknowledged that the Winnebago transfer to Dakota was "one among the hundred swindles the poor red devils have been subjected to." But he would only reluctantly cooperate with the commissioners. When, before the 1865 campaign, Governor Edmunds had asked to join Sully in his talks with peace-minded Sioux waiting at the various posts, Sully told Pope he would "try to eucher [Edmunds], for I don't want him to get the credit of our work."[7]

The acknowledged disaster of Connor's expedition, Sully's ineffectual ramble through Dakota, and post–Civil War reorganization of the nation's military forces made the commissioners' work urgent. Their anticipated arrival and the chaos it created dominated the final issue of the Fort Rice

[6]Chaput, "Generals, Indian Agents, Politicians," 274; "Report of Commission to Treat with Sioux of the Upper Missouri," 28 Oct. 1865, CIA annual report, 537; Adams, Harney, 240; Utley, Frontiersmen, 309, 312–15, 337; Doolittle to Sec. of War, 24 July 1865, 1118, and Pope to McCook, 10 May 1865, 385–86, both in OR, vol. 48, pt. 2; McCook to Levering, 27 April 1865, OR, vol. 48, pt. 1, p. 223; and Doolittle report.
[7]Sully to Curtis and Pope to Sully, 6 June 1865, 800, and Sully to Pope, 14 June 1865, 887–88, all in OR, vol. 48, pt. 2; and Gue, History of Iowa, vol. 4, Iowa Biography, 147.

Frontier Scout. On September 29 a Lakota delegation arrived openly boast-
ing of killing ten soldiers during one fight with Cole's and Walker's men.
However, editor Adams wrote how delighted everyone was to welcome
Two Bear's Yanktonais and Bear Rib's Hunkpapas, who had "proved their
good faith and loyalty during the Winter and Spring." Two Bear, he wrote,
was "as full of wit as ever."[8] Red Horse, an Oglala orator traveling from
camp to camp advocating peace, was the officers' breakfast guest. When
three Cutheads arrived, Adams remarked, "Verily, it savoreth much of a
peace with the Aborigines." He waxed poetic when Fire Heart's Sihasapas
and some Sans Arcs appeared on the hills behind the fort. "Against the
amber of the sky like some caravan of Arabia, crossing the desert," they
waited as Charles Galpin went to greet them. Then, wearing "gay robes"
and on fancy saddles, they "came riding in chanting a wild melody, fifty
abreast, like well-disciplined cavalry." Adams found them dashing despite
how "wild and uncultivated" he judged them to be.

More Sihasapas, Oglalas, and Hunkpapas, including Bear Rib's uncle
Running Antelope and The-Man-That-Has-His-Head-Shaved—the
latter who, with Sitting Bull, had led the July attack on Fort Rice—set
up their tipis on bottomlands near the fort's sawmill. Adams enthused
that the commissioners would find at Fort Rice "the largest collection
of Indians ever congregated at one time in Dakota."

Amidst this hubbub, Black Tomahawk came with the mail. Wagons
bearing potatoes, a scurvy antidote, followed soon after, and on October 9,
their former commander, now Brevet Brigadier General Charles Dimon,
surprised the First USV. After the companies at Forts Berthold and Union
returned to Fort Rice at the end of August, he would accompany the First
to Fort Leavenworth, where they would muster out. The Fourth USV would
remain on the Upper Missouri a little longer. No soldiers garrisoned Fort
Union, but Captain Bassett and Company C remained at Fort Berthold.
Company A under Captain S. G. Sewell would occupy Crow Creek after
Thornton's three companies moved to Fort Randall. Companies E and
F were to serve under Lieutenant Colonel Pattee at Fort Sully until the
Fourth USV and Seventh Iowa mustered out in June 1866.[9]

---

[8]Quotes in this paragraph and the following one are from "Local Items," (*Fort Rice*) *Frontier
Scout*, 29–30 Sept. 1865. Iron Horn (not Horse, as the *Scout* has it) and Grindstone signed an 1868
treaty as Hunkpapas. The Miniconjou chief Iron Horn was their contemporary.

[9]Ibid., 2–9 Oct. 1865; Pattee, "Reminiscences," 347; Tucker-Butts, *Galvanized Yankees: Face
of Loyalty*, 202, 209, 214–16, 222; Dee Brown, *Galvanized Yankees*, 109, 114–15; and "Local Items:
Arrival of the Expedition," *The* (*Fort Sully*) *Independent*, 16 Sept. 1855 [*sic* 1865]. Larned's diary,
10 Oct.–6 Nov. 1865 entries, 270–71, chronicle Fort Rice events after the *Scout*'s publishers left.

THE UPPER MISSOURI DOOLITTLE DELEGATION COMPRISED Major General Curtis, Brigadier General Sibley, Governor Edmunds, former Indian Agent Henry Reed of Iowa, Wisconsin legislator Orrin Guernsey, and Omaha newspaperman and Indian Bureau northern superintendent Edward B. Taylor. At the Yankton reservation, Struck-by-the-Ree gave them an earful: The Yanktons' first two agents, Redfield and Burleigh, had "filled [his] belly with lies." The agent "puts his foot on me as though I were a skunk." The chief wanted his agents to go with him to Washington and swear on a Bible how much tribal money and goods had "been stolen and who stole it." Burleigh, in particular, drew his wrath for transgressions against his starving people. Struck-by-the-Ree pointed to the "black spots you see on the hills before you"; they were graves of his people. When Yanktons receive anything from whites, "it is given as you would throw it to a hog," he said. The president "promised that we should be raised up, but his young men put their feet on us and keep us down; that is the way the white man treats us."[10]

Medicine Cow supplemented Struck-by-the-Ree's indictments. "I think all the work Doctor Burleigh had done was done for himself. . . . When he came there he only had a trunk, but now he is high up-rich." When the 1858 treaty promised the Yanktons money, a school, and a blacksmith shop, his young men wanted such opportunities to learn. He spoke of the Yankton scouts: "When Burleigh told us to be soldiers we became soldiers . . . but we were not paid for being soldiers." They had a new agent, P. H. Conger, but "he is like a man in the middle of the prairie." Because Burleigh "cleaned the agency of everything," Conger had no cattle, wagons, or plows. "Everything has melted away like a snow bank in the summer's sun."[11]

In their report, the commissioners praised the Yanktons for their fidelity and lamented that, instead of being prosperous after a considerable infusion of money, "no improvements worthy of the name" were apparent. Furthermore, the commissioners had to issue provisions to keep the band from starving. Their condition was "disgraceful to the government and

---

[10]"Report of Commission to Treat with Sioux of the Upper Missouri," 28 Oct. 1865, CIA annual report, 537; Morton & Watkins, *History of Nebraska*, 438; Hosmer, "A Trip," in Hakola, *Frontier Omnibus*, 305; Utley, *Lance*, 70; "Local Items," (*Fort Rice*) *Frontier Scout*, 12 Oct. 1865; Struck by the Ree's speech in Doolittle report and in Calloway, *Our Hearts*, 96–98; and Doolittle report, 372, 286.

[11]Calloway, *Our Hearts*, 99–100; Doolittle report, 372, 286; *General Sully's Company of Yankton Scouts* 3–4; Edmunds to Dole, 20 Sept. 1864, CIA annual report, no. 115; and Burleigh to Dole, 21 Oct. 1864, CIA annual report, no. 129, 261, 284–85.

ruinous to the material interests of this well-disposed band." Because
of this misadministration, they must hunt for subsistence and, without
reassurance and encouragement would give in to despair and perhaps
initiate another "formidable Indian war."[12]

At Fort Sully, the commissioners first addressed the entire congregation, then held separate councils with each band, with Zephyr Rencontre and Charles Degre interpreting. After Lone Horn made a cautious
speech for the Miniconjous on October 8, Lame Deer argued forcefully
for removing military posts in Sioux country. He also asked for powder,
lead, and better prices from traders and wondered why it was necessary to
sign a paper. Why was just discussing these issues together not enough?

Their country was part of the United States and could not be left for
just Indians, Edmunds replied. Citizens must be able to travel unmolested
through it. Soldiers would stay and, although Indians could expect help
with food, clothing, schools, and tools, they would not receive ammunition. The most difficult issue concerned roads through Sioux country.
Lame Deer spoke passionately about how soldiers drove away game and
asked why whites did not take other routes to the mines. Finally, the
Miniconjous signed, spurning a reservation, but recognizing the "exclusive jurisdiction of the United States" and agreeing to cease all hostilities. They would prevent other bands from molesting whites' persons or
property and would withdraw from all routes, extant and future, and
would allow no harm to travelers on them.

For its part, the government would provide $30 per lodge for twenty years.
Once twenty lodges lived on a reservation, they would receive an additional
$25 each lodge for five years for buying tools and agricultural supplies.
When a hundred lodges were established, the government would hire a
farmer and blacksmith to teach their skills to Indians. The Lower Brulés
agreed to the same things and in addition agreed to live on a ten-mile by
twenty-mile reservation on the west side of the Missouri river, beginning
at the mouth of White River and including the ruins of Fort Lookout.[13]

J. Allen Hosmer, who sat in on the Two Kettle talks, recorded part of
Eagle Woman's brother Two Lance's two-and-a-half-hour-long speech
in his journal. Two Lance rejected planting in favor of continuing to
hunt. He wanted no additional forts or roads in Indian country. Couldn't
whites see, he asked, that if buffalo leave, the "red man goes too[?]" The

---

[12]"Report of Commission to Treat with Sioux of the Upper Missouri," Commissioners to
Harlan, 28 Oct. 1865, CIA annual report, 537–42.

[13]Ibid.; and Kappler, *Indian Affairs*, vol. 2, *Treaties*, 883–84 (Miniconjous), 885–87 (Lower Brulés).

Sioux would be peaceful toward whites only if they left them alone. According to Hosmer, Two Lance "came forward and touched the pen six times" for six complaints he had against the government. The Two Kettle akicita Whirling Heart, whom Hosmer thought seemed "vexed" by Two Lance's talk, asked "who's afraid to touch the pen[?] I'll touch it with my hands and feet" and did so.[14]

Newspaper dispatches from Fort Sully mentioned with what great trepidation Indians signed these papers. In addition, a careful reading of the transcripts indicate that, rather than signing because they agreed with the requirements of the treaty, some of the spokesmen, as Two Lance seems to have done, may have signed primarily as testament to their own words.

Their version of the 1865 treaty promised the Two Kettle band formal restitution for Puffy Eyes, the chief murdered in 1863 with the six others near Fort Randall. The government would pay $500 to Puffy Eyes' widow and surviving seventeen children and the same to the band "in common, as indemnity for killing said chief."[15]

By October 20, Sihasapas and Sans Arcs had also signed, neither band agreeing to reservation life.[16] General Curtis meantime sent word to Pattee to bring the delegation of Sioux waiting for commissioners at Rice to Fort Sully. Persuading them would take some doing. Pattee remarked, "When an Indian makes a bargain with a white man he expects the white man to keep his word. It is next to an impossibility to make a new bargain." Besides, they objected to riding their horses the 180 miles to Fort Sully, rendering them useless for the winter buffalo hunt. If they walked, Pattee promised to take plenty of provisions and a few horses for hunting any buffalo they encountered. He pointed out that consuming food during the trip would free room in the wagons for the footsore and weary. Lastly, he promised them "a good time all the way down and back." After three days in council, the Sioux relented, and with Charles Galpin to interpret and a three-soldier escort, Pattee's delegation left Rice on October 18. The next day, a partial solar eclipse occurred that was probably what Two Bear's daughter Pretty Shawl, born about 1860, recalled many years later: "Our people thought the sun was dying and were very badly frightened."[17]

---

[14]Hosmer, "A Trip," in Hakola, *Frontier Omnibus*, 289–90, 305–306; see Commissioners to Harlan, 23 Oct. 1865, 536, and "Report," 28 Oct. 1865, 537–42, both in CIA annual report, no. 15.

[15]Kappler, *Indian Affairs*, vol. 2, *Treaties*, p. 897.

[16]Hosmer, "A Trip," in Hakola, *Frontier Omnibus*, 306–307; and Kappler, *Indian Affairs*, vol. 2, *Treaties*, 896–97 (Two Kettle), 898–99 (Sihasapas), 899–901 (Sans Arc). James Gordon's *Chicago Tribune* and *St. Paul Press* dispatches quoted in Doane Robinson, "Ending the Outbreak," 447–55.

[17]Albers and Tweton, *The Way It Was*, book 5, *Native People*, 82.

The Two Kettle chief Four Bears (Eagle Woman's nephew) and his headmen joined Pattee's party at Hidden Wood Creek. More Indians joined at Swan Lake Creek. On October 22, a fierce snowstorm delayed them at the Little Cheyenne River. With only one eight-foot-square tent among them, some Indians rigged up brush shelters. The next night nearby Indians invited the travelers into their lodges. After two days, the storm abated enough for travel, although snow drifted forty inches deep in places. When they met some Fourth usv mail carriers heading for Fort Rice with only one blanket apiece, Pattee ordered the tearfully grateful soldiers back to Fort Sully with his party. That night another Indian camp provided hospitality and shelter. Finally, on October 26, Pattee delivered to the commissioners seventeen chiefs and forty headmen representing, he thought, about 12,000 people.[18]

Pattee called the talks at Fort Sully a "war of diplomacy" and a "battle of the giants." His delegation, with Bear Rib, Running Antelope, Fire Heart, Crow Feather, Bone Necklace, and White Swan among the seasoned speakers, had plenty to say. The Sihasapa chief Fire Heart, his knee stiff from a bullet wound acquired while fighting Sully in the badlands, was particularly unhappy. The 1851 Laramie Treaty designated his band's country as bounded on the north by the Heart River and on the south by the Cannonball and he "did not want any white men in it." Verbal sparring concluded when "Crow Feather seized the pen in both hands and after rolling it between them for nearly a minute" signed the treaty. After the others, none opting for reservations, signed on October 28 and 29, Pattee's delegation began the long trip back to Fort Rice.[19] There, Dr. John H. Vivian, surgeon for the newly arrived Fiftieth, wrote his hometown newspaper on November 1 that at a small-scale confab held at Fort Rice, the Indians agreed to meet commissioners again next spring. Before leaving for winter quarters, they asked for food, ammunition, and powder, but they received only food.

In an October 24 telegram, General Curtis told Pope the attendees "all complain of our encroachments on their hunting grounds and our lines of emigration through their buffalo grounds, but they want peace." However, since chiefs found it difficult to control their young war-minded men, troops must remain on watch. Pope forwarded Curtis's

---

[18] Pattee, "Reminiscences," 345–47, 348–49; and Hosmer, "A Trip," in Hakola, *Frontier Omnibus,* 308–309.

[19] Pattee, "Reminiscences," 348–49; and Kappler, *Indian Affairs,* vol. 2, *Treaties,* 897, 901–903, 903–904, 905–906, 906–908. Some Yanktonai treaty signers were clearly Hunkpapas, and some Hunkpapas signed as Yanktonais. Cf. band affiliations with sub-chiefs listed in "Harney treaty," 24–26, and with signatories of later treaties in Kappler.

communication to General Grant.[20] In their summary communication from Fort Sully, the commissioners relayed the Indians' accusations and told how they "appeared to regard a restoration of kind relations with the United States in the light of interest or profit to themselves, and not inspired by more humane or generous sentiments." Distinctly and palpably, the chiefs manifested "antagonism of the two races in views, habits, and modes of life." Humanity and sound policy, the commissioners wrote, demanded that the evils they complained of be corrected.[21]

After the others left, General Sibley, who previously had lobbied to have the former Minnesota Indians represented to the commission, traveled to the Crow Creek Reservation, where he learned the Sissetons and Wahpetons wanted more than the government was willing to grant—restoration of their full treaty rights. The Mdewakanton chief Passing Hail, a farmer when in Minnesota who had opposed the 1862 war, summarized his people's situation: "At Redwood they took all the young and smart men and put them in prison, and they took all the chiefs and women and children and put them in Fort Snelling. They done with us as they would grain, shaking it to get out the best and then . . . took everything from us and brought us over here with nothing."[22]

Passing Hail told of inadequate food and the horrible communal soup, adding that "white folks do not eat animals that die themselves; but the animals that died here were piled up with the beef here and were fed out to us." When starving women and children tried to obtain scraps during butchering, the soldiers whipped and imprisoned them. When the agent wanted work done, he paid for it with rotting food. Because their annuity goods arrived while the men were hunting, Passing Hail suspected the agent timed it that way. As it was, he tossed "a dress for each woman and a blanket for each family" out an upper story window. "We heard afterwards . . . the agent traded some of our goods away, and we suppose he traded them for robes and furs." Otherwise "there would have been plenty to go round, and the women would not have been crying with cold." According to the president's laws, Passing Hail said, "we have changed ourselves to

[20]Vivian, letter to the editor, *Mineral Point (Wis.) Weekly Tribune*, 13 Dec. 1865; Vivian sketch in Butterfield, *History of Iowa County Wisconsin*, 878; and Pope to Grant, 24 Oct. 1865, OR, vol. 48, pt. 2, p. 1243.

[21]"Report," Commissioners to Harlan, 28 Oct. 1865, CIA annual report, 537–42. The Upper Yanktonais with Pattee signed the treaty on 28 Oct. 1865. Like the other 1865 Fort Sully treaties, it was ratified 5 March 1866 and proclaimed 17 March 1866. Kappler, *Indian Affairs*, vol. 2, *Treaties*, 905–906.

[22]Gilman, *Henry Hastings Sibley*, 208; and Hosmer, "A Trip," in Hakola, *Frontier Omnibus*, 310. Passing Hail speech in Calloway, *Our Hearts*, 100–101. See Gary Anderson, *Kinsmen*, 234, 255; and Gary Anderson, *Little Crow*, 119, 121, 155.

white men, put on white man's clothes and adopted the white man's ways, and we supposed we would have a piece of ground somewhere where we could live; but no one can live here and live like a white man."

On his own reservation earlier, Struck-by-the-Ree had defended the Dakotas to the commissioners. "They did wrong," he said, but with good reason. "For long winters and summers they had been cheated and robbed by the agents and traders. They complained, but the Great Father would not make it right. Their hearts became bad; they thirsted for blood; they got plenty. We have the same cause to kill as our friends in Minnesota. But this [indicating his crucifix] keeps my heart right. I will not let my young men fight. The Yanktons have never killed a white man."[23]

The commission report called the reservation Santees helpless creatures who "have been kept in a condition of semi-starvation" since arriving at Crow Creek. "Several hundred have died from actual want, or from disease superinduced by it." Of the thousand who remained, only ten percent were men, mostly aged or infirm. The commissioners urged prompt and effective relief for "these wretched dependents" of the government's mercy. They praised Sioux who rescued captives and worked as scouts but who received inadequate compensation for such service. Correcting this injustice might induce others "to pursue a like course." After studying the report, the congressional committee concluded that outrageous behavior by whites had caused most Indian wars.[24]

Although they spoke mainly with chiefs who were already peaceable, the Upper Missouri Doolittle commissioners considered their 1865 work successful; in March 1866, Congress ratified nine Sioux treaties. However, their most valuable work was uncovering injustices Indians suffered. Once published, their findings swung the pendulum of popular opinion in the Indians' direction. All the same, conditions did not improve for Upper Missouri Sioux. While his regiment settled in at Fort Rice, Dr. Vivian wrote his hometown newspaper: "Into this country, so wild and savage, we are sent . . . to feed redskins with mouldy flour and maggoty bacon, and to build store houses in which to put other and newer stores, to keep till they too get mouldy and rotten, or until the rats, who are in myriads, eat them up. Truly this like all Indian wars is a great humbug, except to the contractors and A.Q.M's [assistant quartermasters]."[25]

---

[23]Doolittle report, 384, 406–407; and Calloway, *Our Hearts*, 97, 100–101

[24]"Report," Commissioners to Harlan, 28 Oct. 1865, CIA annual report, 537–42; and Lamar, *Dakota Territory*, 21.

[25]Kappler, *Indian Affairs*, vol. 2, *Treaties*, 887–91, 892–95; and Vivian, letter to the editor, *Mineral Point (Wis.) Weekly Tribune*, 13 Dec. 1865.

Chapter 17

Regulars Replace Volunteers

WILLIAM LARNED EXPRESSED LITTLE SYMPATHY IN HIS JANUARY 27, 1866, diary entry for the 3,500 "quite poor and nearly starving" Indians living within six miles of Fort Rice. They came "to bury the hatched" in order to allay starvation, but in his opinion, their poverty was due to their "Supreme Shiftlessness," scarce buffalo, and what he considered their lack of skill in hunting other game. He accused these Hunkpapas, Miniconjous, Sans Arcs, and Sihasapas of stealing "everything they can lay their hands on."

The Larneds and Eagle Woman Galpin and her family went one day to visit friends in Two Bear's band. At Two Bear's tipi, they found warriors with their faces painted black, ready to retaliate for the Lakotas stealing "on their credit." After their social call, the Yanktonai war party escorted the Larneds and Galpins to a hill where they could watch the attack. The 900 or so Lakotas "offered no resistence & the casualties were ponies & dogs shot & Tipis cut to pieces," Larned wrote. Post commander Colonel Clark and Dr. Vivian were visiting the Sihasapa chief Fire Heart when a long knife slit open the tipi from above Clark's head to the ground, "passing near his back." Clark ordered the vandalism stopped, but when Frank La Framboise told him the cause, he let the Yanktonais "administer their laws in their own way." His hands-off policy possibly encouraged the next day's break-in at the sutler's store, where flour and peltries disappeared.[1]

Not everyone suffered. Riding past a Sihasapa camp south of the fort late in January 1866, Larned noticed "tipis large and new—ponies fat & in good numbers for the number of lodges." Bountiful 1865 harvests rewarded white settlers; in addition, since Sully left, peace had reigned in the territory except for an October 10, 1865, incident where Indians attacked people putting up hay in southeastern Dakota and killed a man.[2]

---

[1]Larned diary, 28–29, 31 Jan. 1866, 273–74; Sidney A. Russell, diary, 1 Dec. 1865 and 28 Jan. 1866, MSS 20328, Fort Rice ND Collection, 1864–1921, SHSND Archives (hereafter cited as Russell diary); and Gray, "Story of Mrs. Picotte-Galpin," pt. 1, 15.

[2]Larned diary, 27–29, 31 Jan. 1866, 273–74; Russell diary, 1 Dec. 1865 and 28 Jan. 1866; (continued)

In February 1866, Lieutenant Colonel Pattee returned from leave to his new command at Fort Sully. After an inspection tour, he reported destitution at several Indian camps near Crow Creek as well as among the 700 or 800 Indians at Fort Sully. Army regulations allowed commanding officers in Indian country to issue small quantities of provisions but not over a long period. Pattee called chiefs to Fort Sully for a talk and issued them 500 pounds of hard bread and some other provisions, then continued to help them over the winter. He wrote Edmunds in February that he was "bored to death" by the Indians, especially the "cursed Brulés," whom he called "the meanest Indians in the country." Although he saw hostility in the Brulés' "every look and jesture," he continued to distribute damaged and condemned provisions to his Indian neighbors until buffalo came within forty miles of the post in March.[3]

By then, Pattee counted 1,900 Indians, including 300 Oglala widows and orphans, living within ten miles of Fort Sully. "These last," he explained, "came from Laramie during the winter and all claim to be war widows. Very many of the children are half white." They may have been the families passed off to Agent Jarrot after the 1865 rebellion in which Captain Fouts was killed near the Platte River. If they were the same people Jarrot sent on up the Missouri, the presence of many mixed-blood children might support George Bent's assertion that soldiers raped the women. At Fort Sully, their Indian neighbors apparently shunned the Oglala widows and children. In May, Pattee wrote Curtis that "the more fortunate ones of the nation true to their Barberous motives seldom render them any assistance." When Fort Laramie's commander, Major James Van Voast, expelled Indians from that post in July 1866, he reported similar behavior from the Laramie Loafer band toward soldiers' deserted families.[4]

Kingsbury, *History of Dakota Territory*, vol. 1, 417–18; and Levering, "Recollections," part 3, 1 July 1873, vol. 11, no. 1. See Tripp and Worst chapters in Goodspeed, *Province and the States*, vol. 6, 247.

[3] GO 42, Dept. of the Missouri, 2 Nov. 1865, OR, vol. 48, pt. 2 p. 1252; *The (Fort Sully) Independent*, 16 Sept. 1855 [*sic* 1865]; Pattee to Cmnd'g Gen'l, Pattee to Asst. Adj. Gen., Dist. of Upper Mo., Pattee to Hiram, and Pattee to Governor, all dated 5 Feb. 1866, Andrews to Litchfield, 22 July 1866, Pattee to Asst. Adj. Gen. and Pattee to F.A.Y.[?], 2 March 1866, and Pattee to Clinton, 25 May 1866, all in FS Selected LS, RG 393, NA; Stone to Edmunds, 5 Feb. 1866, and Pattee to Edmunds, 18 Feb. 1866, both in CIA annual report, 165–66; Kappler, *Indian Affairs*, vol. 2, *Treaties*, 14 Oct. 1865, 885–87; and Pattee, "Reminiscences," 349.

[4] Pattee to F.A.Y.[?], 2 March 1866, and Pattee to Asst. Adj. Gen., Dist. of Upper Mo., 31 May 1866, both in FS Selected LS, RG 393, NA; Marshall, *Lakota Way*, 106, 173, 180–95; Hyde, *Spotted Tail's Folk*, 120–21, 121n3; Hyde, *Life of George Bent*, 209; McChristian, *Fort Laramie*, 272; and McChristian, "Fort Laramie and the U.S. Army," 389–90. Pattee's tally: Brulés, 420 persons; Lower Yanktonais, 240; Two Kettles, 231; Miniconjous, 126; Sihasapas, 147; Sans Arcs, 140; Hunkpapas, 84; Upper Yanktonais, 84; Oglala, 84; Santee, 40; Oglala widows and children, 300.

Upriver, by March, twenty-seven Fort Rice soldiers had scurvy. The garrison dug for roots to ward off this debilitating vitamin deficiency disease, but after only nine months at the post, forty-three Fiftieth Wisconsin volunteers died—all but one of disease. Relief had to wait until ice broke up on the Missouri. The first steamboat to dock at Fort Rice on April 19 brought a woman downstream who apparently had lived with Indians since the Minnesota war. "A good looking girl," Corporal Sidney Russell wrote in his diary, but he did not name her. By the end of May, the first upriver-bound boat brought a vanguard of Thirteenth Infantry Regiment regulars to relieve the volunteers.

Fort Rice would be headquarters for the regiment, comprising two battalions. Thirteenth Infantry companies would construct Fort Buford at the Yellowstone–Missouri confluence; Camp Cooke near Fort Benton, Montana; and Fort Stevenson near Fort Berthold. They would also garrison Forts Randall, Thompson, and Sully as well as small posts at Firesteel Creek and Sioux Falls.[5]

Early during post–Civil War military reshuffling, a worried Governor Edmunds petitioned Major General William T. Sherman, head of the Division of the Mississippi at St. Louis, for military protection. In charge of a vast area including states north of the Ohio River (although the Ohio Department was soon dropped) and territories west to the Rocky Mountains, Sherman assured Edmunds that emigrants and settlers would have all the protection possible. "No people know better than you of Dakota, that the volunteer army is now substantially out, and that our regular army is too small to do more than guard key points."[6] Meanwhile, Sherman sent inspectors to all U.S. territories between the Mississippi River and the Pacific Ocean to devise plans for peopling them and protecting future settlers.

Colonel Delos B. Sackett, assigned to visit and inspect Montana and the Missouri River military posts along the way, found Fort Randall so crawling with vermin that men preferred sleeping on the parade ground. Spring flooding washed away a storehouse and some corn. Nevertheless, the post commander condemned the few remaining sacks of damaged corn and, along with some "caked and musty" flour and spoiled and maggoty bacon and ham, issued it to the starving Indians near the post.

[5]Russell diary, 6, 11, 18, and 28 March 1866, and 3 April through 3 June 1866; Pattee, "Reminiscences," 345–50; Athearn, *Sherman*, 50, 121; Quiner, *Military History*, 868; Love, *Wisconsin in the War*, 1122; Goe, "Thirteenth Regiment"; and Wherry, "Types and Traditions." See "Log of the Steamer W.J. Lewis," 330, 337.

[6]Athearn, *Sherman*, 10, 34; and Kingsbury, *History of Dakota Territory*, vol. 1, 414.

Sackett approved; this would "save issuing good provisions to them, as they eat the bad with as much if not more relish than they do the good."[7]

After inspecting Fort Sully, Sackett agreed with Lieutenant Colonel Gustav Heinrichs from Department of the Missouri headquarters, who considered the fort to be of "no importance whatever under the present circumstances." Furthermore, Pattee's personal style and his undisciplined soldiers annoyed Sackett, in whose opinion "it would be a great thing for the service, and for the Indians" when regulars replaced all volunteers. Because Sackett arrived at Fort Sully when peace commissioners were due, the Indians took Sackett for one. He complained of being "compelled to shake hands and be hugged by every dirty buck I met." After listening to their complaints about broken government promises, Sackett was convinced that "Indian wars and massacres" would end only when the military—for the "good of the government and the salvation of the red man"—had sole control of Indian affairs.[8] In July, Lieutenant Colonel George L. Andrews abandoned the post and moved his garrison some twenty-five miles up the Missouri to a site on its east bank to begin constructing a new Fort Sully.

Moving on, Sackett found Fort Rice badly located. By this time, Indians awaiting the 1866 commissioners doubted they would arrive and were "bold, defiant, and somewhat troublesome." Sackett agreed with "all persons here who know anything about Indians," who expected Sioux to resume hostilities as soon as the commissioners left.[9]

Sackett considered Fort Berthold, still garrisoned in early June 1866 by Captain Bassett's Fourth USV Company, the best post, but he disagreed with Sully that protecting Rees, Mandans, and Hidatsas from Sioux was a valid reason to keep troops there. "I hardly believe in using troops to protect Indians from Indians; we have as much as we can do to protect white men from the Indians." He considered it good if Indians would "use each other up." Even while acknowledging that Indian women successfully raised corn on the bottomlands, Sackett saw no potential for agriculture in the territory. "The more I see of Dakota the more I am convinced the government should donate every foot of it to the Indian, and the Indians should be well recompensed in addition, if they agree to

---

[7]Sackett, *Report of Delos B. Sackett*, 14 May 1866 (hereafter cited as Sackett report).

[8]Barnes to Heinrichs, 17 May 1865, 486; Heinrichs to Pratt, 10 June 1865, 848; SO 120, Dist. of N. Kan., 14 June 1865, 886, all in OR, vol. 48, pt. 2; Price, "Colonel D. J. Dill," 30, River Falls Area Research Center, University of Wisconsin; Deland's n76 to Frederick Wilson, "Old Fort Pierre and Its Neighbors," 371–72; Sackett report, 28 May 1866; Pattee to Clinton, 25 May 1866, FS Selected LS, RG 393, NA; and Pattee, "Reminiscences," 349.

[9]Pattee, "Reminiscences," 345–50; Athearn, *Sherman*, 50, 121; Sackett report, 9 June 1866.

remain and live within its borders." On June 11, Sackett inspected Fort Union and the confluence area and proclaimed the site Sully chose in 1864 the best location for Fort Buford.[10]

ALTHOUGH THEIR PURPOSE WAS TO TRAVEL HIGHER UP THE Missouri to make treaties with non-Sioux tribes and, along the way, persuade Sioux headmen who had not signed the ratified 1865 treaties to do so, the 1866 Northwest Indian Commissioners did not neglect Indians who already signed. Cold weather, high water, and a steamboat fire that destroyed some annuity goods delayed the vessel carrying farming supplies and implements. Furthermore, the commissioners had to explain that annuities for the new treaties would not arrive until fall. However, they did have the last 1851 Laramie Treaty goods with them.

At Fort Randall, they met Brulés to whom the Yanktons had lent land for planting, notwithstanding that their own reservation was upriver. One chief complained of waiting on the borrowed Yankton land all spring for promised help while his people grew poor and resorted to eating their horses. Now, he feared, it was too late to plant corn. "My fingernails are too short to work the soil with and we have no other implements." When another chief pointed out his people's lack of clothing, Curtis said the commissioners would "do all we can" to have some sent to them. Meanwhile, they left them gunpowder and bread.[11]

At Fort Sully, Curtis was horrified at the Indians' circumstances. Deep snow precluded hunting over the winter, forcing them to eat "hundreds" of their ponies. Otherwise, they lived on dried buffalo meat "and not much of that." They expected a government-sponsored feast upon the commissioners' arrival, but congressional restrictions instituted in March 1864 amended an 1834 law to forbid the army to feed Indians coming to sign a treaty. Unlike Pattee and Sackett, Curtis witnessed no stealing among these hungry Indians. Yes, they would "run like chickens to gather the offal from the slop buckets that are carried from the garrison kitchens," but rather than steal, they would touch nothing until soldiers told them they could scavenge from spillage caused by well-fed rats breaking into sacks of corn meant for livestock that, this year, had plenty of grass

---

[10]Sackett report, 11 June 1866.

[11]Quotes from "Proceedings of a Board Appointed to Negotiate a Treaty" (listed under "Misc. MP" in bibliography), pp. 1, 3 (hereafter cited as "1866 Northwest Indian Commission Proceedings").

to eat. Curtis lamented the strict military policy by which "not a pound can be issued to the craving Indians, whose hunting grounds we occupy." Furthermore, a December 1865 congressional resolution only authorized the president to redirect already appropriated funds for schools and the like to feed and clothe destitute Indians.[12]

After opening addresses, Edmunds, Reed, and Curtis offered the printed copy of the 1865 treaty for the Indians' perusal. Hearing their own words read to them, some chiefs and headmen said they doubted what they said ever reached the president. It was obvious many did not fully understand what they had signed. Two Lance, for example, believed signing the treaty meant soldiers would leave; instead, more came to replace the others.

When Two Bear told them approximately half the 400 lodges assembled were starving, the commissioners immediately sent them pork and hardtack. Other headmen aired familiar complaints of starvation, scarce game, trespassing whites, cheating traders, and dishonest agents. Bone Necklace still wanted to live on land Yanktons had sold in 1858, despite knowing whites populated it now and most game was gone. Curtis told Bone Necklace, "The Great Spirit made these lands for the white man and the red man; and the Great Spirit made the game for both. The Indians kill ten thousand buffalo where the white man kills one. We are sorry to see that they are getting scarce. A great many died last winter from the cold." The president wanted Indians to live well by hunting and farming. "You say this road is yours, but you agreed last year to let the roads be travelled by the whites; and your Great Father sends you goods because you did so." Everyone—white or Indian—lived under the president "and we must have peace together."[13]

Fool Dog reminded the commissioners that some Fool Soldiers who rescued Santee prisoners received only part of the $50 each due them. Curtis promised to try to pay more "as you were very gallant and captured the first prisoners." When the Two Kettle chiefs also brought up Fool Soldier rewards, the commissioners awarded $20 each to fourteen men

---

[12]All quotes from Curtis to Cooley, 30 May 1866, CIA annual report, no. 63, 167. The 1834 trade and intercourse legislation incorporated ideas concerning Indian trade and treatment derived from an 1829 report to the secretary of war by William Clark of the Lewis and Clark expedition and Michigan governor, Lewis Cass. See Cohen, *Handbook of Federal Indian Law*, Act of 15 March 1864, 13 *Stat.* 29, p. 517, and Resolution of 21 Dec. 1865, 14 *Stat.* 347, p. 519; Sec. 16 of the Trade and Intercourse Act of 30 June 1834 deals with rations. See Cohen, *Handbook*, 6–7, 71, 71n42–44, 75, and 4 *Stat.* 729, 492–93; Prucha, *Great Father*, 103–105; and F.A. Walker, "Indian Question," 334–35, 372–74.

[13]"1866 Northwest Indian Commission Proceedings," 19.

for rescuing eight whites from the Santees. The Sihasapa chief The Shield lobbied for pay for men in his band who also brought in a captive woman.[14]

At the mouth of the Cheyenne River, a delegation of Sisseton and Wahpeton Sioux on their way to the Fort Rice talks hailed the commissioners' boat and came aboard. The group, led by former Santee Indian agent Joseph Brown, included Gabriel and Joseph Renville, Scarlet Plume, Iron Man, and Paul Mazekutmani. They said they represented Indians who, before the 1862 conflict, had farmed in Minnesota. Afterward, they fled to the Turtle Mountains but soon surrendered at Fort Wadsworth, where the men had worked as government scouts. "For four years we have had no resting place," their spokesman said, and they wanted to settle and plant on land between Fort Wadsworth and the Minnesota border about a hundred miles from the nearest white settlement. They wanted their children in school, learning to "work like the whites."

The delegates presented the commissioners with a cogent, comprehensive document setting out their objectives that, essentially, matched the terms of the abrogated 1858 treaty. They reminded the commissioners how Sissetons and Wahpetons helped Sibley during 1862 and reminded Commissioner Curtis that while commanding in Minnesota in 1865, he had witnessed their fidelity as scouts.

Because the commissioners wanted to make peace with recalcitrant Santees, which this group clearly did not represent, the commissioners believed oral negotiations with any Santees waiting for them at Fort Rice would be more fruitful than this impromptu negotiation. However, the delegation reported that the Sisseton chief Standing Buffalo was afraid to bring in his forty lodges, and White Lodge's and Sleepy Eye's Sisseton bands remained militant and unlikely to sign any treaty.[15]

At the formal meeting at Fort Rice, Brown and his Sisseton and Wahpeton farmers expounded on what they wanted—essentially, to resume life as before the 1862 conflict. Curtis explained how, according to the new treaty, they—like other Sioux—would qualify to have a resident farmer, a schoolhouse, and other things they asked for when 200 families settled on their reservation. The group requested a copy of the treaty to study and, afterward, submitted another document enumerating their objections: They could represent only the so-called surrendered members of those bands. They could not agree to cease hostilities toward U.S. citizens because if they did, they would be admitting they once were

---

[14]Ibid., 29, 1–40, 55–88, 95.

[15]Ibid., 41–54. For a history of Santee acculturation, see Gary Anderson, *Kinsmen*, 103–104, 167–72.

hostile to whites when they were not. They could not relinquish rights to Dakota lands in Dakota Territory other than those in the reservation they proposed because the delegation had no power to do so even if so inclined. They did not come to Rice to sell land but to ask for government assistance and compensation for losses and privations so they might live as farmers. They wanted annuity restoration under the abrogated 1858 treaty, "which secured to each farmer individual rights to lands and other property; provided mills, blacksmiths, carpenters, schools and teachers, and enabled the farming Indian to devote his time and energies to the cultivation of the soil" without resorting to hunting for subsistence.[16]

Furthermore, they realized that any money they received would come from land cession rather than as direct government aid. "We cannot consent to receive assistance from that source." They objected to selling the Sissetons' and Wahpetons' "entire landed interest" and were convinced that doing so would lead to war. Militant Sioux would kill Sissetons and Wahpetons and, in addition, steal so many horses the loss would probably exceed what the government paid for the land.

They pointed out that they were responsible for the security frontier settlers now enjoyed. They could guarantee its continuance with reasonable government aid. They reaffirmed their desire to preserve peace and said they would use their influence to prevent "hostile demonstrations against the government or people (ourselves included) of the United States."

Commissioner Curtis asked Colonel Clark to interrogate individual delegates about Brown's role in bringing them to Fort Rice. A storekeeper now at Fort Wadsworth, Brown had picked the delegation, but he did not include any former militants whom the commissioners wanted most to see. Curtis asked the Indians what they thought Brown hoped to gain by this omission. Although their suspicions might have grown out of the question, they indicated they did wonder about Brown's comment that if he could not get satisfaction from the commissioners, he would take the Indians to Washington. Someone said that, instead of being afraid to attend this council, Standing Buffalo and the others knew of it and wanted to make peace. Actually, certain chiefs' exclusion might have been Sully's fault. He had advised Brown in a letter to "take charge" of and choose the representatives in the delegation. Colonel Clark, who read that letter, advised the commissioners to make permanent peace with Santee militants separately. "No white man who has had anything

---

[16]All quotes of Brown's delegation are from "1866 Northwest Indian Commission Proceedings," 84–85.

to do with them, and no Indian who has made peace prior to this time, should be recognized as their representative, as they [the militants] look with suspicion on all such characters."[17]

Governor Edmunds told Brown's delegation the commission could only give all Indians the same terms and could do nothing about their former Minnesota property. The offer was $20,000 for all their Dakota Territory holdings, reserving a 600-square-mile area where the government would protect them. Edmunds warned them they would have no more Dakota Territory lands to sell if they signed this treaty. Nevertheless, the commissioners "think it is very unwise in you not to accept the terms offered." When Brown presented a bill for $668 for bringing his delegation to the Upper Missouri, the commissioners referred him to the commissioner of Indian Affairs for reimbursement.[18]

Indeed, the Sissetons and Wahpetons presented the government with a special case. Before the 1862 war, many had adopted white culture, including agriculture and Christianity. In fact, they were advancing toward the ideal existence the government professed to envision for all Indians. Now, in attempting to be fair to all parties, the government was holding back Indians who were trying to do what was asked.

At Fort Rice, the other Sioux expressed satisfaction with the 1865 treaty but raised similar issues to those presented at Fort Sully. Fire Heart acknowledged that the president was "head man in the whole country" but argued that he, Fire Heart, was "head man out here." If the government moved the military post downriver, he would "touch the pen three times again." Curtis retorted that without Fort Rice, even more Indians would have starved over the winter. The post would stay. Despite the misunderstandings and equivocations they heard, the commissioners wrote Indian commissioner Cooley from Fort Rice that the Indians showed "every indication of confidence in us instead of distrusting us as they did last fall."[19]

THE THREE AFFILIATED TRIBES AT FORT BERTHOLD WERE concerned about protection from the Sioux, but the commissioners would council with them after they returned from Fort Union. At the mouth of the White Earth River, some Yanktonais hailed the commissioners' boat. The-Man-that-Holds-the-Enemy and Big Head's brother

[17]Ibid., 55–88.
[18]Ibid., 89–94, 96–98.
[19]Ibid., 29, 1–40, 55–88, 95.

Bob-Tail-Bear said they spoke for some 300 lodges, including Medicine Bear's Yanktonais, the deceased Big Head's band, some Assiniboines, and a few Santees camped a few miles upriver. The commissioners told these ambassadors they would hold council with the Sioux at the nearby camp but would meet Assiniboines at Fort Union.

At the camp, the commissioners found no Santees among the others. After Curtis briefly explained the treaty, Medicine Bear insisted that whites had caused the war. He wanted soldiers to go and traders to return. He wanted guns, ammunition, and food. Governor Edmunds asked him if whites had harmed his people since last fall's treaty signings. No, but Indians avoid Fort Rice because whenever they come near it, "soldiers stick their big guns at them." The president will not send powder "until peace is made," Edmunds warned.[20] When Medicine Bear balked at signing, the commissioners left provisions and continued to Fort Union.

From Fort Union on July 10, the commissioners invited Santees camped at Wood Mountain north of the international border to meet them either at Union or Berthold. Accurate numbers were important in making treaty disbursements; they discovered here some thirty local lodges of inter-married Assiniboine and Yanktonai people not counted as Yanktonais. They saw that Long Soldier's Hunkpapa band was eking out a living by hunting small game below the Yellowstone and Missouri confluence and by trading. Other Hunkpapas who traded at Fort Union considered the militants Four Horns and Red Horn their head chiefs. These last knew about the treaty but said they had been too far away to come to the 1865 conferences. Edmunds sent them a message: if Four Horns, Red Horn, Big Heart, and Black Moon came now to sign, Hunkpapas would be free to trade anywhere. After awhile, the ambassadors returned with more headmen, but those four chiefs were not among them. Reportedly, they had feared that Crows (also slated to meet with the commissioners) might steal their horses.[21]

The meetings at Fort Berthold began on July 23, but a Sioux attack

---

[20]Ibid., 110–11.

[21]Ibid., 99–106, 106–14, 119, 126, 131–37; "Agreement with Arikara, Grosventres, and Mandan," 27 July 1866, in Kappler, *Indian Affairs*, vol. 2, *Treaties*, 1052–56; "Treaty with Crow nation of Indians," 16 July 1866, Kappler, vol. 5, pt. 4, *Laws and Treaties, Unratified Treaties*, 699–702; "Treaty with the Assiniboines," 18 July 1866, Kappler, vol. 5, pt. 4, 702–705; and Larpenteur journal, 29 Apr., 16 June, and 10–16 July 1866. Red Horn, Four Horns, Running Antelope, and Loud-Voiced-Hawk were honored in 1851 as the Hunkpapa's first shirt-wearers. Big Heart may be the Oglala or Brulé chief a.k.a. Burnt Thigh (Seechah). It is unclear which of two Hunkpapa chiefs named Black Moon the commission wanted to see. Another Black Moon a.k.a. Loves War was a Miniconjou chief. See Vestal (Campbell), *Sitting Bull*, 83, and Papandrea, *They Never Surrendered*, 3–4, 14, 19–20, 38.

interrupted them on the second day. Rees killed five attackers and, according to the commissioners' interpreter, Charles Larpenteur, displayed the corpses' severed hands and feet during a victory scalp dance. On July 25, the Hunkpapa chief Running Antelope seemed to be the only Sioux present. He may have come in response to the invitation the commissioners issued at Fort Union, but perhaps he was living there at the time. At about this time Running Antelope disgraced his office as Hunkpapa shirt-wearer by eloping with another man's wife to the Ree village. However, in council he spoke for the Sioux. He said he punished his people caught stealing Fort Berthold Indians' horses, but some young Berthold men "have no ears" for warnings about stealing Sioux horses. Therefore, he wanted guns and ammunition so his people could defend themselves. Governor Edmunds expressed annoyance at his interruption, but Running Antelope persisted, demanding that money be taken from Dakotas' annuities for damages they inflicted on Lakotas. He warned, "The Santees will be your enemies and ours too." After the three tribes signed a never-ratified agreement, the commissioners considered their 1866 business concluded.[22]

Running Antelope was not the only Sioux resentful of Santees. At Fort Rice, the commissioners listened to some Yanktonais who had planted on the James River for the past fifteen years and wanted to continue planting there—on land Santees now claimed. One Yanktonai, indicating the Sissetons present, wondered why, given that they dressed like white men, they did not "stay where they belong and farm their lands, instead of coming over here to frighten our buffalo."[23] By "where they belong," the Yanktonai may have meant Minnesota. When several Upper Missouri Indians said they wanted to send the Santees back to Minnesota, the commissioners explained that although Minnesota had expelled them, Dakota Territory had not.

Continuing homeward, the commissioners stopped to see how Santees from Crow Creek were faring at their new Nebraska reservation. Created by executive order in February, it was located a few miles upriver of Fort Randall at the confluence of the Niobrara and Missouri Rivers. The population included the remaining 177 Davenport prisoners President Johnson pardoned in April 1866. In Iowa, the 177 had lived as whites;

[22]"1866 Northwest Indian Commission Proceedings," 89–94, 96–98, 150, 177, 208; Goodspeed, *Province and the States*, vol. 6, 250; Andrews to Litchfield, 22 July 1866, Fort Sully Selected LS, RG 393, NA; "Record of Events," July 1866, Fort Sully PR, reel 1238, M617, NA; Larpenteur journal, 23–28 July 1866; Utley, *Lance*, 21–22, 73; and Vestal (Campbell), *Sitting Bull*, 83.
[23]"1866 Northwest Indian Commission Proceedings," 72.

therefore, many no longer wanted to abide by tribal customs. Furthermore, according to Passing Hail, the residents did not arrive in time to plant. They had no timber for building houses or fences, and their few cattle ate everything they did plant. In addition, they had no horses, guns, or ammunition with which to hunt. Consequently, they did not like this location. The commissioners urged them to build mound houses, stay the winter, and look for a new location next spring.[24]

DURING THIS PERIOD, THE INDIAN BUREAU WAS IN TURMOIL. Since spring 1866, animosity between Dakota Territory's non-voting House of Representatives delegate Burleigh and acting Indian commissioner Cooley was palpable. Burleigh, accusing Cooley of corruption and misuse of funds, impeded his Senate confirmation. Cooley, whose office had investigated Burleigh's conduct as Yankton agent, accused Burleigh of personal bias against him. The current issue, however, was evaporating Indian funds. In defending himself to Indian Affairs Committee chairman Doolittle, Cooley argued that, without congressional funding for the several 1865 treaty commissions, he had drawn heavily on contingency funds to pay for them. The Senate confirmed Cooley in April 1866, but he resigned in November.[25]

Meanwhile, in a June 1866 speech in the U.S. House, Burleigh declared the Indians' fate as sealed "as was that of the Canaanites before the advancing armies of Israel as they moved forward to possess the promised land of their inheritance." However, in September 1866, the Third Battalion, Thirteenth Infantry, was called to duty to protect Indians, not march against them. Bothered by borderland mixed-bloods luring his young men away from his peaceable band with contraband goods, Two Bear sent a runner to Fort Rice for help in extricating his band from their clutches. Lieutenant William M. Wherry, with four infantry companies and a mounted detachment, succeeded in driving the mixed-bloods across the border and bringing Two Bear's destitute band back to Rice. Even so, many starved or froze to death over the winter of 1866–67.[26]

In the meantime, Brevet Lieutenant Colonel William D. Rankin's

[24]Riggs, *Mary and I*, 202–206; "1866 Northwest Indian Commission Proceedings," 55–88, 208, 209–12; Meyer, *History of the Santee Sioux*, 242; and U.S. Bureau of Indian Affairs, *Papers Relating to Talks and Councils*, 23–24, 205–16.

[25]Kvasnicka & Viola, *Commissioners*, 94–95, 104–105.

[26]Lamar, *Dakota Territory*, 104. Lamar quoted from *Cong. Globe*, 39th Cong., 1st sess. (8 June 1866), 3056; Wherry, *Types and Traditions*, vol. 37, 519; Meyer, *History of the Santee Sioux*, 144–45, 154–55.

Thirteenth Infantry soldiers had built Fort Buford on the Missouri's north bank opposite its confluence with the Yellowstone. Sitting Bull detested this new post even more than he hated Fort Rice. His band harassed it constantly and in December 1867 killed three citizens, stole horses, and occupied the icehouse and sawmill, firing at the fort while Sitting Bull banged incessantly on the saw blade. Finally, the fort's twelve-pounder gun compelled the Indians to leave. Periodically over the next three months, Sioux pestered the garrison, killing another citizen and three local Indians. The army's other new post, Fort Stevenson, established in June 1866 a dozen miles from Fort Berthold, also vexed the Lakotas. Like Buford, it was on the north Missouri riverbank, but both were near popular Sioux campsites south of the river. Also, the soldiers' presence at both inhibited Sioux from trading with local Indians at Forts Berthold and Union. Meanwhile, the Thirteenth became, with two companies added to its original eight, the Thirty-first Infantry Regiment. The army was on the Upper Missouri to stay, and the Indians knew it.[27]

In sum, the year's peace efforts were not fully successful. The true militants would stay militant, and the others were no longer naive enough to expect much in the way of help, although some demanded it. The commissioners, and Fort Rice Commander Clark, regarded the sophisticated arguments that the farmer Santees presented with suspicion; they did not like the fact that this white man, Brown, represented Indians in such a lawyerly way. They ignored, in their reports, some of the Indians' obvious misunderstandings and confusions and appeared not to make much effort to dispel them. Notwithstanding the vagaries of steamboat travel, and the consequent late or non-delivery of farm equipment and supplies, no one suggested alternative sources of such products or any compensation for them. No one seemed to perceive evil in a government policy that found it acceptable to allay Indians' abject hunger with spoiled food rather than finding some way to decently feed and clothe them. What of the long-term cost of using money meant to ensure the Indians' future (education funds, for example) to ward off starvation? Advocates like Joseph Brown were scarce among the white population but were needed. Meanwhile, the Indians were on their own, stuck with agents who represented the government to them and not the other way around.

[27]Fort Buford PR, June, Aug., Oct., Dec. 1866, and Jan., Feb., March, Apr., June 1867, reel 158, M617, NA; Rankin to Thomas, 29 June 1867, Fort Buford LS, RG 393.4, NA; Sackett report, 2 July 1866; Kimball and Matthews, "Locality and History of Fort Buford," 1–3; Larpenteur journal, 16 June 1866, 12, 14, and 16 July 1866, 15 Oct. 1967, and Thompson's note 32, 496; Utley, *Lance*, 71–72; Larson, *Gall*, 59; and Wood, "Gen. Régis de Trobriand," 4.

Chapter 18

A Contagion of Change

During their sojourn on the Upper Missouri, volunteer soldiers believed they had come to punish Santee Sioux for the 1862 Minnesota conflict. By the time they left, the struggle was about roads, especially railroads, which could move people, cargo, and mail swiftly to and through Indian Country. Railroads could also bring in troops and keep them well supplied.[1] For some Sioux band chiefs and war leaders, whether or not to fight or accede to whites' demands to get out of the way was a decision crucial to the very existence of their demoralized, starving, desperate people.

The Platte River Brulés and Oglalas met the 1866 commissioners in their home country. Since John Bozeman had opened it in 1862, his trail was the shortest way—although his trail extended 600 miles, it shaved 450 miles off a Utah route—to the Montana mining areas from the emigrant trail. General Grenville Dodge described it to Pope: "From Laramie to Powder River, then to Virginia City [Montana], is an excellent wagon road; good grass, water, and wood all the way, and the most direct road that can be got." Since 1859, the Sioux assumed ownership, through conquest of the Crows, of most of the country it traversed. The Crows, who still owned the northwestern reaches of it, shared the Sioux's opinion of Bozeman Trail travelers as trespassers. Both tribes treated them accordingly. Some Sioux winter counts for 1864 depict Crows, perhaps in reference to an alliance formed because of their mutual opposition to whites traveling the route.[2]

Over the summer of 1866, Colonel Henry B. Carrington, who was head of the new Mountain District in General Philip St. George Cooke's Department of the Platte, was to establish forts along Bozeman's trail

---

[1]For the railroad's significance, see Athearn, "Firewagon Road," 3–19.

[2]Dee Brown, *Fort Phil Kearny*, 18–19; Athearn, *Sherman*, 38–39, 55; and Dodge to Pope, 15 Sept. 1865, OR, vol. 48, pt. 2, p. 1229. For a summary, see *Sioux Tribe v. USA*, 42 Indian Claims Commission 214 (1865), Docket 74, "Additional Findings of Fact," 233–55. For the Sioux–Crow truce, see Rzeczkowski, "Crow Indians and the Bozeman Trail," 30–33.

to protect white travelers.[3] When Carrington and his Eighteenth U.S. Infantry battalion were a day away from Fort Laramie, the Brulé chief Standing Elk, traveling to meet the commissioners, visited his camp. Learning Carrington's mission, Standing Elk reminded him the Indians did not give permission for forts, and, besides, the commissioners were at Fort Laramie to negotiate about that very thing. He and Spotted Tail and the aging Little Thunder expected to sign the treaty; the Powder River country was of less concern to them since they usually hunted along the Platte and Republican Rivers, but Standing Elk warned Carrington that Red Cloud's Oglala warriors, the Miniconjous, and others would not surrender the trail without a fight.[4]

At Fort Laramie, Colonel Henry E. Maynadier, the Raynolds Expedition veteran who now commanded Fifth usv soldiers due for discharge, hosted the council.[5] When Red Cloud realized a road would go through despite Indians' objections, he made an impassioned speech and left angry. The three Brulé chiefs signed for their delegations, as did the Oglala chief Big Mouth and headmen of the Laramie Loafer band.

The Oglala American Horse and several other 1865–66 winter count keepers recorded the Fort Laramie meeting with glyphs of a white man with lines connecting two deer heads to his mouth. (Maynadier's name sounded like "many deer.") Believing he accomplished something important, Doolittle commissioner E. B. Taylor wired Indian commissioner Cooley: "Satisfactory treaty concluded. Most cordial feeling prevails." However, because Red Cloud and other militants did not sign them, Congress never ratified the documents.[6]

On June 28, Carrington and his men left Fort Laramie to establish Fort Reno near Connor's 1865 Powder River post. By July 13, his soldiers were also building Fort Phil Kearny 150 miles north of Fort Laramie. In response, Red Cloud mustered some 3,000 Lakota, northern Cheyenne, and northern Arapaho warriors and began his war. On July 16, they killed two soldiers. In August, Carrington's men started building Fort C. F. Smith, ninety miles north of Phil Kearny and about forty-five miles

---

[3]Dee Brown, *Fort Phil Kearny*, 18–19; and Athearn, *Sherman*, 38–39, 55.

[4]Dee Brown, *Fort Phil Kearny*, 20, 38–39; and Carrington, *Ab-Sa-Ra-Ka*, 72.

[5]Meyer, *History of the Santee Sioux*, 144–45, 154–55; Dee Brown, *Fort Phil Kearny*, 18–19; and Athearn, *Sherman*, 38–39, 55.

[6]Utley, *Indian Frontier*, 99–101; American Horse winter count, 1865–66, in Candace Greene and Thornton, *Year the Stars Fell*, 257. Moses Red Horse also recorded 1865–66 as "Many Deers Made Peace." See Karol, ed., *Red Horse Owner's Winter Count*, 65, and *Sioux Tribe v. USA*, 42 Indian Claims Commission 214 (1865), Docket 74, "Establishment of the Powder River Road."

southeast of present Billings, Montana. Although they may have only been present sporadically during the summer, by fall the Miniconjou bands whose chiefs were Brave Bear, White Hollow Horn, and Black Shield were committed to forcing the forts out of the Powder River country. "Harney chief" Lone Horn and Makes Room, one of the ten subchiefs he picked in 1856, as well as the war leader High Backbone, also joined the coalition; by autumn, the Miniconjou camp on the Tongue River numbered a hundred lodges. Motivated to honor the dying wish of their beloved leader, White Swan, to make war on all whites, whom he hated apparently because a white man had once burgled his lodge, they proposed a winter attack on Fort Phil Kearny. The Indians continued harassing the posts and anyone traveling between them until, in December 1866, they scored a major victory by wiping out Brevet Lieutenant Colonel William J. Fetterman's eighty-one-man command. It was the greatest loss, so far, for U.S. troops during Indian warfare.[7]

Congress immediately ordered an investigation into the Fetterman affair and appointed General Sully and Samuel F. Tappan of Colorado to do it. Tappan, a former abolitionist, was an officer with the First Colorado at the time of the Sand Creek assault, but he had no part in it. Their report, released in March 1867, blamed higher-ups, especially department head Cooke, and recommended abandoning the Bozeman Trail in favor of defending the Platte emigrant route. It also advocated reserving 80,000 square miles of country drained by the Missouri and Yellowstone Rivers for the Indians. Despite his opinions in the Doolittle questionnaire and his preference expressed in a letter to interior secretary Browning to drive out the Sioux and negotiate with the original owners, the Crows, Sully signed off on the report's recommendation to organize a separate cabinet-level Indian department. However, Congress adjourned without taking action.[8]

[7]Andrist, Long Death, 97–107; Olson, Red Cloud, 41–50; Calitri, "Shattering," 45–59; and Monnett, Where a Hundred Soldiers Were Killed, 87, 94, 120–24, 138–40, 142, 152, 181. Fort Phil Kearny, Wyo., was named for Gen. Philip Kearny, the nephew of the namesake of Fort Kearny, Neb. General C. F. Smith died on the Tennessee River in 1862.

[8]Dee Brown, Fort Phil Kearny, 18–19; Athearn, Sherman, 38–39, 55, 111; Tappan to Chivington, 6 June 1864, 252, and "Troops in Dept. of Kansas," 620, both in OR, vol. 34, pt. 4; "The Grant and Tappan Indian Policy," Daily Rocky Mountain News, 6 Nov. 1865; Zwink, "E. W. Wynkoop," n42; Olson, Red Cloud, 52–57; Larson, Gall, 62; Keenan, Wagon Box Fight, 14; Utley, Frontier Regulars, 113, 126n12, and Indian Frontier, 108–109; and Rzeczkowski, "Crow Indians," 40. Some investigation documents were suppressed until 1887. See Calitri, "Shattering" for a 2004 reassessment. The commission's official reports are in "Information Touching [on] the Origin and Progress of the Indian Hostilities on [the] Frontier," 40th Cong., 1st sess., 1868, S. Doc. 13, serial 1308. For U.S. territorial policy, see Lamar, Dakota Territory, 3–26.

Nationwide, the Fetterman affair revived the perpetual national debate about what to do with Indians who were in the way of national expansion. Early in 1867, new Indian commissioner Lewis V. Bogy wrote Secretary O. H. Browning that the Powder River Indians had reason to complain about the 1866 treaties. How could the government expect Sioux to give up their prime hunting grounds while hunting was how they made their living? Only two solutions would work: destroy the Indians or remove them from the path of white settlement. Removal would cost too much, and war would inhibit settlement; thus, Bogy advised moving them to reservations, where they could become self-sufficient within a few years. Meanwhile, Nebraska became a state in 1867, and a January 9, 1867, act of Congress made the portion of Dakota Territory west of the 104th parallel part of the new Wyoming Territory.[9]

ON THE UPPER MISSOURI, THE INDIAN COMMISSIONERS LEFT THE Buford construction site in August 1866 after promising the local Indians ammunition and guns for hunting. Lieutenant Colonel Rankin, obeying incompatible military policy, would give them neither. In response, the neighborhood Sioux promised to "wipe every soldier on the Missouri River out of existence." On January 1, 1867, they launched an attack that only the post's twelve-pounder cannon-fire ended. For a time, Rankin could not send out mail. Because Black Tomahawk and other Indian couriers were trustworthy, the Thirteenth's Lieutenant Colonel Andrews hired more Indian mailmen to better serve the growing number of forts, but their jobs were dangerous. A northern "pony express" established in 1867 to carry mail between Minnesota and western Montana failed because of Indian attacks all along its route.[10]

Political upheaval also affected Upper Missouri affairs. After removing Governor Edmunds in 1866, whom Burleigh accused of defrauding Indians, President Johnson appointed Burleigh's father-in-law, Andrew Jackson Faulk, governor and, consequently, ex-officio superintendent of

---

[9]*Sioux Tribe v. USA*, 42 Indian Claims Commission 214, 19 July 1978, Docket 74, "Additional Findings of Fact," 236–40; and Athearn, "Firewagon Road," 3–19.

[10]Fort Buford PR, June, Aug., Oct., Dec. 1866, and Jan., Feb. 1867, reel 158, M617, NA; Athearn, "Fort Buford 'Massacre,'" 675–84, and *Sherman*, 117–26; Andrews to Charles, 14 June 1866, Cooley to Maj. 13th Inf. Commanding Fort Rice D.T., 18 June 1866, and Andrews to Litchfield, 25 June and 22 July 1866, all in FS Selected LS, RG 393, NA; "Record of Events," July 1866, Fort Sully PR, reel 1238, M617, NA; and Gray, "Northern Overland," 58–73.

Indian Affairs for Dakota. A former Yankton Agency trader, Faulk advocated establishing a new reservation that would restrict Indian country to an area north of the Cheyenne River and that would stretch west to the Rocky Mountains.[11]

Early in 1867, Faulk accompanied a group of Sioux chiefs and headmen, including Struck-by-the-Ree's Yanktons and Joseph Brown's delegation of Indian farmers, to Washington. All went well for Brown's group until Scarlet Crow disappeared. After two weeks, someone found the former Sibley scout dead, an apparent suicide, although many suspected murder. However, the trip resulted in the Sisseton and Wahpeton bands ceding their Dakota holdings while retaining 918,780 acres east of Fort Wadsworth as the Lake Traverse Reservation and also reserving land between Devils Lake and the Sheyenne River as the Devils Lake (later Spirit Lake) Indian Reservation. The treaty terms gave the Indians title to the land, reserved the government's right to build roads through it, and required Indians to work to earn food, clothing, animals, and farm implements. Indians could earn patents on reservation land allotted in 160-acre tracts by cultivating fifty acres within five years. The treaty intended the Devils Lake reservation for the roaming Santee bands and the mixed Yanktonai, Santee, and Cuthead bands. They would merit an agent when 500 Indians settled there, but by fall 1867, only fifty-seven households, or about 250 people, had come. When more arrived over the winter, a relief mission became necessary to sustain them.[12]

The 1867 Sisseton and Wahpeton treaty did not restore the 1858 treaty, but it did include a formal apology: "Whereas Congress, in confiscating the Sioux annuities and reservations [after the 1862 conflict] made no provision for the support of these, the friendly portion of the Sissiton [sic] and Warpeton [sic] bands," and because "they have been suffered to remain homeless wanderers, frequently subject to intense sufferings from want of subsistence and clothing to protect them from the rigors of a high northern latitude," even while "at all times prompt in rendering service when called upon to repel hostile raids and to punish depredations committed by hostile Indians upon the persons and property of the whites;" they would be given the means to "return to an agricultural

[11]Wesley Wilson, "Doctor Burleigh," 96; and Goodspeed, *Province*, vol. 6, 251–52.

[12]Schuler, *Fort Sisseton*, 38; McCormack, "Soldiers and Sioux," 13–14; Viola, *Diplomats in Buckskin*, 133–34, 162–63, 164–65, 217n36; "Treaty with the Sisseton and Wahpeton Bands, 1867," in Kappler, *Indian Affairs*, vol. 2, *Treaties*, 956–59; and Meyer, *History of the Santee Sioux*, 199–209, 220–21. Meyer detailed 1857 treaty effects in chaps. 10 and 11, pp. 198–239.

life." In 1867, the army authorized an Enlisted Indian Scout program whereby Indians received the same pay and obeyed the same rules as regular soldiers. Fifteen such scouts worked at Fort Wadsworth.[13]

Even as whites won Dakota Territory lands that Indians ceded between 1865 and 1867, they still coveted the Black Hills. Because Dakota Territory's legislative body's actions were under federal auspices, Governor Faulk convinced territorial lawmakers to press Congress to try to buy them and open them to white settlement. Few doubted the mysterious mountains held mineral wealth. In spring 1867, a group of mostly former Union soldiers met at Yankton to discuss how to open the area to miners, but General Sherman did his duty and forbade them to invade Indian Territory. Widely quoted Sioux City newspapers blasted Sherman, who, one said, "by a high handed and extraordinary use of his power as military commander, has for the past two years prevented the opening up and development of this region." Another called Sherman a "brainless and peaky-headed vagrant" who knew as much about Indians and frontiersmen as a Missouri River shovel fish (probably what is known today as a paddlefish).[14]

When news of the Fetterman disaster in what was then still the western part of Dakota came during a territorial legislative session, the delegates immediately asked Congress for more military posts and a bill to establish a territorial militia.[15] Then a rumor about a massacre at Fort Buford spread across the country. According to the story published April 1 in a St. Louis newspaper and attributed to the wife of an army officer based in St. Louis, the Sioux supposedly killed all the soldiers at the fort, burned Colonel Rankin at the stake, raped his wife, then set her atop a horse to fend for herself in the wilderness. Papers across the country repeated the story, and even the military's *Army and Navy Journal* printed the false report. When Sherman, who lived in St. Louis, could not learn her name, he concluded the rumor was a prank. Another fabrication circulated in May 1867—that Indians had killed everyone aboard the steamboat *Miner*, then destroyed the boat. Added to real incidents—a Thirteenth Infantry lieutenant's wife recorded in her diary in April that an Indian's arrow had killed the *Deer Lodge*'s pilot—these

---

[13]Schuler, *Fort Sisseton*, 38; Kappler, *Indian Affairs*, vol. 2, *Treaties*, 957; and Goodspeed, *Province*, vol. 6, 246, 251–53.

[14]Athearn, *Sherman*, 178–79.

[15]Lamar, *Dakota Territory*, 151; Kingsbury, *History of Dakota*, vol. 1, 864; Wesley Wilson, "Doctor Burleigh," 96; and Goodspeed, *Province*, vol. 6, 251–52.

rumors amplified emotions already inflamed by the Fetterman affair, causing a public outcry against the military as ineffectual in handling threats to westward expansion. Sympathy for Indians also evaporated as frantic requests for more regular troops continued apace with Indians' attacks at points along the emigrant corridors and their vandalism of telegraph and railroad lines. Territorial governors wanted authority to raise militias, but without federal funds available to offer volunteers an attractive wage, local enthusiasm for such groups dissipated. Governor Faulk established a cavalry militia, but it saw no action.[16]

STRUCK-BY-THE-REE'S INTENT WHILE IN WASHINGTON WITH FAULK early in 1867 was, among other things, to persuade Interior Secretary Browning to allow a Catholic mission on the Yankton reservation. Father De Smet was in Washington for the same reason, but Indian commissioner Bogy was more concerned with the recent Fetterman disaster and persuaded the priest to take an assignment with General Grant's wartime aide, Seneca Indian Ely S. Parker, and General Sully. The three would serve as government envoys extraordinary.[17] Their task was twofold: convince leaders of holdout bands to sign a treaty and learn more about Oglala and Miniconjou activity concerning the Bozeman Trail. Arriving on the Upper Missouri earlier than the generals did, De Smet visited the Yankton agency then went on to Fort Thompson to talk to the Brulés, Two Kettles, and Yanktonais sojourning there. They told him of their dilemma concerning their own militant kinsmen, whose invitations to "take up the hatchet against the whites in defense of the land of their birth" always came with "insults and menaces." They also complained that government representatives, "affable and prodigal of speeches and promises in behalf of our Great Father," arrived yearly, yet their "fine words" and "pompous promises" came to nothing.[18]

At Old Fort Sully, Parker and Sully, who brought with him four Thirty-first Infantry companies to bolster Fort Buford's garrison, caught up with

---

[16]Fort Buford PR, June, Aug., Oct., Dec. 1866, and Jan., Feb. 1867, reel 158, M617, NA; Athearn, "Fort Buford 'Massacre,'" 675–84, and *Sherman*, 117–26, 129, 137–48, 177–86; Canfield, "An Army Wife," 64; Utley, *Indian Frontier*, 108–109, 112–17, and *Frontier Regulars*, 132–34; and Kvasnicka and Viola, *Commissioners*, 105–106.

[17]GO 42, Dept. of the Missouri, 2 Nov. 1865, OR, vol. 48, pt. 2, p. 1252.

[18]Chittenden & Richardson, *Life, Letters*, vol. 3, 874.

De Smet. The soldiers' presence could only compromise any message of peace the three envoys espoused, but it did make manifest the government's determination to keep a continued Upper Missouri military presence. Before continuing to Forts Berthold and Union, De Smet sent runners to ask roaming Sioux bands to meet them at Old Fort Sully on their return downriver.

They spoke at Berthold with the three non-Sioux tribes, then continued to Fort Union. Only a few structures remained, and those were outside its walls; the old trading post was being demolished to build Fort Buford.

Upper Missouri merchants were not immune during this postwar contagion of change; the Gregory, Geoway, and Bruguier trading firm, as well as the Hubbell and Hawley firm, sold out to Durfee and Peck in 1867, when steamboats carried a record 8,000 tons of cargo and 10,000 passengers to and from Fort Benton. Veteran trader Charles Larpenteur, whose Durfee and Peck store was still at Union, noted in his diary that Sully, Parker, and De Smet arrived June 28 and, while waiting in vain to speak with the Santees, attended the local July 4 celebration. Even now, the Yanktonai chiefs Medicine Bear and Bob-Tail-Bull, as well as some Sihasapas and Hunkpapas including Sitting Bull, did business here. In his book (but not in his journal), Larpenteur reported a conversation that probably took place in October. Sitting Bull supposedly said he "killed, robbed, and injured too many white men to believe in a good peace" and preferred dying with his "skin pierced with bullet holes" to settling on a reservation. He admitted trying to enlist Assiniboines and peaceable Sioux, whom he accused of making themselves "slaves to a piece of fat bacon, some hard-tack, and a little sugar and coffee," to join his fight. "Look at me, see if I am poor, or my people either. The whites may get me at last . . . but I will have good times till then."[19]

After waiting in vain for the Santees and Crows, the three envoys turned back. Reaching Old Fort Sully on July 24, they learned that Indians indeed came to meet them but lost patience and left to hunt. De Smet wanted to go after them, but when that proved impractical, he vowed to return in 1868 to see what he could do for peace. In his official

[19]Larpenteur, *Forty Years*, 358–60; Larpenteur journal, June 1867–January 1868 entries, especially 15–19 Oct. 1867; Yoemans ("spy"), (*Fort Rice*) *Frontier Scout*, 17 Aug. 1865; Joseph Hanson, *Conquest of the Missouri*, 64–65; Lass, "History and Significance," 21–40; Hubbell Papers, MNHS Archives; Gregory [&] Bruguier [&] Geoway Papers, Fort Union Papers, MNHS Archives; Thompson, *Fort Union Trading Post*, 88–89, 100; Crawford, *Exploits*, 154–56, 153n3 and 155n4; and Goodspeed, *Province*, vol. 6, 251–52.

report, De Smet concluded, "If our Indians become enraged against the whites, it is because the whites have made them suffer for a long time." The others journeyed to Washington in September to report their findings.[20]

ON JULY 20, 1867, CONGRESS CREATED YET ANOTHER FORMAL commission to look into Indian matters the previous commissioners and envoys had uncovered. This year they would focus on three tasks: Discover and remove the causes of war; secure settlements and make transcontinental railroad construction safe; and suggest or set in motion a plan to "civilize" Indians. On the Upper Missouri, they were determined to persuade all Indians east of the river—Yanktonais and Santees—to settle on the Lake Traverse, Devils Lake, or Santee Reservations. On August 6, Generals Sherman, Harney, and Sanborn, Department of Dakota commander Major General Alfred H. Terry, Indian Affairs Committee chairman Senator John B. Henderson, and Fetterman investigator Tappan met at St. Louis to elect Nathaniel G. Taylor—the new Indian commissioner—chairman.[21]

Governor Faulk joined them in Dakota, where Long Mandan complained to them about government goods not reaching his Two Kettle band. Sherman explained: the army fed its soldiers; the Indian Bureau should feed Indians. Long Mandan told Sherman how some Sioux feared coming near the forts; Sherman responded that soldiers in the neighborhood had to be on guard at all times, but he assured Long Mandan that the soldiers would not harm Indians. Sherman held up the Cherokees, who owned farms and lived in houses, for Sioux to emulate. If the government provided materials and instructions, Long Mandan said, his people would use them. Sherman asked: Were his people willing to cut wood for steamers? Yes. Did Long Mandan object to steamboat travel through Sioux country? He did not, personally, but other Indians did.[22]

---

[20]Chittenden & Richardson, *Life, Letters,* vol. 3, 863–92; Carriker, *Father Peter John De Smet,* 208–15; Unknown author [possibly Henry M. Stanley], "A Big Powwow with Friendly Chiefs," and "Our Indian Troubles," *New York Herald,* 24 Sept. 1867; and Gray, "Story of Mrs. Picotte-Galpin," pt. 1, 17–18.

[21]Prucha, *Great Father,* 156, and *Documents,* 104–108; and "Annual Report," 7 Jan. 1868, CIA annual report, 26–50.

[22]Chittenden & Richardson, *Life, Letters,* vol. 3, 863–92; Prucha, *Great Father,* 155–57; and "Annual Report," 7 Jan. 1868, CIA annual report, 26–50.

POSTWAR RECONSTRUCTION AND THE TRANSCONTINENTAL RAILROAD competed for congressional attention with the hit-and-run war Red Cloud and his allies waged over the Bozeman Trail. Through it all, railroad crews continued to work, and in October, the Kansas Pacific hired William F. Cody to kill twelve buffalo a day to feed its laborers. In less than eighteen months, by his own count, he killed 4,280 and earned the sobriquet "Buffalo Bill."[23]

Without Sherman—General Christopher C. Augur, commanding the Department of the Platte since January 1867, replaced him—the commissioners traveled by rail to track's end at North Platte, Nebraska, where Oglala and Brulé chiefs, including Spotted Tail, Man-Afraid-of-his-Horse, Big Mouth, Standing Elk, and Swift Bear, asked for and received guns and ammunition for hunting. In their January 7, 1868, report of this meeting, the commissioners defended their decision: "We are now satisfied, whatever the criticisms on our conduct at the time . . . that had we refused the ammunition demanded at this council, the war on their part would have continued."

The commissioners, minus De Smet, who returned to the Missouri in order to board a steamer for Fort Rice, moved on to Fort Laramie. When Red Cloud and other militants snubbed them, Harney and Sanborn were furious. Journalist Henry Morton Stanley, his African exploits in the future, traveled with the commissioners. When interpreters spoke for Indians in council, he noticed that Harney paid attention while other commissioners did not try to hide their boredom. The Indians did not know the other commissioners, but Stanley saw that most knew Harney or knew his reputation for toughness.[24]

The commissioners' next destination was Fort Harker, near the railroad terminus in Kansas, to deal with southern tribes. Notwithstanding numerous stage station attacks that spring and General Winfield Hancock's controversial burning of a deserted Cheyenne and Lakota village, the commissioners made a series of treaties that helped clear the way for the transcontinental and Kansas Pacific railroads moving west respectively toward California and Denver.[25]

In his October 1, 1867, annual report, Sherman wrote that the only way to restrain Indians was to convince them the army did not fear "to strike

---

[23]Utley, *Frontier Regulars*, 124–25, 129nn42–43, 133; Hyde, *Red Cloud's Folk*, 159; Cody, *Life of Buffalo Bill*, 161–62; and Chittenden & Richardson, *Life, Letters*, 900.

[24]Adams, *Harney*, 254–57, 262–63, 278–80.

[25]Sherman, "Annual Report, 1 Oct. 1867" (listed under "Misc. MP" in bibliography); and Utley, *Cavalier*, 51–52.

them in their most vulnerable points, viz., their property and families."
He asked that the government not pay reparations for Hancock's assault
on the village because it would make the army appear weak.[26]

In the same report, Sherman predicted that the "belt of country"
through which the two railroads ran would fill up with Americans who
would "permanently separate" northern and southern Indians and "allow
us to direct our military forces on one or the other at pleasure, if thereafter they continue their acts of hostility." Sherman again criticized the
Indian Intercourse Law of 1834, which, in this context, mandated the
army to "eject by force the white population" from Indian lands as "utterly
inapplicable" to ensuring settlers' safety on the plains. Because towns
and settlements were "daily occuring" in western Dakota where no civil
government existed, Sherman urged Congress to "provide an efficient
civil government, or empower the military to exercise such authority
where the civil authority is manifestly inadequate." As it was, the nearest
civil authority for the vast region populated by the Sioux was at Yankton.
Meanwhile, the 1867 commission's January 1868 report of its visits with
Plains Indians presented a remarkable historical summary of relentless
white-on-Indian injustice and heralded changing American attitudes.[27]

---

[26]Sherman, "Annual Report, 1 Oct. 1867"; and Stimson, "Indian Question," 399.

[27]Sherman's 1 Oct. 1867 report; Chittenden & Richardson, *Life, Letters,* vol. 3, 863–92; Prucha,
Great Father, 155–56. See also U.S. House, *Report to the President by the Indian Peace Commission,*
7 Jan. 1868, 15–17, 20–22, 26–50.

Chapter 19

The Sioux Treaty of 1868

IN JANUARY 1868, DR. HENRY M. MATTHEWS, FORMER POST surgeon at Fort C. F. Smith, representing the government, met with the Sioux and their allies at the Bozeman Trail's Fort Phil Kearny. If the Indians ceased hostilities toward Americans over the winter, come spring, commissioners would discuss a new treaty with them at Fort Laramie or elsewhere. However, he warned, this was a "last offer, and if you reject it, the white father will be very angry. He loves you, but is not afraid to punish you."[1] The chiefs he spoke with were not the militant leaders Matthews wanted to see. Similarly, one chief remarked that since the president sent Matthews as a surrogate, Red Cloud would come to talks only when the president appeared.

By spring, transcontinental track reached Cheyenne and would soon be in Utah, making an old Utah to Montana land route attractive again and the Bozeman Trail forts less important. Four weeks before the spring 1868 treaty talks began at Fort Laramie, General Grant told General Sherman to close the forts if he thought it wise. Consequently, the commissioners (minus Sherman and Henderson, who were testifying at President Johnson's impeachment proceedings) promised in March to destroy them and send away their garrisons within two months. The subsequent treaty that was hammered out at the spring talks reserved the Lakotas' current Yellowstone and Powder River country hunting grounds for them to share for "so long as the buffalo may range thereon, in such numbers as to justify the chase." Sherman later commented, "I think it would be wise to invite all the sportsmen of England & America this fall for a Grand Buffalo hunt, and make one grand sweep of them all. Until the Buffaloes & consequent[ly] Indians are out from between the Roads we will have collisions & trouble."[2] With their main objective met, the southern Sioux overlooked the treaty's details, which would soon bedevil them.

---

[1]Belden, *White Chief*, 389–90.
[2]Athearn, *Sherman*, 197.

The Hunkpapas, Sihasapas, and Sans Arcs who roamed the Yellowstone country north of where Red Cloud's Oglala and Brulé warriors held sway were concerned with forts along the Missouri River. With individual exceptions, they did not participate in Red Cloud's war. More important to the Upper Missouri Sioux was that the new treaty delineated the Great Sioux Reservation proper, which was essentially composed of present South Dakota west of the Missouri. The commissioners, determined to persuade militants to sign, invited Sioux to Fort Rice to do so. When Running Antelope stopped by Fort Stevenson in April 1868 on his return from the Yellowstone River, he told General Philippe Régis de Keredern de Trobriand the winter was severe and nearly all the chiefs of bands wintering there were willing to attend a peace conference, except the Hunkpapas Black Moon, Four Horns, Red Horn, and Sitting Bull. Lone Horn's Miniconjous, the Sans Arcs, the Lower Brulés, and some Santee bands, he said, planned to surrender at military posts. These Lakotas suffered more than bad weather. De Trobriand noticed Running Antelope had severely gashed his body in mourning for a son lost to disease.[3]

De Trobriand had arrived at his Fort Stevenson headquarters in 1867 to take overall command of Thirty-first Infantry troops, now incorporating companies of the Thirteenth, at Fort Buford and the new Devils Lake post, Fort Totten, 131 miles from Stevenson. A French nobleman by birth but a naturalized American, De Trobriand was a multitalented soldier, artist, writer, and American Civil War veteran. Among the first Sioux he met were Running Antelope, known for "his unvarying attachment to the whites," and his nephew, Bear Rib, whom the general described as chief of the friendly Hunkpapas. His description of their clothing reveals it to be as transitional as the times: both wore new blankets, colored cloth shirts, and eagle feathers in their braided hair. Bear Rib's braids were wrapped in fur. A strip of red cloth draped his shoulders and nearly touched the ground. His blue cloth pants sported a red band and rows of metal buttons. Running Antelope wore large copper earrings, a red kerchief around his neck, and a brown frock coat. According to De Trobriand, Bear Rib was Mato-cu-wi-hu's youngest son; an older brother died of disease soon after their father's assassination. The general,

---

[3]David Miller et al., *History of the Assiniboine and Sioux*, 68; Athearn, *Sherman*, 194–98; Belden, *White Chief*, 399–402, 407; De Trobriand, *Military Life*, 259–60; De Trobriand, *Army Life*, 255, 259–62; and De Trobriand journal, 31 March and 2 April 1867 entries.

impressed with Running Antelope's intelligence, assumed he was acting as "regent" because of his nephew's youth.[4]

Given what Running Antelope told De Trobriand, it was a propitious time for De Smet to attempt to meet personally with militant leaders on their turf. When De Smet petitioned Congress for expense money to make his trip, commission member Harney added his favorable recommendation to Sherman's. The priest and Harney had met in 1850 on a steamboat journey between New Orleans and Memphis, when, in exchanging views about Seminoles and Plains Indians, they formed a lasting friendship.[5]

At Fort Rice, De Smet's friends tried to talk him out of his journey. Failing that, Charles and Eagle Woman Galpin, Running Antelope, Bear Rib, and Two Bear (who had adopted the priest as his koda) were among the seventy men and ten women Eagle Woman later said she chose to accompany the priest. They left on June 3. The Yanktonai Blue Thunder drove De Smet's carriage, its dashboard emblazoned with a large black cross. At the end of a day's travel, the Indians would "talk and argue on the affairs of the day, tell stories, [and] . . . laugh and joke" until bedtime. On one occasion, Galpin translated when the priest entertained Two Bear, Running Antelope, Mad Bear, and Bear Rib with tales of his extensive travels.[6]

Disputes inevitably arose. When someone accused Blue Thunder of theft, De Smet sympathized, conceding that wrongful accusations happened often, and he recommended a good night's sleep. The prescription worked. Another time, when Running Antelope and Two Bear argued over choosing a campsite, De Smet soothed them with a feast of sugared rice in his tent. Soon the two were laughing together. Mostly, the trip was enjoyable. When they stayed in camp all one day because Galpin was ill, the young men fished, smoked, or slept to pass the time.

De Smet, suffering from Grave's disease and feeling unwell, asked Galpin to keep a journal for him to use in accounts he would write later. One day, Galpin recorded Two Bear's long speech "on the great merits of the expedition." He "spoke most earnestly, that favorable results

---

[4]Wood, "Gen. De Trobriand," 4–7, 9; De Trobriand, *Army Life*, 104–11, 117–18, 124–26; Wherry, "Types and Traditions"; De Trobriand journal, 16 Oct. 1867, 92, 95–96; and Fort Stevenson PR, July & Oct. 1867, reel 1227, M617, NA.

[5]Adams, *Harney*, 105–106, 179, 186–91; and Pfaller (ed.), "Galpin Journal," 3–4.

[6]Pfaller, "Galpin Journal," 12; and Garraghan, "Father De Smet's Sioux Peace Mission," 141–63.

might ensue," but Galpin thought Running Antelope expressed "more enthusiasm, if not equal sincerity, on the same subject." Another time, Two Bear proved his reputation as a braggart when, faced with finding a campsite in a heavy evening fog, he boasted of being probably the only man in the country, perhaps even in the world, who could find his way at night or in a fog. Sure enough, he did find a beautiful spot.[7]

Near the Little Missouri River crossing, the travelers paused at a burial scaffold to mourn a warrior who died fighting the Crows. By now, De Smet seemed to be winning over the few skeptics among his escort. One evening, White Ghost, who had fought whites, visited De Smet's tent. According to Galpin, he "coldly put forth his hand" and said, "Sir, since we left I have been studying you. I have made up my mind that you are a great and good man, and withal a very brave one. As I have always thought well of the brave, it does my heart good to look at you."[8]

Generally, the weather was good but sometimes sweltering in this "Moon When the Ponies Shed." Traveling became harder near the Little Missouri badlands. On June 9, De Smet sent ahead four men with tobacco, the accepted invitation to important talks. When they did not return within a week, Two Bear spoke to the disheartened group, urging them not to despair in their important mission of peace. Finally, on June 16, the envoys returned with eighteen warriors who said Four Horns accepted De Smet's tobacco. One warrior expressed pleasure at De Smet's presence and confirmed the Powder River bands' willingness to listen to him. If they would not disclose the location or bring soldiers there, these men would escort the delegation to the camp. That settled, Running Antelope invited them to his tipi for a feast. Eagle Woman years later recalled this meeting differently: someone in the party told her Sitting Bull intended to kill the entire Fort Rice delegation when they arrived at the camp, but even after she told her husband and the priest of the threat, they decided to proceed.

On June 19, within view of Powder River, the head chiefs Four Horns and Black Moon led some 500 warriors toward them.[9] De Smet unfurled

[7]Vestal (Campbell), *Sitting Bull*, 98; Chittenden & Richardson, *Life, Letters*, vol. 3, 903–905, and vol. 4, 1221–22; Terrell, *Black Robe*, 365–68; Carricker, *Father Peter John De Smet*, 219–21; Pfaller, *Father De Smet in Dakota*, 67–68, and "Galpin Journal," 8–10; and Utley, *Lance*, 99. Two Bear characterization in Pell to Sully, 26 Oct. and 1 Nov. 1864, OR, vol. 53, "Supplement," pp. 599–602.

[8]Pfaller, "Galpin Journal," 12.

[9]Chittenden & Richardson, *Life, Letters*, vol. 3, 909–12; Pfaller, "Galpin Journal," 15–16; Holley, *Once Their Home*, 304–306; and Vestal (Campbell), *Sitting Bull*, 100.

a religious banner—his "standard of peace"—with an image of Virgin Mary on one side and the name Jesus on the other. Eagle Woman recalled how he wept and his hands shook as he donned his vestments. The odd banner gave the reception committee momentary pause, but they advanced toward the priest and, after what Galpin described as a convivial reunion between the groups, led the Fort Rice delegation into camp through a well-dressed crowd of perhaps 5,000. According to Eagle Woman, however, this meeting was considerably less amiable. She remembered well-armed Powder River Indians dressed for war and wearing black war paint. She recalled them ordering Thunder Hawk, armed and riding between her and De Smet, to move back, but Thunder Hawk refused to leave them unprotected as the warriors "took charge" of the Fort Rice group. As their horses walked slowly toward the camp with Galpin carrying the priest's banner, a man broke from the oncoming Indians to greet Eagle Woman, and when the major chiefs rode up, they also greeted her warmly before greeting the others. When someone warned her to stay away from the white men in case someone decided to kill them, she disregarded the precaution. Galpin gave Pizi (Gall) the priest's banner to hold for a moment, but Pizi, misunderstanding, kept it (and still had it years later). Then Eagle Woman heard someone cry "*Ouspa!*" ("Hold him!") as someone stopped Gray Eagle's brother from taking aim with an arrow. A Miniconjou man shouted that he would have killed her and the whites had they come to his camp.

Nevertheless, all made it safely to the camp, and because the priest was too tired to speak then, war chief Sitting Bull offered him and the Galpins his lodge to rest in. De Smet awoke after a nap to find Black Moon, Four Horns, Sitting Bull, and another war chief, No Neck, watching over him. A guard of twenty akicita was always with De Smet and the Galpins because, according to a code these Sioux had adopted, anyone who lost a kinsman to a white man had the right to revenge by killing the first white person they encountered. Blue Thunder's presence among De Smet's party was also problematic because, as a scout, he had fought his own people. The warrior White Gut threatened him, "Last time I shot you in the leg; this time I'll kill you." Later, Little Soldier told Sitting Bull biographer Stanley Vestal (Walter Stanley Campbell) that White Gut wanted to kill De Smet even more than he wanted to kill Blue Thunder. Although Galpin must have known he, too, was in danger, he wrote instead about how Eagle Woman "was called to every lodge in the village and was treated with great respect and kindness."[10]

On June 20, 1868, talks began in a shelter made up of many lodges joined together to accommodate a crowd. Galpin described how De Smet "was escorted to a spot in the center where four buffalo robes had been spread for seats." Four Horns and Black Moon, holding their pipes, sat facing them. The 500 warriors sat behind war chiefs Sitting Bull, White Gut, Pizi, and No Neck, while onlookers filled the remaining half-acre space. After dancing, singing, and other ceremonial preliminaries, a head chief introduced De Smet. In a letter later, the priest summarized what he told them: He had "disinterested motives" in coming to warn them they were no match for the American military and to point out that their war could only be one of attrition. He urged them to listen to the commissioners at Fort Rice tell how the government would help them with farms and education. He assured them they would not have to give up all their land.[11]

Black Moon believed De Smet's words were sincere, but this cruel war begun by Cheyennes and Eastern Sioux, he said, left his country desolate and impoverished. Buffalo were scarce; he blamed whites for killing more of the Indians' animals than they needed for food and for decimating their forests. "We have been forced to hate the whites. Let them treat us like brothers and the war will cease." Black Moon admitted De Smet showed them "a glimpse of a better future," and he offered to forget the past and send representatives to Fort Rice to hear the commissioners. "[If] their words are acceptable, peace will be made."[12]

In his turn, Sitting Bull admitted he shed the blood of many white men but only after whites provoked war and had been unjust to Indian families. He would heed De Smet and, "whatever is done by others, I will submit to, and for all time to come be a friend of the whites." He sat, then turned to the assemblage of onlookers behind him to ask if they had heard him. They responded enthusiastically, and he added that he would sell no land to whites, whom he wanted to stop harvesting trees, especially oaks, which "stand wintry storms and summer heats, and like ourselves seem to flourish by them." The cheering lasted several minutes.[13]

---

[10]Pfaller, "Galpin's Journal," 16–17. For No Neck, see Papandrea, *They Never Surrendered*, 6–7; Vestal (Campbell), *Sitting Bull*, 100–101; Terrell, *Black Robe*, 368–72; Carricker, *Father Peter John De Smet*, 221–22; De Smet report of 1868 Powder River talks, box 1, Sanborn Papers, MNHS Archives (hereafter cited as De Smet report); Holley, *Once Their Home*, 303–10; and Slaughter, "Leaves," 227, 239, 258, 273.

[11]Chittenden & Richardson, *Life, Letters,* vol. 3, 915; and De Smet report.

[12]Chittenden & Richardson, *Life, Letters,* vol. 3, 101–102.

[13]Quotes from Pfaller, "Galpin's Journal," 19.

When order was restored, Two Bear explained he had accompanied De Smet "not only to see some of the old comrades I traveled the warpath with, but to hear you talk, and see how you treat this, in my opinion, our best friend. The Whites love and respect him, so do I." The chiefs and braves escorting the priest, Two Bear said, represented some 700 lodges and were committed to following De Smet's advice to be "guided by the men sent by the President to accomplish something definite for our future good." Two Bear would "leave with a heart full of joy, with hopes that you may ever continue to be friends with the Whites, and that this cruel war that has so long been hanging around us will soon be over."[14]

Running Antelope blamed the current trouble on the Santees but said the day's council gave him pleasure and hope for the future. He would return to his Fort Rice camp with a lighter heart, and he assured his audience those who met the commissioners would "not return displeased."[15]

On June 21, De Smet and his party, accompanied by approximately 300 Powder River people, left on their 350-mile return journey. Galpin stopped making diary entries, explaining in his last that De Smet had resumed his own journal.[16] As they neared Fort Rice, De Smet sent ahead a courier with his and Galpin's accounts of the council. In his, Galpin alerted General Terry of De Smet's frailty. The messenger brought back Terry's note offering the priest the commissioners' and the nation's gratitude. When De Smet rode into Fort Rice, a long line of Sioux held their feathered lances high in tribute. Now the conference could begin.

On July 2, 1868, the delegation joined Generals Terry, Harney, and Sanborn and the thousands of Indians who had come to Fort Rice to discuss the proposed treaty. Interpreters included Frank La Frambois, Basil Clement, Louis Agaard, Charles Primeau, and Nick Janisse. Ben Arnold, who spoke and understood Sioux, watched as "dozens of shorthand writers, clerks, news reporters, and interpreters took advantageous positions and others took what was left." Father De Smet took no part in the conference except to sign the documents as a witness.[17]

Harney spoke first. The president wanted Indians to live peacefully, to have homes, churches, plowed fields, and schools so their children would "learn to read and write and grow up in the ways of civilization."

---

[14]Ibid., pp. 19–20.

[15]Ibid., pp. 20–21.

[16]Pfaller, "Galpin's Journal," 19–21; Garraghan, *Jesuits*, 79–80n21; De Smet report; and Chittenden & Richardson, *Life, Letters*, vol. 3, 915–17.

[17]Chittenden & Richardson, *Life, Letters*, vol. 3, 919–22; Terrell, *Black Robe*, 372–77; Carricker, *Father Peter John De Smet*, 222–27; and Larson, *Gall*, 67–69, 73.

The government, he said, was run by good men who made laws which "must be obeyed by everyone." He complimented the Indians' own great men for whom he had "respect for their natural intelligence and understanding." Reminding them that every nation had good and bad people, Harney defined the good as those who were obedient to the law, the bad as disobedient. "You are today living in a country owned by the 'Great Father.' You are his children. He wants you to live on the piece of land reserved for you and live at peace."[18]

Harney announced that although the Bozeman Trail forts would close, the Upper Missouri forts would be "kept as a protection to the country, to preserve law." He delineated the proposed reserve's boundaries in his unequivocal style, telling the Indians they would relinquish all land east of the Missouri, leaving them the country "between the Missouri on the east, the Yellowstone on the north, the Big Horn mountains on the west, and the Platte River on the south, from Platte Bridge eastward to the forks of the North and South Platte . . . thence north to the Niobrara and down it to the Missouri." He assured them no white men would be allowed on the reserve, no white man's livestock could graze there, and no hunters or immigrants could traverse it. Harney detailed the more mundane treaty points regarding distributions of clothing, food, farm implements, household items, and tools. They would receive rations semimonthly. They would have cows for milk and oxen to use for plowing and then later, mares, wagons, and harnesses.

It is not clear from Arnold's account that Harney got across the finer points of the treaty. Did the Indians realize, for instance, that although the Sioux, Arapahos, and Cheyennes could hunt west of the Black Hills "so long as the buffalo may range thereon in such numbers as to justify the chase," that the government did not expect this to be a long period of time? Did they realize that in order to receive the food aid and agricultural help the treaty promised, they would have to move near the Missouri River? Did they realize they had to allow "railroads, wagon roads, mail-stations, or other works of utility or necessity which may be ordered or permitted by the laws of the United States" within the reserve's borders? They may not have realized that provisos in the treaty chipped away at Sioux sovereignty and were meant to destroy the traditional Sioux way of life in order to facilitate their assimilation into contemporary American life.[19]

[18]Harney's speech is in Crawford, *Exploits*, 146, 162–66.
[19]Ostler, *Plains Sioux and U.S. Colonialism*, 49–51.

As the highest-ranking delegate from the militant bands, Pizi rose to speak first. While the Hunkpapa band was trading at Fort Berthold in the 1866–67 winter, the part Hunkpapa, part Arikara Bloody Knife, for his own reasons, had convinced Captain Bassett to order his Fourth usv soldiers to capture Pizi and, if he resisted, to kill him. Bloody Knife led the soldiers to Pizi's tipi, and when Pizi emerged, a soldier bayoneted him through his side. After being stabbed twice more, he fell unconscious in the snow and the soldiers left him for dead. Although Pizi survived, the incident was important enough that Long Soldier included it in his 1866–67 Hunkpapa winter count.[20]

The official record of Pizi's Fort Rice speech is less interesting than Arnold's translation, which he accompanied with a description of Pizi as "striking" and evincing "a proud and independent spirit." He began speaking slowly and distinctly, then "became more impassioned" until he was "the impersonation of defiance, of one wronged and dishonored." Pauses and dramatic gestures punctuated his indictment of the Great Father's broken promises. The wounds the soldiers at Berthold inflicted were not healed, he said, and threw off his long skin robe to stand before his audience in only his embroidered broadcloth breechcloth and beaded moccasins decorated with dyed porcupine quills. "Your hands are red with blood," he told the whites while stretching out his arms dramatically to allow everyone to see blood trickle from one of his wounds. Pizi vowed never to shake hands with the commissioners or sign a treaty until the forts were gone and steamboats stopped traveling the Upper Missouri.[21]

Arnold, who perhaps did not realize that Running Antelope was not representing the Powder River group, thought that Running Antelope was a more polished orator and more "ornate and conciliatory" than Pizi, but he deemed Antelope "less rugged and fearless" and less a leader. Running Antelope praised Harney in his speech, saying that, except for De Smet, he had "never met a white man with any sense" since meeting him in 1856. He said he liked Galpin, too, and wanted him to remain in Indian country as a trader.

---

[20]Crawford, *Exploits*, 165–66; and Chittenden & Richardson, *Life, Letters*, vol. 3, 918. De Smet heard the story directly from Pizi. See also Larson, *Gall*, 56–57; Innis, *Bloody Knife*, 33, 40–41, 46–47; Taylor, *Kaleidoscopic Lives*, 143–59; De Trobriand, *Army Life*, 265–66, 265n30; De Trobriand journal, 11 Apr. 1868; Candace Greene and Thornton, *Year the Stars Fell*, 259; and Canfield, "An Army Wife," 58.

[21]Cf. Pizi's speech in Vanderwerth, *Indian Oratory*, 184–85; Crawford, *Exploits*, 170–71; and Vestal (Campbell), *New Sources*, 225–29. Vestal reprinted the official version; Crawford's (a.k.a. Arnold's) translation is his own and first-hand, though possibly literarily embellished.

The Indians asked the commissioners to persuade the Yanktons to allow their reservation to become part of the new reserve. The Lakotas also wanted the Yanktonais to give up their James River hunting grounds and move to the Great Sioux Reservation. (Some Yanktonais did relocate, but the Yanktons kept their reservation separate.)

Despite his ebullient speech, Pizi (as Man-Who-Goes-in-the-Middle) signed the treaty. Arnold guessed Pizi only signed because the commissioners "almost put the chiefs and headmen under duress by the display of presents" they gave those who touched the pen. Whatever his reasons for signing, Pizi did return to Black Moon's camp loaded with presents. The Senate ratified the treaty that became known as the Laramie Treaty of 1868 on February 16, 1869, and President Johnson signed it into law eight days later.[22]

IN MAY 1868, GENERAL SULLY TOOK OVER THE DISTRICT OF THE Upper Arkansas and, unlike his predecessors, gave the Cheyenne the guns and ammunition that had been promised to them at their treaty signing. Because Sioux, Arapaho, and Cheyenne warriors were attacking white settlements along the Solomon and Saline Rivers—stealing livestock, killing whites, and raping white women—Sully's generosity displeased Sherman and his new Department of the Missouri commander, General Phil Sheridan. Sheridan subsequently prepared a campaign and assigned Colonel George Forsyth to punish the perpetrators.

On September 17, Cheyenne Dog Soldiers and their allies seriously wounded Forsyth in a battle on an island on the Arikaree fork of the Republican River and killed Lieutenant Frederick H. Beecher. Cheyenne chief Roman Nose and several other Indians also died during the Battle of Beecher's Island. Afterward, General Sherman wrote his brother John, a U.S. senator, that "the more [Indians] we can kill this year, the less will have to be killed the next war." He was convinced "they have all to be killed, or be maintained as a species of paupers."[23]

---

[22]Kappler, *Indian Affairs*, vol. 2, *Laws and Treaties*, 1006n3; Crawford, *Exploits*, 170–74; *Sioux Tribe v. USA*, 42 Indian Claims Commission 214, Docket 74, "Additional Findings of Fact," 250; Vestal (Campbell), *New Sources*, 225–30; Gonzalez and Cook-Lynn, *Politics of Hallowed Ground*, 345.

[23]Athearn, *Sherman*, 152, 224–25; Hutton, *Phil Sheridan*, 32–33, 38, 46–47; W.T. Sherman to John Sherman, 23 Sept. 1868, quoted in Athearn, *Sherman*, 223.

Sully, commanding from his ambulance bed while campaigning against Cheyenne and Arapaho raiders on the Cimarron River, encountered difficulties similar to those the 1865 Connor expedition endured. When Sully retreated to Fort Dodge, Sheridan asked Sherman for more men and more aggressive field generals. Sherman complied, and Sully was "unassigned" for a time. In November 1868, Black Kettle, who had survived Sand Creek, died along with his wife and many others when Lieutenant Colonel George A. Custer attacked a Sioux and Cheyenne camp on the Washita. The troops destroyed Indian property and imprisoned many people. Meanwhile, on the same campaign, Indians wiped out Major Joel Elliott's Seventh Cavalry detachment.[24] Such incidents encouraged vengeance, not peace. Nevertheless, several important headmen and chiefs signed the 1868 treaty that fall.

In October, the commissioners met in Chicago to debate future Indian policy. Tappan and Taylor, minus Henderson, argued for keeping the Indian Bureau separate under the U.S. Department of the Interior whereas the generals wanted the military to take over Indian matters. General Grant, the Republican nominee for president, who was there to observe, told a reporter that protection of settlers and emigrants was paramount, even if that meant the Indians' extermination.

The commissioners did reach consensus on one thing: the treaty system was not working. This was not a new thought. In an 1864 article in the *North American Review*, a writer named Whipple expressed succinctly what many American citizens, by 1868, realized, "We treat as an independent nation a people whom we will not permit to exercise one single element of that sovereign power which is necessary to a nation's existence." The 1868 treaties were some of the last made with American Indians.

In a November 23 letter, Harney summarized the 1868 treaty terms for General Sherman: War would stop. The reservation would be for the exclusive use of the Sioux. The government would provide subsistence and assistance to encourage Indians to abandon their nomadic lifestyle and adopt civilized ways. The Sioux, in turn, would settle on reservations and accept government support and instruction. The government's policy now was to maintain peaceful relations with Indians, who, it assumed, would benefit from civilization and Christianity. Moreover, the treaty

---

[24]Hutton, *Phil Sheridan*, 48–49; Welsh, *Medical Histories*, 327–28; Sully, *No Tears*, 216–18; Sherman, "Annual Report, 1 Oct. 1867"; Stimson, "Indian Question," 389; Utley, *Indian Frontier*, 122–27, and *Cavalier*, 52, 68–71, 75–76.

would save the country millions of dollars and thousands of lives. If Congress did not ratify it, Harney warned, a new war might ensue and end only with the Indians' extermination.[25]

Appointed commander of the military district enclosing this vast Great Sioux Reservation, Harney was to supervise and control the Sioux and "all issues and disbursements to them" subject only to his division commander, Sherman. However, for anything concerning the military, he reported to Department of Dakota commander Terry. Harney established his headquarters at Whetstone Creek on the Missouri fourteen miles below new Fort Sully. Ben Arnold, who, with friends, contracted to construct his buildings, noticed the Indians' confidence in Harney and how they "looked upon what he said as law." Indeed, Parmenus Turnley, who knew Harney since their days at Fort Pierre, once called Indians Harney's "favorite foe, and paradoxical as it may appear, about his only congenial friend[s]." Sitting Bull's biographer Vestal said the Sioux "respected [Harney's] common sense and straight-forward methods." Several old Indians assured Vestal that Harney was the "only white man they had ever met who could talk sense or tell the truth," except Father De Smet. They remembered Harney predicting, while at Pierre, that "within ten years, the Sioux and the whites would be fighting again." Had not Sully's fight at Killdeer Mountain and Red Cloud's war fulfilled that prophecy?[26]

The government shut off trade on the Platte River to force Spotted Tail's band north to the Great Sioux Reservation, but they would not live on the Missouri River. Instead, they successfully lobbied Harney for a location on the reservation near the forks of the White River. Only Sioux who frequented Forts Sully and Rice used the new Cheyenne River and Grand River agencies to claim rations due them by the treaty. No one wanted to live at the Whetstone location; the Upper Missouri Sioux considered it too far from their usual haunts. However, by late November, Harney persuaded the Laramie Loafer band to settle there. Sherman insisted, futilely, that roaming Indians like Sitting Bull's band go to their assigned agencies. Instead, less than two months after the talks on the Powder River, Sitting Bull led an attack on Fort Buford, killing three men and stealing the horse herd.

---

[25]*Sioux Tribe v. USA*, 42 Indian Claims Commission 214, Docket 74, "Additional Findings of Fact," 252–53. By an 1871 law, the government would never again recognize a group of Indians as an "independent nation, tribe, or power with whom the United States may contract by treaty."

[26]Crawford, *Exploits*, 166, 174–76; Turnley, *Reminiscences*, 130; and Vestal (Campbell), *New Sources*, 218–19.

Harney quickly spent the money Congress appropriated, then used his own to continue the work of forcing Indians to adapt to and ultimately adopt white culture. Communications between Harney and General Sanborn during this time have Harney begging for additional funding. In June 1869, Sherman replaced him with three army officers to oversee the three Sioux agencies within the Great Sioux Reservation. When Captain Poole, assigned to the Brulés and Oglalas at Whetstone, called on Harney for advice, Harney told him, "They are children, and you must deal with them as such."[27]

North of the reservation, trouble continued. On September 19, Harney stopped at Fort Rice to borrow an officer and a military escort to labor for a few months at the Grand River agency. While they were gone, some Sihasapas came to Rice to beg for food. The same day they arrived, a wood-chopping detail found the body of a private shot through the heart. That night, during a heavy rain, the post surgeon reported soldiers responding to an Indian alarm. The steamboat *Benton* also reported "Indian trouble as bad as ever" at Fort Buford.[28]

PRESIDENT ULYSSES S. GRANT, ELECTED IN NOVEMBER 1868, advocated a peace policy toward Indians that followed a plan his Seneca Civil War aide, General Parker, began drafting in 1867. To implement it, Grant appointed Parker commissioner of Indian affairs. Parker's plan had the War Department administering the Indian Department and instructing Indians to settle on reservations to learn farming or ranching. Believing peace-minded Quakers' anti-war views would influence Indians, Grant and Parker recruited Quakers as Indian superintendents and agents. This new peace policy made Indians subservient government wards with few human rights and no redress in U.S. courts.

In an effort to establish unity of purpose, the roaming Sioux made Sitting Bull head chief of all their bands. Unity would not be enough,

[27]Olson, *Red Cloud*, 83–85; Hyde, *Red Cloud's Folk*, 170; Fort Buford PR, May, Aug., Sept. 1868, reel 158, M617, NA; Carricker, *Father Peter John De Smet*, 228; Harney to Sanborn, 7 and 10 Aug. 1868, Sherman to Sanborn, 9 and 21 Aug. 1868 and 7 Jan. and 7 July 1869, in Sherman letters, box 1, Sanborn Papers, MNHS Archives; J.W.T., "Indian Question," dated St. Paul, Minn., 26 May 1869 in *New York Tribune*, 3 June 1869; Adams, *Harney*, 254–57, 282–83, 265–73; and Mattison, "Indian Reservation System," 146–47; and Poole, *Among the Sioux*, 15 ("They are children" quote).

[28]Dr. Washington Matthews, in *Medical History of Fort Rice*, journal entries 19 & 26 Sept., 14 Nov. 1868 (under "Misc. MP" in bibliography); and "Log of the Steamer Benton."

however, to safeguard their home country. The first transcontinental railroad was completed on May 10, 1869. Soon others would crisscross Indian country.[29]

THOSE WHO SETTLED IMMEDIATELY ON THE GREAT SIOUX Reservation saw 1868 as a turning point in their lives. Interviews conducted in the 1920s with elderly Sioux revealed how wrenching the attendant change was for them. Many separated their lives into two parts: the time when they were "hostile" and after they had "become white men."

Joseph Bob-Tail-Bear, brother of the deceased Big Head, offered this overview of his lifetime: Before 1868, "the Indian was brave, fought the enemy with bow and arrows, stone war clubs, and some of the young braves took the scalps of the enemy." Then the "white man came all around the camps and shot the Indians and took their guns, knives, and horses, also burned their tents or teepes, took some of the Indians prisoners. . . . The white man tried to kill all the Indians but today some of us lived to see the civilisation of some of the Indians." Even so, he remembered the grandfathers predicting younger Indians would fight again because the white man's laws would make them suffer. "I am not ashamed to tell you . . . that what my father and grandfathers told us in their lectures is all true." Bob-Tail-Bear, himself, predicted Indian children would live to see whites buy all the Indian land and chase them from it. Despite his misgivings, he tried to adapt to reservation life, even serving on the Indian police force for a year. At first, he lived in a log cabin north of Standing Rock. "I was quiet and didn't cause any trouble with any one, up until now. Today I am old and live neighbor to a white man." His fourth wife—he had "donated away [divorced] three women in the hostile days"—was dead; now he lived alone in the house he had occupied for thirty-one years.

The interviewer suggested the men answer his questions in a way that would tell their children and grandchildren about their lives. Bob-Tail-Bear advised his progeny to educate their children and "keep civil relations." They should "Christianize" themselves and their children.

---

[29]Utley, *Indian Frontier*, 129–34; see overview in Garfield, "Indian Question in Congress," 29–34; Pfaller, *Father De Smet in Dakota*, 63–64; Adams, *Harney*, 278; and Vestal (Campbell), *New Sources*, 228.

"Today this is the life I lead, to be moral and be awful careful with your reputation, and . . . be responsible [for] your own life."[30]

IN SPITE OF 1868 PROMISES THAT INDIAN LAND WOULD BE inviolate, within a few years mobs of people were passing through the choicest Sioux hunting grounds on their way to the Black Hills. Almost as soon as the treaty went into effect, Captain P. B. Davy, a Minnesota man who led several expeditions overland to the Montana mines, tried to organize a company to explore the Black Hills where rumors, not only of gold, but also of coal, iron, and timber wealth tempted whites. The government quashed Davy's and others' illegal expeditions, but eventually sporadic waves of potential exploiters became an unstoppable tsunami.[31] By 1877, whites had taken the Black Hills, and a decade later the Great Sioux Reservation was further diminished.

As the years wore on, trouble between whites and Indians became more complicated, but because the conflicts often remained local, they went unnoticed by the wider world until some upheaval like the Battle of the Little Bighorn or the Wounded Knee events of 1890 and the 1970s caught the public's attention. Against all the odds nineteenth-century observers gave them, the Sioux have increased in numbers, retained their identities, and revived or preserved their traditions. Today Sioux use advanced college degrees and the federal court system to redress some of the "terrible justice" visited upon them since first contact with Europeans.

---

[30]Bob-Tail-Bear interview in Murphy Collection, SHSND Archives.
[31]Crawford, *Exploits*, 166; and Parker, *Gold*, 21.

Chapter 20

Conclusion

AN UNNAMED SIOUX AT THE 1868 FORT RICE MEETING VOICED how Harney's 1855 invasion of Sioux country, the Santees' 1862 war, and the attendant Sully expeditions had at first melded, then corroded, an age-old unity forged by tradition and tempered through time. In the past "whenever Indians wished to do anything, they all tried to do it together. Now our nation is divided. What caused this? The whites."[1]

What can we conclude about the overall effects of the interaction between soldiers and Sioux chiefs on the Upper Missouri during the period 1854–68? General Harney's 1855 invasion of the Upper Missouri Sioux country eventually sent the entire Sioux Nation—including the southern, northern, and Minnesota bands—spiraling into instability. The subsequent advent of American soldiers required them all to make major adjustments to a new social order.

Of the panoply of officers who touched their lives, Harney seems to have impressed the Sioux most favorably. Like most of his countrymen, he was paternalistic; nevertheless, the Sioux respected him because he said what he meant and did what he said. In 1879, H. A. Stimson, member of a committee of missionaries formed to study the "Indian Question," recalled that in 1868 Harney told the Sioux, "If my Government does not keep this agreement, I will come back and ask the first Indian I meet to shoot me." Stimson pointed out, however, that "General Harney does not revisit the Sioux."[2]

General Sully, even as he waged total war against the Sioux, appeared to respect them, and yet some of his comments indicate ambivalence. Some few officers, after extended contact in circumstances other than war, shed preconceptions and prejudices about the Sioux (and other Indians) in the face of reality. In his journal, General De Trobriand reflected, "The longer I live among these children of the desert and the more I read the official documents relating to Indian affairs, the more I have modified the ideas I

---

[1]Vestal, *New Sources*, 228.

[2]Adams, *Harney*, 270–73. Stimson, "The Indian Question," 397. See entire essay, 395–401. Stimson cites Bishop Whipple in *Faribault Democrat*, 5 Jan. 1877, for the Harney quote.

brought with me. The sum total of the wrongs done to these poor redskins surpasses any conception."[3] Yet here is pity and paternalism, not respect.

When Indians killed soldiers, the soldiers' comrades sometimes felt justified in exacting vengeance from any Indian they encountered just as the Powder River Sioux considered it justice to avenge their people by killing the first white person they saw. War tends to skew a society's normal sense of justice; warriors of any culture are encouraged to depersonalize the enemy. Sully ordering enemy heads severed and the Sioux condoning indiscriminate revenge: these were counter to the norms of each society while at peace. Later, but not too late to be relevant to this discussion, Major James M. Walsh of the North-West Mounted Police came to know well Sitting Bull and his followers during their sojourn in Canada. He judged them to be "very intelligent people possessing a strong sence of justice." He pronounced them "very capable of judging between right and wrong, truthful and honorable, faithful as a friend."[4]

How people interpret the past is often more important than what actually happened. For example, the 1853 amendment to the 1851 Laramie Treaty that some Sioux chiefs signed limited the original's duration to ten years (with five added by the president), rather than the fifty years discussed at the Horse Creek council. Either being unaware of, discounting, or not understanding the amendment, the Oglala Man-Afraid-of-his-Horses spoke in 1868 of the treaty General Mitchell made in 1851 as binding the government to provide annuities for the longer period. Years later, Spotted Tail also spoke of the 1851 treaty as a fifty-year promise.[5] In his 1870 Cooper Union address, Red Cloud said,

> In 1868 men came out and brought papers. We could not read them, and they did not tell us what was in them. We thought the treaty was to remove the forts, and that we should then cease from fighting. But they wanted to send us traders on the Missouri. We did not want to go to the Missouri, but wanted traders where we were. When I reach Washington, the Great Father explained to me what the treaty was, and showed me that the interpreters had deceived me. . . . I have tried to get from the Great Father what is right and just. I have not altogether succeeded.[6]

The Sioux would soon lose the Black Hills, their hunting grounds west of there, and, after winning their pyrrhic victory at the Little Bighorn

---

[3]David Miller et al., *History of the Assiniboine and Sioux*, 54–55; De Trobriand, *Army Life*, 87–91, 255, 259–62; and De Trobriand journal, 31 March, 2 April, and 22 Sept. 1867.

[4]LaDow, *Medicine Line*, 55.

[5]Anderson, "Controversial Sioux Amendment," 207–10.

[6]Vanderwerth, *Indian Oratory*, 188–89; and Ostler, *Plains Sioux and U.S. Colonialism*, 51.

battle, they would forfeit their guns, horses, and even more freedom. Later, they would sacrifice yet more reservation land. The list of Indian relinquishments is long.

American soldiers' military conflict with the Sioux ended in the 1890s, yet fewer than two decades passed until Sioux, even while being denied U.S. citizenship, began serving with distinction alongside U.S. soldiers in a new century's wars. Yanktons were among the first American Indians to flummox the enemy by using their own language as code in both World Wars.

Today, many Sioux live traditionally and worship in their own way, although most are comfortable in the ambiance of the twenty-first century. American Indians became citizens by law in 1924, and if courtroom battles attracted the same attention nineteenth-century military conflicts did, it would be obvious that some Sioux still fight to obtain justice. Even though the Sioux Nation won an $88,345,465 settlement for the Black Hills in 1980, they have vowed, as a sovereign entity, not to accept the money or the substantial interest it has accrued in trust since then. Instead, they want the Black Hills, which their lawyers continue to argue are theirs by the 1868 treaty.

It was this last treaty—after 1868 the documents resulting from negotiations with Sioux leaders and the U.S. government were called "agreements"—that has proved a benchmark. Restoring all it promised would not solve the Sioux's modern dilemmas, although it has figured in a few. In 2003, when a white army recruiter assaulted a young Oglala woman, she sued the government. Her lawyer won using the provision in the 1868 treaty promising government reimbursement for losses due to "bad" white men committing "wrong against the person." In federal claims court on April 28, 2009, Judge Francis M. Allegra ordered the government to pay her $600,000 in damages.[7]

The treaty's influence continues, as does the struggle for justice. Admittedly, Mato-cu-wi-hu and his son Bear Rib, Two Bear, Struck-by-the-Ree, Lone Horn, G. K. Warren, W. F. Raynolds, W. S. Harney, John Pattee, and Alfred Sully lacked the charisma of a Custer, a Crazy Horse, a Sitting Bull. Yet many of these lesser-known participants in Upper Missouri history during those consequential years between 1854 and 1868 have influenced generations.

---

[7]*Elk v. US*, Docket 96, 1–37; and Gruchow, "Native Woman Wins Unprecedented Case," *Argus Leader*, 30 April 2009.

Bibliography

The bibliography is organized in sections as follows: archival resources; government documents; articles, books, and papers; Internet resources; and legal documents.

Archival Resources
Custer National Cemetery, Little Bighorn Battlefield National Monument, Montana

"Record of Interments at Post Cemetery at Fort Rice, D.T."

Fort Union Trading Post National Historic Site (NHS) Library, Williston, North Dakota

Larpenteur, Charles. Journal. 2 vols., F 598 T46. [Erwin N. Thompson's annotated typescript of Larpenteur's journal.]

"Two Interesting Stories of Company I, 30th Infantry, Recruited in Eau Claire." June 28, 1927. Vertical file, HRF 0004. [Clipping from an unnamed Eau Claire, Wis., newspaper.]

U.S. Army. *General Orders, 1st U.S. Vol. Inf., 1862–1865*. Vol. Inf. F 594 U6 vol. 1. [The bound volume of photocopied handwritten papers also includes some 30th Wisconsin Volunteer Infantry orders.]

Henry E. Huntington Library, San Marino, California

Sweeny, Thomas William. Papers. SW 850.

Minnesota Historical Society (MNHS) Archives, St. Paul

Aldrich, Leonard. Papers, 1862–66, 1903. P950.

Brackett, Alfred B., Papers, 1861–68. P1568.

Cambell, George T., Papers. A/-C174.

Dakota Conflict of 1862 Manuscript Collection. P1369 and M582, 4 reels. Duplicated at SHSND as MSS 4378. [Diaries, letters, and reminiscences from

Sibley's 1863 and Sully's 1863, 1864, and 1865 NW Sioux expeditions.] U.S. War Department, Fort Ridgely documents.

Doud, George W., Diaries. P2240.

Dwelle, Merrill. Papers. A/.D989.

Fisk, Andrew J., Papers. P622 M538.

The Fort Sully Independent, 1:1, 16 Sept. 1855 [*sic* 1865] in Brackett Papers P1568.

Gregory, Bruguier and Geowey. Papers. Fort Union Papers, 1863–77. BC2.3/. G822bg.

Hatch, Edwin A.C., Papers. P1437.

Hubbell, James Boyd. Papers, 1834, 1865–1906. A/m.H876.

Jenkins, David N., Papers. P2115.

Marshall, Eugene. Letters in Brackett Papers P1568.

McLaren, Robert Neil. Papers, 1862–77. A/.M161.

Northrup, George W., Letters, 1852–65. A/m.N877g.

Overholt, Nicholas. Diaries, 1863–65. M374

Patch, Edward. Diary, 1846–63. A/.P294.

Regan, James C., Song. Co. A, Brackett's Minnesota Battalion in Brackett Papers P1568.

Rice, Ebenezer A., Diaries, 1864. M646.

Sanborn, John B., Papers, 1854–98. P1981.

Smith, J.A., Papers, 1828–93. P1329.

Sully, Alfred. Copy of Sully's GO 78, 30 Aug. 1864, Camp 39 in Brackett Papers P1568.

Washburn, Edson D., Diaries, 1863–65. P2244.

Watson, Charles Herbert. Letters, 1862–65, 1913. P958.

Historical Society of Missouri, St. Louis

Marsh, Elias Joseph. "Account of a Journey to the Northern Reaches of the Missouri River" [Handwritten journal]. C2599.

Montana State Historical Society Archives Collections, Helena

Benedict, Gilbert. Papers, 1865–67. SC 410.

Chouteau, Charles P., Report to Secretary of War John B. Floyd, 1859. Small Collection. SC 532.

Hilger, Nicholas. David Hilger Papers, 1867–1935. SC 854.

"Log of the *Shreveport*." In La Barge, Harkness & Company records, 1862–67. Fldr 2/2 SC 359.

Wilcox, Alvin H. "Up the Missouri River to Montana in the Spring of 1862," in "Alvin H. Wilcox Reminiscence, 1901–1904." SC 981 and MF 63B.

Nebraska State Historical Society, State Archives, Lincoln

Furnas, Robert Wilkinson. Papers, Furnas Journal, 1862–63, 1844–1905, SG 10. RG1, Microfilm reel 14, 13799.

New York State Library and Archives, Albany

Warren, Gouverneur Kemble. The Gouverneur Kemble Warren Papers, 1848–82. SC10668.

State Historical Society of North Dakota (SHSND) Archives, Bismarck

Beede, Aaron McGaffey. *Heart in the Lodge: "All a Mistake."* [Stage play booklet.] 1915. Filed as 812 B392.

Carter, Theodore. Manuscript. N.d. MSS 20007.

De Trobriand, Philippe Regis Denis de Keredern, Comte. "Vie Militaire Dans le Dakota." Translated by George Francis Will as "Army Life in Dakota." 1926. Typescript in de Trobriand Papers, 1866–69. MSS 10020.

Fort Rice ND Collection, 1864–1921. MS 10655. [Compilation of small manuscript collections.]

Libby, Orin Grant. Papers. A85.

Murphy, Henry. Henry Murphy Collection, 1926–28. [Biographical sketches of Indians.] MSS 20063.

Orland, Ole W. Papers, June 1864–October 1864. MSS 20442.

Patton, Charles E., Papers, 1861. MS 20028.

Porter, Hal P. Hal P. Porter scrapbooks, ca. 1941–54. [Miscellaneous materials in 3 volumes concerning the 1863 Whitestone Hill fight, MSS 10548.]

Wade, William Vose. Paha sapa tawoyak'e/William V. Wade. MSS 20038.

"Whitestone Battlefield: A History from 1863 to 1976: Historic Celebration at Whitestone Park on July 4–5, 1976." Dickey, N.Dak.: Whitestone Battlefield Park Bicentennial Year Celebration Committee, 1976. Filed as 978.454 W588, Dickey.

Zahn, Frank. Collection. MSS 10162, fldr 41P-008/3.

River Falls Area Research Center,
University of Wisconsin, River Falls

Johnston, James. Papers, 1837–1929. ca 1920, 1929. SC 307.

Price, Leonard R. "Colonel D. J. Dill and the Thirtieth Wisconsin Infantry on the Indian Frontier in the Civil War." Master's thesis, 1976.

Thomas, George. Diaries, 1862–75. SC 21.

South Dakota State Historical Society (SDSHS) Archives, Pierre

Deland, Charles E. Papers, 1890–1935. H69-5.

English, Abner M., Collection. H85.78.

Robinson, Doane. Collection, 1856–1946. H74.9.

Running Antelope. Letters, 1870–72, in H75-089, Box 3541B, Manuscript Collections. [Autobiography prepared for W.J. Hoffman at Grand River Agency, Great Sioux Reservation, 1873. Discussed in Mallery, *Picture Writing*, vol. 2.]

Wisconsin Historical Society Archives, Madison

Bryant, Edwin Eustace. Papers, 1864–88. SC 2819.

Clark, John G. "Colonel John G. Clark" [biographical sketch]. Wisconsin Writers Program Writings and Research Notes, 1935–42, box 14.

Hoyt, Otis. Papers, 1792–1921. File 1854 May 9. Oversize.

Meacham, Edgar A. Miscellaneous records of Civil War regiments, 1861–66, 1886. [Fort Thompson Crow Creek agency order book, Series 1204.]

Regimental Muster and Descriptive Rolls 1861–65. [Red books and Blue books for 30th Wisconsin Volunteer Infantry Regiment, ser. 1142, reel 16, and ser. 1144, reel 7. Original ledger books, identifiable by cover's color.]

Russell, Sidney Augustus. "Diary of Sidney Augustus Russell [d]uring service with Co. H, 50th Reg. Inf., Wisconsin Volunteers, Mar. 2 '65–June 14, '66." Wisc. Mss 239S. [Also MSS 20328 at SHSND.]

Yale Collection of Western Americana,
Beinecke Rare Book and Manuscript Library, New Haven, Connecticut

Dimon, Charles A.R., Papers. WA MSS S-1308.

Martin, Lambert A., Papers. WA MSS S-1036.

Raynolds, William Franklin. William Robertson Coe Collection. WA MSS 393.

GOVERNMENT DOCUMENTS

U.S. Bureau of the Census (in chronological order)

U.S. Bureau of the Census. "1860 U.S. Federal (8th) Census for Dakota Territory." RG 29, Reel M653, National Archives.

U.S. Bureau of the Census. "Indian Census Rolls, Standing Rock Reservation, 1885–1940." Reel 547, M595, RG 75, National Archives.

U.S. Department of the Interior
Annual Reports of Commissioner of Indian Affairs
(cited as CIA annual reports)
(in chronological order)

U.S. Department of the Interior. Bureau of Indian Affairs. *Annual Report of Orlando Brown.* 31st Cong., 1st sess., 1849. S. Doc. 1, serial 550, 937–1176.

U.S. Department of the Interior. Bureau of Indian Affairs. *Annual Report of George W. Manypenny.* 33rd Cong., 2nd sess., 1854. S. Doc. 1, serial 746, 211–544.

U.S. Department of the Interior. Bureau of Indian Affairs. *Annual Report of George W. Manypenny.* 34th Cong., 1st sess., 1855. S. Doc. 1, serial 810, 321–576.

U.S. Department of the Interior. Bureau of Indian Affairs. *Annual Report of J. W. Denver.* 35th Cong., 1st sess., 1857. S. Doc. 11, serial 919, 289–696.

U.S. Department of the Interior. Bureau of Indian Affairs. *Annual Report of Charles E. Mix.* 35th Cong., 2nd sess., 1858. S. Doc. 1, serial 974, 353–669.

U.S. Department of the Interior. Bureau of Indian Affairs. *Annual Report of A. B. Greenwood.* 36th Cong., 1st sess., 1859. S. Doc. 2, serial 1023, 373–820.

U.S. Department of the Interior. Bureau of Indian Affairs. *Annual Report of William P. Dole.* 37th Cong., 3rd sess., 1862. H. Doc. 1, serial 1157, 169–576.

U.S. Department of the Interior. Bureau of Indian Affairs. *Annual Report of William P. Dole.* 38th Cong., 1st sess., 1863. H. Doc. 1, serial 1182, 129–634.

U.S. Department of the Interior. Bureau of Indian Affairs. *Annual Report of William P. Dole.* 38th Cong., 2nd sess., 1864. H. Doc. 1, serial 1220, 147–651.

U.S. Department of the Interior. Bureau of Indian Affairs. *Annual Report of D. N. Cooley.* 39th Cong., 1st sess., 1865. H. Doc. 1, serial 1248, 169–772.

U.S. Department of the Interior. Bureau of Indian Affairs. *Annual Report of D. N. Cooley.* 39th Cong., 2nd sess., 1866. H. Doc. 1, serial 1284, 1–362.

Other Congressional and BIA Reports
(in chronological order)

U.S. Department of the Interior. U.S. Bureau of Indian Affairs. Letters Sent, 1858. M298, Reel 60, MNHS Archives.

U.S. Senate. *Condition of the Indian Tribes: Report of the Joint Special Committee Appointed under Joint Resolution of March 3, 1865.* 39th Cong., 2nd sess., 1867. S. Rep. 156 (known as the Doolittle Report).

U.S. Department of the Interior, U.S. Bureau of Indian Affairs. *Papers Relating to Talks and Councils Held with the Indians in Dakota and Montana Territories in the Years 1866–1869.* Washington D.C.: U.S. Government Printing Office, 1910.

U.S. Senate. *Report to the Senate on the Origins and Progress of Indian Hostilities on the Frontier*. 40th Cong., 2nd sess., 1867. S. Doc. 13.

"Records of Special Commission to Investigate the Fetterman Massacre and the State of Indian Affairs, 1867." M740, RG 75, National Archives. [Includes Dr. C. M. Hines's testimony to the special commission.]

U.S. House. *Report to the President by the Indian Peace Commission*. 40th Cong., 2nd sess., 1868. H. Doc. 97.

U.S. Department of War
National Archives and Records Administration (NARA)

National Archives Branch Depository, Washington, D.C. Records of the Adjutant General's Office, 1780s–1917. RG 94.

National Archives Branch Depository, Washington, D.C. Records of United States Army Commands, 1784–1821. RG 98.

National Archives Branch Depository, Washington, D.C. Records of United States Army Continental Commands, 1821–1920. RG 393.

Miscellaneous Military Papers

Billings, John S. *Report on Barracks and Hospitals with Descriptions of Military Posts*. Circular No. 4, War Department General Surgeon's Office. New York: Sol Lewis, 1974.

Campbell, Albert H. *Report Upon the Pacific Wagon Roads*. 35th Cong., 2nd sess., 1857. H. Doc. 108.

"Council with the Sioux Indians At Fort Pierre" [and related documents]. 34th Cong., 1st sess., 1856. S. Doc. 94 and H. Doc. 130.

Engagement Between United States Troops and Sioux Indians. 33rd Cong., 2nd sess., 1855. H. Doc. 63.

General Alfred Sully's Company of Yankton Sioux Indian Scouts. 57th Cong., 1st sess., 1901. S. Doc. 298, vol. 20 [misc. doc.]

Kimball, James P., and Washington Matthews. "Locality and History of Fort Buford, Dakota Territory." In *Medical History of Fort Buford*, vol. 198. RG 94, Adj. Gen.'s Office, National Archives.

Letter from the Secretary of War Transmitting in Response to Resolution of February 11, 1887, Report of Colonel Carrington on the Massacre Near Fort Philip Kearny. 49th Cong., 2nd sess., 1887. S. Doc. 97.

Medical History of Fort Rice, 1864–1878. Series 31141 at SHSND Archives. RG 94, Adj. Gen.'s Office, National Archives.

Pope, John. *Report of an Exploration of the Territory of Minnesota*. 31st Cong., 1st sess., 1850. S. Doc. 42.

"Proceedings of a Board of Commissioners Appointed to Negotiate a Treaty or Treaties with the Hostile Indians of the Upper Missouri." 1866. Manuscript 20485 at SHSND Archives.

Raynolds, William F. Raynolds expedition official reports. 40th Cong., 1st sess., 1868. S. Doc. 77.

"Records Relating to Investigation of the Ft. Philip Kearny or Fetterman Massacre." Reel 1, M740, RG 75, National Archives. [Also in Special Case files, NARA records microfilmed by SDSHS Archives, reel 1582.]

Sackett, Delos B. *Report of Delos B. Sackett.* 39th Cong., 2nd sess., 8 May 1866. H. Doc. 23.

Secretary of War. "Expedition of Brigadier General Sully against the Northwest Indians" (appendix). 38th Cong., 1st sess., vol. 5. H. Doc. 97.

Sherman, W. T., Gen. "Annual Report of Lt. Gen. W. T. Sherman, 1 Oct. 1867." In *Report of the Secretary of War, 1867.* 40th Cong., 2nd sess., 1867. H. Doc. 1, pt. 1, serial 1314.

Sully, Alfred, Gen. Abstracts of letters from Sully to Asst. Adj. Gen., Dept. NW, 30 June 1864 and 21 July 1864. Filed together at RG 393, P 601 CB 1864, National Archives.

Testimony of Col. H. B. Carrington, 18th U.S. Inf. before the Commission investigating his operations in Dakota and the Mountain District, 1866. Special Case files, NARA records microfilmed by SDSHS Archives, reel 5035.

Articles, Books, and Papers

Adams, George Rollie. *General William S. Harney, Prince of Dragoons.* Lincoln: University of Nebraska Press, 2001.

Albers, Everett C., and D. Jerome Tweton, eds. *The Way It Was, North Dakota Frontier Experience.* Book 5, *Native People.* Fessenden, N.Dak.: Grass Roots Press, 2002.

Ambrose, Stephen E. *Crazy Horse and Custer: The Parallel Lives of Two American Warriors.* New York: Anchor Books, 1996. First published 1975 by Doubleday.

Anderson, Gary Clayton. *Kinsmen of Another Kind, Dakota-White Relations in the Upper Mississippi Valley, 1650–1862.* Reprinted with new material. St. Paul: Minnesota Historical Society Press, 1997. First published 1984 by University of Nebraska Press.

———. *Little Crow: Spokesman for the Sioux.* St. Paul: Minnesota Historical Society, 1986.

Anderson, Gary Clayton, and Alan R. Woolworth. *Through Dakota Eyes: Narrative Accounts of the Minnesota Indian War of 1862.* St. Paul: Minnesota Historical Society Press, 1988.

Anderson, Harry H. "The Controversial Sioux Amendment to the Fort Laramie Treaty of 1851." *Nebraska History* 37 (Sept. 1956): 201–20.

Andreas, A. T. *Andreas' History of the State of Nebraska*. Chicago: Western Historical Co., 1882.

Andrist, Ralph K. *The Long Death: The Last Days of the Plains Indians*. Norman: University of Oklahoma Press, 1964.

Antrei, Albert. "Father Pierre Jean DeSmet [*sic*]." *Montana The Magazine of Western History* 13, no. 2 (April 1963): 24–43.

Armstrong, Moses K. *The Early Empire Builders of the Great West*. St. Paul, Minn.: E.W. Porter, 1901.

———. *History and Resources of Dakota, Montana and Idaho*. 1866. Reprint, Fairfield, Wash.: Ye Galleon Press, 1967.

Athearn, Robert G. "The Firewagon Road." *Montana The Magazine of Western History* 20, no. 2 (April 1970): 2–19.

———. "The Fort Buford 'Massacre.'" *The Mississippi Valley Historical Review* 41, no. 4 (March 1955): 675–84.

———. *Forts of the Upper Missouri*. 1967. Reprint, Lincoln: University of Nebraska Press, 1972.

———. *Sherman and the Settlement of the West*. 1956. Reprint, Norman: University of Oklahoma Press, 1995.

Bakeman, Mary H., comp. and ed. *Legends, Letters and Lies: Readings about Inkpaduta and the Spirit Lake Massacre*. Roseville, Minn.: Park Genealogical Books, 2001.

Bandel, Eugene. *Frontier Life in the Army, 1854–1861*. Translated by Olga Bandel and Richard Jentre. Edited by Ralph P. Bieber. Philadelphia: Porcupine Press, 1974.

Barbier, Charles P. "Recollections of Ft. La Framboise in 1862 and the Rescue of Lake Chetak Captives." In *South Dakota Historical Collections*, vol. 11, compiled by the South Dakota State Historical Society, 232–46. Pierre, S.Dak.: State Publishing Co., 1922.

Barbour, Barton H. *Fort Union and the Upper Missouri Fur Trade*. Norman: University of Oklahoma Press, 2001.

Beam, D. C. "Reminiscence of Early Days in Nebraska." In *Transactions and Reports of the Nebraska State Historical Society*, vol. 3, 292–315. Fremont, Neb.: Hammond Bros. Printers, 1892.

Beck, Paul N. *The First Sioux War: The Grattan Fight and Blue Water Creek, 1854–1856*. Lanham, Md.: University Press of America, 2004.

———. *Inkpaduta, Dakota Leader*. Norman: University of Oklahoma Press, 2008.

Belden, George P. *The White Chief, or Twelve Years among the Wild Indians of the Plains, from the Diaries and Manuscripts of George P. Belden, the Adventurous White Chief, Soldier, Hunter, Trapper, and Guide*. Edited by James S. Brisbin. Cincinnati and New York: C. F. Vent, 1870.

Bergemann, Kurt D. *Brackett's Battalion, Minnesota Cavalry in the Civil War and Dakota War.* St. Paul: Minnesota Historical Society Press, 2004.

Bettelyoun, Susan Bordeaux, and Josephine Waggoner. *With My Own Eyes.* Edited by Emily Levine. Lincoln: University of Nebraska Press, 1998.

"Biography of Old Settlers." In *Collections of the State Historical Society of North Dakota,* vol. 1. Bismarck, N.Dak.: Tribune St. Printers & Binders, 1906.

Bluemle, John P. *The Face of North Dakota.* Bismarck: North Dakota Geological Survey, 1991.

Boller, Henry A. *Among the Indians, Eight Years in the Far West, 1858–1866.* Edited by Milo Milton Quaife. Lakeside edition. [1867?]. Reprint, Chicago: R. R. Donnelly & Sons, 1959.

Boutin, Loren Dean. *Cut Nose Who Stands on a Cloud.* St. Cloud, Minn.: North Star Press, 2006.

Bowers, Alfred W. *Hidatsa Social and Ceremonial Organization.* Lincoln: University of Nebraska Press, 1992.

Bray, Edmund C., and Martha Coleman Bray, eds. *Joseph N. Nicollet on the Plains and Prairies: The Expeditions of 1838–39, with Journals, Letters, and Notes on the Dakota Indians.* St. Paul: Minnesota Historical Society, 1976.

Bray, Kingsley M. *Crazy Horse: A Lakota Life.* Norman: University of Oklahoma Press, 2006.

———. "Teton Sioux Population History, 1655–1881." *Nebraska History* 75, no. 2 (Summer 1994): 165–88.

Bristow, David L. "Inkpaduta's Revenge: The True Story of the Spirit Lake Massacre." *The Iowan,* January–February 1999. http://www.davidbristow .com/inkpaduta.html.

Brown, Dee A. *Fort Phil Kearny: An American Saga.* New York: G. P. Putnam's Son, 1962.

———. *The Galvanized Yankees.* Lincoln: University of Nebraska Press, 1986.

Brown, Mark H. *The Plainsmen of The Yellowstone: A History of The Yellowstone Basin.* 1961. Reprint, Lincoln: University Nebraska Press, 1969.

Buck, Daniel. *Indian Outbreaks.* 1904. Reprint, Minneapolis, Minn.: Ross & Haines, 1965.

Buechel, Eugene, and Paul Manhart, trans. and eds. *Lakota Dictionary, Lakota–English / English–Lakota, New Comprehensive Edition.* Lincoln: University of Nebraska Press, 2002.

Burlingame, Merrill G. *The Montana Frontier.* 1942. Reprint, Bozeman, Mont.: Big Sky Books, 1980.

Burstein, Andrew. *The Passions of Andrew Jackson.* New York: Alfred A. Knopf, 2003.

Butterfield, C. W. *History of Iowa County, Wisconsin.* Chicago: Western Historical Company, 1881.

Calitri, Shannon Smith. "'Give Me Eighty Men': Shattering the Myth of the Fetterman Massacre." *Montana The Magazine of Western History* 54, no. 3 (Autumn 2004): 44–59.

Calloway, Colin G., ed. *Our Hearts Fell to the Ground: Plains Indian Views of How the West Was Lost.* Boston/New York: Bedford/St. Martin's Press, 1996.

Canfield, Sarah. "An Army Wife on the Upper Missouri: The Diary of Sarah E. Canfield, 1866–1868." In *The Centennial Anthology of North Dakota History, Journal of the Northern Plains*, edited by Ray H. Mattison, 59–71. Bismarck: State Historical Society of North Dakota, 1996. First published 1953 by *North Dakota History*. Page references are to the 1996 edition.

Carley, Kenneth. *The Dakota War of 1862, Minnesota's Other Civil War.* 1961. Reprint, St. Paul: Minnesota Historical Society Press, 1976.

Carricker, Robert C. *Father Peter John De Smet: Jesuit in the West.* Norman: University of Oklahoma Press, 1995.

Carrington, Margaret. *Ab-Sa-Ra-Ka, Home of the Crows.* Philadelphia: J. B. Lippincott & Co., 1868.

Cash, Joseph H., and Herbert T. Hoover, eds. *To Be an Indian: An Oral History.* St. Paul: Minnesota Historical Society, 1995.

Chaky, Doreen. "Fossils and the Fur Trade: The Chouteaus as Patrons of Paleontology." *Gateway Heritage* 19, no. 1 (Summer 1998): 22–31.

———. "Wisconsin Volunteers on the Dakota Frontier." *Wisconsin History* 80, no. 3 (Spring 1997): 162–78.

Chaput, Donald. "Generals, Indian Agents, Politicians: The Doolittle Survey of 1865." *The Western Historical Quarterly* 3, no. 3 (July 1972): 269–82.

Cheney, Roberta Carkeek. *Sioux Winter Count: A 131-Year Calendar of Events.* Happy Camp, Calif.: Naturegraph Publishers, 1998.

Chittenden, Hiram Martin. *The American Fur Trade of the Far West.* 2 vols. Lincoln: University of Nebraska Press, 1986.

———. *History of Early Steamboat Navigation on the Missouri River: Life and Adventures of Joseph La Barge.* Minneapolis, Minn.: Ross & Haines, 1962.

Chittenden, Hiram Martin, and Alfred Talbot Richardson., eds. *Life, Letters and Travels of Father Pierre-Jean De Smet, S.J., 1801–1873.* 4 vols. New York: Francis P. Harper, 1905.

Clow, Richmond L. "Mad Bear: William S. Harney and the Sioux Expedition of 1855–1856." *Nebraska History* 61, no. 2 (Summer 1980): 132–51.

Cody, William F. *The Life of Hon. William F. Cody, known as Buffalo Bill, the Famous Hunter, Scout and Guide: An Autobiography.* 1879. Reprint, London: Senate, 1994.

Cohen, Felix S. *Handbook of Federal Indian Law.* 1941. Updated edition, Buffalo, N.Y.: William S. Hine Co., 1988.

Collins, Ethel A. "Pioneer Experiences of Horatio H. Larned." *Collections of the State Historical Society of North Dakota* 7 (1925): 1–58.

Coyer, Richard Joseph. "'This Wild Region of the Far West': Lieutenant Sweeny's Letters from Fort Pierre, 1855–1856." *Nebraska History* 63, no. 2 (Summer 1982): 232–54.

Cozzens, Peter, ed. *Eyewitness to the Indian Wars, 1865–90.* Vol. 5, *The Army and the Indian.* Mechanicsburg, Penn.: Stackpole Books, 2005.

———. *General John Pope: A Life for the Nation.* Urbana: University of Illinois Press, 2000.

Cozzens, Peter, and Robert I. Girardi. *The Military Memoirs of General John Pope.* Chapel Hill: University of North Carolina Press, 1998.

Crawford, Lewis F. *The Exploits of Ben Arnold, Indian Fighter, Gold Miner, Cowboy, Hunter, and Army Scout.* Norman: University of Oklahoma Press, 1999. First published 1926 as *Rekindling Camp Fires* by Capital Book Co.

Culbertson, Thaddeus A. *An Expedition to the Mauvaises Terres and the Upper Missouri, 1850.* Lincoln, Neb.: J & L Reprint Co., 1981. First published 1852 in *Bureau of American Ethnology Bulletin* 147.

Custer, Elizabeth B. *"Boots and Saddles" or Life in Dakota with General Custer.* Norman: University of Oklahoma Press, 1961.

De Girardin, E. "A Trip to the Bad Lands in 1849." Translated by Elizabeth Conrad and S. M. Stockdale. *South Dakota Historical Review* 1, no. 2 (Jan. 1936): 56–58.

Deloria, Ella C. "Dakota Texts." In *Publications of the American Ethnology Society*, vol. 14, edited by Frank Boaz. New York: G. E. Stechert & Co., 1932.

———. *Speaking of Indians.* 1944. Reprint, Lincoln: University of Nebraska Press, 1998.

———. *Waterlily.* Lincoln: University of Nebraska Press, 1988.

DeMallie, Raymond J., ed. *The Sixth Grandfather, Black Elk's Teachings Given to John G. Neihardt.* Lincoln: University of Nebraska Press, 1984.

DeMallie, Raymond J., and Douglas R. Parks, eds. *Sioux Indian Religion.* Norman: University of Oklahoma Press, 1987.

Denig, Edwin Thompson. *Five Indian Tribes of the Upper Missouri: Sioux, Arickaras, Assiniboines, Crees, Crows.* The Civilization of the American Indian series. Norman: University of Oklahoma Press, 1961.

De Trobriand, Philippe. *Army Life in Dakota: Selections from the Journal of Philippe Regis Denis de Keredern de Trobriand.* Translated by George Francis Will. Edited by Milo Milton Quaife. Detroit, Mich.: Lakeside Press, R. R. Donnelley and Sons, 1941.

———. *Military Life in Dakota: The Journal of Philippe Regis de Trobriand.* Translated and edited by Lucille M. Kane. St. Paul, Minn.: Alvord Memorial Commission, 1951.

DeVoto, Bernard A., ed. *The Journals of Lewis and Clark.* 1958. Reprint, New York: Houghton Mifflin, 1997.

Dickey County (N.Dak.) Historical Society. *A History of Dickey County, North Dakota.* Dickey County Historical Society, 1930.

Diedrich, Mark. *Dakota Oratory: Great Moments in the Recorded Speech of the Eastern Sioux, 1695–1874*. Rochester, Minn.: Coyote Books, 1989.

———. *The Odyssey of Chief Standing Buffalo*. Minneapolis, Minn.: Coyote Books, 1988.

Diessner, Don. *There Are No Indians Left but Me! Sitting Bull's Story*. El Segundo, Calif.: Upton, 1993.

Doud, George W. "Doud Diary." In *South Dakota Historical Collections*, vol. 9, 471–74. Pierre, S.Dak.: Hipple Printing, 1918.

"Drifting Goose's Village." *Museum News* 15, no. 1 (Jan. 1954): 2. Published by the W. H. Over Museum, University of South Dakota. On file at SHSND.

Drimmer, Frederick, ed. *Captured by the Indians: 15 Firsthand Accounts, 1750–1870*. 1961. Reprint, New York: Dover Publications, 1985.

Drips, J. H. *Three Years among the Indians in Dakota*. New York: Sol Lewis, 1974.

Drum, Richard C. "Reminiscences of the Indian Fight at Ash Hollow, 1855." *Collections of the Nebraska State Historical Society* 16 (1911): 143–51.

Dyer, Frederick H. *A Compendium of the War of the Rebellion*. Dayton, Ohio: Press of Morningside Bookshop, 1908.

Eggleston, Edward. "George W. Northrup: The Kit Carson of the Northwest." Edited by Louis Pfaller. *North Dakota History* 33, no. 1 (Winter 1966): 5–21.

Ellis, Elmer, ed. "The Journal of H. E. Maynadier, A Boat Trip from Fort Union to Omaha in 1860." *North Dakota History Quarterly* 1 (Jan. 1927).

Ellis, Richard N. *General Pope and U. S. Indian Policy*. Albuquerque: University of New Mexico Press, 1970.

English, Abner M. "Dakota's First Soldiers." In *South Dakota Historical Collections*, vol. 9, compiled by the South Dakota Historical Society, 241–335. Pierre, S.Dak.: Hipple Printing, 1918.

Ewers, John C. *Indian Life on the Upper Missouri*. Norman: University of Oklahoma Press, 1968.

"Exploring the Black Hills: The Explorations of Captain William Franklin Raynolds, 1859–1860." *South Dakota Historical Review* 4, no. 1 (1973): 18–62.

Farb, Robert C. "Military Career of Robert W. Furnas." *Nebraska History* 32, no. 1 (March 1951): 18–41.

———. "Robert W. Furnas as Omaha Agent." Pts. 1 and 2. *Nebraska History* 32, no. 3 (Sept. 1951): 186–203; and 32, no. 5 (Dec. 1951): 268–83.

Foster, Mike. *Strange Genius: The Life of Ferdinand Vandeveer Hayden*. New York: Roberts Rinehart Publishers, 1994.

Frazer, Robert Walter. *Forts of the West: Military Forts and Presidios and Posts Commonly Called Forts West of the Mississippi River to 1898*. Norman, University of Oklahoma Press, 1965.

Gard, Wayne. *The Great Buffalo Hunt, Its History and Drama, and Its Role in the Opening of the West*. 1959. Reprint, Lincoln: University of Nebraska Press, 1968.

Garfield, Marvin H. "The Indian Question in Congress and in Kansas." *Kansas Historical Quarterly* 2, no. 1 (Feb. 1933): 29–44.

Garraghan, Gilbert J. "Father De Smet's Sioux Peace Mission of 1868 and the Journal of Charles Galpin." *Mid-America: An Historical Review* 13 (October 1930).

———. *The Jesuits of the Middle United States*. Chicago: Loyola University Press, 1938.

"Gazetteer of Pioneers and Others in North Dakota Previous to 1862." In *Collections of the State Historical Society of North Dakota*, vol. 1, 355–80. Bismarck, N.Dak.: Tribune State Printers & Binders, 1906.

"General John Blair Smith Todd." In *South Dakota Historical Collections*, vol. 7, compiled by the South Dakota Historical Society, 493–513. Pierre, S.Dak.: State Publishing Co., 1914.

Gilman, Rhoda R. *Henry Hastings Sibley, Divided Heart*. St. Paul: Minnesota Historical Society Press, 2004.

Goe, James B. "Thirteenth Regiment of Infantry." In *The Army of the United States: Historical Sketches of Staff and Line with Portraits of Generals-in-Chief*, edited by Theophilus Francis Rodenbough and William L. Haskin, 575–85. New York: Maynard, Merrill, & Co., 1896.

Goetzmann, William H. *Army Exploration in the American West, 1803–1863*. Austin: Texas State Historical Association, 1991.

Gonzalez, Mario, and Elizabeth Cook-Lynn. *The Politics of Hallowed Ground: Wounded Knee and the Struggle for Indian Sovereignty*. Champaign: University of Illinois Press, 1998.

Goodspeed, Weston Arthur, ed. *The Province and the States: A History of the Province of Louisiana under France and Spain, and of the Territories and States of the United States Formed Therefrom*. 7 vols. Madison, Wisc.: Western Historical Association, 1904.

Goodrich, Thomas & Th [*sic*] Goodrich. *Black Flag: Guerilla Warfare on the Western Border, 1861–1865*. Urbana: Indiana University Press, 1999.

Goodwin, Carol G. "The Letters of Private Milton Spencer, 1862–1865: A Soldier's View of Military Life on the Northern Plains." *North Dakota History* 37, no. 4 (Fall 1970): 233–70.

Gray, John S. "Bloody Knife: Ree Scout for Custer." *Chicago Westerners Brand Book* 17, no. 12 (1960–61): 89–96.

———. "Honore Picotte, Fur Trader." *South Dakota History* 6, no. 2 (Spring 1976): 186–202.

———. "The Northern Overland Pony Express." *Montana The Magazine of Western History* 16, no. 4 (Autumn 1966): 58–73.

———. "The Santee Sioux and the Settlers at Lake Shetek." *Montana The Magazine of Western History* 25, no. 1 (Winter 1975): 42–54.

———. "The Story of Mrs. Picotte-Galpin, a Sioux Heroine." Pts 1 and 2. *Montana The Magazine of Western History* 36, no. 2 (Spring 1986): 2–21; 36, no. 3 (Summer 1986): 2–21.

Greene, Candace S., and Russell Thornton, eds. *The Year the Stars Fell: Lakota Winter Counts at the Smithsonian.* Washington, D.C.: Smithsonian Institution, 2007.

Greene, Jerome A. *Fort Randall on the Missouri, 1856–1892.* Pierre: South Dakota Historical Society Press, 2005.

———, ed. "Lt. Palmer Writes from the Bozeman Trail, 1867–68." *Montana The Magazine of Western History* 28, no. 3 (Summer 1978): 16–35.

Greene, Jerome A., and Douglas D. Scott. *Finding Sand Creek: History, Archeology, and the 1864 Massacre Site.* Norman: University of Oklahoma Press, 2004.

Gue, Benjamin F. *History of Iowa from the Earliest Times to the Beginning of the Twentieth Century.* Vol. 4, *Iowa Biography.* New York: The Century History Company, 1903.

Hafen, LeRoy R., ed. *Mountain Men and the Fur Trade of the Far West.* 10 vols. Glendale, Calif.: Arthur H. Clark Co., 1968–72.

Hafen, LeRoy R., and Ann W. Hafen, eds. *The Far West and the Rockies Historical Series 1820–1875.* Vol. 12, *Powder River Campaign and Sawyer Expedition 1865. A Documentary Account Comprising Official Reports, Diaries, Contemporary Newspaper Accounts, and Personal Narratives.* Glendale, Calif.: Arthur H. Clark Co., 1961.

Hakola, John W., ed. *Frontier Omnibus.* Missoula: Montana State University Press; Helena: Montana Historical Society, 1862.

Halaas, David Fridtjof, and Andrew E. Masich. *Halfbreed: The Remarkable True Story of George Bent, Caught Between the Worlds of the Indian and the White Man.* N.p.: Da Capo Press, 2004.

Hampton, H. D. "Powder River Expedition, 1865." *Montana The Magazine of Western History* 14, no. 4 (Autumn 1964): 2–15.

Hanson, Charles E., Jr. "The Fort Pierre–Fort Laramie Trail." *Museum of the Fur Trade Quarterly* 1, no. 2 (Summer 1965): 3–7.

Hanson, James A. *Little Chief's Gatherings: The Smithsonian Institution's G. K. Warren 1855–1856 Plains Indian Collection and The New York State Library's 1855–1857 Warren Expedition Journals.* Crawford, Neb.: The Fur Press, 1996.

Hanson, Joseph Mills. *Conquest of the Missouri: Being the Story of the Life and Exploits of Captain Marsh Grant.* New York: Murray Hill Books, 1946. First published 1909 by A. C. McClung & Co.

Harkness, James. "Diary of James Harkness, of the Firm of LaBarge, [*sic*] Harkness and Company." *Contributions to the Montana Historical Society* 2 (1896): 343–61.

Hart, Herbert M. *Old Forts of the Northwest.* Seattle: Superior Publishing, 1963.

Hasselstrom, Linda. *Roadside History of South Dakota*. Missoula, Mont.: Mountain Press, 1994.

Hassrick, Royal B. *The Sioux: Life and Customs of a Warrior Society*. Norman: University of Oklahoma Press, 1964.

Heard, Isaac V. D. *History of the Sioux War and Massacres of 1862–3*. New York: Harper & Brothers, 1864.

Hilger, Nicholas. "General Alfred Sully's Expedition." *Contributions to the Historical Society of Montana* 2 (1896): 314–28.

Historical Records and Studies. Vol. 24. New York: United States Catholic Historical Society, 1934.

History of Western Iowa: Its Settlement and Growth. A Comprehensive Compilation of Progressive Events Concerning the Counties, Cities, Towns and Villages—Biographical Sketches of the Pioneers and Business Men, with an Authentic History of the State of Iowa. Sioux City, Iowa: Western Publishing Co., 1882.

Hodges, William Romaine. *Carl Wimar: A Biography*. Galveston, Tex.: Charles Reymershoffer, 1908.

Hodgson, Thomas C. *Personal Recollections of the Sioux War with the Eighth Minnesota, Company F*. Transcribed by Robert Olson. Roseville, Minn.: Park Genealogical Books, 1999. Originally published in the *Dakota County (Minn.) Tribune*, 1887–91.

Holley, Frances Chamberlain. *Once Their Home or Our Legacy from the Dahkotahs: Historical, Biographical, and Incidental from Far-off Days, Down to the Present*. Chicago: Donohue and Henneberry, 1891.

Hoover, Herbert T. "Yankton Sioux Tribal Claims against the United States, 1917–1975." *Western History Quarterly* 7, no. 20 (April 1976): 125–42.

———. "A Yankton Sioux Tribal Land History." 1995. Unpublished manuscript in I. D. Weeks Collection at University of South Dakota at Vermillion. Cited in *Yanktons v. Gaffey* documents. See http://www.sdbar.org/Federal/1998/1998dsd022.htm.

Howard, James H. "Dakota Winter Counts as a Source of Plains History." *Bureau of American Ethnology Bulletin* 173, no. 61 (1960): 335–416.

Howe, Craig, and Kim TallBear. "Introduction." In Oak Lake Writers, *This Stretch of the River*.

Hoxie, Frederick E., ed. *Encyclopedia of North American Indians*. New York: Houghton Mifflin Co., 1996.

Hunter, Louis C. *Steamboats on the Western Rivers: An Economic and Technological History*. 1949. Reprint, New York: Dover, 1993.

Hurt, Wesley R. "Additional Notes on Dakota House Types of South Dakota." *Museum News* 15, no. 1 (Jan. 1954): 3. (Published by the W. H. Over Museum, University of South Dakota.) On file at SHSND.

Hutton, Paul Andrew. *Phil Sheridan and His Army*. Lincoln: University of Nebraska Press, 1985.

Hyde, George E. *Life of George Bent, Written from His Letters*. Edited by Savoie Lottinville. 1968. Reprint, Norman: University of Oklahoma Press, 1968.

———. *Red Cloud's Folk: A History of the Oglala Sioux Indians*. 1937. Reprint, Norman: University of Oklahoma Press, 1975.

———. *A Sioux Chronicle*. Norman: University of Oklahoma Press, 1956.

———. *Spotted Tail's Folk*. 1961. Reprint, Norman: University of Oklahoma Press, 1974.

Innis, Ben. *Bloody Knife: Custer's Favorite Scout*. Edited by Richard E. Colin. Bismarck, N.Dak.: Smoky Water Press, 1994.

Iowa Adjutant General's Office. *Roster and Record of Iowa Soldiers in the War of the Rebellion: Together with Historical Sketches of Volunteer Organizations, 1861–1866*. 6 vols. Des Moines, Iowa: E. H. English, 1908–11.

Jackson, Donald. *Custer's Gold: The United States Cavalry Expedition of 1874*. 1966. Reprint, Lincoln: University of Nebraska Press, 1977.

Jackson, Helen Hunt. *A Century of Dishonor: A Sketch of the United States Government's Dealings with Some of the Indian Tribes*. 1881. Reprint, New York: Barnes & Noble Publishing, 2006.

Jacobson, Clair. "The Battle of Whitestone Hill." *North Dakota History* 44, no. 3 (Summer 1977): 4–14.

———. "A History of the Yanktonai and Hunkpatina Sioux." *North Dakota History* 47, no. 1 (Winter 1980): 4–24.

Jensen, Richard E., and James S. Hutchins, eds. *Wheel Boats on the Missouri: The Journals and Documents of the Atkinson–O'Fallon Expedition, 1824–26*. Helena: Montana Historical Society Press; Lincoln: Nebraska State Historical Society, 2001.

Johnson, Dorothy M. *The Bloody Bozeman: The Perilous Trail to Montana's Gold*. 1983. Reprint, Missoula, Mont.: Mountain Press Publishing, 1992.

Jones, Robert Huhn. *Guarding the Overland Trails: The Eleventh Ohio Cavalry in the Civil War*. Spokane, Wash.: Arthur H. Clark, 2005.

Jordan, David M. *"Happiness Is Not My Companion": The Life of General G. K. Warren*. Bloomington and Indianapolis: Indiana University Press, 2001.

Josephy, Alvin M., Jr. *The Civil War in the American West*. New York: Random House Vintage Books, 1993.

Kappler, Charles J., comp. and ed. *Indian Affairs: Laws and Treaties*. Vol. 2, *Treaties, 1778–1883*. Washington, D.C.: Government Printing Office, 1904.

———, comp. and ed. *Indian Affairs: Laws and Treaties*. Vol. 5, *Laws, Compiled from December 22, 1927 to June 29, 1938*. Washington, D.C.: Government Printing Office, 1904.

Karol, Joseph H. *Red Horse Owner's Winter Count: The Oglala Sioux 1786–1968*. Marin, S.Dak.: Booster Publishing, 1969.

Kautz, August V. "From Missouri to Oregon in 1860: The Diary Of August V.

Kautz." Edited by Martin F. Schmitt. *Pacific Northwest Quarterly*, July 1946, 193–230.

Keenan, Jerry. *The Wagon Box Fight: An Episode in Red Cloud's War*. New York: De Capo Press, 2000.

Kelly, Fanny. *My Captivity Among the Sioux Indians: A Pioneer Woman's Firsthand Story of Frontier Experience during the Opening of the West*. 1871. Reprint, Secaucus, N.J.: Carol Publishing Group, 1993.

King, James T. "The Civil War of Private Morton." *North Dakota History* 35, no. 1 (Winter 1968): 9–19.

Kingsbury, George W. *History of Dakota Territory*. 5 vols. Chicago: Clarke Publishing, 1915.

Kudelka, Susan Mary. *March on the Dakota's [sic]: The Sibley Expedition of 1863*. Gwinner, N.Dak.: McCleery & Sons Publishing, 2003.

Kurz, Rudolph F. *Journal of Rudolph Friederich Kurz, An Account of His Experiences Among Fur Traders and American Indians on the Mississippi and the Upper Missouri Rivers During the Years 1846 to 1852*. Translated by Myrtis Jarrell. Edited by J. N. B. Hewitt. 1937. Reprint, Lincoln: University Nebraska Press, 1970.

———. *On the Upper Missouri: The Journal of Rudolph Friederich Kurz, 1851–1852*. Edited and abridged by Carla Kelly. Norman: University Oklahoma Press, 2005.

Kvasnicka, Robert M., and Herman J. Viola, eds. *The Commissioners of Indian Affairs, 1824–1977*. Lincoln: University of Nebraska Press, 1979.

LaDow, Beth. *The Medicine Line: Life and Death on a North American Border*. New York: Routledge, 2002.

Lamar, Howard R. *Dakota Territory, 1861–1889*. 1956. Reprint, Fargo: Institute for Regional Studies, North Dakota State University, 1997.

Langford, Nathaniel Pitt. *The Discovery of Yellowstone Park*. 1905. Reprint, Lincoln: University of Nebraska Press, 1972.

Larpenteur, Charles. *Forty Years a Fur Trader on the Upper Missouri*. Edited by Milo Milton Quaife. 1933. Reprint, Lincoln: University of Nebraska, 1989.

Larson, Robert W. "Chief Gall and Abe Lincoln's Railroad." *North Dakota History* 74, nos. 3 and 4 (Summer and Autumn 2007): 7–27.

———. *Gall, Lakota War Chief*. Norman: University of Oklahoma Press, 2007.

Lass, William E. "The History and Significance of the Northwest Fur Company, 1865–1869." *North Dakota History* 61, no. 3 (Summer 1994): 21–40.

———. *A History of Steamboating on the Upper Missouri River*. Lincoln: University of Nebraska Press, 1962.

———. "The 'Moscow Expedition.'" *Minnesota History* 39, no. 6 (Summer 1965): 227–40.

———. "The Removal from Minnesota of the Sioux and Winnebago Indians." *Minnesota History* 38, no. 8 (Dec. 1963): 353–64.

Lawrence, Elden. "The Missing Voices." In Oak Lake Writers, *This Stretch of the River*, 31–34.

Lee, L. P. *History of the Spirit Lake Massacre*. New Britain, Conn.: L. P. Lee, 1857.

Letellier, Louis Dace. "Louis D. Letellier." Edited by Constant R. Marks. In *South Dakota Historical Collections*, vol. 4, compiled by the South Dakota State Historical Society, 217–53. Sioux Fall, S.Dak.: Press of Mark I. Scott, 1908.

———. *Louis Dace Letellier: Adventures on the Upper Missouri*. Edited by Carla Kelly. Williston, N.Dak.: Fort Union Association, 2002.

Levering, N. "Recollections of the Early Settlement of North-Western Iowa." Pts. 1 and 2. *Annals of Iowa* 11, no. 1 (Jan. 1873); 11 no. 3 (July 1873).

Lingk, Ray W. "The Northwestern Indian Expedition . . . The Sully Trail 1864, From the Little Missouri to the Yellowstone River." *North Dakota History* 24, no. 4 (Oct. 1957): 181–200.

"Log Book of Steamer W.J. Lewis." In *Collections of the State Historical Society of North Dakota*, vol. 2, compiled by the State Historical Society of North Dakota, 314–42. Bismarck, N.Dak.: Tribune State Printers & Binders, 1908.

"Log of the Steamer Benton from Missouri, to Fort Benton, Idaho." In *Collections of the State Historical Society of North Dakota*, vol. 2, compiled by the State Historical Society of North Dakota, 285–313. Bismarck, N.Dak.: Tribune State Printers & Binders, 1908.

"Log of Steamer Robert Campbell, Jr., from St. Louis to Fort Benton, Montana Territory." In *Collections of the State Historical Society of North Dakota*, vol. 2, compiled by the State Historical Society of North Dakota, 267–84. Bismarck, N.Dak.: Tribune State Printers & Binders, 1908.

Lounsberry, Clement A. *Early History of North Dakota: Essential Outlines of American History*. Washington, D.C.: Liberty Press, 1919.

Love, William DeLoss. *Wisconsin in the War of Rebellion*. Chicago: Church & Goodman, 1866.

Luce, J. C. "The Battle of White Stone Hill." In *South Dakota Historical Collections*, vol. 5, compiled by the South Dakota Historical Society, 417–19. Pierre, S.Dak.: State Publishing Company, 1910.

Mallery, Garrick. *Picture-Writing of the American Indians*. 2 vols. 1893. Reprint, New York: Dover Publications, 1972.

———. *Sign Language among North American Indians*. 1881. Reprint, Mineola, N.Y.: Dover Publications, 2001.

Manypenny, George W. *Our Indian Wards*. 1880. Reprint, New York: Da Capo Press, 1972.

Maroukis, Thomas Constantine. *Peyote and the Yankton Sioux*. Norman: University of Oklahoma Press, 2004.

Marsh, Elias, J. "Trip up the Missouri River from St. Louis to Fort Benton, June and July and August, 1859 on the Steamers 'Spread Eagle' and 'Chippewa.'" *South Dakota Historical Review* 1 (Jan. 1936): 79–127.

Marshall, Joseph M., III. *The Journey of Crazy Horse*. New York: Viking, 2004.

———. *The Lakota Way: Stories and Lessons for Living, Native American Wisdom on Ethics and Character*. New York: Penguin Compass, 2001.

Mattison, Ray H., ed. "The Fisk Expedition of 1864: The Diary of Wm. L. Larned." *North Dakota History* 36, no. 3 (Summer 1969): 227–38.

———, ed. *Henry A. Boller: Missouri River Fur Trader*. Bismarck: State Historical Society of North Dakota, 1966. Reprinted from *North Dakota History* 33, no. 3 (Spring 1966): 260–315; 33, no. 4 (Summer 1966): 160–219. Page references are to the State Historical Society of North Dakota reprint edition.

———. "The Indian Reservation System on the Upper Missouri, 1865–1890." *Nebraska History* 52, no. 3 (Sept. 1955): 1–48.

———. "Report on Historical Aspects of the Oahe Reservoir Area, Missouri River, South and North Dakota." In *South Dakota Historical Collections*, vol. 27, compiled by the South Dakota Historical Society, 1–159. Pierre, S.Dak.: State Publishing Company, 1954.

McChristian, Douglas C. *Fort Laramie: Military Bastion of the High Plains*. Norman, Okla.: Arthur H. Clark, 2008.

———. "Fort Laramie and the U.S. Army on the High Plains, 1849–1890." Manuscript available at National Park Service Historic Resources Study, Fort Laramie National Historic Site, February 2003.

McCormack, J. Michael. "Soldiers and Sioux: Military Life among the Indians at Fort Totten." In Larry Remele (ed.), *Fort Totten Military Post and Indian School 1867–1959*, 9–22. Bismarck: State Historical Society of North Dakota, 1986.

McDermott, John D. "The *Frontier Scout*: A View of Fort Rice in 1865." *North Dakota History* 61, no. 4 (Fall 1994): 25–35.

McLaird, James D., and Lesta V. Turchen. "The Dacota Explorations of Lieutenant Gouverneur Kemble Warren, 1855–1856–1857." *South Dakota History* 3, no. 4 (Fall 1973): 359–89.

McLaughlin, James. *My Friend the Indian*. Boston: Houghton Mifflin, 1910.

———. *My Friend the Indian; or, Three Heretofore Unpublished Chapters of the Book Published under the Title of My Friend the Indian*. Edited by U. L. Burdick. Baltimore: The Proof Press, 1936.

McLaughlin, Marie L. *Myths and Legends of the Sioux*. Bismarck, N.Dak.: Bismarck Tribune, 1916.

Meyer, Roy W. *History of the Santee Sioux, United States Indian Policy on Trial*. 1967. Reprint, Lincoln: University of Nebraska Press, 1993.

Meyers, Augustus. "Dakota in the Fifties." In *South Dakota Historical Collections*, vol. 10, compiled by the South Dakota State Historical Society, 130–94. Pierre, S.Dak.: Hipple Printing Co., 1920.

———. *Ten Years in the Ranks, U.S. Army*. 1914. Reprint, New York: Arno Press, 1979.

"Michael DeSomet—Sioux guide, a.k.a. Joseph DeSomet Lewis." *North Dakota History* 67, no. 3 (2000): 24–37.

Miller, David, Dennis Smith, Joseph R. McGeshick, James Shanley, and Caleb Shields. *The History of the Assiniboine and Sioux Tribes of the Fort Peck Indian Reservation, Montana, 1800–2000.* Poplar, Mont.: Fort Peck Community College and Montana Historical Society Press, 2008.

Miller, George L. "The Fort Pierre Expedition." In *Transactions and Reports of the Nebraska State Historical Society*, vol. 3, 120–24. Fremont, Neb.: Hammond Brothers, 1892.

———. The Military Camp on the Big Sioux River." In *Transactions and Reports of the Nebraska State Historical Society*, vol. 3, 110–18. Fremont, Neb.: Hammond Brothers, 1892.

Milligan, Edward A. *Dakota Twilight, The Standing Rock Sioux, 1874–1890.* Hicksville, N.Y.: Exposition Press, 1976.

Minnesota in the Civil and Indian Wars 1861–1865. 2 vols. St. Paul, Minn.: Pioneer Press, 1890.

Moe, Richard. *The Last Full Measure: The Life and Death of the First Minnesota Volunteers.* St. Paul: Minnesota Historical Society Press, 1993.

Monnett, John H. *Where a Hundred Soldiers Were Killed: The Struggle for the Powder River Country in 1866 and the Making of the Fetterman Myth.* Albuquerque: University of New Mexico Press, 2008.

Morgan, Lewis Henry. *The Indian Journals 1859–62.* New York: Dover Publications, 1992. Originally published 1959.

Morton, J. Sterling, and Albert Watkins. *History of Nebraska, From the Earliest Explorations of the Trans-Mississippi Region.* Edited by Augustus O. Thomas. Lincoln, Neb.: Western Publishing and Engraving, 1918.

Myers, Frank. *Soldiering in Dakota among the Indians in 1863–4–5.* 1888. Reprint, Freeport, N.Y.: Books for Libraries Press, 1971.

Nicolay, John G. "The Sioux War." *Continental Monthly* 3, no. 2 (Feb. 1863): 195–203.

Nowak, Timothy R. "From Fort Pierre to Fort Randall: The Army's First Use of Portable Cottages." *South Dakota History* 32, no. 2 (Summer 2002): 95–116.

Oak Lake Writers. *This Stretch of the River: Lakota, Dakota, and Nakota Responses to the Lewis and Clark Expedition and Bicentennial*, edited by Craig Howe and Kim TallBear. Sioux Falls, S.Dak.: Pine Hill Press, a publication of Oak Lake Writers Society, 2006.

Oehler, C.M. *The Great Sioux Uprising.* New York: De Capo Press, 1997.

"Official Correspondence Relating to Fort Pierre." In *South Dakota Historical Collections*, vol. 1, compiled by the South Dakota Historical Society, 381–440. Aberdeen, S.Dak.: News Printing Co., 1902.

Official Records of the Union and Confederate Navies in the War of the Rebellion. Washington, D.C.: U.S. Government Printing Office, 1917.

Olson, James C. *Red Cloud and the Sioux Problem*. Lincoln: University of Nebraska Press, 1965.

Oneroad, Amos E., and Alanson B. Skinner. *Being Dakota: Tales and Traditions of the Sisseton and Wahpeton*. Edited by Laura L. Anderson. St. Paul: Minnesota Historical Society Press, 2003.

Ostler, Jeffrey. *The Lakotas and the Black Hills*. New York: Viking Penguin, 2010.

——.*The Plains Sioux and U.S. Colonialism from Lewis and Clark to Wounded Knee*. Cambridge, U.K.: Cambridge University Press, 2004.

Overholser, Joel. *Fort Benton: World's Innermost Port*. Fort Benton, Mont.: Privately published, 1987.

Papandreau, Ronald J. *They Never Surrendered: The Lakota Sioux Band that Stayed in Canada*. First Lightning paper ed., 3rd rev. ed. La Vergne, Tenn.: Book-Surge Publishing, 2009.

Parker, Watson. *Gold in the Black Hills*. Lincoln: University of Nebraska Press, 1966.

Pattee, John. "Reminiscences of John Pattee." In *South Dakota Historical Collections*, vol. 5, compiled by the South Dakota State Historical Society, 273–350. Pierre, S.Dak.: State Publishing Co., 1910.

Paul, R. Eli., ed. *Autobiography of Red Cloud: War Leader of the Oglalas*. Helena: Montana Historical Society Press, 1997.

——. *Blue Water Creek and the First Sioux War, 1854–1856*. Norman: University of Oklahoma Press, 2004.

Paulson, Howard W. "Federal Indian Policy and the Dakota Indians: 1800–1840." *South Dakota History* 3 (Summer 1973): 285–309.

Paxson, Lewis C. "Diary Kept by Lewis C. Paxson, Stockton, N.J., 1862–1865." In *Collections of the State Historical Society of North Dakota*, vol. 2, compiled by the State Historical Society of North Dakota, 102–63. Bismarck, N.Dak.: Bismark Tribune State Printers & Binders, 1908.

Pearson, Dean A. *Fort Dilts: The Story behind the Story*. Bowman, N.Dak.: Dean A. Pearson, 2001.

Perret, Geoffrey. *Lincoln's War: The Untold Story of America's Greatest President as Commander in Chief*. New York: Random House, 2004.

Pfaller, Louis B. *Father De Smet in Dakota*. Richardton, N.Dak., 1962.

——, ed. "The Galpin Journal: Dramatic Record of an Odyssey of Peace." *Montana The Magazine of Western History* 18, no. 2 (April 1968): 2–23.

——. "The Peace Mission of 1863–1864." *North Dakota History* 37, no. 4 (Fall 1970): 292–313.

——. "The Sully Expedition of 1864 Featuring the Killdeer Mountain and Badlands Battles." *North Dakota History* 31, no. 1 (Jan. 1964): 25–77.

Poole, DeWitt Clinton. *Among the Sioux of Dakota: Eighteen Months' Experience as an Indian Agent, 1869–70*. 1881. Reprint, St. Paul: Minnesota Historical Society Press, 1988.

Price, Catherine. *The Oglala People, 1841–1879: A Political History*. Lincoln: University of Nebraska Press, 1996.

Prucha, Francis Paul. *Documents of United States Indian Policy*. Lincoln: University of Nebraska Press, 1975.

———. *The Great Father: The United States Government and the American Indians*. Abridged ed., 1984. Reprint, Lincoln: University of Nebraska Press, 1994.

Quiner, Edwin Bentley. *Military History of Wisconsin: Civil and Military Patriotism of the State, in the War for the Union*. Chicago: Clarke & Company, 1866.

Ramsey, Alexander. *Message of Governor Ramsey to the Legislature of Minnesota, delivered at the extra session September 9, 1862* (booklet). St. Paul: Press Printing, 1862.

A Report of the Proceedings of a Council Held at Fort Pierre by General Harney with a Delegation of Nine Tribes of Sioux Indians. Fairfield, Wash.: Ye Galleon Press, 1972.

Rezatto, Helen Graham. *The Making of the Two Dakotas*. Lincoln, Neb.: Media Publishing, 1989.

Riggs, Stephen R. *Mary and I*. Minneapolis: Ross & Haines, 1969. First published 1880.

———. *Tah-koo Wah-kan, or, the Gospel among the Dakotas*. 1869. Reprint, Ann Arbor: University of Michigan Library, 2001.

Roberts, Frank H. H., Jr., ed. "River Basin Surveys Papers." In *Bureau of American Ethnology Bulletin*, no. 176. Washington, D.C.: U.S. Government Printing Office, 1960.

Roberts, Gary L. "Condition of the Tribes—1865: The McCook Report." *Montana The Magazine of Western History* 24, no. 1 (Winter 1974): 14–25.

Roberts, Jack. *The Amazing Adventures of Lord Gore: A True Saga from the Old West*. Silverton, Colo.: Sundance Publishing, 1977.

Robinson, Doane. "Ending the Outbreak." In *South Dakota Historical Collections*, vol. 9, compiled by the South Dakota State Historical Society, 409–70. Pierre, S.Dak.: Hipple Printing, 1918.

———, ed. "Fort Tecumseh and Fort Pierre Journals." In *South Dakota Historical Collections*, vol. 9, compiled by the South Dakota State Historical Society, 70–239. Pierre, S.Dak.: Hipple Printing, 1918.

———. *A History of the Dakota or Sioux Indians*. Minneapolis, Minn.: Ross & Haines, 1956. First published 1904 in *South Dakota Historical Collections* (vol. 4) by the state of South Dakota. Page references are to the 1956 edition.

———. *History of South Dakota*. 2 vols. Indianapolis, Ind.: B. F. Bowen & Col., 1904.

———. "The Rescue of Frances Kelly." In *South Dakota Historical Collections*, vol. 4, compiled by the South Dakota State Historical Society, 109–17. Sioux Falls, S.Dak.: Press of Mark I. Scott, 1908.

————. "Tales of the Dakota: One Hundred Anecdotes Illustrative of Sioux Life and Thinking." In *Collection of the State Historical Society of South Dakota*, vol. 14, compiled by the South Dakota State Historical Society, 1–517. Pierre, S.Dak.: Hipple Printing Co., 1928.

Robinson, R. G. *Rotting Face: Smallpox and the American Indian.* Caldwell, Idaho: Caxton Press, 2001.

Robinson, Will G. "Digest of Reports of the Commissioner of Indian Affairs, 1853–1869." In *South Dakota Historical Collections*, vol. 27, 160–515. Pierre, S.Dak.: South Dakota State Historical Society, 1954.

————. "Digest of Reports of the Commissioner of Indian Affairs as Pertains to Dakota Indians, 1873–1875." In *South Dakota Historical Collections*, vol. 20, 307–500. Pierre, S.Dak.: South Dakota State Historical Society, 1958.

Robrock, David P. "The Seventh Iowa Cavalry and the Plains Indian Wars." *Montana The Magazine of Western History* 39 (Spring 1989): 2–17.

Ronda, James P. *Lewis and Clark among the Indians.* 1984. Reprint, Lincoln: University of Nebraska Press, 1988.

Rowan, Richard D., ed. "The Second Nebraska's Campaign against the Sioux." *Nebraska History* 44, no. 1 (March 1963): 3–53. [Includes Furnas and Pierce diaries of Sully's 1863 campaign.]

Rzeczkowski, Frank. "The Crow Indians and the Bozeman Trail." *Montana The Magazine of Western History* 49, no. 4 (Winter 1999): 30–47.

Schuler, Harold H. *Fort Pierre Chouteau.* Vermillion: University of South Dakota Press, 1990.

————. *Fort Sisseton.* Sioux Falls, S.Dak.: The Center for Western Studies, 1996.

————. *Fort Sully, Guns at Sunset.* Vermillion: University of South Dakota Press, 1992.

Schultz, Duane. *Over the Earth I Come: The Great Sioux Uprising of 1862.* New York: St. Martin's Press, 1992.

Scott, Kim Allen, and Ken Kempcke. "A Journey to the Heart of Darkness: John W. Wright and the War Against the Sioux, 1863–65." *Montana The Magazine of Western History* 50, no. 4 (Winter 2000): 2–17.

Shambaugh, Benjamin F., ed. "Iowa Troops in the Sully Campaigns." *The Iowa Journal of History and Politics* 20 (1922): 364–443.

Sides, Hampton. *Blood and Thunder: An Epic of the American West.* New York: Doubleday, 2006.

Slaughter, Linda. "Fort Randall." In *Collections of the State Historical Society of North Dakota*, vol. 1, 423–29. Bismarck, N.Dak.: Bismark Tribune State Printers & Binders, 1906.

————. "Leaves from Northwestern History." In *Collections of the State Historical Society of North Dakota*, vol. 1, 200–92. Bismarck, N.Dak.: Bismark Tribune State Printers & Binders, 1906.

Smith, G. Hubert. "Fort Pierre II, 39st217 a Historic Trading Post in the Oahe Dam Area, South Dakota." In "River Basin Surveys Papers," no. 18, edited by Frank H. H. Roberts, Jr. In *Bureau of American Ethnology Bulletin 176*. Washington, D.C.: U.S. Government Printing Office, 1960.

Smith, Rex Alan. *Moon of Popping Trees, The Tragedy at Wounded Knee and the end of the Indian Wars. . . 1851–1891, Seen in the Light of Inevitable Historical Change*. New York: Reader's Digest Press, 1975.

Southwell, Kristina L., ed. *Walter Stanley Campbell Collection, The University of Oklahoma Libraries Western History Collections, Inventory and Index*. Norman, Okla.: Associates of Western History Collections, 2001.

Spence, Clark C. "A Celtic Nimrod in the Old West." *Montana The Magazine of Western History* 9, no. 2 (Spring 1959): 56–66.

Sprague, Donovin Arleigh. *Images of America: Standing Rock Sioux*. Charleston, S.C.: Arcadia Publishing, 2004.

Standing Bear, Luther. *My People the Sioux*. 1928. Reprint, Lincoln: University of Nebraska Press, 1975.

Stanley, David S. *Personal Memoirs of Major General D. S. Stanley, U.S.A*. Cambridge, Mass.: Harvard University Press, 1917.

Stewart, Rick, Joseph D. Ketner II, and Angela L. Miller. *Carl Wimar, Chronicler of the Missouri River Frontier*. Fort Worth, Tex.: Amon Carter Museum, 1991.

Stimson, H. A. "The Indian Question." *The American Missionary* 33, no. 12 (Dec. 1879): 395–401.

Stolzman, William. *How to Take Part in Lakota Ceremonies*. Pine Ridge, S.Dak.: Red Cloud Indian School, 1986.

Sully, Langdon. *No Tears for the General*. Palo Alto, Calif.: American West Publishing, 1974.

Sunder, John E. "Frederick G. Riter: Fur Trader and Weather Observer." *North Dakota History* 34, no. 2 (Spring 1967): 157–60.

———. *The Fur Trade on the Upper Missouri, 1840–1865*. Norman: University of Oklahoma Press, 1965.

Swagerty, William R. "'Uncle Sam Is a Weak Old Fellow.' Northern Plains Indian Response to American Fur Company Activities, 1826–1854." In *Fur Trade Symposium 2000 Proceedings, Indians and Traders: Entrepreneurs of the Upper Missouri*. Williston, N.Dak.: Fort Union Association, 2001.

Taylor, Joseph Henry. *Kaleidoscopic Lives*. Washburn, N.Dak.: Washburn Fiftieth Anniversary Committee, 1932.

Terrell, John Upton. Black Robe: The Life of Pierre-Jean DeSmet. Garden City, N.Y.: Doubleday & Co., 1966.

Thompson, Erwin N. *Fort Union Trading Post: Fur Trade Empire on the Upper Missouri*. Williston, N.Dak.: Fort Union Association, 2003.

Todd, John B. S. "The Harney Expedition against the Sioux: The Journal of Capt. John B. S. Todd." Edited by H. Mattison. *Nebraska History* 43, no. 1 (March 1962): 89–130.

Toponce, Alexander. *Reminiscences of Alexander Toponce*. 1923. Reprint, Norman: University of Oklahoma Press, 1971.

Tucker-Butts, Michèle. *Galvanized Yankees on the Upper Missouri: The Face of Loyalty*. Boulder: University Press of Colorado, 2003.

Turnley, Parmenas T. *Reminiscences of Parmenas T. Turnley: From Cradle to Three Score and Ten*. Chicago: Donohue and Henneberry, 1892.

Tuttle, Edmund B. *Three Years on the Plains: Observations of Indians 1867–1870*. Norman: University of Oklahoma Press, 2002. Originally published as *The Boy's Book about Indians*, London: Routledge, 1870. Page references are to the 2002 edition.

Unruh, John D., Jr. *The Plains Across: The Overland Emigrants and the Trans-Mississippi West, 1840–60*. Urbana: University of Illinois Press, 1993.

Utley, Robert M. *Cavalier in Buckskin: George Armstrong Custer and the Western Military Frontier*. Norman: University of Oklahoma Press, 1988.

———. *Frontier Regulars: The United States Army and the Indian, 1866–1891*. Lincoln: University of Nebraska/Bison Book edition, 1984. First published 1973 by McMillan.

———. *Frontiersmen in Blue: The United States Army and the Indian, 1848–1865*. 1967. Reprint, Lincoln: University of Nebraska Press, 1981.

———. *The Indian Frontier of the American West 1846–1890*. Albuquerque: University of New Mexico Press, 1984.

———. *The Lance and the Shield: The Life and Times of Sitting Bull*. New York: Ballantine Books, 1993.

———. *The Last Days of the Sioux Nation*. New Haven, Conn.: Yale University Press, 1963.

Vanderwerth, W. C., comp. *Indian Oratory: Famous Speeches by Noted Indian Chieftains*. Norman: University of Oklahoma Press, 1971.

Van der Zee, Jacob. "Neutral Ground." *Iowa Journal of History and Politics* 13, no. 3 (July 1915): 311–48.

Van Nuys, Maxwell. *Inkpaduta: The Scarlet Point*. Denver, Colo.: Van Nuys, 1998.

Vestal, Stanley [Walter Stanley Campbell]. *New Sources of Indian History 1850–1891: A Miscellany*. Norman: University of Oklahoma Press, 1934.

———. *Sitting Bull, Champion of the Sioux: A Biography*. Norman: University of Oklahoma Press, 1989. First published 1932 by Houghton Mifflin.

Viola, Herman J. *Diplomats in Buckskin: A History of Indian Delegations in Washington City*. Bluffton, S.C.: Rivilo Books, 1995.

Wakefield, Sarah. *Six Weeks in Sioux Tepees*. Helena, Mont.: Globe Pequot Press, 2004. First published 1863 by Atlas Print.

Walker, F. A. "The Indian Question." *The North American Review* 116, no. 239 (April 1873): 329–89.

Walker, James R. *Lakota Belief and Ritual*. Edited by Raymond J. DeMallie and Elaine Jahner. 1980. Reprint, Lincoln: University of Nebraska Press, 1989.

———. *Lakota Society*. Edited by Raymond J. DeMallie. Lincoln: University of Nebraska Press; Denver: Colorado Historical Society, 1982.

The War of the Rebellion: A Compilation of the Official Records of the Union and Confederate Armies, a.k.a. *Official records of the Union and Confederate Armies*. Series I, 53 vol.; Series II, 8 vols.; Series III, 5 vols.; Series IV, 4 vols. Washington, D.C.: U.S. Government Printing Office, 1885.

Ware, Eugene F. *The Indian War of 1864*. 1911. Reprint, Lincoln: University of Nebraska Press, 1994.

Warren, G. K. "Explorations in Nebraska and Dakota." In *South Dakota Historical Collections*, vol. 11, compiled by the South Dakota Historical Society. Pierre, S.Dak.: State Publishing Co., 1922.

Warren, Gouverneur Kemble. *Explorer on the Northern Plains: Lieutenant Gouverneur K. Warren's Preliminary Report of Explorations in Nebraska and Dakota, in the Years 1855-'56 '57*. Reprint, Washington, D.C.: U.S. Government Printing Office, 1875. First published 1858.

Watkins, Albert. "The Oregon Recruit Expedition." *Nebraska State Historical Society Collections* 17 (1913): 127–45.

Way, Frederick, Jr., comp. *Way's Packet Directory, 1848–1994*. Athens: Ohio University Press, 1983.

Welsh, Jack D. *Medical Histories of Union Generals*. Kent, Ohio: Kent State University Press, 1996.

Welch, James, and Paul Stekler. *Killing Custer*. New York: W. W. Norton, 1994.

Werner, Fred H. *With Harney on the Blue Water: Battle of Ash Hollow, September 3, 1855*. Greeley, Colo.: Werner Publications, 1988.

West, Elliot. "The Shadow of Pikes Peak." In *A New Significance: Re-envisioning the History of the West*, edited by Clyde A. Milner II, 205–11. New York: University of Oxford Press, 1996.

Wherry, William M. "Types and Traditions of the Old Army with the Thirteenth Infantry in Dakota." *Journal of the Military Service Institutions of the United States* 37 (July 1905): 519–26.

Whipple, H. B. "The Indian System." *The North American Review* 99, no. 205 (October 1864): 34–39.

White, Helen McCann. *Ho! For the Gold Fields: Northern Overland Wagon Trains of the 1860s*. St. Paul: Minnesota Historical Society, 1966.

White, Richard. "The Winning of the West: The Expansion of the Western Sioux in the Eighteenth and Nineteenth Centuries." *The Journal of American History* 65, no. 2 (Sept. 1978): 319–43.

White Bull, Joseph. *Lakota Warrior*. Translated and edited by James H. Howard. 1968. Reprint, Lincoln: University of Nebraska Press, 1998.

"The Wiciyela or Middle Dakota," *Museum News* 27, nos. 7–8 (July–Aug. 1966). Published by the W. H. Over Museum, University of South Dakota. On file at SHSND.

Williamson, John P. *An English–Dakota Dictionary*. 1902. Reprint, St. Paul: Minnesota Historical Society Press, 1992.

Wilson, Diane. *Spirit Car: Journey to a Dakota Past*. St Paul: Minnesota Historical Society Press, Borealis Books, 2006.

Wilson, Frederick T. "Old Fort Pierre and Its Neighbors." In *South Dakota Historical Collections*, vol. 1, edited by Charles E. DeLand, compiled by the South Dakota State Historical Society, 259–81. Aberdeen, S.Dak.: News Printing Co., 1902.

Wilson, Wesley C. "Doctor Walter A. Burleigh: Dakota Territorial Delegate to the 39th and 40th Congress; Politician, Extraordinary." *North Dakota History* 33, no. 2 (Spring 1966): 93–103.

———. "General John B. S. Todd, First Delegate, Dakota Territory." *North Dakota History* 31 (July 1964): 189–94.

Wischmann, Lesley. *Frontier Diplomats: The Life and Times of Alexander Culbertson and Natoyist-Siksina'*. Spokane, Wash.: Arthur H. Clark, 2000.

Witte, Stephen S., and Marsha V. Gallagher, eds.; William J. Orr, Paul Schach, and Dieter Karch, trans. *The North American Journals of Prince Maximilian of Wied*. Vol. 2. Norman: University of Oklahoma Press; Omaha, Neb.: Joslyn Art Museum, 2010.

Wood, W. Raymond. "The North Dakota Artwork of General Régis de Trobriand" (2–3), "General Régis de Trobriand: A Brief Biography" (4–12), and "The North Dakota Artwork" (13–30). *North Dakota History* 73 nos. 3 and 4 (Fall and Winter 2006 [combined issue]): 2–30.

The World Almanac of the American West. New York: World Almanac, 1986.

Zens, M. Serena. "The Educational Work of the Catholic Church among the Indians of South Dakota from the Beginning to 1835." In *South Dakota Historical Collections*, vol. 20, compiled by the South Dakota State Historical Society, 299–356. Vermillion: University of South Dakota, 1940.

Zwink, Timothy A. "E. W. Wynkoop and the Bluff Creek Council, 1866." *Kansas Historical Quarterly* 43, no. 2 (Summer 1977): 217–39.

INTERNET RESOURCES

Cornell University. "Making of America" database. http://cdl.library.cornell .edu/moa/.

Iowa History Project. Contains documents pertaining to Iowa history that are out of copyright. http://iagenweb.org/history/.

Knudsen, Dean. "Civil War Rosters." http://www.civilwarroster.com/index
.html.

Library of Congress. *A Century of Lawmaking for a New Nation: U.S. Congressional Documents and Debates, 1774–1875.* http://memory.loc.gov/ammem/amlaw/.

Linder, Doug. "Famous Trials Page." http://www.law.umkc.edu/faculty/projects/
ftrials/ftrials.htm.

National Park Service. "Civil War Sailors and Soldiers System." http://www
.itd.nps.gov/cwss/.

"Soldier's Pay in the Civil War." In *Civil War Dictionary* [source given as Mark M. Boatner]. http://www.civilwarhome.com/Pay.htm.

Standing Rock Tribal Tourism Office. "Standing Rock Tourism." http://www
.standingrocktourism.com/history/chiefs.asp.

U.S. Naval Observatory. Provides astronomical data, such as the time of past eclipses and so forth. http://aa.usno.navy.mil/data/docs/RS_OneDay.html.

Legal Documents
(in alphabetical order)

Elk, Lavetta v. US, case *1:05-cv-00186-FMA.*
  Docket 96, filed 4/28/09, 1–37. 70 Fed. Cl. 405, April 2006.
The Sioux Tribe, et al., plaintiffs, v. USA, defendant, 15 1865.
  Docket 74, Indian Claims Commission, decided 27 Aug. 1865, "Findings of Fact."
  Docket 74, 42 Indian Claims Commission 214, decided 19 July 1978, "Establishment of the Powder River Road," and "Additional Findings of Fact."
Yankton Sioux Tribe et al. v. United States. [Papers relating to this case date from 1828 through 1987 and are on file at the I.D. Weeks Library, Archives and Special Collections, University of South Dakota, accessible online at http://
www.usd.edu/library/.]
  Docket 332A, "Interlocutory Order," 12 Jan. 1962. Yankton claim dismissed.
  Docket 332B, U.S. Claims Commission. 29 Ind. Cl. Com. 143, 9 Nov. 1972.
  Yankton claim granted.
  Docket 332C, U.S. Claims Commission. 41 Ind. Cl. Com. 160. Grants motion for rehearing 24 Ind. Cl. Com. 208. 27 Dec. 1977.
    Vaughan, Jack C. *Colonel Alfred Jefferson Vaughan: The Frontier Ambassador.* Dallas, Tex.: Jack C. Vaughan, 1957.
    Vaughan to Cumming, 6 March 1854: plaintiff's exhibit No. 54-17.

Index

References to illustrations are in italic type.

CPSIA information can be obtained
at www.ICGtesting.com
Printed in the USA
LVOW04s2346290416

485938LV00011B/56/P